W9-AEB-191

THE WHY OF FASHION

THE WHY OF

by Karlyne Anspach

THE IOWA STATE UNIVERSITY PRESS, AMES, IOWA

FASHION

KARLYNE ANSPACH, professor of home economics at the University of Illinois, holds the B.S. degree from Iowa State University, the M.A. degree from Columbia University, and the Ph.D. degree from the University of Chicago. Miss Anspach has a unique combination of education and training in the fields of apparel design and consumption economics. She was a fashion designer for Nelly Don Dress Company; a student at L'Ecole de la Chambre Syndicale de la Couture Parisienne (French haute couture official training school); and in 1966 she spent three months in Bangkok studying the fashion consciousness of Thai women, as a beginning to a cross-cultural examination of fashion. Besides this book, she has to her credit numerous journal articles, and was a contributing author for the book "Unit Method of Clothing Construction."

Thomas G. Kovacs, instructor of graphic design at the University of Illinois, prepared the jacket artwork and the illustrations appearing in this book.

© 1967 The Iowa State University Press
Ames, Iowa, U.S.A. All rights reserved

Composed and printed by
The Iowa State University Press

First edition, 1967

Second printing, 1969

Standard Book Number: 8138–1796–x

Library of Congress Catalog Card Number: 67–29679

To my Mother, ALICE SYKES ANSPACH

The corn maidens swished their ribbon skirts—
Coquetting with plumed hair.

ALICE ANSPACH

PREFACE

Fashion has played an important role in American life since the founding of the nation. The intensity with which fashion is sought by people on many levels of society is evidence of its impact on modern life and the significance of this element of dress. This book was developed from a felt need for a text that brings together in one book the present knowledge of fashion while still keeping a historical perspective on fashion development. It uses an interdisciplinary approach, applying concepts from social psychology, sociology, economics, and communication to the clothing area, and integrating these concepts with current research and social-historical facts.

Appropriate for courses concerned with fashion analysis; studies in consumer behavior; the social, psychological, and economic factors of dress; or historic costume (including American dress); it presents a "total" cultural approach to the evolvement of national styles, with the overall purpose of developing greater understanding of fashion.

Fashion in all its important dimensions is considered. To develop each dimension adequately the book is divided into three parts: fashion as a social need; fashion as an economic commodity; and fashion as a symbol of American life.

Fashion is viewed first as a social phenomenon involved with the why of human behavior. Then the element of fashion in dress is examined to see how it affects the economic system and is, in turn, affected by it. These

two factors—the social and economic effects of fashion—
ultimately lead to an examination of why prevailing styles
in dress become a symbol of the nation's life.

My initial scholarly interest in fashion was stimulated
by graduate work in the economics of consumption at the
University of Chicago under the guidance of Professor
Margaret Reid. Discussions on fashion at a graduate seminar led by professors Elihu Katz and David Riesman encouraged further study. The specific idea for this book
developed from student discussions and readings in a seminar on fashion which I conduct at the University of Illinois. The seminar is basically an analysis of "Why We
Dress as We Do."

For critical assistance and encouragement in the preparation of this book I acknowledge a deep debt to Dr.
Margaret Reid, University of Chicago, and to my colleagues at the University of Illinois and Iowa State
University.

KARLYNE ANSPACH

CONTENTS

Introduction

NATURE OF FASHION

With the first hint of a change of season the American
woman feels impelled by an unseen force to hurry to her
favorite dress shop. There the wife of a Chicago doctor rejects
this and selects that; the daughter of the local pharmacist in
Prairie City molds her body into a flat rectangle similar to one
pictured in a New York newspaper; the rush chairman of a
college sorority at Oklahoma University is charmed by a gaily
colored tube. These women are fashion conscious. In response
to a subjective need for fashion they have adopted fashion's
form.

The term "fashion" is used in different ways by the sociologist, the historian, the economist, and the public at large.
Confusion results unless a distinction is made between three
uses of the word: (1) as a social phenomenon, (2) as a commodity, and (3) as a symbol.

Fashion as a Social Phenomenon

In the broadest sense, fashion, like custom, can be defined
as the accepted way of talking, walking, eating, and dressing that is adopted by a group of people at a given time. However, unlike custom, which tends to preserve things as they are,
fashion honors change. Custom venerates the past while
fashion respects the present. As one fashion evolves into another, some of the old is retained and something new is added.
It is the *new element* that marks the new fashion. The central
problem in fashion thus becomes the introduction, acceptance,
and adoption of change. Why do some groups adopt these

changes faster than others? Why do styles in fashion vary from group to group and time to time? To answer these questions, fashion must be viewed as a social phenomenon—a study in group behavior.

MAJORITY AND MINORITY FASHIONS. Fashion movements vary in size; they cover small or large groups. Society in general is frequently visualized as one large group and the terms "popular fashions" or "mass fashions" refer to the fashion choices made by the majority of this group. When smaller groups prefer other things, these choices may be thought of as fashions of minority groups or subgroups. For example, teen-age fashions in dress are the styles preferred by young people of high school and college age. High fashions are the styles preferred by a small group of women of recognized taste and authority in the fashion world. Such a group may include women of wealth and position, buyers acting for their clientele, editors of fashion magazines, and fashion writers. Thus small groups choosing from among many items may favor certain styles which become for them "their fashion." Some of these minority fashions may later triumph and become the majority fashion for society in general. Other minority fashions represent only the residual demand left after a fashion has run its course, as in the continuing demand for classics. However, the minority group whose choice is accepted by the majority is the innovator of fashion.

INTRODUCTION OF FASHION. It is not always clear how fashion goods are introduced. Much is known about how original styles from high fashion designers filter down and become popular fashions. But little is known about how the styles from other groups reach the majority. For example, popular new dances and musicians' slang have come from the Negro subculture. In the 1960's short skirts and boots were popularized by the teen-agers of England long before they were shown in Paris by Courreges, a high fashion designer. But it has never been explained just how or why blue jeans and head scarves became such popular fashions in the United States.

Fashion innovation may be studied either by tracing to the source a past style that became a mass fashion or by following a current style to see if it emerges as a fashion. The difficulty rests in the fact that fashion has no objective truth. Once identified, fashion then begins to fade and is no longer fashion. Moreover, a description or formula for one fashion will not fit any other fashion; the content of fashion is constantly changing.

FASHION CYCLES. The term "fashion" is technically correct only when a choice is accepted by the majority of a group.

However, to show the relative position of different items on the scale of group acceptance, fashion is thought of as having a life cycle or wavelike motion. It rises, reaches a peak, and declines. A dress style which has not yet been accepted by a group, but soon will be, is an "incoming fashion." One which is accepted and fulfills the definition of the term is "fashion at its peak." A style which was a group choice but is now in less demand is an "outgoing fashion." A fashion can last a long or short period of time—for centuries or for weeks. The rate of fashion change is called the "tempo of fashion."

Taking this all together, fashion as a social phenomenon has several characteristics. It involves change and the acceptance of change by groups. It has a cyclical movement: it rises, reaches a peak, and falls. It has no objective truth; when it has been accepted by the majority of a group it begins to fade. Fashion movements cover small or large groups, short or long periods of time.

Fashion as a Commodity

Another dimension is present in the definition of fashion as "the accepted way." The term "accepted way" involves two problems: the problem of acceptance we have just discussed, and the problem of "the way." What is the best way to express fashion? Why do some objects become fashion goods whereas others do not? This feature of fashion refers to the tangible form of fashion which can be imitated or bought and sold on the market. When the retailer says he sells fashion he is selling the appearance of fashion, the shape of fashion— fashion as a commodity. It is in this sense that Paul Nystrom, the economist, describes fashion as nothing more or less than the prevailing style at a given time.[1] Because he uses the word "style" and style implies distinguishing characteristics that are generally recognized, this term "the prevailing style" is useful to identify fashion as a commodity.

Fashion can be recognized in most areas of life. Teen-age jargon is fashion in speech. The Model T Ford typifies fashion in cars. But dress remains the most sensitive medium for fashion transmission, an area so sensitive that the word fashion is often taken to mean only fashion in dress when used by women's magazines, department store buyers, and the public at large. For that reason this study of fashion will concentrate on fashion in dress.

Fashion as a Symbol

The total idea of fashion cannot be fully developed without examining fashion as a symbol. It is the form of fashion or fashion as a commodity that comes to have symbolic meanings. The dress of a nation reflects the core of beliefs of the nation and becomes a collective symbol of social identity. Each successive fashion in dress seems to represent fully the spirit of the times.

Why do fashion styles become a symbol of the culture? A clue to the answer to this question lies in the interdependent relationship between the cultural environment, the need for fashion, and the production of fashion goods. This relationship can be viewed as the circular *flow of fashion*.

FLOW OF FASHION. The need for fashion is socially developed —the result of cultural conditioning. It is experienced by individuals as a vaguely felt need, somewhat amorphous in character. Once the need arises, however, products are offered to satisfy this need; some are accepted and become fashion in tangible form. In the process of fashion acceptance, suggested ideas attract the attention of many people. While satisfying the demand for familiar qualities, they also awaken new responses by presenting something strange. An unfamiliar quality is an inherent part of any incoming fashion. Once fashion is adopted, however, the newly awakened responses become part of the person's life style and the fashions now seem to symbolize the spirit of the culture. Thus fashions act to reshape the culture from which they spring. By changing the cultural environment they promote new attitudes and values which, in turn, arouse new needs, and the circular flow of fashion begins again.

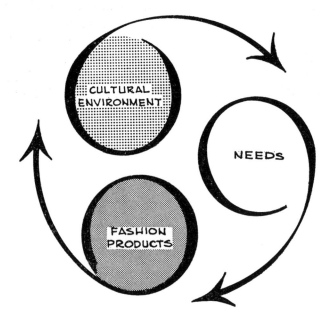

Viewed in this way a study of fashion becomes more than a classification of styles or a frivolous discussion of clothing; it becomes, instead, a study of the needs, values, and habits of the people, a study of the structure of the society.

Book Organization

In this book, fashion in all its dimensions is considered, but to adequately develop each dimension the book has been divided into three parts: Part I, Fashion: A Social Need; Part II, Fashion: An Economic Good; Part III, Fashion: A Reflection of American Life.

Part I concerns fashion as a social development; Part II involves the production and distribution of fashion goods on the market; and Part III examines ways in which popular styles in dress reflect life in America.

The dominant concern of this book is with "whys" not

"whats." Fashion is viewed as a social phenomenon involved with the "why" of human behavior. Although, to ignore the "what" of fashion, or fashion as a commodity, is to ignore the only tangible evidence we have that fashion as a social phenomenon exists. Therefore, dress fashions are frequently used as examples. In addition, the element of fashion in dress is examined to see how it affects the economic system and is, in turn, affected by it. These two factors—the social and economic effects of fashion—ultimately lead to an examination of why prevailing styles in dress become a symbol of the nation's life.

1

FASHION: *A SOCIAL NEED*

1

THE RISE OF FASHION

Imitation and emulation between social groups and between persons prompt the rise of fashion, while a belief in the value of change sustains acceptance of fashion throughout the society. A technical culture that permits abundance and waste gives added impetus to fashion realization.

Theoretically, man's wants are unlimited. They vary among people and places from time to time, but the urgency of wants does not appreciably diminish as more are filled. When man has satisfied his physical needs, his psychologically grounded desires take over. He demands high fashion clothing, foreign-made cars, and original paintings rather than food for hunger or clothes for warmth.

Needs are both relative and absolute. Absolute needs are those we have no matter what the condition of our fellowman. The terms implies a measurable standard. A space suit for rocket flight must meet an absolute standard of performance under set conditions. This type of need can be measured. But those needs which are relative, those we feel only in relation to another commodity or person—social needs—cannot be measured in absolute terms. Status, values, self-esteem, and all the things with which fashion is concerned can only be determined relatively. For this reason it is difficult to know when this type of need has been met.

Fashion arises primarily to identify status. All social institutions created by societies to regulate ways of acting, any formal or informal subsystems within the larger society, automatically create membership and positions which are forms of status. Each status, or defined social position, conveys certain rights and privileges. For example, a "wife" has duties and

3

privileges that are different from those of a "mother" or a "daughter." Some positions are nonranked, others are ranked as superior or inferior. The word "girl" designates a nonranked status, but phrases such as "an elite," "a common man," or "poor white trash" carry connotations of rank. Each form of status acquires characteristic markings.

A social position is understood by reference to other social positions with which it is directly or indirectly connected. How does one status compare with another? What are the symbols, rules, and skills of those who exercise stated duties within a defined social location? Since status is relatively determined, it is the comparative ranking of groups, individuals, and commodities as superior or inferior that initiates the fashion movement.

In 1903 Gabriel Tarde, a French sociologist living in a world of aristocrats, described the *imitation of the superior by the inferior*. He believed that imitation of ideas usually precedes imitation of their expression—that progress moves from *within to without*. For example, French literature predominated over Europe in the seventeenth century before French arts and fashions made their tour of the world. According to Tarde: "Before imitating the act of another we begin by feeling the need from which this act proceeds, and we feel it precisely as we do only because it has been suggested to us. The examples of persons or classes as well as localities that are thought superior will prevail over the example of inferior persons, classes or localities."[1]

Tarde sensed that even though an idea starts at the lowest level of society, its expansion will depend upon some high social elevation. He visualized the spread of fashion as a social water tower from which "a continuous waterfall of imitation" could descend.[2] Today, this is called the vertical flow of fashion, whereby ideas that become fashion are initiated in upper status levels and flow in a vertical direction from superior to inferior social groups.

Another early sociologist Georg Simmel, a German, reasoned that fashion needs interpersonal and intergroup relationships in which admiration is mixed with hostility. There must be not only a desire to copy and be like the other, but also a desire to be different and distinct from the other.[3] Thus, fashion arises not only to differentiate groups and per-

1 / FASHION: A SOCIAL NEED

The fashion movement may be vertical between upper- *and lower-status groups* or
horizontal *between groups of equal rank
and members of the same group.*

sons from one another but also to link them with a common bond. This happens when subgroups adopt their own designs within the prevailing fashion trend.

In general, then, fashion arises where differentiated social groups exist. The fashion movement may be vertical, between upper and lower status groups, or it may be horizontal, between groups of equal rank or members of the same group. The initiating spark is the social need of people to be like others and yet to be distinct from others. It follows that a stratified society (or a society composed of varied groups) that allows mobility between and within groups will favor the general rise of fashion. Such factors as the ranked difference between groups, the closeness of group contacts, and the rate of mobility from one group to another will all affect the fashion movement.

Democratization of the Elite

Sociologists and observers of the social scene have outlined the operations of elites in America. While there is considerable distance from the bottom to the top levels of the socioeconomic scale, American society should not be viewed as one large pyramid with a moneyed, well-born aristocracy or elite at the top. There are many peaks, each having its own elite. C. Wright Mills identified three: the political, military, and economic elites. Russell Lynes adds the intellectual, the underworld, the small business, labor, cafe society, and celebrities of the big media. Within each peak are different levels, each topped by an aristocracy of its own. As elsewhere, choice has multiplied. Movement can be up or down within one's own pyramid, or sideways between pyramids. Horizontal movement can be more important today than vertical movement.

Fashion flourished historically at the courts of kings among an aristocratic elite of inherited positions. The introduction and wearing of new fashions was an established privilege of those who held superior rank. Today, we have many elites, and fashion is the privilege of most American women who desire it. Why did these different elites rise in America? Why did fashion become democratized?

ARISTOCRATIC ELITES. The early settlers from England brought
with them a strong inherited sense of social stratification
with all its trappings in dress, in feasting, and in the
attraction of the landed gentry for city life. They tried to
follow the Old World pattern in the new land.

Aristocracy in Boston revolved around the figure of the
Royal Governor. The "Governor's set" led the social and intellectual life of the colonies. Its members adopted many of
the courtly customs and ceremonies of British royalty and
formed their own royal court. Samuel Sewall noted in his
diary as early as October 18, 1687: "As I came home from
Roxbury, I met the Governor's Lady riding in her coach
hitherward. The same day the Governor's Lady arrived, word
came that Captain Phips was Knighted, so we have two ladies
in town."[4]

In March, 1734, a quantity of Nassau silks of the "colour
provided for the royal wedding" was quickly dispatched to
Boston from London, so their ladies might have them "as soon
as some of ours."[5]

Like all newly formed aristocracies, that of Boston sought
to advertise itself and its position by great displays of mag-
nificence. Prosperous businessmen purchased "a coach and six
horses richly harnassed"; North End merchants built elegant
three-story brick houses. Men wore "silver laced coats and gold
wrought caps," and they carried this ostentation to the grave.
A funeral required mass gifts of black gloves. At the funeral
of Andrew Faneuil, 3,000 pairs were distributed; often several
hundred would be given. Mourning-rings were a great expense; 200 were given at one Boston funeral in 1738, and these
rings cost over a pound each.[6]

If Boston was splendid, New York was even more brilliant. The merchant aristocracy was conspicuous for its command of all the social graces. Governor Frances Lovelace
wrote to King Charles in 1668: "I find these people have the
breeding of counts, and I cannot conceive how such is acquired."[7] Class feeling was very open, as shown by the haughty
and sensitive air of the aristocrat or the dogged prejudice of
poorer folk. In addition, there was a tendency for town gentry
to sniff derisively at country bumpkins who came to town.

New York was a more cosmopolitan city than Boston.
Eighteen different languages were spoken there by 1643. Jews

from Holland and Brazil arrived in 1654, and many French Walloons and English settlers came four years later. Although the Dutch were in the majority when the English took over, most people conversed equally well in three languages—Dutch, English, or French—and they always followed French fashions. The Dutch groups were the most frugal, industrious, and wealthy; the English, especially those involved in trade, the most extravagant and showy.[8]

In the South, the ladies of Annapolis, Baltimore, or Charleston also ordered rich damasks and brocades from London. As the planters grew wealthy, they competed with the merchants. However, most of the cultural developments that pushed American society into the stream of world events came in the towns. It was here the burgeoning middle class, striving to move up, developed power and status symbols of its own.

MIDDLE CLASS ELITES. In England, the various classes—rich and poor, nobleman, gentleman, yeoman and laborer, each with a multitude of traditions—were given a lawful status which could not easily be destroyed nor safely ignored. But in America the social scale was much shorter—from an indentured servant to the middle gentry—and there it abruptly stopped. Few members of the British upper classes came to America. No nobles emigrated. Even the second Lord Baltimore, by whose means Maryland was founded, stayed in England. The few squires or gentlemen who did come became leaders in the New World. But the yeomen were the most numerous and necessary migrants to New England. Heirs of the sturdiest English fighters, the archers of Agincourt and Crecy, they were also farmers fit to conquer the forests of America. They had *no counterpart in other lands.*[9] Positioned between the nobility and the gentry and the laborers or peasants, they were thinkers as well as doers.

This population, composed almost entirely of middle and lower classes, used with meticulous care such prestige distinctions as there were. The titles "Mr.," "Gent," and "Lady" amazed the British Mrs. Trollope, visiting America in 1827. She observed, ". . . in mentioning each other they constantly employed the term 'lady,' and they evidently had a pleasure in it . . . the lady over that way what takes in washing . . . and the laborers on the canal were invariably denominated 'them gentlemen.' . . ."[10] The place at the table, the seating in the church, the position in the college classroom, and all such minor matters were regulated with a sensitivity to status, equaled only by the minuteness of the difference on which it was based.

The function of the meetinghouse to "rank the orders" lives on in the fiction of Harriet Beecher Stowe. "At the head stood the minister and his wife, whose rank was expressed by the pew next to the pulpit. Then came Captain Broune, a retired English merchant and ship owner. . . . Next came the pew of Miss Mehitable Rossiter, who, in right of being the only surviving member of the family of the former minister, was looked upon with reverence in Oldtown. . . . People who have *ruffles round their hands,* and rode in *their own coaches,* and *never performed any manual labor,* might be said to constitute in Oldtown our House of Lords . . . the minister, Captain Broune, and Sheriff Jones."[11]

While snobbishness raged in the small Puritan villages of New England, still, within households, there was little distinction between master and man or mistress and maid. All ate at the same table and warmed themselves by the same fireplace. Almost every household, especially in the country, had the help of a slave, an indentured servant, or the daughter of some neighbor—a "hired girl." There was little stigma attached to this work, and unmarried girls of fairly good families frequently went out to service. The outlying communities offered more opportunity for the average man to escape from his class than did the growing towns.

However, in the cities a new type of elite came into being, one which placed little emphasis on outward show of status symbols, whose identification required a knowledge of the inner man. From the city of Philadelphia, Benjamin Franklin went forth to the Court of France. There was something irresistibly appealing in the picture of "the provincial tallow-chandler's son, dressed in his plain garb of homespun, standing unabashed in the presence of the gorgeously arrayed decadent nobles of France."[12] Franklin was the pioneer and prototype of the poor and aspiring; his rise was due to industry and application, not to sheer genius. As he became the apotheosis of the self-made man, the embodiment of all those virtues that were inspiring—personal achievement and public service—

the social barriers between classes in America inevitably came down.

"NEW" ELITES. Meanwhile, American industrialization, a new aid to economic growth, joined hands with urbanization to create new pyramids of power. In the "Gilded Age" (1860–1914) arose the financier, the "robber barons of American Business," as they were called by Theodore Dreiser. In his book, *The Financier*, he characterized this type at the turn of the century: "He believed sincerely that vast fortunes were to be made out of railroads if one only had the capital and that curious thing, a magnetic personality—the ability to win the confidence of others. Other men want money, but not for money's sake. They want it for what it will buy in the way of simple comforts, whereas the financier wants it for what it will control—for what it represents in the way of dignity, force, power."[13]

The new American aristocrats, much more civilized and sophisticated than before, and very wealthy, came to Europe with no sense of inferiority. For the first time, American influence was felt abroad.

It became fashionable to merge American millions with European blue blood, often impoverished. One of the first of these weddings was that of Anna Gould, youngest daughter of the railroad magnate, Jay Gould. She came to Paris at the age of eighteen. Two years later she married a playboy marquis, Boniface de Castellane; Gould reportedly presenting a dowry of fifteen million dollars. Boni, as he was called, built his bride a pink marble copy of Queen Marie Antoinette's little Trianon palace on a fashionable avenue of Paris. After eleven years he had spent three million dollars of her money and incurred huge debts. She threw his clothes from the house, and he obtained a Vatican annulment of the marriage.[14]

While New York was *the* social center in the United States, many smaller cities had their own society, living in a relatively grand way. Mansions from this period linger on. Standing on top of the hill overlooking the main avenue, they were looked up to by the citizens of the towns. In the heart of the Midwest, sixteen-mule teams hauled building materials from the Mississippi River—walnut and rosewood for the thick, high-arched doors and windows, and mahogany for the continuous ribbon of wood running from floor to floor in the grand staircase. A table-center bouquet for an opening night might cost $700, and the toilette of the ladies was often as brilliant as that to be found in Chicago, Boston, or Philadelphia.

In this same spirit, in a small prairie town, spunky Florence Bund starched her cotton petticoats till they made a noise like silk when she walked. This was to signal that she, too, wore rustling silk and taffeta petticoats beneath her dress.

As might be expected, increased immigration emphasized one previously unnoticed type of elite, "the native American." Each new wave of immigrants made those who were here before seem more American by comparison, and the social distance between groups was determined more and more on the basis of length of residence in America. Hostility, based on strangeness and protection of "I-was-here-first" rights, placed the newest arrivals on the defensive and on a lower social scale. To move from an "immigrant" to an "American" was to climb one of the many status pyramids found in a country that believed in mobility through individual effort.

This is the same process that is repeated when a new person tries to move from the out-group to the in-group: the freshman in college; the would-be member of the club; the last person to be hired by the boss; the new neighbor. The newcomer's position is subtly marked by the degree of social distance maintained between him and the others in the group.

Some superior status for all—everyone a possible elite— this seems to be America's goal. And if this goal is not reached by birth or inherited wealth, then it can be attained by earned wealth or an expense account sheet, through occupational power or by artificial distinctions of club membership.

The first American aristocrats were of the European cut— wealthy landowners, cultured and well born, the Governor Winthrops and the Thomas Jeffersons. Soon came the merchant aristocracy, haughty and showy. But also squeezing in were the "noble barbarians," plain men of personal achievement and public service, the Benjamin Franklins. Then were added the commercial giants of trade and enterprise, the John Jacob Astors. And following these came the fabulously wealthy elites of industrialization and urbanization—the Du Ponts, Vanderbilts, and Rockefellers. Infiltrating at every chance were the "native Americans," the established residents. We can add the entertainment celebrities, the underworld leaders, labor executives, writers, space scientists, pollsters, and economic advisers to the president.

With so many models to copy, imitation in the Tarde sense of moving from inward need to outward expression runs rampant. Veblen chose the word emulation, that invidious comparison that prompts us to outdo those with whom we class ourselves. Current writers prefer to think of not imitation or emulation, but a striving to catch up with the living standards of others. Fashion, easily recognized, and now, easily acquired, often becomes one of the first outward expressions of this inner social need.

DEMOCRACY IN FASHION. Fashion is not new to America. What is new is the change from an aristocratic conception of fashion for the few to a more democratic conception of fashion for the many. The age of the common man began with the reign of Queen Victoria. A degree of soberness settled over England and America as they turned their attention to everyday affairs and comfortable family life. But not France. The elegant French bourgeois with no title and inherited estates felt the need to assert himself by some other means. And that means was fashion. Almost every novel by Stendhal or Balzac describes the smartness of a man and the toilette of a woman.

Conditions were favorable for the appearance of a grand couturier. A wise English tailor with a superb knowledge of cut, Charles Frederick Worth, linked himself with the imperial economic policy of France: the promotion of the fabric industries. Because he designed silk dresses for Empress Eugénie, the number of silk looms in Lyon doubled between 1860 and 1871. Worth was the innovator who industrialized fashion by linking the creative designer to clothing manufacturers and a foreign clientele of merchants. He made elite fashion "big business." Since women of means and those of title met on an equal footing, both came to Worth. The pains he took to give society the best in dressmaking skills and artistic genius resulted in the triumph of French gowns abroad. Paris became the sole arbiter of high fashion.

Curiously enough, while France was establishing a business of exclusive fashions for the few, America was launching a ready-to-wear industry that would bring fashion into the homes of every community in America and spill over into world markets. Fashion moved from custom-made to ready-made goods. By developing different grades of merchandise—cheap, medium, better, and high—the ready-to-wear industry began to tempt even the most fastidious customers.

The same three factors that produced tremendous national wealth—the factory, the city, and the immigrant flood—also produced the ready-to-wear industry. The invention of the sewing machine and the cutting knife, together with the waves of immigrant German, Austrian, and Hungarian tailors around 1880, pushed the cloak and suit industry ahead.

The success of the clothing industry in the democratization of fashion was partly revealed over forty years ago by Robert S. Lynd and Helen Merrell Lynd's sociological study, *Middletown*. An employer commented, "I used to be able to tell something of the background of the girl applying for a job by her clothes. Now, I have to wait until she speaks, shows a gold tooth, or otherwise gives me a second clue."

At school in Middletown, the girls from working-class homes wore dresses that used to be considered party dresses. They felt abused if they had to wear the same dress two successive days. One mother sent her thirteen-year-old to school dressed in lisle hose and gingham, but the girl seemed like an "object of mercy," so she changed to silk dresses and silk hose.[15]

The prevalence of the distinctive jangling beads and short skirts of the 1920's showed that fashion was infiltrating all sections of the community. Fashion became popular.

Upton Sinclair in his novel, *Oil*, describes the inner turmoil of Mrs. Groaty, the wife of a night watchman. She used to "take in" washing to help support her seven children, but was soon to preside at a meeting in her home to discuss oil rights. Having no suitable clothing for the occasion, she acquired an evening gown of yellow satin. "Now she felt embarrassed because there was not enough of it, either at the top where her arms and bosom came out, or below, where her fat calves were enclosed in embroidered silk stockings. . . ." But, "It was what 'they' were wearing, the saleswoman had assured her, and Mrs. Groaty was grimly set upon being one of 'them.' "[16]

Today, the prevailing informality of manners, clothes, and taste makes the popularization process more complete. A democracy of clothes has been established. The status element of fashion no longer recognizes the barriers of class.

The Mobile Middle Class

The middle class has been inherently more restless than the upper or lower classes. Mobility-minded members of the middle class imitate those above (and below), move from one status group to another, and bring new symbols of their own into the upper classes. Established groups of elites are then forced to change in order to maintain their "different" quality. Since fashion feeds on imitation and differentiation, it is plain that a dominant middle class will favor the rapid growth of fashion.

The upper class, already at the top and not wanting to move down, may only move sideways. They see no advantage to "change"; in fact, change may ruin them. The lowest class, already at the bottom, and with horizontal movement bringing only momentary relief, may only go up. But they are hampered by lack of knowledge and lack of means* They are unequipped for a struggle that requires a "future" rather than a "now" orientation; they often view change with suspicion and apathy. Located in between these two extremes, the middle class, alert and thinking, may move in any direction.

Conditions in America encourage status mobility. Few positions have remained fixed long enough to enter by birth or by well-established sequences of training or achievement. We emphasize: (1) change in systems of positions, and (2) mobility of individuals by achievement. Changes in technology break up expected status characteristics by altering the occupations about which they grow up, and mobility brings large numbers of new kinds of people into various positions.

* The study, "Stratification in a Prairie Town," by J. Useem, P. Tangent, and R. H. Useem (1942) showed that women in the top strata of the town were "more preoccupied with dress and current styles and were more critical of what others wore than women of low status who neither discussed the matter often or evaluated others by their clothes." [17]

The confusion in status that results calls for some generally recognized system of identification. Fashion often serves this purpose.

The strong American middle class that arose in the early part of the nineteenth century was composed of teachers, merchants, and office workers who wanted clothes of good appearance at low cost. Furthermore, large numbers of immigrants who came with few clothes found clothing an important means of gaining social acceptance in unfamiliar surroundings.

Emigrants to America left communities that were whole and integrated—one church, one state, and a hierarchy based on occupation and status. In the Old World, individuals had fixed roles and expectations. They were located at a precise point in the social structure. However, those who came to America were among the least fixed. They were dissenters, servants, captives, and victims of economic disaster. In America they entered a life of spatial and social mobility.* Constant territorial expansion caused the development of one frontier after another. These new communities often failed to create a strong, integrated leadership and relied on the voluntary actions of smaller groups operating within the fragmented sectors of the whole. People banded together to sponsor any cause toward which they felt concern. The state was weak, its authority tentative, so individual groups were strong.

The American population was so heterogeneous— Quakers, Presbyterians, Anglicans, Jews, Catholics; Yankees, Germans, Irishmen, Italians, and the like—that no single set of institutions could serve the social and cultural needs of all the people. It was a fragmented rather than a whole society.

In large cities, community life developed within ethnic groups to satisfy the need for intimate association with others. While at first these people achieved group identity by dressing

*In 1952, W. Lloyd Warner conducted a nationwide sociological research to test the hypothesis that there was less mobility than in the past. The results of over 8,000 questionnaires and interviews on the social origin of the present elites were compared with a similar study by Taussia-Joslyn in 1928. Warner found that the trend is toward openness in the occupation and status structure. There has been an increasing competition among all ranks for higher positions and a reduction in the proportion of those born to high position who stay there. This suggests that America is still a land of opportunity and the sons of men in less prestigious positions are likely to be more mobile today than they were in the 20's. Only the avenue of mobility has changed. Today's avenue of advancement is by higher education.[18]

as they had back home, this practice gradually changed as the need to be accepted as an "American" overtook them. Because they lived so close together, all classes emulated and imitated each other. The application of the democratic principle established their right to have the same general appearance as their more affluent countrymen, and the economic opportunities they found in the new country enabled them to fulfill individual demands.

EMPHASIS ON INDIVIDUAL WORTH. Private ownership in a free-enterprise system reemphasizes the importance of the individual. It is expedient to develop individual differences where there is danger of absorption or obliteration by competition and where individual achievement is highly valued. Dress and housing, easily seen criteria for judging differences between people, become sharply accented.

Conversely, in a communal society where emphasis is on the socializing impulse, there is little, if any, accent on fashion or individual dress. It is hoped that similarly dressed (and housed) people will exhibit relative similarities in their actions. This is seen in some of our socioreligious groups such as the Pennsylvania Amish.

So much attention has been given to the dehumanizing of man by machine that the ways in which machinery has enhanced individual personality are sometimes undervalued. Technology brought in an objective view of life. Because it stripped nature of all subjective and human characteristics it more sharply defined the concept of man's individual personality. We now see the inner man and the outer man, the subjective and the objective. This reemphasis of the individual is in line with the philosophy of the Christian religion and the eighteenth-century liberal political ideas which stress the worth of man and initiate the idea of progress.

EMPHASIS ON CHANGE AND PROGRESS. A belief that change is progress promotes the acceptance of fashion and sustains fashion as a popular institution. Each new fashion, such as a prettier color, a smarter style, a better fit, seems to offer the promise of more reward than the preceding one. It embraces the theme of promise that has been crucial in American development.

Promise and progress have fused. In the eighteenth century "progress" was linked to change, and was accompanied by faith in the goodness of man and the ability of reason to create an earthly utopia. Christian philosophy indoctrinated man with the thought of an ultimate happy destiny, while experimental science opened up the engaging prospect of indefinite improvements in this life. Men admired their ancestors less, stressed their contemporaries more, and expected even more of their descendants. There was a vision of "additive betterment," accumulated through the years—more and richer land, more and higher education, more and prettier gowns.

Supporting this belief were three genuinely new features embodied in the vision of the American frontier: a sense of physical spaciousness, a resultant sense of opportunity, and a chance for trial and error free from old restrictions. The frontier, acting as a psychological safety valve, offered new hope to the unsuccessful, to the adventurous, to the young, and to the newly arrived; it generated plasticity in behavior, self-confidence, and self-reliance.

Looking back from the twentieth century on the achievements of Western society—economic recovery after war and depression, rising income, speedier travel, improved health, increased leisure—the world is seen as a universe in perpetual flux. It is "a universe in which the idea of things as well as the things themselves arise out of temporary conditions and are transformed with the modification of the conditions out of which they arose." Thus progress, while still containing the idea that man can, by deliberate purpose and rational thought, construct a more "just" society, becomes merely temporary insight, useful for the brief moment in which it flourishes. There is no final good, no absolute standard of value.[19]

This same idea is implied by the term "objectless craving" used by David Riesman in discussing consumer behavior. He suggests that the object itself, that is, the exact color, form, or texture it assumes, is unimportant; only the striving for something that is "approved by others" is important.[20] This explains the desire for fashion goods which have no objective identification but are "the accepted way" used by a group at a given time. Fashion goods are socially useful items as long as they remain in the current fashion cycle, but they have no absolute standard of value.

The Material Orientation

While the need for fashion is socially developed, the technological and economic systems of the society produce the materials for fashion. The technical culture in America inspires attitudes favorable to fashion development. A material orientation and an acceptance of abundance and waste sustain fashion as well as business.

EMPHASIS ON MATERIAL OBJECTS. There are several factors that put America in the forefront of the current industrial revolution and placed the emphasis on the production and consumption of material goods. Historically, the economic situation in Europe was different from that in America. European society was static in the sense that riches were reserved for a few individuals while the masses existed at a subsistence level. The ordinary man had little chance of acquiring great wealth; there were too many people eager to share in a limited supply of riches. The few ordinary men who did accumulate wealth tended to hide it to avoid both the ill will of others and the tax collector.

But in America the situation was reversed; riches were abundant and people were scarce. Work was rewarded more in proportion to the effort expanded. Since labor was in demand, the more a man worked and the harder he worked, the more wealth he accumulated. Then, too, the religious beliefs of the Pilgrims and Puritans did not hamper but reinforced the gospel of work; men were not born good, they "made good."

American wealth went into an improved standard of living, something that cannot be easily hidden. Improvements in education, health, housing, and clothing are publicly observable. Furthermore, Americans tended to equate the welfare of individual members of the community with the welfare of the community as a whole. An improved level of living for individuals was thought to lead to better conditions for all.

As a democracy we are governed by the ideal of economic

liberty, the sense that there should be no economic slavery, servitude, or dependence. We tend to think that one way of making people self-reliant, interested in personal as well as national achievements, is to raise the level of living; and where there is a high standard of living, people can afford to wear clothing which enhances their self-esteem and upholds their dignity in the eyes of others. It is thought that a well-dressed population, while not necessarily a happy one, has a chance to be happier than an ill-dressed one.

For all ideal possibilities, Jacques Barzun reminds us, presuppose material supplies. Man cannot live without food, clothing, and shelter. The "values" we talk so much about require tangible formulation in books, paintings, music, or theater. And equally concrete are feelings, thoughts, and policies, for unless they are embodied and active in human beings, they remain dreams or mere words.

This material orientation toward creature comforts rather than intellectual uplift is the outgrowth of modern technology in a free-enterprise system. Technological change alters wants, and causes goals to shift in various ways: Decreasing the cost and increasing the supply of some items makes more goods available to more people; introducing new articles such as cars, refrigerators, and television sets stimulates wants that had previously gone unnoticed; creating more efficient forms for existing goods makes the old forms seem obsolete; inventing such things as central heating changes our basic ideas of hygiene and subsequently our entire way of life.

Business, interested in a quick return, develops a passion for inquiry that shows. Forced into continuous improvement by competition, business supports research for better ways of producing better things, more substitutes, and more choices at competitive prices. With a quantitative orientation we optimistically believe that if "some" is good, "more" should be even better.

America before 1880 was incurably optimistic. It was a zesty and boisterous America, featuring exaggerated jokes and exaggerated dress. A change of fortune might, at any moment, put into your hands all the things you could only envy before. A chance spin of the wheel—gambler's luck—with an adroit mixture of wits and hard work could do the trick. It would transform rags to riches.

This theme was dramatized by Horatio Alger, Jr., whose books inspired boys and girls for decades. In *Tattered Tom* and *Ragged Dick,* the fresh and buoyant spirit and the sturdy independence of the hero or heroine, plus chance, always surmounted the most unsavory circumstances. These were Cinderella stories in contemporary settings, and a change in dress inevitably alerted the reader to the changed circumstances.

Moreover, this fiction was based on fact. Benjamin Franklin, Andrew Jackson, and Abraham Lincoln had all risen from a low estate to high places. Today we continue the Horatio Alger and the Cinderella legends. If no longer obvious in private industry, they are still blatant in the entertainment world. This partly explains our hero worship of sports and film stars, many of whom rose while very young from complete obscurity into the limelight. The average person can vicariously share in their success and relive the rags-to-riches dream. Opportunists and go-getters willing to take a chance have been, and still are, vital to economic expansion in the United States. It takes optimism to risk, for risk can mean waste and failure as well as success.

ECONOMY OF ABUNDANCE AND WASTE. Technology brought in a revolutionary attitude toward the material world. This new attitude discards old traditions and rules found wanting after testing, and supports the idea of "indefinite perfectibility." The young Frenchman, Alexis de Tocqueville, when visiting America in 1831, recorded this episode. "I accost an American sailor and inquire why the ships of his country are built to last for only a short time; he answers without hesitation that the art of navigation is every day making such rapid progress that the finished vessel would become almost useless if it lasted beyond a few years. . . ."[21]

Spurred on by the relative abundance of natural and social resources, we became an acquisitive society with a passion for wealth. Wealth became the yardstick of success. People were willing to work hard and their occupation determined their way of life. The Lynds' study of Middletown showed the attitude of the average person: "One's job is the watershed down which the rest of one's life tends to flow in Middletown. Who one is, whom one knows, how one lives, what one aspires to be . . . are patterned for one by what one does to get a living and the amount of living this allows one to buy."[22]

Wealth increases aspirations by making a variety of values possible. Some people feel free only in proportion to the money they possess. Without money they are stopped cold when it comes to fulfilling themselves. Sufficient capital allows them to try the new and fail, to make a poor decision—to waste. They have risked only a small part of their resources. With too little capital, failure can mean ruin. It follows that in the area of clothing, wealth allows trials of new fashions, some of which will be quickly outmoded while others may be discarded as failures.

Abundance and waste go together. In 1893 Henry Adams stated that the American wasted money more recklessly than anyone ever did before; he spent more to less purpose than any extravagant court aristocracy; he had no sense of relative values, and knew not what to do with his money when he got it, except use it to make more, or throw it away.[23] These were the families who became social leaders a decade or so later and gave the incentive for the widespread imitation and emulation that caused Veblen to write his *Theory of the Leisure Class* in which he viewed fashion as conspicuous waste.

The question arises: In an industry-based society, is the highest efficiency reached through what superficially appears to be waste? Our rapid large-scale consumption accelerates the replacement of plant and tools, always at a higher technical level. Old machinery becomes obsolete when something better emerges. Business competition and the accuracy with which performance can be measured exert pressures for change. Seen in this way, obsolescence as a process is wealth producing, not wasteful. What is needed is a method for getting rid of products we have outmoded.

The consumer faces the same pressures for change from the better performance of new products, new status symbols, and social competition. His house, his furniture, his clothes become obsolete. Getting rid of these outdated products brings on waste in the popular sense of "not using things up." A woman buys a new dress before the old one is worn out; a man buys a new car while the old motor is still in good condition. It is a short-run sacrifice of economic waste for a long-run gain of social efficiency. Fashion not only allows waste but makes waste an approved way of meeting social needs. Waste, from an individual point of view, should mean money spent but not enjoyed nearly as much as if spent in some other way.

Conclusion

The need for fashion arose in response to the social and economic pressures placed on individuals and groups by society. It became one of the meaningful ways by which human beings adjust to one another, and must be understood like any symbol, rule, or skill, if a person is to function capably within his own group or any of the statuses available to him. While the current image of fashion is always changing, fashion itself remains constant, and inevitably becomes a status symbol.

The conditions that stimulate demands for fashion goods from a large number of people appear to be the presence of many models to follow, a rising level of income that permits increasing expenditures for clothing, and a desire for approval in a society that emphasizes individual worth. The democratization of fashion, by giving everyone the same silhouette, has tended to narrow the gap between the socially underprivileged and the privileged while still retaining the fine distinctions of the social code.

2

THE FUNCTIONS OF FASHION

Fashion functions for the individual, the group, and the
nation. When Seventh Avenue sells fashion it is selling
something consumers want. We have seen how social and
economic conditions foster a need for fashion, but how does
fashion help the individual adjust to society?

The Individual

NEED FOR FASHION. The final test of a culture lies in the
quality of the setting it provides for the individual personality to form itself. The discovery of identity is a
crucial phase of the interaction of culture and the personality.
A girl may pause and reflect, Who am I? Where do I go from
here? She is engaged in a search for self which is part of the
maturing process. An awareness and acceptance of one's self, a
self capable of maintaining a "give and receive" relationship
with others, is necessary for the development of a creative individual.

George Mead defines knowledge of self as an awakening in
ourselves of the group of attitudes which we are arousing in
others. We identify ourselves by the attitudes others take
toward us and by the attitudes we take toward ourselves. It
follows that we seem to have not one but many selves. A
policeman in his uniform is a friend to the law abider, but an
enemy to the lawbreaker; he is a direction-giver to the tourist;
and simply a man-on-the-job to himself. Each self-identity is
dependent on the situation involved.

External self-identification is not the total person, just as a word is not the thing it represents. Our gestures, conduct, and dress—the signs of our identity—are presented to others to interpret in the same way we present words in a conversation. We are sending a message. If the meaning we intended to communicate is the one that is received, we have shared an idea with someone. If, on the other hand, the message received is not what we intended, if people view us differently from what we have in mind, we have failed.

Some overlapping field of common experience is necessary before a sign can have the same meaning for different people. A group of California coeds found this out when they tried to please some Japanese visitors. When the International House in Berkeley, California, was first opened, the American girls dressed for dinner in Japanese kimonos. To their chagrin, a young Japanese woman stood up and left the dining room, protesting that people should not come into the dining room in their underwear. The coeds had purchased their kimonos unaware that there was a difference between the underwear kimono and the overwear kimono. Countless other similar incidents occur when people find themselves in unfamiliar environments.

In any society, people seek the approval of some of their fellows and try to be successful by some shared standards of achievement. They try to resolve the conflict between individuality and conformity. The prodigious problem of human behavior in social terms is summarized by Ernest Becker: how to bring people to act together without endangering the fragile self-system of each. Man has to discover how "to confront a multitude of individuals with each other and still permit them all the conviction (the fiction) *that each is an object of primary value in a world of meaningful objects.*"[1]

While society has helped man by providing him with a conventional code of manners such as the Japanese bow, the French *Bon Jour,* the American smile, the intricacies of the social code are hard to master. This code calls for constant adaption to changing factors and each incident requires a new definition of the situation.

Clothing is of major importance in defining a situation. It can be considered part of society's social code. Gregory Stone noted that from birth to death, each change in a significant life situation requires a change of wardrobe, and even in daily life, each separate activity requires a change of dress.[2] A person's appearance *"announces* his identity, *shows* his values, *expresses* his mood, or *proposes* his attitudes."[3]

To be spectacular in figure and face, a delight for all the men in the office, and still be dressed with a decorum that offends no employer or customer of the company is a working girl's problem. This conflict between our own taste and the standards of the group is part of the complex background of suitable dress.

These two divisions of mental influence on dress are referred to by Ernst Harms as the "psycho-individual" and the "psycho-social": one is oriented toward the individual's own impulses, the other toward the situation.[4] Fortunately, fashion provides a way to resolve the conflict between the two.

USE FOR FASHION

To Express Personality. In the interests of self-security we try to function in society without anxiety; we seek the compromise that allows us to exercise our individual difference within the group. This complex need is characterized by psychologist Edmund Bergler as involving three reputations concerned with dress: (1) the reputation of belonging; (2) the reputation or mental impression every woman wants to convey to others; (3) the reputation or unconscious impression of herself which she wants to convey first to her inner conscience and later to the environment.[5]

These three needs or reputations are relative. They depend on the particular situation, on what other people are doing within the situation, and on the individual impulses of a person to make the symbols, rules, and skills of the group with which she wants to be connected part of herself. How fashion functions for the group will be discussed more fully in the following section. Here we are concerned with the mental impressions each individual wishes to convey with her clothes. These impressions can be viewed either as terminal values, enjoyed for their own sake, or as instrumental values, cultivated because they lead to something else.

The mental impressions we wish to convey to others are social values that have been classified and labeled. However, the interpretation of these values constantly shifts. You might wish to be well dressed, chic, pretty, arty, neat, warm and friendly, or noticeably different. These are qualities concerned with mood and interpersonal relationships. They arise from our own impulses as well as from the situation.

Ernst Harms gives some typical impulses of the human mind in relation to dress. The strongly volitional type of person lays great stress on the shape of her clothing, choosing arrogant and puffy dress. This type uses loud and complementary colors. The emotional type stresses harmony and fitness of color, the "well-suited" colors. The intellectual prefers subdued tones but has a marked color sense. She attaches a great deal of value to decorations and ornaments which are carefully chosen for personal or characteristic qualities, although they may not be used artistically.[6] The act of choosing dress is an emotional experience for the wearer. The results of this act make up her external surface. She expects the observer, through empathy, to make the same objective evaluation of her appearance as she has herself.

An illustration of empathy—the ability to go "out and into" something which attracts us—given by Esther Warner in her book, *Art,* demonstrates our personal involvement with clothes. She tells of her friend in Africa, an old African chief, who wanted a new hat. When she offered him the pith helmet she was wearing he turned it down. "Your hat is a turtle hat," he said. "It would make me feel that I crawl on the ground. . . ." But, when he brought out an old top hat and stood under it, he said, "I am tree-tall." With that hat he could talk to the trees. For him, it was truly a hat.[7]

As the overall fashion cycle changes its character from a lady-like New Look to the youthful shapeless chemise, to the casually classic, to the daring exposure of the topless bathing suit or a ten-inch mini-skirt, it gives people of different orientations an opportunity to find fuller self-expression through their clothes. Fashion continually rises and flourishes in response to new subjective demands.

Self-confidence rather than self-expression is the basis for those mental impressions we wish to convey first to ourselves and then to others. We may need to convince ourselves that we are attractive, efficient, capable of "good taste." Fashion can protect us from psychologically grounded fears that are socially engendered. It protects us from obscurity; from ridicule if we are "different," or if we lack taste. It protects the anxious and immature inner self from outer attack. It allows the dependent personality to follow others and be relieved of responsibility. It supports the timid by making acceptable styles they would like to wear but lack the courage to try. A fashion which enhances self-esteem and makes us feel competitively equal or superior to our associates *works for us* and helps diminish anxiety.

To Define Status. Although emotion may play a part in designing the dress to suit the person and the occasion, it is intellect that directs the actual choice of the correct garment for defined social situations. By reading the cues of others as well as our own, we are able to make a quick appraisal and determine which form of the social code to use. We must be aware of such elements as power difference, social distance, and prestige distinction.

Seeman and Evans, who studied apprenticeship and attitude change at the University of California, used a scale of stratification composed of three status elements: power difference, social distance, and prestige distinction.[8] These concepts help explain the subtle differences that separate social groups and individuals.

Power difference refers to "the degree of influence and decision-making in the work of the unit."[9] This is the basis for *The Power Elite* of C. Wright Mills—the overlapping cliques of politicians, army officers, and corporation officials who make decisions of national importance. It is also the element that causes chills in the wife of the salesman on his first job as she dresses for a social engagement at the home of the boss.

Social distance refers to the "degree of closeness, friendliness, intimacy, or informality of the relationship."[10] Think of the woman viewing her wardrobe and musing: "This dress is right for the family . . . the new one is better for the club . . . but I'm to be a guest in a group I don't even know. . . . What shall I wear?"

Prestige distinction is the amount of deference that is expected or the general emphasis upon ranked status symbols.[11] A Washington hostess knows the protocol of seating arrangements for government officials, where to place the Secretary of State in relation to the French Ambassador. In many homes there is also protocol: Father sits in *his* chair to read the paper and recover *his* identity.

Clothing, being peripheral and easily seen, permits fast assessment of a situation, and the element of fashion in clothes adds a status dimension of its own. Fashion can identify status difference from the lowest rung on the ladder to the top. This is because there is, within fashion itself, a hierarchical relationship between high fashion, mass fashion, and past fashion.

High fashion is the prevailing style chosen by women of recognized taste and authority in the fashion area. They may be editors of fashion magazines, influential buyers, or women of wealth, social position, or fame, who have acquired reputations for chic.* They love beautiful clothes; they are, in the words of *Vogue,* "the elegants." They wear their taste like a trademark and their number is relatively small.

While it may seem, in some cases, that the wearer gives distinction to the fashion, it is equally true that the fashion, made with skill under the trained eye of a creative designer, contributes its share of distinction to the wearer. This reciprocal give-and-take makes the fashion seem doubly desirable. High fashion, future oriented, and placed at the beginning of the fashion cycle, often directs the mass fashion. High fashion is given high status.

Mass fashion, on the other hand, is the prevailing style chosen by an anonymous group of consumers, large in number, some with chic and some without. (Even a distinctive fashion on a person lacking chic seems less desirable.) Because of the variety of tastes involved and the lower quality of fabric and construction required for popular price, mass fashion appears less desirable than high fashion. A person with chic may do more for a mass fashion than it does for her. Distinction is more dependent on the wearer than on the fashion.

This does not mean that a mass fashion lacks status. The mere fact that it *is fashion,* representing now in time, gives it status over yesterday. When you are in fashion you are right for today's life—you know what it is all about, you look new.

A dress out-of-fashion is at the end of the fashion cycle and the bottom of the status scale. It can only depend on the

---

* A *chic* person is a term used in the fashion world to designate someone who appreciates herself as a symbol of taste in fashion. To this person, quality in clothing means excellence in design, becomingness, and a high degree of fashion.

talent and ingenuity of the wearer, or some inherent quality over and beyond fashion for distinction. Without these, it is a has-been, to be cast aside, for it is of little social value to the wearer. In connection with our idea of progress, we rank time. The future is high in status, the present is medium high, and the past is low. A discerning eye picks up these subtle time differences between fashions at different stages in the fashion cycle and uses them as rank and status symbols.

Research on the shopping behavior of homemakers, conducted by Gregory Stone and William Form in a county seat town in south-central Michigan, underscores the importance of clothes to status in an everyday situation. The investigators found that the type of clothing worn by the homemaker while shopping for clothes was conditioned by her social position in the community; that the higher her social status, the more likely she would be "dressed up"—wearing a good dress, or a suit, and high-heeled shoes. This was particularly true when the women viewed a shopping situation as enhancing their social status and self-esteem: when they felt that the way they dressed affected the service the salesclerks gave them.[12] In another sense, this study also seems to illustrate "role-playing," a concept used by social psychologists to help explain the interpersonal relationships within a social situation. Dress and fashion are significant symbols used to identify roles as well as status.

To Play a Role. The concepts of role and status are often confused. Lloyd Warner believes that status emphasizes membership and place in a social universe and is defined in a relational context, whereas role emphasizes personality and is defined by reference to how individuals act or are believed to act by those around them. The role an individual plays is the way he defines himself as a person; it accents how he stylizes his behavior. Warner emphasizes that role is essentially a product of personality traits, real or attributed, while social status is a product of the interconnection of social relations. In America, such terms as "clubwoman" for an individual active in civic affairs, or "little mother" for the girl who protects others designate personality roles.[13]

Roles are learned. When children "make-believe"—play at pretending to be a storekeeper or a cowboy—they project

themselves through imagination into another's role. They realize how it feels to be that person and view themselves through the eyes of the pretend personality. Adults act in a similar way; in different situations they play different roles. Role-playing is a way of seeing how each person in a group looks on the other members of the group and on himself in an expected role. It can be used in the process of self-identification; that is, by role-playing, we can react through anticipation to our own self-symbol.

Of all the roles we play, there is general agreement that the age-sex role is the most important. This, in turn, determines our position in the family as wife, mother, father, or husband. For men, the occupational role supports their sex role. The more successful they are in their job, the more desirable they seem as husbands and fathers. And they often adopt the identity of their occupational group. We seldom mislabel "the Professor" in his conventional tweeds, carrying a leather briefcase, slipping into a topcoat that almost matches, and putting on *a hat*. In the same way we know "the Businessman" in his more formal suit tailored with precision, his topcoat perfectly matching, and the entire ensemble, including the hat he wears and the attaché case he carries, strictly in fashion. The degree of fashion present and the type of fashion selected can identify horizontal groupings on the same level as well as vertical groupings between levels in our social relationships.

Unlike men, identity for women is not so easy. An occupational role outside the home may conflict with the feminine role women have been trained to assume. Success for a woman does not mean success in a job, but success in finding and keeping a husband. The test of her femininity, as Margaret Mead said, is her ability first to attract and keep several men and then finally one man. The continual query "Who do you date?" is simply a check on the popularity of each girl by her peers, on her success as a woman.[14]

Each girl strives for the feminine ideal—to be fascinating . . . young and glamorous . . . beautiful . . . attractive to men. This is what women want to be. Fashion, because it defends the rights of imagination and represents public taste, is able to personify the prevailing ideal of femininity.

(1967): A young eccentric dashed into the gay party.

She wore a leopard-print dress; gloves to match; low-heeled shoes; beige, patterned stockings; and pounds of sandy-blond hair. She spun away with everything flying, flying hair and flying dress . . . never missing a dance.

(1907): A demure girl, radiantly charming, entered the church in a wine-red dress, high-necked, with velvet bands edging the bodice yoke, her gored skirt clearing the floor by one inch. She wore white gloves and a white beaver hat (*real* beaver) with a white ostrich plume whose tip curled over the broad brim of the hat toward the back. A young man looked . . . and said quietly to himself . . . There's my girl.

The radar equipment of each girl, in David Riesman's language, is tuned in on the reactions of her peer group. She imitates and emulates those girls who attract men, those most approved by others, and therefore, most successful. Attractiveness is something that can be acquired with skill and money; there is no excuse for relaxing in despair.

The results of the Katz and Lazarsfeld study, *Personal Influence,* showed fashion interest was at its peak among young single women under 35 years of age who were looking forward to marriage.[15] Girls feel that the more attractive they are the better their chances for the right marriage or a job promotion. When a conflict arises between the occupational demands of the Staid Office Executives and the current image of feminine glamour, fashion steps in as peacemaker to solve the problem. Sweaters and knit dresses, colorful blouses and smooth-fitting skirts allow the individual display of seductive curves while satisfying the group demands of business to "cover up."

The Group

NEED FOR FASHION. People emulate "better" taste and so upgrade their own. But it is not the president of the company that the workingman wants to imitate nor the wealthy matron that his wife wants to emulate. Rather, sociologists points out that as a rule *consumers emulate tastes within reach*—people in their own group. The Texas schoolgirl copies the dress of an admired member of her family or the ideas of her respected friends, not the fashions worn by a New York debutante.

Each group is concerned with maintaining conformity within and establishing difference without, between their groups and others. As a group develops a style of living, this becomes the group image. William H. Whyte, Jr., in his study of new suburbia, found the community united in a code of inconspicuous consumption; it was an offense to display worldly goods. To maintain group harmony, each member tuned in to see when consumption was ostentatious and when it was style leadership.[16]

The "reference group" concept of social psychology gives us perspective. One person is a member of many groups—a part of many wholes. A college student may be a female of one age group, a member of a family and a community, a member of the student body, a dorm girl, and a member of a corridor group. She may be a Methodist, a Chinese, and an American. At the same time she may wish to belong to a sorority, become a career girl, or, above all, become a member of the young married set.

We act in relation to the group to which we are most committed. This can be a group in which we are a member or a group in which we hope to hold membership. The group from which we draw our beliefs, motivations, and actions in a specific instance is the "reference group."

USE OF FASHION. Fashions in dress are classified according to such factors as occupation, activity, and age. They become group standards. These standards, codified as symbols, are shared by all members of the group. The symbols have a common meaning for each member and come to be a shorthand method of communication. A reciprocal exchange of symbols permits members of the group to communicate faster and better with each other than they can with other groups. For example, the mathematical concepts or key language that mathematicians share identify their group and hold the group together, while an unusual fashion in dress may identify and hold together a group of surfboard riders in California. Overlapping areas of common experience strengthen the solidarity and exclusive character of the many groups found in a complex society.

Occupational Groups. More and more, man is occupational

man. He is what he does. For many people the occupational group is the most important reference group.

The *Wall Street Journal* for December 11, 1964, devoted a front-page column to the lively controversy in the nation's offices on above-the-knee skirts. "The knee does *not* show in business," declared the president of a Chicago employment agency. This was at a time when skirts were reaching a new high, going to two or three inches above the knee, even shorter than during the 20's.

In general, the business world, dependent on the opinion of customers for success or failure, adopts a policy that will be acceptable to most people. It wishes to appear sensible and sober, worthy of trust and confidence. For this reason business rejects the extremes of fashion—the latest styles from Paris as as well as the outlandish hairdos and trick clothes of the off-beat crowd.

The degree of conservatism in the business image varies with the type of business. Banks are among the most conservative in standards of dress. A spokesman for a Chicago bank observed that most of their employees soon learn to dress so as "to fade into the background." Even stores that are glad to sell fashion take a dim view of their employees' wearing too much of it. Bergdorf Goodman, an elegant New York women's specialty store, reminded its employees that "we don't want our salespeople mistaken for customers."[17] Airlines take a new look each year at the hostesses' uniform. While keeping a relatively modest dress, some companies follow fashion up and down, in and out. Others lag sedately behind. The unexpected twistings and turnings of fashion play their part in enhancing or sabotaging a company image.

The relation between the employees' attitude to clothing and the company image was studied by Form and Stone at Michigan State College in 1955. They found that the meaning of clothing varied with the type of occupation and the social standing of the occupation. White-collar workers valued clothing as a symbol which could be used to impress and manipulate others. They "dressed up" to impress the personnel manager when applying for a job. Men in higher prestige positions purchased more clothing and spent more for it than men in lower positions. There was widespread belief among white-collar employees that dress was related to success on the job. However, manual workers appeared to be unaware that people judged them by their clothing. They wanted durable clothes that facilitated work performance and felt the use of clothing was restricted by the job demands.[18]

According to this study there was general satisfaction with the occupational dress. Both businessmen and manual workers were reluctant to change. Men in business felt deviations would impair customer relations; "the public" would disapprove. Manual workers felt the immediate members of their work group would ridicule them. For one group the social control was "indirect and impersonal"; for the other it was more "direct and interpersonal."

Peer Groups. When Riesman said that for "other-directed" people their contemporaries are the source of direction—either those known to them or with whom they are indirectly acquainted through friends and the mass media—he restated the reference group concept in a more limited way. That is, he proposed that the peer group is the most important reference group.

Although the word peer refers to contemporaries for any age group, young people, especially, because of their search for self-identity, may have a feeling of direct participation only with people like themselves. They may say to themselves: I belong here, with my peers who have the same needs and inclinations as myself.

At the same time that membership in a peer group satisfies the need to belong to something bigger than oneself, it also poses a threat to individualism. Kenneth Benne suggests that "peer groups normally unite (defensively or offensively) against the symbols of authority, and from this fact flows the identity-destroying effects of the group on its members, its punishment of individual variations, its exaltation of uniformity." The group stereotype in forcing members to deny parts of themselves gives them an invalid self-image before their own self and the world.[19]

Each off-beat "live" group gets a label and a "look." They reject the accepted fashion image and introduce their own unexpected twist; with exaggerated styles they call attention to themselves. Between 1963 and 1964 some English groups, including the Beatles, the Stones, and the Mods, became fashion

Brigitte Bardot

innovators. The Beatle haircut—a long bob for men, brushed forward toward the eyes—was the fashion rage. In London dance spots the girls seemed modest and demure until you noticed that a striped green chiffon dress on a well-built blonde had no sides at the top. *Women's Wear Daily* reported, "It's all sort of like Oliver Cromwell doing the twist with Queen Victoria."[20]

Not long before, in 1960, Brigitte Bardot made St. Tropez, a little French Riviera fishing village, the center of a Bardot cult. Here the young French crowd gathered, the girls in their bone-tight pants and their Bardot trademark—a heavy mane of hair elaborately draped on top of the head and caught by a barrette, the long locks falling in disorder over the shoulders. Heavy black eye liner, their only makeup, made their eyes stand out from the face. The total look was one of elaborately planned neglect.

We have had the beatnik age, the rock 'n roll period, the jitterbug stage, and the jazz era—a whole series of young, vibrant images. In these rebellions of youth against the established authority, "conventional fashion" is symbolically replaced by the "group fashion." The new authority (the group sterotype) may then exert a more rigid control over the members of the group than the authority it replaced.

A group organized for *achievement,* not offense or defense against authority, finds differences in ability and talent lend strength to the group. A good baseball team cannot be all pitchers; it requires a variety of abilities in the interest of the game. These groups develop an internal division of labor to achieve their common purpose. Even here, however, once a uniform is donned, there must be constant vigilance against the stultifying effect of a group stereotype that forces people to deny parts of themselves.[21]

Prestigious Groups. Upper-status groups are concerned with prestige-ranking symbols—rare goods that come in limited supply. They feel that superior social groups should be adorned with superior dress. They look for luxury goods, rare high fashion garments designed by creative couturiers, executed by skilled workmen in the best quality fabrics, and made to fit perfectly the body of one person.*

The price of rare goods is high, partly because the limited supply is desired by people who can afford to pay high prices, and partly because the greater skill that is required to produce excellence in dress is paid for on a level with greater skill in other fields. Thus, high fashion designs, like first quality plays, may be available only in large cities. There, the social pressure, concentration of wealth, and large numbers of shoppers create sufficient demand to make it worthwhile for some distributor to supply this type of goods.

The cultured wife of a wealthy broker, banker, artist, or architect may live in the fashionable surburban countryside. Although she lives in the country, she has city tastes. She might summer in Maine, winter in Palm Beach, jet to Europe once a year, and go to New York for the best plays. And she

---

* Dwight E. Robinson, a business economist, defines rarity as a limited supply of something unusually excellent. He believes that while sensory gratification *may* be an attribute of any luxury goods, rarity is a necessary condition.[22]

would probably patronize a high fashion designer or couturier who would help her select "superior" taste symbols.

Norman Norell, one of America's top designers, says that such women *know* about fashion and quality. It takes know-how—first, to select excellence in dress, and second, to make a dress or suit yours alone. A woman has to have her own touch, some "wonderful accessory" that "makes her uniform different."[23] These observations suggest that a sense of self-expression, fashion, and excellence direct the taste of the upper-status woman that Norell serves. In short, she has the ability to select luxury goods and use them in a distinctive or rare manner; that is, she is able to define one person, herself.

Taste, generally speaking, means a "preference for" something. Thus, everyone has taste. But in a more particular sense, taste is often described as the ability to discern and appreciate that which is beautiful and appropriate—the marriage of the aesthetic and the practical. Viewed in this way, taste may be an end in itself. The real reason for having taste is to increase capacity for enjoyment and understanding. However, taste for taste's sake is cultivated by many people who do not enjoy the things they have taste about. They are only concerned with taste as an approved symbol of a prestigious group.

In *The Tastemakers,* Russel Lynes notes that there is no reason to improve taste if "taste continues to be a set of mannerisms that one learns from a book of cultural etiquette."[24] But as long as taste is necessary for membership in a high-status group it will be used as a means to an end—a tool in mobility. Only those people who see taste for what it contributes to the enrichment of life will seek it as an end in itself.

One important attribute of taste is quality, a psychological value that varies to some extent with each person. One woman may prefer one brand of lipstick over another. But, for each group or society, standards of quality tend to arise. These are determined by the people of recognized taste, training, experience, background, and interest in a particular area. Clare McCardell, a creative American fashion designer, said that occasionally she would buy a good dress for her young daughter so the child could experience quality in clothes. She was giving her child a background for fashion judgment. Quality becomes, then, a combined evaluation of individual taste and the recognized standards of an authoritative group.

What constitutes "superior" taste is relative to a society. Harriet Martineau, a cultured English woman who came to America in 1834, considered the dress and manners of young women at the fashionable watering places on Long Island ostentatious and vulgar. "When I saw the young ladies tricked out in the most expensive finery, flirting over the backgammon board; tripping affectedly across the room, languishing with a seventy-dollar cambric handkerchief . . . I almost doubted whether I was awake."[25] Today, she would be more likely to find members of the upper-strata groups casually dressed than overdressed and their manners would be correspondingly natural and relaxed.

The Nation

NEED FOR FASHION. The nation needs to help people prepare for change. The central problem for the individual in today's society is developing flexibility in behavior. The ideal personality appears to be one so adaptive to changes through time, space, and empathy that displacement is its permanent mode.

In an industry-based society, change is inevitable. Advancing technology alters wants for material goods by introducing new or more efficient products and by lowering the cost of existing items. It breaks up expected status characteristics by introducing new occupations around which status symbols are formed. It redistributes wealth. By various means, technology initiates and supports social change. A technological nation must reinforce a desire for mobility and change within the society.

At the same time, each society has a need for stability or social order. A complex society of many small groups and diverse symbol systems, such as ours, also tends to develop an opposing but necessary system—an overall symbol system that everyone understands. Generalized public symbols arouse common sentiments, values, and beliefs and act to maintain national solidarity while permitting subgroup diversity. The overall fashion trend can be viewed as such a symbol. It becomes a recognized standard and affects individual groups in a general way, causing each group to develop its fashions either in accord with or opposed to the prevailing mode.

USE OF FASHION

Prepares People for Change. Fashion prepares people for change in a nation where progress is dependent on change. Openmindedness in temporary things, such as shortening or lengthening skirts, may lead to openmindedness in things of more lasting importance. As constant changes in the form of fashion prod people to continually revise their taste, fashion becomes a force for mobility and fluidity in a nation's social structure.

So, too, imitation which results in emulation has a potent effect on the spread of new ideas—it expands the structure of human wants. We see this in the struggle of the "have-not" nations to copy the "have" nations, to achieve a high level of living for masses of the people rather than a few. The drive for *economic democracy* may have begun (a condition the United States has almost achieved). Poverty has two aspects: (1) the lack of better things for better wants; and (2) the lack of better wants for better things. However, the degree of satisfaction derived from the consumption of the same goods under varying conditions cannot be measured and will be different for each person involved, for "the good life" is a relative concept.

Fashion, by designating rank and status, helps to provide men with the motives to excel by striving for positions of higher prestige and power. It encourages the rivalry and competition needed in a free-enterprise system that believes in social mobility. The fashion area offers a relatively harmless arena for emulative drives. As Veblen suggests, the display of fashion goods by a man's wife may take the place of the display of several enemy heads in more primitive cultures. They each serve to designate the defined social position of the male. Relatively speaking, fashion provides a conventional (nonrevolutionary) way for individuals to rise in status and expend their aggressive drives.

Fashions of the Western world allow each person to change his group identification according to the needs of his own personality. Indirectly, Horatio Alger, Jr., impressed this on his readers in 1871 with the young heroine, Tattered

Tom. "When she wore her old tatters she was quite ready to engage in a fight with any boy who jeered at her, provided he was not too large. Now (in her new school clothes) she would hesitate before doing it, having an undefined idea that her respectable dress would make such a scene unbecoming."[26]

Retains Social Order. Through fashion, people know where they stand in relation to others, who they are, and how to act. Fashion is a nonverbal communication between all members of the society. An understanding of fashion symbols allows one to go freely about the society. However, a limited knowledge restricts his movements. The outward symbols in clothing are constantly changing. If he does not know the cues he does not recognize the change. A person has to really be "in-the-know" to catch the subtle nuances of fashion in the upper-class groups today.

Mass fashion or popular fashion surmounts group barriers and becomes a national symbol available to everyone. Although all dresses may not have quality, they can have fashion. And fashion in clothing is often the first symbol a newcomer or an isolated group will display of the shared pattern of beliefs and behaviors that make up the nation. Fashion helps to construct a common subjective life in a pluralistic society. Changes in fashion can make a thing seem modest or immodest, proper or improper, and if they last long enough, such changes can affect the standards of modesty and propriety throughout the society.

The dress of a nation symbolizes the spirit of the nation, yet that spirit, as represented by dress, is open to different interpretations.* For example, Joyce Carey noted that the educated and enterprising European peasant breaks away from the traditional national costume because he feels it is a badge of servitude and backwardness. So, too, when young African chiefs leave the tribe for the outside world, they tend to adopt Western dress; to them Western dress is not the mark of a mass mind but the mark of a free and independent mind.[27]

Fashion aids in various ways to retain balance in the social order. When fashion breaks convention it becomes an outlet for curiosity and imagination. It causes excitement and

* Fashion as a reflection of American life is discussed in Part III of this book.

relieves boredom. The topless bathing suit of 1964 gave the public a "new kick," mainly in the feature columns of the newspapers. The "monokini," as one lawyer named it in contrast to the "bikini," was especially "in" with the rich girls, partly because they had private beaches and bail money, and partly because they were sometimes bored. Too much leisure and too many years of affluent calm can create a degree of boredom that may become a bane to a society. When comfort and security come comparatively quickly for most people, with little struggle or effort, a vague uneasy boredom can set in. The novel and the new give superficial relief, although they do not cure the basic ailment.

Because consumers want fashion (even discounters use fashion, not price, to upgrade their items), the "rag market" becomes Big Business. It is a major source of income for the nation.

After the French Revolution, Napoleon Bonaparte saw that fashion would be productive only if it were identified with change. During his regime, clothing was changed three times a day and jewelry was designed for each toilette. To women whom he saw more than once in the same dress Napoleon would say, "Madame is that the only dress you possess?"[28] This economic attitude led to the founding of the haute couture by Charles Frederick Worth who linked fashion to the textile industry and made high fashion a business.

In this country, the Industrial Revolution, urbanization, and the immigrant floods brought mass production of all types of fashion apparel. It was not long before the fashion industry became one of the most competitive industries in the free-enterprise system and a source of national wealth. It has remained competitive: a fairly homogeneous product, sold by large numbers of sellers to numerous buyers, with little or no discrimination. Today, fashion can be thought of as part of the social code, representing a solution to many anxiety-creating problems. As a symbol, fashion helps people know who they are and where they stand in relation to others. It is used by individuals to express personality, to define a situation, and to play a role. Fashion also answers the needs of small groups for identity and status in a complex society, yet binds them together with nationwide sentiments and common beliefs. Fashion helps people prepare for change and offers a nonrevolutionary way for individuals to rise in status; at the same time it helps retain the social order. As fashion circles the globe in exports and imports, it expresses the worldwide interdependence of people and narrows the cultural gaps.

The phenomenon of fashion clearly arises in answer to the social needs of society. The changing form of fashion—fashion products that are bought and sold on the market—is largely determined by the economic conditions of society.

2

FASHION: *AN ECONOMIC GOOD*

3

ECONOMICS OF FASHION

Once a social need for fashion arises, the economic resources of the nation will be directed toward producing, distributing, and consuming fashion goods. The astute managers of the Paris Fashion House of Dior sensed that this would happen in Russia long before there was any pronounced market for high fashion goods and took forward-looking steps to promote affluence and style of Soviet citizens.

As new industries arise to produce fashion goods, they help to increase the national circulation of wealth. This is evident in France where the prestige of haute couture is responsible for volume sales in French perfume, and in major cities of the United States where thousands of factories turning out mass-produced clothing employ thousands of workers. More money for more people both accelerates the social need for fashion and permits the sale of more fashion goods; the entire process becomes self-perpetuating.

Consumer outlays for clothing and accessories amounted to almost $35 billion in 1963, about 9 per cent of total personal consumption expenditures in the United States.[1] By 1964 a marked increase in the industry had begun which was expected to bring the total outlay for fashion goods in 1967 to over $50 billion, making this market second only to food among all consumer markets. The increasing proportion of young, fashion-minded adults in the population and rising personal incomes suggest that even greater expenditures lie ahead. While the apparel industry is not ranked with the steel industry as vital to the national economy, nevertheless, as one of our major industries, it contributes in a significant way to the circulation of wealth.

Circulation of Wealth

Industries pay money in the form of wages, interest, and rent in return for the productive services that individuals sell or loan them—personal skills, savings, land, equipment. At the same time, individuals, as consumers, pay money to industry in return for produced goods and services. In this way wealth circulates.

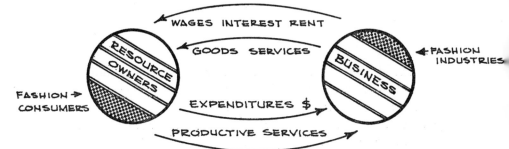

When the customer murmurs "I'll take it," and the retail clerk asks "charge or cash?" this activity typifies an exchange of goods on the market. One form of property, a coat, is given in exchange for some other form of property, money. It is this act of exchange that makes fashion goods a subject for economic investigation.

In addition to acts of exchange, economics is concerned with three other types of human activity: production, distribution, and consumption. Production is the transformation of raw materials and labor into products. It consists of services rendered, just as distribution is another type of service—the transportation of goods from one spot to another. Thus, a wool coat, as an economic good, is the sum total of the services of the farmers who raised the wool, the transport workers who carried it to the mill, the processors, the manufacturers, the retailers, and all persons who helped make the coat available on the market. In this sense, when the consumer pays for garments at the store he is paying for a bundle of services.

Acts of consumption are of interest to the economist because the consumer's "taste" or "preference for" one product over another is the only reliable measure of consumer demand. There is no satisfactory test of quality in a produced product except the test of intelligent preferences. That is why Norman Norell, a top American designer, feels that the criterion of a design is that it is accepted and worn by the general public.

The economist studies, but does not judge, choices. He is concerned with who produces what, who consumes what, and who exchanges what.

In total, the economic process can be viewed as a choice-making process in a scarcity situation. That is, the economists assume that human wants are limitless, but the means to satisfy these wants—time, labor, and capital—are limited. So, goals must be established. First, decisions as to which wants to satisfy, in what quantity, and at what time; and second, decisions as to the best way of producing goods while using the least resources. All alternative ways are considered and the consequences of each compared. The responsibility for the final choice rests with the person who makes the product.

The study of fashion as an economic good becomes, then, the study of the best way to meet the socially developed need for fashion products. In the past it was possible for individual craftsmen, such as the patient dressmaker or the skilled tailor, to meet the fashion demands of individuals and family groups. Today, the story of fashion apparel is the story of how hundreds of designers, manufacturers, and merchandisers meet the many varied demands of a vast market.

Analysis of Fashions on the Market

The market at any one time is composed of the fashion of the majority (the official "fashion") and minority or subgroup fashions. When a style is "the fashion," the demand for that style is at a peak. The designs being sold in that style outnumber any other. It is this style that buyers hope to stock in sufficient numbers to handle the volume of demand, and the one most manufacturers would like to produce. When the trade records sales of these styles, they are called "best sellers." The word "ford" is also used to designate a style so popular it will be copied in clothing lines at various price levels.

Other styles, such as the "incoming" and "outgoing" fashions and the classics, are the minority fashions, favored by some women but not by most. The problem of the producer and distributor is calculating just how great this demand will be. It is easy to place a style in "past" phases of the fashion cycle but very difficult when the process is in operation. The seller must decide "now" if a style is on the upswing, on the decline, or in its peak of demand. The very definitions of the terms make the dilemma apparent. A fashion is the style favored by the majority, and this can be accurately known only for a past market. The dilemma, however, is not quite as severe as it seems. Although it is difficult to forecast accurately, the volume of sales and the rate of growth or decline in relation to possible total volume can be indicators for well-informed estimates as to which stage a fashion is in. The difficulty, as David Riesman states so succinctly, "is much the same problem as the pollsters predicting who will win the election before it is held. They can be wrong." Various factors in society mold consumer preference and choice. The social factors have been discussed in Part I of this book; in this chapter the emphasis will be on economic factors.

Economic Factors in Society That Affect Fashion and Style

The size of fashion movements and their rapidity of change are greatly affected by economic factors. Machine technology has made possible mass production and quick turnover. Producing an item in large numbers may result in economies of scale which lower the cost of production. If the same dress design is repeated thousands of times and economies of scale result, it can be sold at a lower price than an original, few of which are produced. A decrease in price acts as a stimulant to increased demand which, in turn, may cause a further drop in price. In this way fashion and dropping prices reinforce each other. An economic system with economies of scale tends to stimulate a majority choice.

A mass demand is further created by vast networks of communication and transportation which bring into one sphere of influence geographically separated individuals. Radio and television, national brand advertising, and fashion services whose analyses appear in numerous newspapers and magazines bring a sameness of influence to their audience regardless of the locality in which they are received. At the same time, more people and goods travel greater distances. This exposure of people to the same ideas results in demands becoming more similar throughout the nation and even throughout the world.

If the same things are to be available to great numbers of people, equality of income is a necessary factor. In this country, per capita income has increased greatly and become more equally distributed. The combination of natural resources with an advanced production and distribution has resulted in an unusually large degree of available goods and other usable wealth. A greater real income allows people a higher range of experimentation and makes them more receptive to new ideas. Their interest in durability lessens, contributing to rapid fashion change. Items are discarded not because they are worn out but because they "seem" old.

The psychological acceptance of change and experimentation has been promoted by new inventions. In the clothing field, the whole series of man-made fibers, such as rayon, nylon, and Dacron, revealed startling new possibilities. "Fur" can be made instead of being grown. In our economy these changes come relatively fast and consumer acceptance is hastened by the great network of advertising and promotion. The public becomes accustomed to rapid change in technology and transfers this acceptance of "change" to fashion, too.

Industry Views Fashion and Style

Since the fashion element in new apparel quickly outmodes the old style, fashion is often looked upon by industry as a source of increased demand. But this can be a problem as well as a blessing. As Nystrom states it: "Consumers not producers make the fashion. . . . The producer or dealer may propose but it is the consumer who disposes. The individual concern whose product most clearly approximates the current requirements of fashion and therefore of consumer demand gets the business and makes the profit."[2]

For the consumer to find what she wants, or want what she finds is as important to the producer and retailer as to herself. The more readily she finds the fashion she is looking for at her price level, the lower are the selling costs. The problem becomes one of communication: How is industry to know which style women will like or how they can induce them to like what they offer?

The consumer communicates to the retail dealer with her purchase. The market she faces does not offer all possible styles. The manufacturer and the retail buyer have already narrowed the choice, but the consumer chooses from what is available.

The diversified mass of manufacturers and retailers—large and small, leaders and followers—use many ways to "tune in" on consumer desires. Foremost among these are analyses of sales records. The sources available for the study of consumer demand are:

1. Unit stock control
2. Competitors' sales
3. Reports from all personnel
4. Reports from customers
5. Reactions to advance promotions and advertising
6. Fashion services
7. Fashion magazines, newspapers, television and radio

Even with this information it is still hard for a retailer or manufacturer to be sure, when he presents a new style, that he is offering what his customers will want. The passing of time brings new desires and new attitudes. The new styles may bear some resemblance to the former fashion; perhaps there has just been a change in Paris from Dior's "A" silhouette to his "H" silhouette.* How can he tell who among his customers will like the new "H" silhouette, which version they are more likely to want, or whether they will want it at all? The sales reports from last season may give hints as to the past popularity of enduring "classic" styles, and the "A" silhouette fashion can be identified in its "incoming," "peak," or "outgoing" stage, but how can one predict the acceptance of an entirely new style?

Riesman, in the article "Autos in America," states that

* The "H" silhouette was introduced by Dior in 1953. The bloused bodice, straight waistline, and straight skirt made it resemble the letter "H."

polling the car owners as to what they like about cars can never help the designer decide what a new car should look like. "Since fashions represent the victory over the majority of what was a moment ago a minority taste, polling the majority cannot serve to create styles, only to confirm them. In fact, people will often verbally reject what they will accept as a *fait accompli*—whether in fashion or in race relations or politics generally."[3]

Past sales can bear a false message. The consumer, through need, may take what is available. This choice may build a desire never to buy that style again. The consumer is "satisfied" when her purchase is so well liked it promotes the wish to repeat this experience in some future purchase.

To further complicate the question of fashion acceptance, there is this factor: The market may be viewed as one large group of "all women," or as many subgroups made up of women with common characteristics. The subgroups may favor certain style or stages in the fashion cycle. Those who prefer "incoming fashions" can be classed as the "high style" group. They look for dresses which are new, that have not yet been accepted by the majority of "all women." These are the women who introduce change. Other groups prefer "classics"—conservative styles which were formerly accepted and for which there is a continuing demand. Still others may favor the "junior miss" type. The classifications can be numerous. These groups separately make up the minority fashions and en masse they compose the total market of "all women."

Fashion for the total market or the majority fashion can be seen as that style which forms a common link between most minority fashions. If back fullness is the majority fashion it will be found in the classics, in the college styles, in the mature styles, but the degree and importance of its use will vary among subgroups, depending on their preferred style.

It is also possible that women grouped by like characteristics find through experience certain combinations of design elements "satisfactory" to them. Such a combination might be a V neck, easy-fitting bodice, natural waistline, slightly flared skirt, cap sleeve, soft texture, and a shade of blue. This becomes for them their favorite personal style. Each time new styles are offered they search for this basic combination. This does not mean they oppose fashion, for fashion brings variations of a theme and relieves monotony, but if the current styles are only empire lines and tubular skirts, members of this group may be discontented. *They may be unhappy if they cannot find within the fashion the basic elements necessary to their personal style.*

Thus, conflicting factors in consumer choice point up the need for industry to continuously check consumer demand. The consumer, choosing alone in a market economy, decides what best fulfills his needs. The consumer as a rational, thinking being, neither passively manipulated by hidden persuaders and wastemakers nor innocently entrapped by Madison Avenue advertising, is the director of production, deciding which products shall be made and who shall make them, which companies shall survive and which shall perish.

Part II of this book traces the development of designing, producing, and merchandising fashions in dress and examines the problems each phase of the industry faces in meeting consumer demand. The area of promotion and adoption of fashion goods is treated as a communication problem between different phases of the industry, between industry and consumers, and between consumers in various stages of adoption of a new style.

4

DESIGN

Before it can become part of the fashion marketplace, a dress must first be designed. This design may become a style, and from several styles a fashion will be chosen. This is a choice-making process that begins with the designer. To answer the question of what determines which models a designer will present, we must focus on three factors that affect the decision: (1) the designer's reason for designing; (2) his understanding of dress; and (3) his sense of business. Two of these factors relate to the individual's view of himself and the social culture in which he lives, while the third concerns his degree of involvement in an economic system that is geared to consumer demand and the profit incentive.

The Designer

It is recognized that the function of design for the creator of design is not the same as it is for the consumer of design. The consumer looks to design for emotional release in fantasy from the tensions of everyday pressures, for physical relaxation and comfort, for social utility, and for enhancement of personal esteem. The creator of design may attempt to share with others some relationship of ideas, form, or matter which he has sensed; to solve a technical problem; to invent new media of expression; to achieve fame or at best notoriety; or simply to make a living.

The style a designer develops indirectly reveals his motivation. For example, Cristobal Balenciaga, the Parisian designer of Spanish descent, who, for over twenty-five years led

Balenciaga

the creative fashion world, consistently presented his ideas of free-form sculpture through the medium of dress. With refined, stark, austere designs he became the master of the elegant contemporary look in clothing. Meanwhile, a fellow couturier, Christian Dior, following his own hobby of architecture, solved the technical problem of keeping a graceful ladylike design in shape on the active form of twentieth-century women by perfecting the use of interlinings. Some of his most successful designs seemed to flow across the body as if the movement had been caught and transfixed at a moment in time. These molded effects were the result of layer after layer of interlinings skillfully cut and sewed by highly trained dressmakers.

In the early 1900's, Nelly Don (Nell Donnelly), one of the first successful American designers of ready-to-wear, felt that housedresses could become a medium for artistic expression and that women could look pretty in inexpensive cotton dresses. Rudy Gernreich, one of America's avant-garde designers, achieved worldwide notoriety in 1964 by challenging conventions and starting a nudity trend with his topless swimsuit. Hidden away in the back rooms of noisy garment factories are hundreds of anonymous designers turning out the useful types of designs the average American woman wants in ready-to-wear. They make a living at designing because they present ideas that many people like.

Dress designers have variously been called shapemakers, engineers of fleeting shapes, designers of the ephemeral, and in more mundane language, masters of a craft with artistic overtones, or stylists in a useful art. All these terms suggest various dimensions of central importance to an understanding of dress.

In the broadest sense, dress is considered by the anthropologist to be any alteration of the physical presence so that others are able to make identification to the one who appears. Thus, it includes not only things made of cloth and cloth substitutes, but also face-painting (cosmetics), hair-dressing, carriage, and degree of obesity and thinness. Within this definition, a designer of dress is someone who plans the alteration of the physical presence in acceptable ways. If the designer works with cloth or cloth substitutes he is a shapemaker: he makes shoulders appear broad or narrow, waists short or long;

he makes people seem aggressive by covering them with large areas of scarlet and black, he makes them appear retiring in silvery pink; by shortening skirts, he makes women seem younger; by lengthening them, older. By altering the apparent size, shape, and tempo of the body he also changes the "presence" or entire social-psychological impact of the person. The designer becomes a "shapemaker" in the fullest sense of the word.

In addition to serving as a vehicle for identification, dress is also a form of ornamental art. Like all art forms, dress is an artificially arranged whole; it is the product of someone's imagination, hard work, and knowledge or experience. As ornamental art, it is created not only to please the eye but also to serve as an assertion of status—to enchance or give special attributes to the wearer. Just as the decoration around the doorway of a cathedral distinguishes it as a special opening, or the paneling and interior design of one office differentiates it from another in some hierarchy of values, so dress characterizes one person or another. Ornamental art has not only a terminal value, that is, it is enjoyed for itself alone, but also an instrumental value; it is "used for" or "leads to" something else. Dress, as ornamental art, must therefore be considered a "useful art."

All works of art have some material aspects that appeal to our five senses and also to our "intuition" (spacial and temporal form). Dress designs can be judged by the same criteria as all other art: (1) material, which includes color and texture; (2) form, the shapes made by the lines of the design; (3) expression; (4) function. A critic of design would ask: Do the four aspects of the design work together to augment each other? Does the art work accomplish what it sets out to do?

Before directing these questions to dress designs, we must understand that the consumer function of garments as seen by the designer is, in general, to suit the life-style of individuals who come from various subgroups in the society. Conse-

A shapemaker changes not only the apparent shape but also the spirit or essence of the body—the romantic; the space age; art nouveau; the young look; Victorian; the "total look"; lady-like.

quently, a dress designed for a woman who wants "elegance," a fashionable unobtrusive simplicity portraying "the best" in all phases of design, will be judged as art on how well it gives form to this feeling. Similarly, a dress intended for a college girl may be designed to convey casual, useful qualities such as physical comfort and easy upkeep, along with a youthful, avant-garde air. If the design embodies this feeling, it can be said to fulfill the criteria of art in regard to expression and function.

In dress, the beauty of design arises primarily from the harmony between certain specific proportions of line and color and the proportions of the body. Woman is the central theme of fashion creation; if she is by-passed and clothing is produced that bears no relation to the female form, it cannot be called art. The artistic element demands that the wearer, the material, color, and other aspects of the design must form *one harmonious unit.*

As an artist, a dress designer senses this need for creating a well-ordered whole. He is a highly motivated critic of his own work. By temperament, he typically enjoys his work and is strongly committed to it; his control consists in making critical judgments about what he has done. When a ready-to-wear manufacturer substitutes a pattern maker for a designer, he has a specialist, not an artist, and aesthetic self-criticism of the work may be lacking. If this happens, the development of designs in dress becomes, literally, "styling in a craft with artistic overtones."

Like any artist, the designer must develop a certain proficiency in handling the media of his craft. The basic problem of dress design is that of molding a flat surface to fit a curved shape, since materials used in making dresses are woven in flat strips, whereas the human body for which the dress is intended is a series of curved shapes. Material can be molded or shaped in many ways, such as shrinking, stretching, darting, gathering. The particular way it will be shaped is a matter the designer must solve. The most creative designers produce "effectively surprising" ideas or recombine old ideas in novel ways that are useful in his culture.

Every dress design contains basic features related to the structure of the human body. Labels or names attached to these features consistently call to mind this relationship. For example, the waistline of the dress is related to the waistline of the body; the neckline of the dress is the opening for the neck of the wearer. In cases where names are not identical in both areas, constant use has tended to make the association almost automatic. The sleeve of the dress covers the human arm; the skirt covers the body area below the waistline. These basic features are present and identifiable in all dresses and can be thought of as the basic parts of dress with which the designer must always work.

Variations and combinations of these basic parts make each design unique. A neckline may be scooped and boat-shaped; it may be normal, round, with a Peter Pan collar; it may end in a soft scarf. The material used in the dress can vary in design, color, or texture. A skirt may have one of several silhouettes. It is the combination of all the basic parts that makes one dress differ from another. The description of a dress as "polka dot, sleeveless, with soft blousing from a natural waistline and a slim tubular skirt" brings an entirely different picture to mind than one described as "princess, with full flared skirt, below-elbow sleeves, and a neat Peter Pan collar."

Scholars who study historic fashions point out that each part of the dress can only be moved *up* or *down, in* or *out*. For example, in some periods the neckline is raised to the level of the eye, while in other periods it is plunged to below the navel. Sometimes it is cut to hug the base of the neck, whereas again it may be rounded out to drop off the shoulders. These fluctuations in design are not the result of a designer's conspiracy, but the effect of fashion. They enable those who study fashion to accurately measure changes in design.

Thus far, in considering dress designers as shapemakers whose job is to alter the physical human presence, we have examined them as creators of an ornamental or useful art who must develop some proficiency in the media of their craft. Now, we will consider them in a third dimension—as "fashion" designers. Since dress is the most sensitive medium for fashion transmission and since fashion is in constant demand, the fashion aspect becomes dominant in dress designs. This is a transitory, ever-changing element and explains why dress designers may be called engineers of fleeting shapes or designers of the ephemeral. Not only does the social need for fashion in a culture vary between groups and between times but the phenomenon of fashion itself has a cyclical movement. It is a recognized fashion law that when a style reaches the peak of group acceptance and becomes a universal fashion, reaction sets in, replacing straight lines with curves and flourishes or short hemlines with long. This ephemeral quality caused Gabrielle Chanel to insist that the French couturiers were not artists, but furnishers. She noted, "A work of art is something that at first seems ugly and becomes beautiful. Fashion first seems beautiful and then becomes ugly."[1] So, a fashion is not meant to last, can only be desirable *now*. Consumers clearly are willing to pay for this impermanent quality, the continual modification of design that represents recent labor and current times. Clearly also, the consumer tends to select products of certain designers over those of others.

What characteristics can be said to make a creative fashion designer? A creative fashion designer must have a flair for the coming style, a sense of an impending revolution in culture, art, and fashion. He must have talent in fitting a formula to the revolution and a sense of timing as to when to present new fashion forms. He must have courage to stand above the current fashions and, once he has grasped the means by which to initiate new fashion forms, the intelligence to pursue it.[2] Finally, he must have luck.

Creative designers with a highly developed sensitivity to fashion present ideas they hope will be chosen by a select group of recognized fashion leaders who readily accept innovations in dress. If successful, these designers are called the "leaders" among designers. There are perhaps one or two a season, sometimes none. Other designers possess only a good sense of timing. They know when to enter and leave the fashion cycle, when a line or color has outlived its day or will shortly do so. They are influenced by the less demanding fashion awareness of the customers they serve and are content to let others initiate the revolutions.

Like all individuals, designers differ in many ways. We have discussed those aspects most pertinent to their craft: reason for designing; creative ability to alter the physical human presence in accepted ways; aesthetic judgment; and fashion sense. These differences will help to decide their choice in design. However, there is one final factor which may be the most significant of all in governing a design decision—the designer's business connection.

While a few high fashion designers own their firms, most designers sell their services to a businessman in return for wages. They agree to perform some function in exchange for money. The businessman wants a product that will minimize his worries by increasing the cash flow of business; that is, a product that will stimulate sales, reduce costs, and eliminate competition.

He is interested in *efficiency* (doing the most with the least) and *volume*. Because turnover increases volume he is sympathetic to the social phenomenon of fashion which hastens depreciation of semidurable products and helps increase the flow of economic goods in and out of the cultural environment. He is used to change, for competition brings pressures to change, and looks upon the rate of change in any area as directly proportionate to the number of possibilities.

He judges all factors in design—the fashion element, beauty, craftsmanship, creativity—with the same criteria: Does it sell? He is less interested in an object for its own sake than as a means to an end, only important insofar as it sustains production and consumption.

Placed in a situation where design is just one phase of a cooperative process, the designer in business tries to shape his design so that it relates most naturally to the manufacturing process being used. He becomes attuned to technical limitations on the manufacturing level and merchandising problems. He asks, Who are my customers? My competitors? Then, through a process of trial and error he solves each of his problems. His mind becomes a filing cabinet of what his customers will (and will not) accept—convertible necklines, medium blue, belted waistlines. To help the retailer, he may key his designs to a promotion idea the store could use. For example, John Weitz, a free-lance designer who made his fashion reputation on clothes for the sports car set, presented a line of beachwear featuring "a swimsuit wardrobe at budget prices."[3] Other designers may reduce labor costs by retaining one simple, easily constructed style year after year, changing only the colors and textures. A designer tries to see his designs from the viewpoint of the consumer, manufacturer, and retailer, as well as in the light of his own inclinations. The result is a three-way compromise between what he would like to make, what will sell, and what it is possible to make.

James Galanos of California, a high fashion designer who contributes imagination and beauty to the American fashion scene, appraises his position as owner and designer of a business: "As designer I make clothes that I think women will wear because they are beautiful, but as the owner of a business, the clothes must sell." Fortunately, in his case, the clothes that have sold have also been those that he considered beautiful.[4]

Still another designer-owner, Norman Norell of Norman Norell, Inc., considered the designer of the most expensive ready-to-wear made in the United States during the 1960's, stated, "I'm more interested in launching a fashion than in creating beautiful things." For him, the criterion of a design is that it be accepted and worn by the general public.[5] Significantly, his statements indicate that the same pragmatic test of functionalism that rules an economic system oriented to efficiency and the profit motive (verification by consequence) also rules fashion designing.

The businessman and the fashion designer have some things in common: Each is less concerned with the ultimate than with the swiftly changing claims of each moment, and each has a respect for the consumer that is unique. The businessman discovers consumer wants in order to satisfy them and sell his goods, for people buy according to their needs. The fashion designer also discovers consumer wants even before they are apparent to business, for he shapes the products that business will sell three to six months after he has conceived them. When his designs are placed in the market, they must reflect *at that time* the life-style pattern of individuals, because fashion is, by definition, the prevailing style *at a given time*. It is no accident, then, that good fashion is good business. An effective designer like a good businessman must be realistic, practical, open-minded, and a good judge of consumer preference.

FREEDOM OF THE DESIGNER. Within the framework of the designing situation, how free is the designer to do what he wants? No designer can do exactly what he wants because he is, first of all, inhibited by the fashion element: He must design what is considered to be most desirable in social behavior at a given time. At the mercy of change, he is prevented from perfecting the same style but *must* change; he becomes a master at designing in an area where ideas of order are constantly changing as fashion moves in unpredictable and independent ways. Only a few, like Chanel, can create one shape —a uniform—and continually refine it. A few others become like Balenciaga, an artist who subtly and constantly changes shapes yet keeps the same feeling. The rest must design within the course of fashion, making numerous variations on a theme.

The designer is limited also by the appreciation of his audience. He cannot say what *he* wants to say, but only what his buyers are able to understand. The largest audience of most designers consists of company salesmen and buyers from retail stores, both of whom feel they represent consumer opinion; they choose the styles they believe their customers will like, always hoping they have chosen a prevailing style or fashion. If the buyer's sense of timing is off, the customers never see designs they might have preferred. Buyers are the designer's biggest worry; they tend to stay on the safe side, selecting only styles that have sold in the past and passing up the more creative models. Designers feel that many buyers lag behind consumers in their taste, thus tending to discourage fresh, creative talent in designing.

Finally, the designer is restrained from producing a self-satisfying piece of craftsmanship by the technicalities of the manufacturing situation which force him to create order within the strict limitations of the company policy. When a firm is not designer-owned (the majority are not), the designer remains anonymous and the dress is labeled with the company name. Since the company owns the designs, it has the right to change them in any way—to simplify for lower costs, or to make the design over in the company image. A designer who walks into a store three months after designing a dress and sees it hanging on a rack may suffer pangs of frustration: Did *I* do that? There is nothing of *me* left in it.

In spite of all these difficulties, designers keep working, and thousands of fashion designs appear each season. Perhaps we are now ready to answer the question with which we began: What determines which models a designer will present? In general, he can only present what he believes, within his understanding of himself and the culture, to be the best solution to the problem, but with this realization: He may do what he wants, but it is society that will determine the value of what he does, for his designs must be woven into everyday life. Fortunately, society provides more than one system of designing and employs various types of talent.

Some form of dress design is found in all countries of the world, and fashion is international. Design ideas in dress move freely between countries and are seldom classified as secret material vital to the nation's security, as are military, political, and scientific matters. Like design ideas, vast quantities of fashion goods are imported and exported every year.

A foreign label can serve to stimulate fashion interest. The air of mystery inherent in the unfamiliar adds to the fantasy element so necessary to fashion goods and excites the imagination. An object that would have gone unnoticed in its natural setting takes on an air of individuality and assumes new dimensions against a strange background. It is this "exclusive" air, this uniqueness, that seems to initiate the imitation and emulation so necessary to the fashion movement. Plainly enough, the entire world becomes a laboratory for fashion design, although the fashions of the Western world are the ones with which we are more familiar.

Before entering into a discussion of the areas for design, and especially a detailed comparison of two prevailing systems, the French haute couture and the American ready-to-wear, we will touch upon some noteworthy clues as to what types of objects are likely to become carriers of fashion and, thus, the materials for design.

The Materials

In general, fashion involves those items which have many functional alternatives. One dress substitutes for another; this season's hat replaces last year's style. It follows that fashion settles on trivial things. Triviality, as defined by Elihu Katz, "does not refer to the amount of emotion, affection, and functional significance surrounding an object but rather to its life-expectancy, its susceptibility to being outmoded." Each object has an estimable life span: stockings a few weeks, a dress a few years. "It is characteristic of fashion that it forces replacement of an object before its life span ends. Such objects are acquired without regard to durability. This is one definition of 'conspicuous consumption.' "[6]

The most visible clothing items are likely to change in fashion more quickly than other garments. You might expect style changes in dresses to be more frequent than in underclothes, unless underclothes indirectly become visible too.

One purpose of women's undergarments has been to accentuate or even to create those desirable feminine features which characterize the sex. The back falsie (bustle) gave way to the front falsie (the padded brassiere), while girdles continue to pull in the waist and smooth the hips. Such garments produce "visible" change in the feminine silhouette and tend to make the underwear business almost as fashion conscious as the outerwear business.

Absolutely unnatural forms may, at least for a time, bear the stamp of fashion. The odd, the extreme, and the unusual arouse the imagination. In contrast, as Simmel suggests, the fashion classic with its air of composure does not offer nearly so many points of attack from which modifications, disturbances, and destruction of the equilibrium can come.[7]

Finally, as we have already indicated, imports are important fashion objects. They often assume a greater value simply because they did not originate in this country. Paris fashions may be created with the sole intention of setting fashion elsewhere. Unlike primitive tribes who view novelty as an evil, we live in a society that has to a large extent removed the feeling of insecurity associated with the new: We are stimulated by things from outside.

This was illustrated when the fabric "bleeding madras" (a rustic type of cotton in rugged irregular plaids with colors "guaranteed to run" after washing, made by the cottage workers of India) became popular for American sportswear through the early 1960's. The commercial value of this fabric, made purely for export to the United States by India, and not highly valued in its own society, caused American technicians, after spending years perfecting dyes that would not run, to turn back the clock and produce a madras-type fabric that bled. Paradoxically, the American-made material was not enthusiastically received by most sportswear manufacturers who preferred the original article. They felt the domestic fabric lacked the glamor of the India madras.

So, in various ways, different objects become carriers of fashion. In countries acclimated to fashion change there are no social upheavals as style follows style; indeed, fashion tends to ignore even the boundary lines of nationality and brings fresh ideas from one culture into another.

A stimulating challenge to craftsmanship is created by the healthy competitive pressure among designers of the industrialized nations of the Western world. France retains her position as top designer for the high fashion world and continues to set the fashion trend; Italy forges ahead in imaginative sportswear and leather goods; and England, at one time sole arbiter of fashions for men, sweeps onto the fashion scene in the 1960's with avant-garde styling for teens. Yet while the giants continue to dominate the fashion arena, the more exotic but less industrialized nations of the Eastern world also furnish inspiration for Western design: Thailand, the Siamese colors and textured silks; India, the handwoven silks and saris; China, the tribute silks, Chinese brocades, and frog fastenings; Japan, the obi sashes, kimono sleeves, and subtle, mysterious prints.

Significantly, each country contributes more richly in one area than another. While France has an abundant supply of skilled workers to construct the intricate designs produced by her master couturiers, American sewing machines hum with ready-to-wear. While Ireland brings linen into fashion, Italy does clever things with straw. Pooling the talents and resources of many nations widens the horizons of design and helps to overcome the technical limitations of each nation. The world, as a design laboratory, opens up boundless horizons for change, assuming that the rate of change is directly proportionate to the possibilities. Widened vistas make it possible for more groups and more varied groups to be satisfied with more fashion products.

The Area

Rather than serving people in general, the systems that produce fashion products are organized to serve subgroups of the population which share easily identified characteristics. The shared *group characteristics then constitute the area for design*. It is the designer's job to plan products that reflect group traits in a way acceptable to most members of the group.

SEX. The first major division of clothing is by the sex of the wearer—men's wear and women's wear. Companies tend to specialize in one area or the other. Even when women began to wear blouses styled identically to men's shirts, they were made by women's blouse companies. It was considered revolutionary that a company which traditionally made shirts for men should also make shirts for women.

The sex factor not only divides garments into two areas but also decides who shall design in each area. Originally, women's clothes as well as men's were made entirely by men tailors. Around 1675, however, a petition to the king of France asked that women be allowed to make petticoats, skirts, and other accessories. The petition claimed that "it accorded with propriety, chastity, and modesty of women and girls that they should be dressed by persons of their own sex." This appeal to morality was decisive. As years passed, the new profession of "milliner" arose and these women alone were allowed to create as their artistic inspiration decreed. They trimmed the dresses made by dressmakers and designed all types of head adornments. Milliners were the first artists in dress.[8]

For a century, then, with few exceptions, the production of fashionable dress for women became the privilege of women designers, while men continued to be tailors. It was Rose Bertin, a fashionable French milliner, who encouraged a love of finery and need for change in sixteen-year-old Marie Antoinette and helped bring dress designing into prominence. However, during the last half of the nineteenth century, when fashion in dress became of commercial concern, men stepped back into this area of design to take a hand in the new industry. Charles Frederick Worth, an English tailor, possessing both artistic genius and a sound business sense, founded what was to become the haute couture in Paris. Today, men continue to dominate the area of high fashion design for women; possibly because most women lack courage to take the risk of failure high fashion involves or, perhaps, because a man is able to see women and their dress more objectively, while a woman tends to design subjectively—*for herself.* Chanel was always her own best model; she was fortunate that her type was one with which great masses of the people could identify. Only a few outstanding women, including Madeleine Vionnet, Jeanne Lanvin, Elsa Schiaparelli, and Gabrielle Chanel, have been able to set fashion trends on the international scene, while many men have done so.

In the area of medium-priced ready-to-wear in America, on the other hand, where fashion and utility are the main appeals, women designers tend to far outnumber men. This may be due, in part, to the climate of opinion in the United States which traditionally considered dress designing to be a "non-masculine" occupation; or it may also be that women, in their roles as wife and mother (the social conscience of the family), are better able than men to sense the everyday functions of dress. Significantly, most successful men designers have a woman stylist on whose taste they depend to keep their designs in line with social behavior, while women designers often need a good male production manager and publicity agent to ultimately succeed in a business way.

AGE, SIZE, FIGURE TYPE. As the production of clothing for women became more industrialized, more specialized areas for design were marked out. Women's wear was grouped by the age, size, or figure type of the prospective wearer. This allowed companies and their designers to concentrate on the needs of small consumer groups within the population.

A representative grouping of ready-to-wear by age would include these labels: infants and children; girls and subteens; juniors; women and misses. A comparable grouping by size and figure type would include: infants and children; girls; subteens; juniors, standard women and misses sizes; proportioned sizes; half sizes; petites; tall girls; larger women.

Grouping by size and figure type allows more specialization than grouping by age. Moreover, in America, there has been a psychological block against grouping by age because of the nationwide accent on youth. This has caused the figure problems of the older person to be handled as a sizing problem.

Most designers work with a figure type in mind. Norman Norell, for example, states that he designs for "the figure type who can wear my clothes." Couturiers sometimes have a favorite mannequin for whom they style their line. In general, the three factors of age, size, and figure type are closely inter-related.

Consider the area of children's clothes. Small children have a distinct body-build compared to adults: Their heads are relatively large in relation to their bodies, they have vanishing waistlines and protruding abdomens that continually expand to hold unlimited amounts of food, and they keep growing up. These factors cause the designers of children's clothes to favor dresses that hang from the shoulders as one-piece shifts or modified princess styles, and to place emphasis on yoke and neck details. These styles are so functionally successful for growing children they have become classic styles that continue year after year.

An observing customer sees the relation of the garment to her body type, thus the designer must achieve harmony between his design and the body shape for which it is intended. Size and figure type is an expandable area of design dependent on our knowledge of body structure.

Helen McCullough, a customer of half-size dresses tells what this label means to her: "Half-size dresses are designed for women with short waists. Most frequently they are made for shorter women, and/or plump women, whose waistline measurements have increased with the years, causing the two largest circumferences of the body—the bust and the hips—to come closer together. With standard length dresses the waist length must be shortened and the hip line lifted."

Furthermore, she seems to feel that if tall women need half-sizes, usually it is only the waist length that needs to be shortened, not the hip height. And alterations for such dresses are easier to make than when both bust and hip lines are involved. "Of course," she adds, "there is considerable difference in the contour of half-size women just as there is in the body structure of all women. . . . Designs in these dresses need good vertical lines."

USE. Still another general classification for clothing is the use to which the garment will be put and the symbolic role it is to play in the mind of the wearer. Here, the first major division is by garments for innerwear and outerwear. Innerwear refers to such items as underslips, brassieres, girdles, nightgowns, and the like—clothing not intended to be seen in public. Outerwear includes dresses, separate skirts and blouses, suits, coats, and all accessories—clothing meant to be seen in public.

A further division of these general groupings is by "use" categories. Blouses, which are functionally versatile and can reflect all types of attitudes, will serve to illustrate this point. Blouses can be used for working or lounging at home; active and spectator sports; school, street, and business wear; cocktail parties, and evening wear. They can be warm or cool, washable or dry-cleaned, and they lend themselves to all types of decoration and texture combinations that reflect personal attitudes and values. A blouse designer could, therefore, specialize in avant-garde overblouses for college students, or he could add individual touches to classic blouses intended for general street wear. The degree of the "imaginative element" versus "utility" the blouse possesses depends on the designer's conception of the symbolic role the blouse is to play in the life of the intended wearer.

LEVEL OF LIVING. A final significant classification of garments for design is by price line. Each company caters to the consumer group in the the population that can afford to buy its products. A ready-to-wear company which sells dresses meant to retail at $2.95 to $10.95 is courting the lower-income groups, while a Paris couture house or a high fashion ready-to-wear company, whose prices range between $500 and $3,500 or more, appeals to the upper-income levels.

In a mobile and expanding society, individual incomes shift. People move, or anticipate moving, from one level to another. If they move up, they may then possess the necessary fee to enter an exclusive Fifth Avenue Salon, or if they prefer to trade with a general department store, their demand for better goods may force that store to "trade-up"; that is, to stock higher quality goods at higher prices. Buyers for the store must contact a new group of manufacturers who make garments at the price level now demanded. In essence, the price line of each firm corresponds to the income level of some customer group.

All companies can be ranked in some hierarchy of quality which corresponds to the price line they produce. Once a designer becomes proficient at one price level he will generally find it difficult to design in another. That is why the couture designer who creates subtle models of intricate cut that are sewed by hand can seldom make the more obvious designs of machine-sewed ready-to-wear. Nor is the reverse likely to happen. Designers on lower-price lines become skilled at adapting an idea so it will be useful to them—they know how much to take off, leave on, or add; they develop a knack in choosing or creating ideas that are effective regardless of the fabric quality. A proficient designer of inexpensive ready-to-wear rarely moves up to haute couture levels. Each becomes a craftsman within the framework of his price level.

No matter what his price level, however, a designer must know quality. The look of quality in fashion goods is judged and priced at each step of the marketing system; first, by the manufacturer, next, by the retailer, and finally, by the consumer.

Quality, as the term is used here, refers to a relative evaluation between two products, one product seeming to possess more preferred features than the other. A customer saying she likes a particular dress because it has "better style," "better lines," or "better color" indicates the garment is being measured by some standard of values in the mind of the person making the selection. While quality is a psychological value, varying to some extent with individual temperament or bias, standards of quality tend to arise for each group in the society —standards initiated by individual members of the group whose opinions are sought and respected by the others.

In time, through consensus, what were once merely individual opinions become accepted standards for the group. *Top quality* in fashion is the quality preferred by a select group of authoritative people in the fashion field—authority acquired through experience, background, interest, and study. A designer learns to evaluate standards of quality and is able to portray, with his designs, the type of quality acceptable to the group for which he designs.

The two systems of design to be compared in the following pages, the French haute couture and the American ready-to-wear, originally stood for the top and the bottom in quality, just as they began at the extremes on the social scale and income levels. The haute couture designed elegant gowns for

French

74

American

empresses and queens at excessive fees, while ready-to-wear firms made coarse work-clothing at minimal cost for laborers.

Today, the two systems are closer together, the couture moves down the quality scale, adding first, boutiques, and next, ready-to-wear outlets, while the ready-to-wear moves up to invade exclusive salons in direct competition with couture garments. But each is still dependent on the other for its existence. American ready-to-wear, in general, looks to the French haute couture for its design ideas and fashion leadership, while the haute couture is dependent on ready-to-wear copies to spread the fame of its originals, and for financial support from commercial buyers.

Specialization by areas of design has not only permitted and encouraged copying of design but has, in fact, made it necessary, if there is to be a universal fashion. Diverse groups are held together by one common bond—the prevailing style at a given time—and within this general shape they develop their own group variations. If there were no similarities in the styles of various groups, we could not distinguish today's fashion; if there were no dissimilarities we could not distinguish one group or person from another. So the designer's task becomes one of endless mediation, partly shifting and partly holding to a steady course, integrating and differentiating at the same time.

The System

Two sytems of supplying fashion goods, French haute couture and American mass-produced ready-to-wear, serve different groups. Both systems are consumer-oriented and use the profit incentive; both will exist as long as there is demand for their product. The difference in the price lines on which the two systems concentrate provides a basic distinction between them. The term "haute couture" has come to symbolize exclusive high fashion designs of the best quality made for wealthy women of exacting tastes, while mass-produced ready-to-wear, in general, stands for medium to poor quality garments that allow almost everyone some fashion at a price they can afford. Of the dresses produced in 1964 in the United States, 47.5 per cent were in the wholesale price range of $6.00

to $15.99 per unit and the largest group of coats produced at wholesale prices were untrimmed coats under $16 (51 per cent).[9] The minimum retail price of a dress from a top Parisian house, during this same period, was close to $500.

HAUTE COUTURE IN FRANCE. Haute couture began with the House of Worth in Paris around 1850, and more than 100 years later, continues to carry on the same system of meticulous fashion production for a luxury trade. It has been copied all over the world, but has never reached the high point of development it did in France.

Strictly speaking, haute couture is officially defined by the trade association which represents it, the Chambre Syndicale de la Couture Parisienne: "Haute couture is any undertaking whose most important activity consists in creating models with the object of selling them to a professional clientele which thereby acquires the right to reproduce them. An haute couture concern of this nature also reserves the right to repeat these models for private customers."[10]

It is evident from this definition that the haute couture exists to be copied. The prestige of the couture house depends on its publicity, which in turn depends on how often and how well its models are copied. With fame, prices on original ideas can be set at high levels, but fame does not come until public acceptance proves that the couturier is able to please the customers. Any designer who maintains a top position does so through public acceptance.

Chanel suits become an international uniform as the result of public realization that Chanel makes an older woman look young and a young woman look chic, that her suits are easy to wear and comfortable, yet fashionable enough for the average spender, and that they can easily be reproduced by mass-production methods.

Private customers come to a couture house for something individual, simple, and well made, often preferring different styles from those selected by the commercial buyers, so that the exclusiveness of the model is not lost. These women, who set the tone the establishment maintains, seem to have two tendencies: (1) either to choose the more original ideas that are difficult to wear, or (2) to make a cautious choice. A hard-to-please French woman has developed her own taste, preferring fluid lines, quiet elegance, and more individuality than Americans. These exacting customers prefer to underdress in tweed suits, cardigans and sweaters, but with a rare distinctive air that maintains their minority high status position.

Fit and *fabric* are two things the couture can provide. Once the customer has selected a model or design, a new garment is proportioned especially for her figure and draped on her own dress form. Stripped to her bra and girdle, her measurements are taken in every conceivable direction, with especial attention to the size and placement of the bust. The most important measurement a Parisian dressmaker takes is the one made from the small bone in the center back of the neck, over the shoulder and down the chest to the highest point of the breast, and from there to the waist. This measurement provides the vertical placement of the bust in relation to the shoulder and the waist. The next measurement records the distance around the body of the entire chest area at the same high point on the bust, making careful note of the distance between breasts. This measurement gives the volume and relation of the breasts to each other. Once all measurements are taken, a dress form is remolded with muslin and cotton to the desired shape. Dress forms for steady customers are numbered and stacked anonymously away on top of cupboards or in out-of-the-way corners of some of the back working rooms of the establishment.

A customer may have the dress made in the fabric of the original design or one of her own choosing. She will consult with her *vendeuse* (saleswoman for the house). Each *vendeuse* is assigned to one customer whom she always serves and with whom she develops a special relationship. Many of these saleswomen of top Paris houses are former customers themselves and represent the house's point of view. No good *vendeuse* would allow her client to buy a dress that is not becoming.

While private customers are necessary to a couture undertaking, the influence of ready-to-wear buyers has been steadily increasing. In some cases, they, rather than private customers, are able to dictate the tone of the house. The original model (the actual garment) or, sometimes, sketches, patterns, and muslin *toiles* (the original idea draped in muslin) are sold to commercial buyers who come to Paris from all over the world. These buyers, representatives of manufacturing firms and retail stores, are charged higher fees than private customers for the same original models. They pay sizable sums for tickets to the prepublic showings, which are then applied as credit toward purchases. With each dress or pattern comes a list of all the specifications—the exact yardage of the materials used; where to obtain the fabric, trimmings, and interlinings; and any other information necessary to accurately reproduce the dress.

The Paris influence on the fashion world is so vast it seems tyrannical, but the size of the haute couture industry is relatively small. The number of important couture houses varies between 20 and 49, sometimes employing at a peak season 8,000 people, and the total export sale of couture garments brings in around $12 million a year.[11] Compare this with the more than 12,000 ready-to-wear firms in New York alone, each one employing from 20 to 250 people, while one large company such as Jonathan Logan grosses over $100 million annually.

In the opinion of the buyers as well as most fashion authorities, only three to five houses of the total haute couture group are considered important each season. The influence of these houses depends almost entirely on the designer for whom the house is usually named. Some brief sketches of well-known houses will give a glimpse of the uncertain course of a Paris couture house.

In 1954 five designers were important: Jacques Fath, Christian Dior, Pierre Balmain, Hubert de Givenchy, and Cristobal Balenciaga. Ten years later, only three names stood out: Dior, Balenciaga, and a new one—Yves St. Laurent. What had happened in that ten-year span?

Jacques Fath, although a young man, died in 1955, and his house, unable to go on under the direction of his wife Genevieve, closed. Christian Dior also died, the victim of a heart attack in 1957. But his house, one of the best organized in Paris as a modern industry, continued to be supported by its worldwide system of enterprises while it adjusted to new designing talent—first, Yves St. Laurent, and later, Marc Bohan. The fame and organization of the Dior enterprises kept the house going after the designer responsible for the reputation was dead. Pierre Balmain, while continuing his own house in Paris, was no longer influential as a creative designer.

Hubert de Givenchy occasionally came to the fashion forefront, especially if his designs were chosen by well-known personalities such as movie star Audrey Hepburn, but he was not consistently influential. Cristobal Balenciaga, alone, continued to maintain his creative leadership and a top position for his house.

The new name to appear on the list of influential designers, Yves St. Laurent, a hard-working, unknown boy of 21, in 1957 rose swiftly to fame as the successor to Dior with his new look, the "trapeze." In 1963, because of personal difficulties, he established his own house, with the backing of a United States southern millionaire, J. Mark Robinson. Robinson handled the finance while St. Laurent had complete fashion authority in the house that bore his name.

In general, a French couturier is an independent designer with a high level of detached perception of any problem. He has general flexibility gained through a range of experience and highly developed ability to communicate. He is usually an artist with a good eye for proportion and highly developed senses. He is deeply engrossed in his work. Since it goes out under his name and he must assume complete responsibility, he believes the original model must be perfect. The hard-working couturier puts forth intense effort to create the 200 to 300 models the top houses show each spring and fall. He treats dressmaking as a fine art, of value in itself, and continually strives for the spirit of "elegance"—design that has been reduced to the irreducible, with nothing included except the basic essentials. An elegant design is executed with skill in quality fabrics and made to fit perfectly the body and spirit of the wearer. Each couturier strives for elegance but gives to it his own distinctive stamp, rarely changed, since to do so would scare away his regular customers.

To qualify for an haute couture house a designer should be able to design garments which express his own ideas. In this way he differs from a dressmaker who executes ideas customers suggest. An haute couture house must show at least 60 models, twice a year, on living mannequins, all of which were designed, produced, and the reproductions made-to-order in its own custom workrooms.

Training. The Chambre Syndicale de la Couture Parisienne,

the trade association founded in 1868 to represent the different branches of French fashion industries and to deal with the administrative and labor problems of its membership, operates a school in Paris for the purpose of training seamstresses, tailors, and minor couturiers to work in the haute couture system and maintain the standards the system requires.

As a student at this school, in the advanced course designed for people who might become couturiers, I was initiated into the backstage life of haute couture and will relate here the philosophy of the system as it appeared to me in my work in the school. Visits to couture houses, both to see the showings out front and the workrooms in the back, convinced me that the methods used at the school, as well as the equipment, arrangement of space, and general attitude, were identical to those used in the top couture houses. A description of the work at the school will portray, in essence, the philosophy the couture strives to maintain.

Around 80 students, mostly in the 18- to 24-age group, were enrolled in the advanced course, which lasted for one eight-month school year from October to June. The classes had an international character; while made up predominantly of French, there was a mixture of nationalities, including Swedish, English, Chinese, Italian, American, Australian, New Zealand, and Greek. In a room of some thirty students, six were boys (excellent sewers).

For daily work, each student squeezed onto a small stool behind a small table, perhaps one yard long, flanked on either side and behind and before with other people on small stools behind small tables. The room was completely filled. Each student spread out needle, scissors, red basting thread and muslin, and this is where he worked, with no talking allowed, for six hours. On dark days a pale light bulb in a green procelain shade glowed faintly over each table. Each student worked on the dress form beside her, as madame, the teacher, passed through the group saying, "I have arrived," "see there," "do like this."

Classes ran from nine to five o'clock, with a two-hour lunch period. Two and one-half days were devoted to *coupe* (cutting and draping), and two full mornings to *dessin* (sketching and painting original ideas). Other courses included French culture and textiles.

Before discussing the techniques taught in the school, I will give you a general picture of the development of a couture garment. First, a designer sketches on paper hundreds of ideas with many themes and many variations of a theme. These ideas are discussed with the top women stylists in the couture house and a joint decision is reached on the nucleus for a new line—*the idea*. A line of clothes for around-the-clock wear will be built on one, two, or as many as seven themes. The line will generally contain a continuation of some ideas from the past line which may not yet have reached the zenith of development, and the introduction of possible new directions fashion can take in the future. The nagging question a couturier must answer is, "What have I done that is new?"

Once the idea for the line is formed, the next step is to translate designs on paper into reality in the workrooms. An experimental design is draped in unbleached muslin *(toiles)*. The muslin design is executed as perfectly as possible and may require over 300 hours of labor, since it will be the pattern for the finished dress. The muslin garment is modeled and carefully examined for beauty of line, proportion, and movement on the body. If it is not satisfactory, it will be worked over or rejected at this point. When the muslin is acceptable, selection is made of a fabric of the right color and texture to express the design idea, as well as the girl to serve as the model in the opening show. The actual dress is then draped on the dress form of the mannequin who will wear the dress. When finished, the dress is modeled and examined again for beauty and perfection of design and construction. It can still be rejected at this step. If satisfactory, the couturier selects the accessories and the dress is shown on the opening date. From then on, its life history depends on public acceptance.

At school, the course that developed skill in creating dress ideas continually emphasized *beauty of line*. A sketch that did not have some new beauty of form was always rejected. Added decoration was only acceptable *if* the cut or spirit of the garment was enriched by this additional texture. At the time, Italy was just emerging as a high fashion center and was frequently discussed at the school. Consensus among the French was that the Italian couturiers would not be a serious threat to the Paris haute couture because "the Italians do not know *line,* they only know sportswear and decoration."

"Line" is important to couture design because the couture house must rely on the subtle intricacies of cut in its garments to distinguish them from ready-to-wear and to guard against unauthorized copying. Color and texture are both more easily seen and more easily copied.

Not only must a design have beauty of line, it must be appropriate. Each garment was designed for a specific use—lunch on the Riviera, at the hunt, before noon in the city, after noon, for the ball, and so on. Each time of the day and each occasion was treated as having its own particular manners: One must be dressed for the hunt, not simply appropriately, but "elegantly" appropriately.

Each idea had a source of design, such as paintings by Dufy or Braque, stories from French literature, or a theme for a masked ball. The designer's idea had to portray the mood of the source. The best students of design were those who were able to suggest with the fewest lines some subtle shape that conveyed a quality of breathless unreachability; a quality that seemed to demode all other designs and that made the viewer yearn for the breeding and manners of kings. Finally, and always, the design must be *in* fashion. After the 1954 spring showings of the haute couture had been held, and the new H line of Dior appeared, the entire school completely changed its *ligne général* in design and draping. Fashion can only be now or tomorrow, not yesterday. If the students' ideas are not "à la mode," they are hopeless. Where before the showings the students were flattening the abdomen, afterwards they were rounding it out with bloused bodices; where before they were making tight skirts, afterwards they were making full pleated ones.

Paralleling the design classes, the draping classes ceaselessly strived to perfect muslin *toiles* with the same feeling of elegance sought in sketch. The entire class was given the same sketched design to drape, each member interpreting the lines in muslin according to his own sensitivity to effects. Each garment was draped on a special haute couture dress form and was made entirely by hand.

Here again, emphasis was placed on beauty of line, harmony with the shape of the human figure, adequate interpretation of the artist's idea, and perfection in fit. The French think *in the round*. A design must flow around the figure and be attractive from the back as well as the front. Since a woman's figure is curved—her stomach rounds out and protrudes—so the garment must be eased and shaped over this curve. Her hips round, so the darts must be placed to shape and mold the skirt pleasingly over the area. The bust is rounded and the shape must never be lost, but rather subtly suggested, even beneath the most casual, bloused top. The bust is never vulgarly displayed as in America, where the women wear dresses that strain tautly from breast to breast. The only rule in placing any line or dart is to enhance the figure pleasingly, and to carry out the effect of the artist's sketch.

These ideas were new to an American who had been taught to think along more rigid lines. In America, darts were straight lines and were placed in certain conventional locations; side seams were straight lines that usually went down the sides of the figure. Women were not supposed to have rounded stomachs that protruded—what were girdles for?—and the French, not the Americans, by popular belief, were the ones who displayed too much.

Besides honoring the shape of women's figures, the French continue to emphasize an idea that seems, sometimes, to be forgotten in America. Not equipment, but the skill possessed in one's own hands was all-important. Work could always be improved and each muslin was treated with the same respect as any artist's sculpture. As a result, the muslins draped by the better students were so well handled that elegance showed through the muslin *toiles* in beauty of proportion, line, and superb handling of the grain and fit. It was all the result of personal skill, while equipment was kept to bare essentials.

In this respect Balenciaga is esteemed for his know-how in textiles; 50 lengths averaging 4 to 6 yards each are said to be sufficient for him to create 20 models, while some couturiers use 200 lengths for an outfit of 1 to 10 models. An entire Dior collection is estimated to take over 4,000 lengths.[12]

All pressing in this school was done by flatirons, which I had seen before only in museums. The irons sat on their own gas plates, and until some student furnished a match and lit the fire under them, no pressing could be done. There were no ironing boards as we know them; a regular board was placed between two saw horses and on this you rested a small elevated pressing board about 10 inches long and 4 inches wide like a miniature sleeve board. The entire garment was pressed on this, because most pressing involved the shrinking and molding of small areas. Yet, I have never seen muslins so perfectly pressed.

St. Catherine's Day. November 25, the day of the protective saint for young girls, and especially seamstresses, brings vacation to the school. On St. Catherine's day every unmarried girl past 25 is supposed to put on a special cap of green and yellow and may ask a boy to marry her—in the same tradition as leap year in America. All seamstresses have a holiday. During my stay, Christian Dior's workrooms were opened for festivities, and those who knew someone working there and could obtain a pass might visit this behind-the-scenes area of an haute couture establishment.

It was truly a seamstresses' soirée. In a gala mood, the girls wore old-fashioned dresses, in sharp contrast to the daily high fashion atmosphere. The workrooms where the seamstresses sit and sew all day for very little salary, by American standards, were completely covered with crepe paper in gay oriental themes, or flower-garden motifs, with huge paper flowers pinned to yards of muslin. These workrooms covered seven floors and every one was decorated differently, and each had its own three-piece dance orchestra, food, and festivity. Trying to visualize the rooms in their normal state, I could see, from the piled-up small tables and stools near the door, that the rooms resembled those at the school, even to the flatirons on their gas jets.

The St. Catherine's day festivities illustrate the strong feeling of group solidarity that develops among the members of a workroom in an haute couture establishment, and the recognition that France gives to the occupation of seamstress by honoring them with a special holiday. It is in these workrooms the couture garments are made, each room being responsible for its assigned designs. All members of the group take pride in *their dress* and are happy or sad at the fate the original model meets when the showings are held and the design, no longer theirs, becomes public property.

A Showing. The haute couture establishments are housed in old French mansions in good residential areas, which is why they are called "Houses." The Dior establishment alone seems to have built an additional annex to hold its many offices and workrooms. If, as a prospective customer, you went to a showing, you would enter through one of the huge decorated grilled doors, always so mysteriously closed on Paris streets, and perhaps find yourself in a small paved courtyard. When you entered the building itself, in all probability the first thing you would see is an accessory shop or *boutique* on the ground floor level. A boutique is a shop where a few garments are sold ready-made (with fittings). In the boutiques, dress prices begin around $150, but these garments, while conceived by the couture designer, have little design compared to the garments shown in the official collections.

From the ground level, you would mount a stairway with a decorative handrail to the second floor level (considered the first floor by the French). Here, the wide halls are studded with salesgirls *(vendeuses)*. These girls may be dressed in casual black jersey tops and black skirts, or dark sweaters and tweed skirts. You pass by and enter the showroom, which may be a simple large room, almost square, with plain walls and fluorescent lights covered with shirred silk to soften the glare, or a rather small informal room decorated with distinction and opening onto a garden. As a member of the audience you sit in one of several straight-back chairs, perhaps five rows deep. The show begins. A woman calls out the number identification of each garment as the mannequin enters and walks quickly across the room. If you are interested, you jot the number down on the white card you were handed for that purpose—a card also containing the name of the *vendeuse* allotted to you. Absorbed by the show selections, you scarcely notice that one and one-half hours have gone by, and the showings are over.

Climate of Opinion. The couturier, whatever his national origin, works best in Paris for many practical reasons. The large group of couture houses furnish the competition that stimulates an established talent and provide a training laboratory for new talent. Most couturiers developed their artistry in the workshop of an older colleague. Christian Dior, before opening his own house, had spent ten years as a designer at

Lucien Lelong, and Yves St. Laurent, in turn, received his training under Dior.

Furthermore, only Paris can provide thousands of gifted girls who have sewing skill in their fingertips, and supply the accessories, jewels, belts, shoes, gloves, embroidery—everything a couturier needs. Then, too, there is no other place with such an appreciative audience—where men as well as women love dress, and a nation is waiting to honor with respect and fame a successful designer.

Elegance has ruled the upper levels of society in France for three centuries, beginning with the reign of Louis XIV, who, to control his idle nobles, bereft of their property by royal decree, initiated the luxurious court life at Versailles. Dressmakers and tailors were organized to produce the royal robes. The beautiful garments covered with delicate embroidery and fine jewels, worn in the daytime, helped to increase the aura of distance associated with royalty by removing the wearer from reality; royalty was, by definition, above the crowds. As important was the fact that a constant change of dress kept the wearers occupied. Meanwhile, the brilliance of the creations spread the reputation of Paris around the world and the era of French fashion leadership began.

Three centuries is a long period of time to treat with respect an industry that in many countries is considered frivolous and ridiculous. Fear of ridicule strangles the creative urge, but in France creativity receives due credit. The couturier believes, as do the French people, that his creation, like an object of art, is valuable and necessary. The perceptive French woman notices hair, hands, gloves, legs, shoes, and composure, while the French man notices the woman and her dress.

Appreciation of dress runs through every level of French society. Only in France would a gnarled seaman, running a boat between Nice and Monte Carlo, sit down beside an American female passenger long enough to say, "Your sunglasses are not pretty, you should get new ones." This happened to me, and his statement was perceptive. The sunglasses I was wearing were men's glasses from the Army Air Force—useful, but unflattering in their style to a woman.

A woman in France is observed and appreciated by men for qualities only another woman would notice in America.

Frenchmen enjoy looking at women, discussing gowns at a ball, or sauntering through a maze of dusty antique shops in some obscure Paris bypath. There is a comradely give and take in discussing objects of art with no self-consciousness involved as to whether it is a "proper" male or female subject. Art is everybody's subject.

It is within this general appreciative atmosphere of selective taste that the handicraft skills are encouraged in France. The main element in couture is handwork, not included in ready-to-wear. Couture appears simpler than ready-to-wear because the hand operations permit greater subtlety of shaping and fit. It may take 30 seamstresses, sharing one sewing machine that is sparingly used, 80 hours to make the simplest design, while a lavish evening dress may require 500 hours. A skilled seamstress is as necessary to a designer as a patron. Without superior handling, a design can be lost, just as both handling and design are hurt if the fabric lacks some degree of excellence. The couture garment is a synthesis of specialized skills, the result of many artisans willing to cooperate to serve a vigorous tradition of craftsmanship. People who can afford to, buy handwork to impress each other, while those who can appreciate it select it for pure aesthetic enjoyment.

The challenge of the changing shapes of fashion is an intellectual exercise to the designer who must ask himself: "How ingenious am I at solving this problem?" It also requires a certain worldly approach. A fashionable style is merely one of many possible surfaces for what may be underneath. After all, one shape is as good as another; it is only the fact that it is fashion that counts.

This intellectual attitude fits in with the general French approach to life. Each individual is credited with being an autonomous person, able to think and act on his own. A conversation, a market exchange, a discussion of politics is considered in France an intellectual exercise between the people involved. The important thing is the spirit of the exercise, not the matter itself, just as style and fashion in dress can be appreciated regardless of content or what is beneath the surface.

Because Paris is a world center for high society, artists and entertainers, buyers and sellers of luxury goods, and because it produces the ideas that become fashion, it acquires an added glamour. Paris is news. This allows anyone who succeeds in the haute couture system to achieve world fame, although, conversely, a mediocre talent may be crushed. The ceaseless variety of life that Paris offers tends to encourage a creative temperament which needs breadth rather than height, needs to experiment without being laughed at, and needs to learn how to communicate intuitive thought.

Challenges. The haute couture faces the problems of high costs, low profits, a limited market, and unauthorized copying or piracy of design. While commercial buyers and manufacturers buy more than ever two types of models—either the most typical of the new fashion or the easiest to reproduce—the private customers who are willing to pay the prices of haute couture diminish each year.

Couture houses have constantly faced this problem. It is hard to increase sales beyond a certain point because of the limited size of the market. High fashion cannot exist without the exclusive appeal of *rare* goods, those goods that possess a desired superior quality plus the element of individuality associated with scarcity. To maintain this exclusive element, high quality garments must be offered at high prices; yet, the higher the price, the fewer the women who can afford them and the fewer the garments sold. Firms producing expensive ready-to-wear in New York also face the same problem. They must depend for a market on specialty shops which buy for quality and on the tastes of their select group of customers.

In addition, the couture houses have slim profit margins. A Dior evening gown which costs a private client $1,400 makes the house only $70 profit on the sale. An economic survey in 1965 revealed that the usual profit margin on couture clothes was about 5 per cent. Collections are costly to produce. Each biannual collection at Dior costs a minimum of $200,000, while Pierre Cardin estimates that his spring collection costs between $120,000 and $140,000, compared with $180,000 for his winter collections.[13]

Because haute couture provides indirect benefits in world markets to French makers of perfume, cosmetics, jewelry, ready-to-wear, and similar items, the French government has, in the past, provided the Paris couture houses with subsidies in various forms. The subsidy is in the form of, sometimes, a tax break; at others, it is a direct subsidy to each house based on the amount of French fabric used in a season.

The French textile industries, also, attempt to woo the couture. For example, in 1959 the French silk industry took double-page ads in the newspaper *Le Figaro* promoting gifts from Paris couturiers. All the items were, of course, silk—dresses, pillows, brocade match boxes.[14] Christian Dior, when he established his house, was backed by $500,000 from the French textile king, Marcel Boussac, who reasoned that the prestige of the haute couture directly affected the sale of textiles from his mills. Textiles industries may furnish fabric free to the couturiers, and receive, in return, the benefits of the publicity from the couture models.

In 1962, as labor and textile costs rose, subsidies were withdrawn, leaving the houses pretty much on their own. Thus, for economic reasons, they go more and more into some type of ready-to-wear which is not made in the couture house but in workrooms located in lower rent areas of the city or suburbs. Many obtain their major source of income from related products that reflect the prestige gained through the fashion collections and are supported almost entirely by sideline sales of perfumes, cosmetics, stockings, and other accessory items. In the huge Dior enterprises, the couture sales are considered to be only one of many departments, bringing in about 9 per cent of the total sales, but it is still the most important department in terms of prestige for the entire Dior operation.

Consequently, while the export sale of couture garments brings to France around $12 million a year, the total export of all French fashion products, including ready-to-wear, perfumes, jewelry, cosmetics, handbags, and the like, is roughly estimated at $375 million. France, it is evident, benefits more from the prestige of its best known product—high fashion—than from the scant profits on the couture collections themselves.[15]

Still another problem to the couture is style piracy. Not everyone who wants to copy a high fashion design is willing to pay for it or to wait until it is released. In spite of all the precautions taken by the houses, piracy or stealing of design ideas is not uncommon. Ideas may leak through a member of the staff, a press agent, clients who secretly sketch other models as they buy one, or underground copy systems—models bought through private clients and rented out as miniature shows. Sometimes, albums of sketches are compiled by guests at the collections who are exceptionally gifted at remembering designs. Fashion photographers may invite manufacturers, retailers, and press friends for a private look at models they are supposed to be photographing for publication a month hence.

While French dressmakers all along the upper-class shopping streets of Paris turn out close copies of couture designs, it is the big United States manufacturers which concern the couturiers. With their large production capacity, the Americans can quickly flood the market with cheap imitations even before the originals go on sale, and French designers have no recourse under United States law.

Design and fashion styling are such important competitive weapons among garment concerns that style piracy is a way of life. Copying the work of creative designers is standard operation for many small firms making cheaper dresses. This is the only way they are able to get quickly into fast-selling styles. Each is set up to handle certain price lines, as we have discussed before. The firm that sells dresses for $70 is equipped only for that price level. Even though the dress with slight variations may sell for $30, they are not organized to handle this, just as the firm selling dresses for $30 is not qualified to reduce the design further and sell it for $8.95. Normally, copying goes from higher-priced firms to lower, if the dress shows signs of public acceptance. Henry Rosenfeld, whose firm grosses $20 million a year copying or "knocking off" more expensive dresses, claims his production is so flexible he can have an item in the stores two weeks after he sees it somewhere.

The haute couture system is threatened also by the makeup of the modern world. The couture's power, vested in individual couturiers and skilled workers, carries on the individuality and personal responsibility of an artisan era. So far, the system has been supported by the French climate of opinion that has always favored the small shop owner over large-scale industry, even in the face of tremendous economic pressures to change. Slowness to mechanize production facilities and thus cut costs has kept France from dominating the ready-to-wear field. One of the best known ready-to-wear producers opened his first factory with 20 workers in the summer of 1964. Before this, his garments were made by 230 contracted seamstresses working in their own homes[16]—a system used early in the 1900's in this country. In contrast, Berlin has been quick to mechanize large factories for ready-to-wear production since World War II.

The couture system is threatened by mass-produced ready-to-wear, not directly, but indirectly by what happens to the taste of people. Demand is both cause and effect. Those accustomed to ready-to-wear made in a confusion of blends and synthetics can no longer identify or judge fabrics. Those who wear clothes that fit approximately and have never experienced the feel of a garment made to *their* body measurements cannot judge fit. Those who will not risk upsetting social harmony by being different from their fellow associates, except in minor ways, will not appreciate or seek the surprising individual element in design.

If the demands of great masses of people with no desire for individuality, no appreciation of fit, little sensitivity to aesthetic qualities or fine workmanship overwhelm the minority who have these perceptions, haute couture, which stands for elegance and manners in dress, may not be desired, even by those who can afford it.

Without the new ideas offered by the couture, all dress might well become standardized. Paris clothes are new and exciting. There is fashion there that cannot be found anyplace else in the world. The French have waged an unceasing battle against the routine, the normal, the already accepted, and stand supreme as the creative motors of the ready-to-wear and textile industries all over the world. What direction the couture will take is uncertain. After all, fashion suggested by a couturier with imagination is only a suggestion which can be adopted or discarded. Each woman adapts her own clothes to herself; she holds the ultimate decision about the future of the high fashion industry.

READY-TO-WEAR IN THE UNITED STATES. Unlike the haute couture system which began over a century ago to supply elegant designs for a small group of wealthy courtiers, the ready-to-wear system developed largely in the present century to furnish fashion for masses of people in the lower- and middle-income levels. It was an outgrowth of widespread cultural changes, rather than the desires of one group.

The period 1879 to 1909, which saw the first census of manufacturing, stands for rapid industrial growth in the United States. The maze of technical developments and the slow but steady rise in prices induced all industries to expand, including the ready-to-wear industry. While improvement in stitching machinery was slow, the percentage of the women's garment industry using mechanized power rose from 11.3 per cent in 1889 to 70.6 per cent in 1910.[17] Garment construction was broken down from the single operator making the entire garment in her home to a task-oriented system in a factory, with a "baster," "operator," and "finisher." The demand for ready-made clothing increased as the margin between the cost of making the garment and materials in the home and prices of the factory-produced goods decreased.

In 1963 a business survey showed consumer outlays for clothing and accessories in the United States amounted to almost $35 billion, or about 9 per cent of the total personal consumption expenditures.[18] It is generally recognized that the United States has brought the mass production of fashion goods to the highest development in the world and leads in the quantity, variety, and quality of ready-to-wear.

The meaning of the term "ready-to-wear" is self explanatory. Before buying these garments a customer may try on the completed dress to judge the becomingness of the design and the degree of fit. Minor alterations, usually in length, can be made to adjust for differences in body build. Because many manufacturers have specialized in various areas of design, it is hoped that a variety of choices will give the customer what she wants in both fit and design, without any changes. She may walk into the store, and walk out wearing the garment she has purchased. The clothing is, as the name implies, ready to wear.

Basically, ready-made garments *save time, energy,* and *money.* They require no waiting on fittings, and eliminate the dressmaking risk of a poor choice inherent in selecting styles without being able to see them on the figure.

The ready-to-wear industry is strictly a business operation, set up to produce as many as are wanted of any particular design, and is totally dependent on its own resources. It must be strongly consumer-oriented and cost-minded to survive the fierce competition between thousands of factories in this country as well as those abroad. The more mediocre the product, the greater the competition will be.

Each manufacturer strives to differentiate his garment from others and lessen competition by giving his product some air of exclusiveness. For example, one suit company turns out classic styles year after year, but always in high quality fabrics with good workmanship and generous seam allowances for fitting. Another suit company, at the same price level, offers more fashion features in its styling, but they are executed in lower quality fabric. In a cost sense, the second firm spends more for the design and labor required to sew styled parts, but saves money on fabrics, while the first company may have no designer at all—just a pattern stylist—and spends more for its fabrics.

Continual cost analysis in the factors of production tends to make the factory owner *more process-minded than design-minded.* The cheapest and quickest garment to make, not the most beautiful, is the best—as long as the customer will accept it and it sells.

Who is the ready-to-wear customer? She is the average American woman who wants comfortable clothes that portray a pleasant personality. She likes to feel properly dressed rather than actually elegant. In fact, the average woman, while wanting to be in fashion—look like "today" in styling—has little technical fashion know-how. Nor does she want to spend any more time and money than she has to on clothes.* Sometimes she lacks a sense of proportion, going from the extremes of beatnik dress to overdress, and accepts eccentricity in design that might be considered humorous in other countries. At other times, her choice is so staple it is monotonous. As she gets older and her size increases she is less willing to accept changes in cut, but remains receptive to changes in color and texture. In general, however, she is relatively easy to dress, slim and well built, and believes she wants timeless, simple, casual clothes.

The designer working under this system may be less crea-

---

* In 1959 a study prepared by the research department of Street and Smith Publications, now a division of Conde Nast, based on 5,452 mail returns from women 15 years of age and older, showed that while the employed woman spent an average of $13.42 for a dress, the non-employed woman paid $11.36. The woman with some college education paid $15.92, the woman with no college education paid $10.73.[19]

tive than in haute couture, but must be more in touch with what has been selling as an indication of what people want. He follows accepted fashion styling rather than initiating ideas for new fashions. His designs are made to please, even though this may mean the same old shirtwaist year after year, with only minor variations.

Because his work goes out under the company name, no one person is really responsible. The garment is an anonymous creation in which the design is just one phase of a process. Company policy may determine the results of the designer's activity before he is ever hired. In many firms a committee made up of the owner, the merchandise manager, and perhaps the head of sales selects the designs that will be used. Consequently, even though seven different designers may work for a company, the styles all seem to be made by one person—the garments acquire a company stamp, rather than a designer's stamp.

A ready-to-wear designer is price conscious as well as product conscious. He tries to do the most with the least, while watching the form of his design become blurred to suit the technical limitations on the manufacturing level. Detail may be more important than form. Ready-to-wear sells from a rack and garments need hanger appeal—something to catch the consumer's eye as she thumbs through dozens of dresses jammed into a limited space.

Once selected, a garment must fit the life pattern of the consumer. Utility rules in ready-to-wear—utility in a technical, social, and physical sense. The garment is made in the quickest way, suits the everyday social life of the customer, and is comfortable to wear. The high fashion fantasy of the couture designer is tamed, moderated, and accepted. The lifetime of a fashion becomes the time it takes to assimilate, rationalize, and functionalize it, in short to water it down from the zenith of haute couture to the lowest level of ready-mades.

The Designing Process. A company may hire one, two, or as many as seven designers, or it may hire none, relying instead on a pattern maker with a sense of style. Although the designer is anonymous to the consumer, she is real and vital to the company as long as she fits into the cooperative enterprise. Like any malfunctioning part of a machine process, she is replaceable. A designer is valuable only as long as she designs garments that sell.

From my experience as one of seven designers, hired by a large ready-to-wear firm making low- to medium-priced dresses, I will describe designing in the ready-to-wear system, as it seemed to me. Like haute couture, the ready-to-wear system, once established, does not radically change through the years. A recent letter from the company assures me that the process remains much the same as when I was there, except for the addition of new figure-type lines.

In general, all ready-to-wear firms have three to five showings a year. The major lines, which may contain around 60 designs, are for spring, fall, and summer, while sometimes a second spring line and a second fall or resort line are added. Preparing these showings and producing the garments take time. Consequently, the designer has been busy designing the garments from three to six months before the customer sees them. The company introduces the new lines with a fashion show on live mannequins, or shows the garments hanging on racks in a showroom to company salesmen and retail buyers. The garments these people select as possible good-selling numbers for their clients are the ones that are then started in the factory production system.

How does the designer know what the customer will want? One of the best ways to find out is to know someone who wears the garments this company produces, perhaps a mother, a sister, or a friend. A mental image of a real person gives the designer a "type" toward which to focus design ideas. It is the same thing as a couture designer who designs for a favorite mannequin, an elegant private customer, or, as Yves St. Laurent does, for his mother. Companies often send their designers on retail store promotions, primarily to acquaint them with the needs of the customers and to acquire a "customer image."

Another way to learn consumer preferences is to look at the sales records. In the company I worked for, each dress was sketched and kept in a book with its own sales record. The records of several years indicated which designs were best sellers. A comparison between best-selling numbers might reveal that they had some design features in common, such as fullness on the shoulder or curving V-shaped necklines. By incorporating these features into new designs, another best-selling number might be created. The final test, however, is always the sales record of each individual design. In this connection, an examination of competitors' merchandise is expedient to see why their designs sell so well.

Once the designer has formed an image of what the customer likes, his next consideration is the latitude in construction permitted by the technical operations. For example, a square corner may be much harder to execute than a curve or a straight line; an all around pleated skirt may take too much yardage. These are the cost limitations design ideas must encompass.

A final limitation is that, in contrast to the French couture designer who starts with hundreds of sketched ideas, the American ready-to-wear designer starts with the fabric. She may be told the company has purchased 20,000 yards of a particular fabric and expects to sell it in dresses at a stated price. It is the designer's job to design a dress that will do this. A sample bolt of goods is brought into the designing booth—a walled-off section on an open factory floor—and there the designer experiments. Perched on a high stool in front of a large table she considers all the limitations within which she must create: the customer image, the technical limits on factory construction, the 20,000 yards of this particular material, and the price line. She tries the material this way and that, she sketches, she forms a plan.

The plan is next turned into reality. The ready-to-wear designer is responsible for showing her idea as a finished dress. She may be the only one to see her sketched idea, or if she is unable to sketch, it does not matter. The thing she must be able to do is make the pattern for her idea and supervise the machine operator who sews it into a completed model.

Most mass-produced garments are cut from flat, not draped, patterns. It is called the "flat pattern" method of designing because the designs, all variations of one standard size pattern, can be laid out flat. Each company has developed its own size standard to keep dresses consistent and to satisfy a particular figure type of customer. As new designs are made, the patterns of the designs are kept in large envelopes for the designers to use. This allows a designer to use parts of an old pattern if her entire idea is not completely new, and to make only the pattern pieces for the styled sections she has created. By not having to make the entire pattern, the design operation is speeded up. Timing can be very important to small companies which are dependent on one or two designs hitting the market at exactly the right place in the fashion cycle of acceptance.

After the dress is designed and accepted by other members of the firm, who pass on whether it represents the company policy, the dress is analyzed for cost and given a stock number. Duplicate samples are made for salesmen, followed by the opening showings of the line. If the dress is favored by salesmen and buyers, it is graded into various sizes (changed from a standard 14 to 10, 12, 16, 18) and is produced in the factory.

There is a steady underlying tension and drama to the designing process. Each step means possible failure or success. Designs can be rejected by the company officials before the salesmen see them; they can be rejected by the retail buyers before the customers see them; and finally, they can be rejected by the customers. *Or,* they can sell by the thousands.

The interests of the company are the designer's interests. She becomes part of a closely knit group and generally feels strongly committed to her work. Whether she "steals ideas" by copying, "adapts" best-selling ideas from higher priced lines, or "creates" her own ideas depends partly on the company policy and partly on her own purpose in designing. If she is committed to expressing something she alone has sensed, she will try to originate, but if she is simply designing to make a living, she will do whatever is the most expedient. In any case, the successful designer for ready-to-wear must possess creative ingenuity to design within so many limitations, a sense of what the ordinary person likes, and enough fashion intuition to keep her designs within the general course of fashion.

Climate of Opinion. The ready-to-wear system of designing reflects the American climate of opinion. Our background lacks a tradition of art but includes the tradition of a machine civilization in a political democracy. By reducing the creative element in dress to its lowest level in order to suit the mass-production system, ready-to-wear has discouraged beauty and individuality in dress design. On the other hand, by building up the commercialization of fashion—transitory art—it has encouraged the adoption of some fantasy elements by almost everyone.

Based, as are most machine industries, on the belief that practical success is what counts, the system does not hesitate to vulgarize dress by making it showy, shocking, or in some way ridiculous, if that will make sales, or encourage fast turnover. On the other hand, it will repeat designs boringly alike, if that seems to be what people want. Without standards of its own, the system simply reflects the tastes of the people it serves.

Artistic awareness is not yet highly developed in most Americans. Art in America tends to cling to a system developed when the West was being settled. The main centers cluster in New York, while trading stations string out along the principal routes to the West. The more prosperous people still make it back East to enjoy a wide selection in paintings, sculpture, and dress. The rest of the population sees very little.

This general lack of artistic appreciation dates back to a colonial culture that took art traditions from the Old World and gave none in return. Absorbed in the hard work of trying to attain in one generation the cultural equipment that was the product of many centuries of civilized effort in Europe, and in an environment adapted only to the level of savagery, the early settlers often exhausted their energies. Taste, manners, and matters of the spirit suffered.

In time, a local pride, narrowness, or provincialism developed. People admired what was close at hand and saw things in the distance rather hazily. They forgot the traditional standards of Europe and developed local standards. Their local standards were based on practical solutions to problems made by people who had to deal with the materials of the environment, even though they might know little or nothing about artistic expression. Sometimes, this false local pride cast a rosy glow over the strange and the shocking; a native oddity or a mediocre product from a foreign country might be elevated to a high position completely out of line with its true merit.

Today, local bias persists. For example, the college student admires her classic neat white blouse but may look askance at a dress made from a hand-dyed batik from Burma. She admires a local teen-age craze but a French haute couture model seems as weird to her as the surface of the moon. Unusual cut makes her uneasy. She cannot relax and treat an artistic individual quality in dress as fun, or design as a mental exercise—something to be enjoyed because it broadens perceptions. It is too unfamiliar. Aesthetic sensitivity is still hard work for many Americans. Art is something students study, a field of ethics that should be learned, a taste for the "finer things of life" one ought to have, rather than a spontaneous reflection of acute personal interest that is a natural part of life.

While many Americans work at acquiring aesthetic perception, most of them are still not willing to pay for skilled craftsmanship in their clothes in the same way they are willing to pay for utility. Often unable to discriminate in quality, they buy their "taste" ready-made. They rely on the designers who planned the garment and the store buyers who selected it to give them taste. But they fail to consider the circularity of the process in the ready-to-wear system. The designer creates and the buyer selects to suit the public taste as recorded on their past sales records; they strive to reflect public taste *as it is*. Meanwhile, the consumer has falsely assumed that she is buying the superior taste of the experts in the clothing field. This demand and cause effect makes it difficult for new group standards of taste to arise and initiate changes in the quality of consumer goods.

Challenges. The greatest challenge to the American ready-to-wear system is the growth of similar systems in France, Italy, Japan, Germany, and other countries. Long accustomed to a near monopoly in this field, America will increasingly face competition from abroad as more and more countries mechanize their garment industries. Each country brings to the system a different climate of opinion and a different set of labor skills. Therefore, the designs they present will vary in quality, expression, and craftsmanship. This is good news for consumers—a wider choice allows more people to be satisfied—but it may hurt the sales of some American firms. However, America, which has traditionally favored the free-enterprise system, should be able to match ideas from abroad with new ideas of her own. Competition has always acted as a spur to growth rather than as a deterrent.

Conclusion

We have seen that designers choose to make different designs under the couture system in France than under the ready-to-wear system in America. They will compromise on their reason for designing, their understanding of the meaning of dress for the people they serve, and their sense of involvement in an economic order. Thus, designers of equal creative talent and perceptive insight, working under two different systems of design, face different problems. The solutions they find to these problems become their designs. Paris designers supply the essence, mood, and overall direction fashion often follows. American designers quickly adapt, interpret, and conceive ideas for ready-to-wear they hope will give the best value in the world.

While differing in many ways, there is one thing these designs share—a universal fashion element. Each design will contain some aspect of the prevailing style that either represents the fashion of today or becomes the fashion of tomorrow, or it will never be produced.

5

PRODUCTION

The manufacturer cuts, sews, and makes the garment, adapting design ideas to the production process. Yet, a dress hanging on the rack in the retail store may scarcely resemble the designer's original model. It has become a manufactured product, the production choice of some producer weighing quality against cost and solving the problems unique to a fashion industry.

The fashion industry is a volatile industry. It requires *styling, timing,* and *flexibility* to handle the upswings and downturns in demand caused by the transitory element of fashion. Unlike the manufacturer of staple goods who adjusts only to long-term technical advances, the producer of fashion goods concentrates on short-term changes.

Fashion production is primarily affected by the routine season-to-season alterations in style that tend to identify this year's fashion as the difference between the new model and the old one it replaces. This makes the designer, or the stylist, an important member of the manufacturing firm.

In addition, the area of garment production is affected by long-term technical developments in the textile industries that supply the fabric for designs. New fibers, weaves, and finishes in fabrics can bring a fundamental change to the nature of fashion in dress.

And, finally, there are the unexpected dynamics of group taste. If California teen-agers spontaneously want "granny dresses" (contemporary mother hubbards with hemlines dropped to the ground), while hemlines of other dresses are rising above the knees, some company will supply them. It takes alert timing to market fashion goods at the peak of public acceptance and requires adjustable production methods.

The factors that cause volatility in the fashion industry increase risk of failure or success. To counteract risk, manufacturers may introduce a stable element into their production. For example, textile mills, which are strongly influenced by fashion in the making of fabrics for garments, add stability to their production by supplying sheeting, toweling, and upholstery fabrics—goods for which there is a more constant demand. Some dress companies make uniforms for institutions in addition to their regular lines, or carry several fashion lines instead of one.

Stability can also be added by creating brand loyalty. Firms that specialize in one area of design build a unique product image toward which a traditional sentiment or sense of loyalty can be developed. Consumers may feel this product in some way possesses qualities superior to other similar products. Brand loyalty arises especially in the sizing area of women's wear where a company will concentrate on one figure type such as half sizes or tall girls, or where shoe companies will specialize in "lasts"—sizings to fit various types of feet.

While he is faced with specialized problems, the fashion goods manufacturer, like any businessman, has the duty of increasing profits by making designs simple and less costly to produce. The producer of fashion goods must use resources efficiently and meet competition in the same general way as any other manufacturer. He considers the same problems: locating his plant near a source of labor supply; negotiating with a union; using as many assembly-line techniques as possible; buying his fabrics and selling his product in the least costly way. He knows there may be larger manufacturers who can undersell him, or smaller companies who can offer more specialized services. Since salability is based on both improved utility and appearance, the public benefits indirectly from efficient business practices.

In the apparel industries, simplification has tended to

The French high fashion couture design is adapted to the mass-production techniques of American ready-to-wear and the everyday needs of the consumer.

eliminate intricate cut which involves costly hand sewing, and to rely instead on texture, color, and applied designs to create interest. As a result, American-made garments seem easier to care for and more comfortable to wear, although less beautiful or individual in design. This "utility" rationalization for change in design, introduced primarily for business reasons, is strongly supported by the American climate of opinion, creating a demand-and-cause interrelationship. Whether the American taste for simplicity in dress, defined as a lack of complicated cut, is the result of industry's influence on taste and its subsequent effect on the style of life, or is the effect of the lifestyle pattern of the consumer on demand, remains undecided. What is clear is that business molds the consumer, and the consumer molds business; the influence goes in both directions.

Working within this dual frame of reference—the volatile nature of consumer demand for fashion goods, and the profit-oriented nature of business—the producer decides what garments to present. This decision, in essence, then determines the character of the United States garment industry. The extent of the American producers' contribution to the fashion industry is suggested by the following opinions and trade demands of fashion experts from outside the United States: "I find Europe nowadays trying to copy everything American. I'm always saying to my European friends—all you do is criticize the Americans, yet all you do is copy them."[1] These are the comments of Brita Behn, a charming Italian-born woman of style. Her remarks illustrate the degree of influence America exerts in the world of fashion.

The nature of the influence is indicated by the sales made by the United States to foreign countries. Leading British retailers come to the United States to buy lingerie, inexpensive women's sportswear, and the medium- and high-priced lines in men's casual wear. They buy in quantity and want fast deliveries. Synthetic fabrics and wash-and-wear items lead the list of desired items, with printed cotton cloth and knitted apparel next in demand. During an interview with an American fashion reporter, the director of a British specialty store explained why he preferred certain American products. "We feel in this country [Britain] that synthetics have been pretty disappointing. Nylon and your other synthetics are always much better than what we can get here."[2]

Even the Russians have looked appreciatively at the United States fashion industry. Members of a Soviet delegation sent to study the American apparel industry were particularly interested in the production of women's raincoats and undergarments, and men's shirts. They paid special attention to the techniques of mass production, noting the efficiency of large American corporations in manufacturing women's foundation garments and medium-priced clothes for teen-agers.[3]

But not everyone sees American fashion in a favorable light. The late Christian Dior expressed another popular view when he said that America represents the triumph of quantity over quality. He saw America as a land where the dominance of mass production results in "a multitude of the mediocre."[4]

The sampling of opinion from outside the United States suggests that the rest of the world considers America's contribution in the fashion area to be the volume production of practical clothing. America offers useful clothes designed for modern life at a price most people can afford.

Technical and Industrial Development

America reached its preeminent position in the world through the efficient use of resources in industrial expansion. Furthermore, the social, religious, economic, and intellectual attitudes of the young dynamic country helped to justify the large amounts of scientific research applied in this country to the advancement and expansion of industry.

CLIMATE OF OPINION. As we have seen, the attitudes of the early residents of this country, coupled with the abundance of natural resources, put America in the forefront of an intellectual and industrial revolution which placed its emphasis on mass production and consumption. The American people moved, as favorable economic conditions developed, from a predominantly rural agricultural nation to an urban industrialized society, although not without opposition from respected leaders.

Thomas Jefferson, in writing his *Notes on the State of*

Virginia, presented a viewpoint toward manufacturers popular around 1781: "We have manufactured within our families the most necessary articles of clothing. Those of cotton will bear some comparison with the same kinds of manufacture in Europe; but those of wool, flax and hemp are very coarse, unsightly and unpleasant: and such is our attachment to agriculture, and such our preference for foreign manufactures, that be it wise or unwise, our people will certainly return as soon as they can, to the raising of raw materials, and exchanging them for finer manufactures than they were able to execute themselves."[5] At that time, Jefferson felt the United States was destined to be an agricultural nation and that agriculture was the most honorable occupation.

Benjamin Franklin, in his pamphlet "Information About America," (1784) noted the general failure of several great establishments producing quantities of linen and woolen goods for sale, goods of equal value being imported cheaper. "Great establishments of manufacturers," he wrote, "require great numbers of poor to do the work for small wages; these poor are to be found in Europe, but will not be found in America 'till the lands are all taken up and cultivated and the excess of people who cannot get land want employment."[6] As Franklin observed, the scarcity and high price of labor was the most serious obstacle to manufacturing. Not until the labor problem was solved by mechanizing related industries did widespread industrialization of fashion finally begin.

INTERRELATED INDUSTRIES. The three main links in the production and distribution of fashion goods—the textile industries, the apparel industries, and retailing—are interdependent. The apparel industries serve as the primary traffic-builders and producers of profitable high-volume sales for the textile industries and for the retailers. They are the chief customers of the textile industries and are, in turn, dependent on the retailers for the purchase and distribution of the goods they manufacture. All three are ultimately dependent on consumer demand.

The enormous expansion of the women's garment industries in America by 1910 was the result of technical and industrial interrelationships. A shift from production of garments in the home to large-scale production in the factory

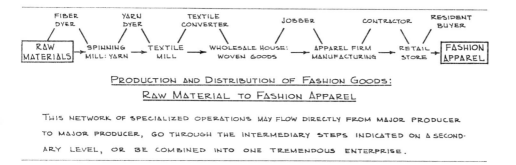

PRODUCTION AND DISTRIBUTION OF FASHION GOODS:
RAW MATERIAL TO FASHION APPAREL

THIS NETWORK OF SPECIALIZED OPERATIONS MAY FLOW DIRECTLY FROM MAJOR PRODUCER
TO MAJOR PRODUCER, GO THROUGH THE INTERMEDIARY STEPS INDICATED ON A SECOND-
ARY LEVEL, OR BE COMBINED INTO ONE TREMENDOUS ENTERPRISE.

is dependent upon a ready supply of cloth, which is dependent on the availability of yarn. Lower costs, which increase consumption and enlarge production, are dependent upon the invention of suitable stitching machinery which, in turn, is dependent on the availability of suitable sewing thread, which is dependent on the development of mechanical combs.

Technological advances start a chain reaction throughout interrelated industries. Sheer wool, for example, did not become fashionable until the mechanization of the combing operation made the worsted industry possible. Form-fitting knitted underwear and thin stockings followed the invention of suitable knitting machinery. As new fibers and new fabrics are created in the research laboratory of the modern textile chemist, new trimmings and advanced styling to suit them are produced by the design units of the garment manufacturer.

Related industries must be sensitive to the changing currents of fashion at every level: the mill level, the manufacturing level, the retail level, and the consumer level. The farther removed the major producer is from the end product (fashion apparel), the more sensitive to public taste his long-range planning must be. Yet long-range fashion planning is more difficult than short-range planning in the volatile fashion fields. A textile stylist who scouts for fashion news is an important asset to the textile industries, just as a designer is important to the garment industries. Unlike the designer, however, she only advises, and is, therefore, not responsible for the decisions made by other members of the firm. The colors, weaves, and fibers selected by the textile industries one or two years in advance of the market sales must receive public acceptance at the time they appear.

In this vein it should be mentioned that the development

of taste is not left entirely to cultural influences outside the fashion goods industry. Each level of the marketing system tries fashion promotion. It is an economic law that a mechanized apparel industry requires the standardization of fashion over a wide area. One function of advertising and other forms of fashion propaganda, given in a later chapter, is to stimulate a desire for the same thing at the same time in a large number of people—to build a like-mindedness among consumers.

To decrease risk in long-term planning and to increase flexibility, some enterprising producers have integrated the major production processes. One firm that makes lingerie and panties for volume distribution buys the acetate and nylon yarns it needs from the primary producer, knits its own material, and dyes and finishes the fabric in its own plants. Furthermore, it has its own designing and styling staff. Eventually the firm hopes to make its own laces and ribbons. This self-sufficiency permits the firm to quickly accommodate its merchandise to the customer's habit of buying when the need arises and not before. It gives fast deliveries on short-term orders from retailers. "We can have the fabric on the cutting table twelve hours after receiving the yarn from the primary producer and put the merchandise on the counter within four days of receiving the yarn," the company president reported.

While this practice seems modern and efficient, it had a parallel more than 300 years ago in the busy "clothier" in London: The clothier, or cloth manufacturer, had become a large-scale contractor, employing specialists at each stage of the operation. He took the wool to the spinner, the yarn to the weaver, and the rough cloth to be washed and stretched and finished to the dyer. The clothier then sold the finished product to the draper. He sold the cloth on the retail market, while a great surplus went abroad. The prosperity of many people depended on the clothier and he depended on his market. By 1642, in England, the integration of industry was underway in the manufacture of cloth. But in America, the integration of industry was centered in the home.

HOMESPUN. Household production of coarse cloth was the rule in early America; finer fabrics came from England. The wool industry was an occupation for the entire family, as this description of a colonial household by Alice Morse Earle illustrates. The setting was in the early evening by the bright firelight. "The old grandmother at light and easy work, is carding the wool into fleecy rolls, seated next the fire; for, as the ballad says, 'She was old and saw right dimly.' The mother, stepping as lightly as one of her girls, spins the rolls into woolen yarn on the great wheel. The oldest daughter sits at the clock-reel, whose continuous buzz and occasional click mingles with the humming rise and fall of the wool-wheel, and the irritating scratch of the cards. A little girl at a small wheel is filling quilts with woolen yarns for the loom, not a skilled work. The father is setting fresh teeth in a wool card, while the boys are whittling hand reels and loom spools."[7]

Spinning was a popular holiday recreation. Women, rich as well as poor, appeared on Boston Common with their wheels. Alice Morse Earle reports that at the fourth anniversary in 1749 of the "Boston Society for Promoting Industry and Frugality," three hundred "young spinsters" spun on their wheels on Boston Common. The art of spinning was so universal it furnished a legal title for an unmarried woman that we still recognize today. And as Earle notes: "Spinster is the only one of all her various womanly titles that survives; webster, shepster, lister, brewster, and baxter are obsolete."[8]

While every farmer's daughter knew how to weave as well as to spin, weaving was not recognized as wholly woman's work as was spinning. Handweaving was a trade to which men were apprenticed. Every town had professional weavers who comprised a universally respected class and were the ancestors of wealthy and influential citizens.

The automatic loom, often regarded as the greatest single achievement in textile machinery during the nineteenth century, was first introduced in 1894. Consequently, household production of cloth steadily declined as the margin between the cost of garment materials and the price of ready-to-wear apparel narrowed, and large-scale production in the factory soon prevailed.

THE TEXTILE INDUSTRIES. The Industrial Revolution in America made its real start in the cotton mills. It was American research that opened up the vast cotton market in the nineteenth century, just as it opened up the markets for man-made fibers in the twentieth century. In the beginning both types of fiber symbolized low social status in comparison with pure silk which had traditionally implied high status. For example, the Chinese peasant wore cotton, but the emperor's gowns were made of silk. The American working girl wore rayon stockings or slips, but she dreamed of owning articles made of silk.

Silk, although always prized, achieved a high fashion rank when Charles Frederick Worth made Empress Eugenie the figurehead of fashion in the luxurious silks from the looms of Lyons, France. Later, silk enjoyed a lush period of demand for hosiery. In the two decades between World War I and World War II, the newly developing synthetics were regarded with suspicion, and silk hosiery was universally popular. Before World War II almost 85 per cent of the world's silk fiber went into hosiery, but it soon gave way to nylon. The decline in the use of silk has paralleled the rise in synthetics. However, the mood or essence of silk lingers on as a "superior" quality to strive for and imitate, just as the spirit of the haute couture hovers over the designers of mass-produced goods. Scientists working with various fibers continually strive to impart a silklike quality to other fibers to raise their apparent quality.

As the production of one fiber increases or decreases in response to new technologies, its long-term effects become an important consideration for the field of fashion. Are fiber characteristics adapted, as in garment design, to general fashion trends before they can be accepted? As we examine in the following pages each dominant fiber type that has been mass-produced in the United States, the effect of the fabric on fashion will be noted. We will observe how each producer meets his competition at home and abroad; how he solves the problems of efficient use of resources necessary to a business that is profit-oriented; and how he solves the specific problem of volatility inherent in a fashion industry.

In general, the major problem to the United States textile industry has been the high cost of labor in this country. Plagued by price competition from abroad, where labor is cheaper, manufacturers have turned to mechanization, but have been unable to compete on the basis of quality and style. Volatility is not the problem for the textile producer it is for the garment producer since the textile industry is stabilized by the production of fabrics other than fashion fabrics in which the fashion element does not fluctuate as rapidly and radically as in dress.

Cotton. The largest single division of the textile industry in the United States is cotton. A breakdown of the total mill output for 1960 shows: cotton 65 per cent; wool 6 per cent; man-made fibers 29 per cent.[9]

Each new development in the cotton area seems to radically change the entire clothing industry. It was the early mass production of cotton fabric that made possible inexpensive ready-made clothing for the laboring classes. The next development, the mercerization of cotton, gave the fabric a silklike quality. This raised the status of cotton and extended its use to better quality garments. Later, shrinkage control gave guaranteed sizing. And finally, the wash-and-wear finish adapted this 5,000-year-old fiber to the "utility" demands of modern life. Today, the largest use of cotton is in apparel fabrics.

When Eli Whitney revolutionized agriculture in 1792 with the invention of the cotton gin, he also elevated cotton to a top quantity, if not quality, position as a dress fabric. Because the cotton gin could clean as much cotton in a day as one handpicker could in a year, cotton was planted in greatly increased amounts. The availability of a large supply of an inexpensive textile fiber changed and cheapened apparel. It was a major factor in bringing fashion to a price everyone could afford.

Mr. Whitney had grasped the fundamental idea behind mass production in 1798 when he suggested interchangeable parts, for only machines can make interchangeable parts; handmade objects are all slightly different. This basic technique of mass production was perfect for a society short of labor and skills. It enabled women, children, and newly arrived immigrant workers to become "the numbers of poor to work for small wages" that Franklin foresaw as necessary for the success of large-scale manufacturing.

At Lowell, Massachusetts, the total number of operators employed in all the cotton manufacturing plants by 1832 was 5,000; 3,800 were women and girls.[10]

Foreign visitors to the textile mills commented on the attractive appearance of girls who worked there. One such account is that of an English woman, Mrs. Harriet Martineau. After visiting a cotton mill at Paterson, New Jersey, in 1831 she wrote: "The girls were all well-dressed. Their hair was arranged according to the latest fashions which had arrived via New York, and they wore calashes in going to and fro between their dwelling and the mill."[11]

The presence of working girls who did not demand high wages helped New England to maintain its position as the center of the cotton textile world until the early 1920's. At that time the mills began to move south. The cotton mill owners discovered they could get laborers to work for longer hours at even less pay in areas where the cotton was grown— South Carolina, North Carolina, and Georgia. Benefits multiplied from the move south: the mills were near the sources of the raw cotton, close to a cheaper labor supply, and faced with lower community taxes.

The southern economy gradually shifted from growing cotton to manufacturing cotton textiles. However, the many advantages the textile manufacturers originally enjoyed have been slowly disappearing as the South becomes industrialized in other ways. Heavy industries, such as missiles and atomic energy operations, electronics, and auto assembly plants, are also moving south. These companies bring with them not only workers used to a high wage level, but also a new group of labor unions. The textile mills, once almost completely nonunionized, now must compete with higher-salaried firms for workers. This factor, added to the increased competition with cheaper foreign textiles and our own man-made fibers, has put the cotton textile mill man in a difficult position.

In the 1960's, for the first time since record-keeping began, American imports of cotton exceeded exports. After World War II, American advisers helped introduce advanced cotton production methods to countries such as India, Pakistan, Egypt, and Mexico. As these countries improved their seed and machinery, production in cotton reached record heights and the price of cotton on the world market fell. Because the price of American cotton was set so high, it could not compete on the world market.

The dilemma of the cotton industry illustrates the difficulties encountered by a "price-supported" industry. During the depression of the 1930's, the United States government, to help the small farmer survive, began propping up the price of cotton with a subsidy. (It has done the same for wheat, corn, and other farm commodities.) When cotton, or any other commodity, is pegged at a certain price, it is not free to move up and down according to the laws of supply and demand and it is not allowed to reach a competitive level through bargaining between the buyers and seller. If production from abroad should soar, the price of cotton in the world market is likely to fall. But because the United States cotton price is not free to fall, the American cotton industry loses buyers to countries which are able to undercut American prices.

The price problems faced by producers of raw cotton have also plagued the cotton textile industry. For a time the government used the "two-price cotton" plan. Under this plan, the government, as well as other sellers, was empowered to buy up surplus United States cotton at the pegged price

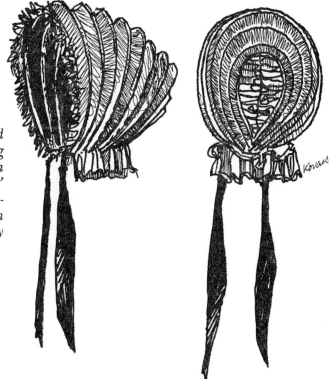

Calash: A woman's hood having hoops like the folding top of a light horse-drawn carriage called a "calash." Some early American versions were made of thin coarse cotton supported by cane hoops.

and sell it abroad at any price it could get. For example, the government might buy cotton at 33 cents a pound, and sell it abroad at 25 cents. But American cotton manufacturers had to buy the cotton at the pegged price (33 cents). This forced the mill owners in the United States to pay more for American cotton than foreign mill owners paid for the same cotton. Thus, foreign textile manufacturing firms gained two advantages over their American counterparts: they could pay their workers lower wages and buy raw cotton at lower prices.

This two-price system was dropped and a "one-price cotton" system was restored temporarily in 1964. Under the new plan, American textile manufacturers were reimbursed by the government for most of the difference between the price they had to pay for cotton from the United States and the price foreign manufacturers paid for cotton on the world market. Instead of dollars, the American manufacturers were given the equivalent value in additional units of cotton taken from the surplus cotton bins of the government. Although this plan improved the competitive position of the domestic cotton textile manufacturer, the sale of raw cotton, because it continued to depend on government price support, remained a problem, with the American taxpayer bearing the burden of government subsidy.

Textile manufacturers have also been aided by efforts to control international trade in cotton through long-term joint decisions between the governments of several countries and through bilateral cotton textile agreements with separate countries. These pacts put limits on the amount of cotton that can come into the United States. However, any government curb on a lower-priced import means higher prices for the American consumer: It amounts to a hidden tax on all Americans to protect one industry. Textile producers say that they would like to have competition on the basis of quality and style rather than simply on a basis of production or raw material cost.

The American cotton industry, unable to compete in labor costs and quantity, is retreating from the fashion element in fabric to the utility element. As fine quality cottons without a "wash-and-wear" finish become a rarity—hard to find, yet still in demand by discriminating tastes—they move up to become high status symbols. The molding qualities of natural fibers without crease-resistant finishes are needed to execute the intricate cut and fit of couture garments. So, the couture-type designer must seek cottons from abroad to supply his needs, but the ready-to-wear designer of low- to medium-priced lines finds a generous supply of fabrics in the United States. In view of its difficulties, there is general agreement among the cotton textile industry leaders that a successful future for the industry depends on a multifiber approach. The industry will need to be able to use all fibers and not be dependent on just one. Today, all new equipment is designed to produce blends with synthetics as well as cotton. Future product improvement and innovation will include easy-care and permanent-press techniques.[12]

Man-made fibers. A man-made or "manufactured fiber," as defined by the Textile Label Law, is "any fiber derived by a process of manufacture from any substance which, at any point in the manufacturing process, is not a fiber." This is in contrast to the term "natural fiber," a fiber that exists as such in the natural state. Man-made fibers offer the textile industry better performance in some characteristics than cotton and greater styling variation. In their various forms they become lower priced functional alternatives or substitutes for most of the natural fibers.

Unlike silk, which came into the modern fashion world in the custom-made garments of the French courts, the man-made fibers, sometimes called synthetics, were first introduced in the volume ready-to-wear markets. The strategy was an economic decision, a matter of the relationship between investment and earnings in the development of a new fiber. The Du Pont Company spent ten years in research and invested $27 million before it produced the first pound of nylon in a commercial plant. The investment in Orlon acrylic fiber was around $25 million at the same stage, and by the time Du Pont began to produce Dacron polyester fiber commercially, it had invested around $40 million. To realize an early return after years of costly research, Du Pont went directly to the general market.[13]

In order to understand the problems in acceptance encountered by the man-made fibers at different levels of fashion, it will be helpful to review the history of synthetics. The first man-made fiber was rayon which came into existence as artificial silk. The name rayon was not adopted until 1924, some 40 years after the introduction of the fiber. The second man-made fiber was acetate, which was introduced shortly after World War I. Since acetate, like rayon, stems from cellulose, it was considered to be in the same class as rayon. And because the term artificial silk implied an inferior substitute, early versions of rayon and acetate were handicapped. For the most part they were used in merchandise that was inferior and was regarded merely as a substitute for silk.

To counteract this attitude, Du Pont pioneered in the creation of a fabric development program. Under the program Du Pont took rayon yarn to France and there had leading mills manufacture fabrics of silk and then identical fabrics of rayon. The two fabrics were placed before designers from America and abroad and designers were asked to select between the two unidentified fabrics. Many designers who would not have thought of selecting rayon did so in this test. This altered their opinion of the fiber, and when they also considered the economic advantages of rayon over silk, rayon became more acceptable to designers. The same thing was true of acetate.

Nylon was the forerunner of the newer fibers and was used initially as a hosiery yarn. World War II coincided with the introduction of nylon, and many vital military uses were found for the fiber, particularly after the supply of silk had been cut off. Because of war orders, nylon was doing a volume business before any normal peace-time development programs had begun. This spurred plant expansion and intensified research into the development of other new fibers.

Unfortunately many of the things done during and after the war in connection with nylon had to be undone. For example, some nylon was used in men's shirts, but no attention was paid to fabric construction, styling, or any other important phase of shirtmaking.

The key attraction of nylon has been functionality, rather than fashion. This is true in hosiery where nylon continues as the predominant fiber, and is equally so in lingerie and nightwear where the strength and laundering ease of the fiber have permitted the introduction of intricately trimmed styles of fragile appearance at a relatively low cost.

Nylon, Dacron (polyester fibers used in easy-care and

wash-and-wear garments), and spandex (a manufactured stretch fiber) are the new fibers that initially offered functionality over and above aesthetics. The three have had wide acceptance on the volume market but a very cautious acceptance in high fashion. Large producers like Du Pont continue to promote fabrics, especially the blends such as Dacron and cotton, among the leading designers of Paris. They eventually hope to have their fibers used in the top salons of dress fashion, as well as in the volume departments of lingerie and hosiery.

Wool. Like cotton, woolen firms have had economic difficulties. The cost of the fiber is high and the cost variations are extreme, while foreign price competition is stiff. The number of mills has shrunk, and the production force has dropped. Creative American designers turn to European woolens for inspiration, while American woolenmakers are diversifying into synthetic and cotton textiles manufacturing in an effort to survive.

What has happened to the companies that once made American woolens a byword in fashion? One such company, Forstmann, which started in 1905 as Forstmann and Huffmann produced luxurious fleeces, the finest quality broadcloths and gabardines. It was the first mill to give characteristic trade names to its fabrics and stabilize production with a product image. It also produced what is regarded as the most expensive fabric ever made commercially—a 32-ounce vicuna which sold for $175 a yard. Another well-known company was Stroock, which entered the field between 1861 and 1873. Stroock made the finest fleeces and face-finished fabrics in the market, and was regarded as the first to make 100 per cent camel hair successfully. Finally, there was Botany, the company that made the best in flannels, challis, and velours.

These, and other great woolen firms have disappeared or have been absorbed by more diversified textile companies. They were unable to adjust to such technological and social changes as the rising competition with the new synthetics which are sometimes combined with wool and often entirely replace it; the competition with cotton which became an all-season fabric; the fashion change from tailored heavy worsted styles to lighter-weight and softer designs; and the sportswear explosion coinciding with the population exodus to the suburbs. Finally, there were firms unable to adapt to the speedup in communication that gives each new fabric almost total, immediate exposure and makes the ready-to-wear industry clamor for the new, the different. Quality woolen mills, used to taking more time for the development and acceptance of their fabrics, could not respond quickly enough; they lacked the necessary flexibility.

As a result the public's belief that imports are better fashion goods than American-made products and the American designer's insistence on "exclusives" have combined to hand Europe first place in the creation of wool fabrics. For the first nine months of 1966 all wool imports were about 19 per cent of total production.[14] In fact, Commerce Department figures showed the total cotton, wool, and man-made fiber imports in 1966 amounted to 2.8 billion equivalent square yards, an increase of 35.7 per cent over 1965 and about 10 per cent of American fabric consumption. Man-made fiber imports hit a record mark. Japan continued to be the leading United States supplier by far in 1966 and sent 445 million square yards of man-made fibers to this country, an increase of 48 per cent over the previous year. Behind Japan was Canada with 63.4 million square yards, an increase of 83 per cent; and Hong Kong with 39.3 million square yards, up 105 per cent.[15]

THE APPAREL INDUSTRIES. The import threat to American apparel manufacturers is not as great as to the textile industries. While retailers of foreign ready-to-wear know that their customers like the crafted handworked production many foreign creators are able to offer, this may bog down when orders come in quantity. Prices are fine, the quality good, the handworking interesting and unusual, but the production and delivery may be terrible. Most retailers prefer to deal with American manufacturers who can be telephoned when needed and who will take back orders that are not right. Convenience, timing, and dependability on delivery dates work in their favor.

Over 150,000 different styles, nearly two thirds of the billions of dollars worth of clothing purchased annually for women and children, originate in New York's garment center. Twenty-two blocks of skyscrapers, untidy lofts, and cluttered streets centering on Seventh Avenue house the thousands of firms that form the nucleus for the factories radiating out to other parts of the country.

In the 1962 *Annual Survey of Manufactures* by the United States Department of Commerce, the apparel industry ranked fifth in number of employees among the twenty types of industries surveyed, tenth in the size of payroll, and ninth in value added to the product by manufacture. The industry is located in or near twelve major cities: New York (the largest center), Philadelphia, Boston, Baltimore, Cleveland, Cincinnati, Chicago, Kansas City, St. Louis, Dallas, Los Angeles, and San Francisco.

Mechanization. The apparel industries have been harder to mechanize than the textile industries. Garment producers face large fluctuations in consumer demand since dress is the most sensitive medium for fashion transmission. Consumer choice in dress involves both the personal factor of individual style as well as the group factor of fashion. Each woman, while wanting to look like her neighbor, also wants to *look different* from her.

The American woman does not like to walk into a room and find someone else wearing a dress exactly like hers. It is like one actor stealing the spotlight from another. And yet, American women feel they have nothing to wear (even with a closet full of clothes) unless they own a dress *somewhat* like those other women are wearing—a dress in this season's style. Today's women demand today's fashions. And that demand keeps the sewing machines humming.

Thus, garment producers must offer enough variety in styling to suit everyone. But a variety of offerings involves the risk of either spreading demand over many designs so that no one design can be produced in large enough quantities to permit economies of scale, or if one or two styles do become desired "best sellers," the designing of those that did not sell was economic waste. This uncertainty in the demand for a product that requires frequent style changes makes it difficult to apply the assembly-line techniques of the factory system to garment production. It is much easier to apply, for example, to the manufacture of sheets which have less personal identification, are more uniform in style, and experience a stable demand.

The mass production of clothing is the result of the efficient use of a European invention, the sewing machine. Since industrialization came to the United States later in the nineteenth century, the Americans were able to profit from the industrial and technical experiences of European nations.

The first sewing machine patent was granted in France to a completely unknown engineer, Thimonnier, who arrived in Paris in 1830 with his invention. It is said he employed 80 people to help him make army uniforms, but was soon mobbed by jealous tailors and his machine smashed. An American, Walter Hunt, who invented the safety pin, introduced the first model similar to the modern sewing machine. His machine featured an eye-pointed needle and a shuttle, but it was not patented. However, another American, Elias Howe, Jr., received a patent on a similar one in 1842. And nine years later, Isaac Singer and two other makers appeared with improved machines. They were promptly sued by Howe, and soon each manufacturer was suing all the others. The "sewing machine war" that followed ended in the Sewing Machine Combination, America's first patent pool. Would-be manufacturers were licensed at so much a machine. The cost of this quasi-monopoly to the consumer is illustrated by the fact that a 40 to 50 per cent drop in price occurred as soon as the patent expired in 1877.[16]

The sewing machine, on which the garment industry depends, has carried small-scale industrialization around the world. Every home that has a sewing machine has production equipment on almost equal terms with any garment factory.

The promotional policy of the Singer Company did much to arouse worldwide interest in the sewing machine. Some of the problems this company has encountered and its ingenuity in solving them are illustrated in the following story: The Sudanese manager of a Singer shop in a Moslem land had difficulty getting the veiled ladies to attend classes. (Setting up sewing classes in underdeveloped countries is the key to new business for Singer.) He decided against going near the secluded Islam ladies. Instead, he approached their husbands and showed them how much more work their wives could do if they knew how to use a sewing machine. Today, he runs thirty sewing schools in the Sudan, and all the students are Moslem wives sent there by their husbands.[17]

Once the sewing machine was in general use, the next advance in the apparel industries came with the invention of the mechanical cutting knife in 1876. The cutters became the aristocrats of the trade. After the patternmaker has translated the sample garment design into separate pattern pieces, one man with an electric knife can cut 300 pieces of fabric at once. The skill of the cutter in guiding a heavy cutting machine through many layers of cloth may mean the difference between profit and loss for the employer.

Before the cutting knife was invented, women far outnumbered men in the cloak factories, the oldest branch of the women's garment industries. Afterwards, men cutters entirely displaced women in cloak shops, just as they pushed women out of the pressing industry when the pressing machine came in.

A further aid to mechanization, electricity, introduced in the early part of the twentieth century, enabled plants to run at night, and provided power for their machines. Present power sewing machines run at incredible speed. In addition, specialized machines do binding, cording, embroidery, overcasting, or any garment construction operation that a plant supervisor thinks can be done in less time, if properly mechanized.

A technological revolution in the apparel manufacturing plants is under way. In 1958 a machine which pressed, folded, and packaged soft goods in one automatic cycle was put in operation at a pajama firm. It was felt the multipurposed machine could process 3,000 dozen pajamas per day, working at capacity.[18] More recently, in 1966, the J. Carrol Wood Manufacturing Company of Texas, manufacturer of work and casual clothes for men, installed a computer-controlled sewing machine, believed to be the first of its kind, that utilizes punched eight-channel tapes in which tabs control the movement of fabrics. In addition, sizing research has made advances in the mechanical grading of patterns (changing the pattern from one size to another). Body dimensions and measurements are placed on tapes, allowing computers to grade patterns quickly and accurately. Eventually, it is hoped that such steps as trial fits and trial cuts may be eliminated.[19]

These innovations emphasize the importance to dress firms of "organizing technics"—coordinating the management acts through the medium of materials handling for greater productivity and profits. For example, a conveyor belt carrying finished garments to a pressing station and pressed garments to a packaging station may cost only $2,000 to install, but may save the company $4,000 a year in management costs.

Growth in more efficient automated production methods in the apparel industries arouses a need for general information throughout the industry. In 1965 the first quarterly publication of the Apparel Research Foundation, Washington, D.C., was distributed to almost 8,000 apparel manufacturers. It reports and evaluates recent machinery shows, new developments such as "durable press," and new equipment like the automated handling of limp fabrics.[20]

The style factor in women's clothing has been the largest deterrent to mass production. Unless there is some "staple factor" in a garment it is difficult to establish section production, the technique used by some manufacturers to compound a small labor advantage. Section work occurs when the total garment construction operation is broken down into parts. Each operator works continually on only one section (perhaps sewing the crotch seam in a pair of slacks), as opposed to the traditional method where one person constructs most of the entire garment.

In section production, the assembly line has three elements —direct flow, smoothness, and balance. The prime purpose is to reduce handling of garments, goods, and machines. The plant is arranged to insure a direct flow of goods, from the arrival of the uncut fabric through to the finished garment. The smoothness of the operation will depend on having the right goods at the right place at the right time. In addition, the laborers must work at a fairly consistent rate of speed. Balance is achieved by apportioning the "timed" operations. Thus, a time-and-motion-study engineer clocks each move within an operation, as well as the entire operation; he may decide it requires three workers to feed one if a bottleneck is to be prevented.[21]

While Henry Ford is recognized as the father of all assembly lines, the first steps in the apparel industry were taken by a man named Schmidt, a shirt producer, who applied mass-production techniques to shirts. His success encouraged others to follow his example, particularly in branches of the industry where styles are less variable—the daytime, housedress, and sportswear divisions.

The more style features a garment has, the more ingenuity it requires for the supervisor of machine operations to break the design down into relatively staple or near staple classifications. The word staple, here, refers to garment operations that are almost the same season after season; a careful division may still leave many variable parts. This variability in design makes it impossible to adopt a straight assembly-line technique in fashion, a problem some companies have solved by sending the unstyled parts of a dress to a section production plant while keeping the styled parts to be worked on by small groups of more experienced workers. The section production system can be applied in modified form to most divisions in the industry except those involved with very high style dresses.

Labor. The garment industry was built on narrow profit margins—sometimes as low as 1 per cent—and cheap labor. Unlike other industries that require large investments in heavy equipment, the garment industry originally needed just one machine, the sewing machine. While the industry is becoming increasingly mechanized, the cost of labor has been the main concern of the industry, as well as its chief competitive weapon.

From the beginning, the clothing industry drew its labor supply from the less skilled members of the population, people with the lowest standard of living. They were often the most recent arrivals in the country and thus were at the bottom of the social scale. In 1880 when immigrant waves of German, Austrian, and Hungarian Jewish tailors took over the New York garment industry, the contracting* system was widespread. Every immigrant and his brother tried to open a shop. Labor was cheap, and sweatshop workers were willing to work long hours in unsanitary conditions for low pay.

But by 1905 a new wave of less docile immigrants, many of them revolutionists from Russia and Italy, swept into the needle trades. Attacking their own countrymen with ruthless competition, these penny-pinching Eastern Europeans and Italians soon pushed out their German competitors. Moreover, once in control, these newcomers enabled New York to corner the cheap clothing market and helped American women earn the reputation of being the best dressed in the world.

* Contractors: manufacturers who do not put out lines of their own, but have the necessary space, machines, and work force to produce for others.

Thirty years later the racial composition of garment workers began to change. By 1937 the workers in New York's dress industry were more than 50 per cent Italian, 32 per cent Jewish, 5 per cent Negro, $2\frac{1}{2}$ per cent Spanish, and $1\frac{1}{2}$ per cent native Americans. While on the West Coast in San Francisco, there was a different mixture: Spanish Mexicans, 27.2 per cent; native Americans, 24.8 per cent; Italians, 20.2 per cent; Russian, 17.4 per cent; and Jews, 10.2 per cent.[22]

As each group of immigrants succeeded economically and moved up the social scale, it discouraged its children from going into the garment business. This left a labor vacuum for the next group of unskilled workers to fill. In 1962 Negroes and Puerto Ricans made up one-fourth of the International Ladies Garment Workers Union's national membership of 400,000; in New York City alone they comprised about one-half of the membership.[23]

Because women will work for lower wages than men, they are in demand in the textile and garment industries. Manufacturers who move out of New York usually relocate in medium-sized towns near labor markets that will accept relatively low wages, often no more than the federal minimum rate. Shrewd businessmen, they realize that the wife of an unemployed coal miner will be grateful for the opportunity to run a power machine in a garment factory.

Paradoxically, fashion, an upper-class status symbol, has become available at a price reasonable enough to extend the market to all, only because of the presence of the lower-class immigrant laborers—workers, who, in fierce competition for jobs, were willing to accept hours and conditions native Americans would not.

Unions. During the period 1900 to 1910 about one-half the garment workers provided their own machines and repairs. According to Florence S. Richards, "As many as 10,000 New York needleworkers had to kick back about 3.5 per cent of their earnings in the spoils system."[24] Contracting produced subcontracting, with, in turn, sub-subcontracting. The entire system resembled a pyramid, supported by a large base; workers on each level profited as they pared the wages of the workers beneath. "Greenhorns" were hired to perform single operations on garments brought in bundles from larger manufacturers. A garment might travel by pushcart to three different factories before completion, much as it still might today. Men worked fourteen to sixteen hours in shops while their wives and children helped with the rush work at home.

From these predominantly Jewish garment workers rose some excellent labor leaders. The International Ladies Garment Workers Union, organized in 1900, became a major union with over 65,000 members after it won two significant strikes in 1909 and 1910 in New York City. When the shirtwaist makers walked out in 1909, it was the largest strike by American women up to that time. Although the strike leaders were men, 75 per cent of the strikers were girls sixteen to twenty-five years old. The men let them do the picketing, get assaulted, arrested, and fined.[25]

Public opinion began to favor the strikers and helped pave the way for the next great revolt in 1910 when 60,000 workers struck. This strike was settled in September with the "Protocol of Peace," a milestone in labor-management relations which drastically improved the years after 1910 for garment workers. The Protocol set the pattern for collective bargaining as a solution to conflicts between man and man, and raised the worker from slavery to "industrial citizenship." From this time on the worker was no longer a victim of circumstances; he could alter circumstances through his own effort.

Through unions, laborers have tried to better their conditions, raise wages, reduce hours, increase the safety and healthfulness of the work environment, and improve provisions made for them when idled by business conditions, accident, illness, or old age.

As long as the wage-earning class accepts the existing order and merely attempts to secure better conditions through bargaining, John R. Commons pointed out (1936): "Its union is not 'class conscious,' in the revolutionary sense of socialism, but 'wage-conscious,' in the sense of separation from but partnership with, the employing class."[26]

The management decisions with which unions "interfere" are usually those that greatly concern their numbers. The issues vary from one situation to another. The Amalgamated Clothing Workers Union (men's clothing) attempts to rigidly control the quality of the garment each firm produces and its choice of subcontractors. This same union has loaned money to small firms in order to help them continue in business, but it is not averse to forcing low wage contract shops out of business.

To equalize unit wage costs among competing firms, the Amalgamated Clothing Workers have sought successfully for many years to establish piece rate systems. The International Ladies Garment Workers Union, which must also do this, at first resisted "piecework" but soon was forced to accept it. Indeed, one of the major functions of the union is determining labor costs. Every single garment to be mass produced is bargained over by representatives of labor and management. The price paid workers for each dart, seam, pleat, and hem is determined. If labor costs are too high the manufacturer may abandon the style for one that takes less sewing.

Bigger than any company it deals with, the ILGWU rarely calls a strike. Instead, it assumes special leadership roles. The union builds factories for employees to use; its engineers increase efficiency; its economists advise on business trends. For example, if the Du Pont Company, in connection with its synthetic fabrics program, needs to know how many dresses are made at what price, it can get the information from the ILGWU. Union leaders know how to make and sell a dress as well as how to administer an organization that collects millions of dollars in dues.

In 1941 manufacturers and union members alike were startled when Julius Hochman, head of the unionized dressmakers in the New York area (largest component of the ILGWU) injected efficiency promotion into union bargaining. Instead of using a request for more pay or a cut in hours as a basis for renewal of the union contract, he asked for a program of efficiency in production and sales promotion. This carried with it the implied threat of a strike against *backward* employers.

In the end his proposals were written into a formal agreement and hailed by the press as a milestone in labor-capital relations. Hochman wanted "efficiency" and "promotion." It was his idea to establish the New York Dress Institute (founded in June, 1941) to promote nationwide dress consciousness. He wanted to make New York the fashion mecca of the world. But first his plan had to be sold to his own union colleagues.

2 / FASHION: AN ECONOMIC GOOD

Then it was "forced down the throats" of the manufacturers.

The cause of unionization had earlier been advanced by the National Industrial Recovery Act of 1933. A portion of Section 7a of this law states: ". . . employees shall have the right to organize and bargain collectively through representatives of their own choosing." (Government support of the workers' right to organize was made even more explicit in the Wagner Act of 1935, and the Taft-Hartley Bill of 1947).

The codes of fair competition developed under NRA made it more difficult for nonunion employers to pay low wages or to undersell their competitors with lower prices. The codes, in turn, reduced the employer's incentive to avoid unionization. In fact, many welcomed the union as a policing agent to prevent chiseling by their cut-throat competition. Unions, such as the clothing unions, which had been frustrated by the opposition of low wage nonunion employers, also received the most benefit from the National Recovery Act.

But, while gaining power, the unions also experienced difficulties during this period. Communists, boring from within during the early 1920's, gained control of some of the local garment unions in a move to take over the national ILGWU. According to Melvin W. Reder, a labor economist, communists made a practice of exploiting the grievances of racial and ethnic minorities in unions with a large immigrant group.[27]

Before long, David Dubinsky, a respected member of the cutters local, threw himself into the fight against the communists and became a decisive force in expelling them. By 1932 he was in such a strong position that he was asked to become president of the national union on his own terms. When Dubinsky took over the ILGWU, it had 40,000 members and was $750,000 in debt. Two years later (1934) the membership stood at 200,000 with a treasury surplus of $500,000.[28] Dubinsky was formally elected president and remained in that office for over thirty years; his resignation became effective April 12, 1966.

The unions are not without internal strife, although it may be muffled. The shifts in ILGWU membership from old to new minority groups bring accusations of discrimination against the union from union members. On another level, many union officials complain that they are underpaid.[29] Yet most of the public programs for the 400,000 workers in the union are admirable. These include: a union-sponsored education program; health centers; vacation resorts in the Pocono Mountains of Pennsylvania; and semi-independent political action.

Curiously, unification among manufacturers in the clothing industry came from their traditional enemy, the union. Today, as the American worker evolves into a middle-class citizen who owns his car and often his home, he does not want economic warfare or even hostile coexistence; he wants to cooperate with the system that has given him all that he has.

Trends in Manufacturing Today

In the women's and children's garment industry there is a noticeable trend toward bigness. Multimillion-dollar corporate enterprises are emerging. More than forty firms are doing enough business to be listed in the New York or American stock exchanges. Among these firms two stand out: Jonathan Logan, Inc., the first garment firm to pass the $100 million mark (in 1963), and Bobbie Brooks, Inc., a close second with an outstanding growth record.

THE LARGE MANUFACTURER. *Size* and *diversity* cut costs and minimize the style hazards for big garment firms. Jonathan Logan, with twelve divisions, covers almost every branch of ladies outerwear. It claims to have been the first to come out with a true junior figure, the figure with a short waist, slim hips, and big bust, which is the silhouette of the Jonathan Logan line. However, if the junior line fails, the company can rely on its R & K line—dresses in women's sizing—or the Betty Barclay fashions, in a different price line. Big companies do not depend on one line.

The built-in stabilizer for Maurice Saltzman of Bobbie Brooks is "multi-category selling." He does the "entire wardrobe" of color-coordinated skirts, blouses, dresses, and suits for the active young adult. He is not dependent on one type of garment. While his suit sales fell off in 1960, sales of dresses, blouses, and skirts soared.

These large firms maintain offices and showrooms in New

York, but manufacture anywhere it is profitable. Because they are in the moderate-price field, fashion styling is not too urgent. They can wait a little for style acceptance in the higher-priced lines before adapting new ideas to fashions for their less demanding customers. Bobbie Brooks quite deliberately avoids the flamboyance of high fashion. Studies have shown that Bobbie Brooks customers are far too conformist to wear avant-garde styles; they want to dress like each other.

The big factories use assembly-line techniques to put a dress together. Each factory worker does a single piece operation—side seams, styled parts, zippers, hems—on a power sewing machine. Jonathan Logan has at least eighteen plants from Canada to Tennessee, including a unique, integrated knitwear plant in Spartanburg, South Carolina, which takes raw material in one door and turns out finished wool dresses at the other.

Big firms which sell to as many as 12,000 retail outlets can afford large-scale promotional programs and national advertising campaigns. With a national sales force, they can seek out the buyer and do not have to wait for the buyer to come to them. Since their brand names are well known and bring steady customer demand, they can make a retailer buy in depth instead of selecting this dress and that.

Big firms can also buy their supplies for less. When a textile manufacturer sells as much as two million yards to one buyer, the manufacturer can afford to reduce the price. One large firm could purchase the entire output of a chemical company or fabricator in a particular fiber or fabric and receive the extra benefit of the fabricator's advertising and promotion. If large firms overbuy, they can always use the goods next year or in another line.

Furthermore, big firms can afford to employ the best in designing talent. And, because they produce so many dresses, they can restyle one in midproduction if changes will make it more salable.

They can afford to take advantage of automation, using computers to handle inventory and keep track of how garments are selling.

Large firms can expand into foreign countries. Even the Iron Curtain parted when Russia imported modern brassieres and girdles from the Finnish licensee of Peter Pan Foundations, Inc. A small quantity of the Finnish-produced brassieres were sent to Leningrad in December, 1964. However, representatives of Peter Pan Foundations were not optimistic that the shipment would find its way into stores, but suspected that it was purchased for examination by Russian manufacturers, or for an exhibition by the committee on exports.[30]

With all the advantages enjoyed by big firms, how do small manufacturers stay in business?

THE SMALL MANUFACTURER. Small concerns exist because there are so many mass markets. Seventh Avenue has dresses from $2.95 retail to $2,000 custom made. Because women want to look alike, yet different, styling still plays the key part in making or breaking apparel manufacturing.

Many retail outlets use the small manufacturer because they do not want brand name merchandise that sells at standard markup prices. They want to put in their own label and use their own judgment on how much to charge.

Also buyers for retail departments, afraid that they will be caught with large quantities of goods that will not sell, order cautiously. Often they would rather buy a little of several items than a large amount of any one design. If a line takes hold, they reorder. If it does not, they do not.

The small firms wait for buyers to come to Seventh Avenue. Their success depends on a few good-selling numbers. When they are lucky they have one, two, or as many as six successful styles a year. If unlucky, they have none, and must sell their goods at a loss.

If a small manufacturer puts out a line that suddenly catches on, he can farm out the orders he cannot handle to a contractor. If he lacks capital to buy his goods or pay his rent and salaries, he "factors his business." That is, if he has a large order from a store, he shows this order to the factor, who lends him the money at interest rates of from 6 per cent to 15 per cent. The factor takes the order, and collects the money from the store.

Small firms have been hard hit by two recent developments. The first is the consolidation of the textile industry. The number of textile mills and converters before World War II has been significantly reduced. And large-scale producers like large-scale buyers do not want to do business with a customer who buys only a few yards here and there. Secondly, big retailing chains are taking over the fashion goods distribution in suburbs and shopping centers where the small specialty shop cannot afford to go. Again, a big retailing corporation likes to be supplied by a producer large enough to fill its needs.

In spite of these difficulties, the low capital investment—$10,000 to $50,000—and the chance of high profits from a dress or coat that "clicks" draws many small competitors into the concrete jungle of Seventh Avenue. The fashion industry remains the most pressure-packed, truly competitive business in the United States with each contestant searching for the slightest competitive edge.

Challenges Facing Manufacturers

As changes occur in technology, demand, and fashion trends, the producer must meet these changes by adopting new methods, adding new lines, or trying new ideas in color, silhouette, and fabric. Only by trying a new idea is it possible to learn the degree of acceptance it will command or the problems it will cause by introducing change. Experiment enables action based on findings. The fashion business requires sensitivity to changes occurring in every phase of the business, and the initiative to take calculated risks.

KEEPING UP-TO-DATE: SIZING. Specializing in the design area of size of figure type has proved to be one successful way to to build a unique product image. Customers like a garment that fits. It is probably the most important factor in selling ready-to-wear apparel. As fit and style improved in ready-to-wear, the local tailor and seamstress lost prestige. Although many people consider the fit of American ready-to-wear good, others view it as inadequate.

Critics of present sizing methods agree that the language of size should describe the physique of the person rather than the size of the garment or the size of the specialized mannequin (model form) on which the producers fit their stock. They emphasize that *the body* should be the basis of any sizing standard for the very obvious reason that garments are made to fit the body.

Professor Charles Colazzo of the marketing department, Northeastern University, Boston, illustrated this point at a press interview during the Fifteenth National Conference on Standards in 1965. He suggested that the men's suit industry might do well to adopt the Dutch system of sizing which is based on four body factors. These are waist girth, height, broadness of hips, and slope of shoulders. He went on to explain that the Dutch, by using eight of the most important basic measurements, have been able to adequately fit four-fifths of the Dutch male population. Under their previous system they satisfied less than half the population although using a similar number of sizes.[31]

The sizing of children's clothing, which is often related to chronological age rather than physical characteristics, can cause the consumer particular aggravation. Since there is little correlation between the physical size of one child and that of another of the same age, the consumer is forced to measure the length and width of the garment to estimate fit. Various attempts to remedy this situation have been made.

In an effort to improve the sizing of children's clothes, the Bureau of Home Economics through the Department of Agriculture, in 1939, took 36 measurements on each of 147,-000 children in all parts of the United States. This study proved conclusively that chronological age is a poor basis for sizing garments and that the existing method should be revised. But there was no general agreement among people in the trade as to which combination of physical characteristics would be most desirable as sizing elements.

Although an analysis of the home economics study showed that a combination of height and weight would best control the variation of all measurements, this concept seemed so revolutionary that few manufacturers would accept it. Instead, some manufacturers tried a combination of height and hip girth measurements which are reasonably easy to take on a child. A few years later others tried a combination of weight, height, and waist measurements. Where this was done, a sizing tag might read: W [weight] 32 1/2 pounds; H [height] 37 inches; W [waist] 21 inches; Size 3—Average Age, 37 months. All this information made a long and complicated sizing label, something many customers would not read.

Another branch of the industry, the mail-order business, was faced with a large number of returns on children's clothes. To stop this costly process, the mail-order houses developed new sizing scales to help mothers order garments in the correct size for their children. Sizes were based on the child's height, weight, and chest measurement. In addition, information on the lengths of such items as coats or dresses was included. Clear and detailed illustrations showed the consumer how and what to measure on each child.

The mail-order houses extended this system to cover other branches of apparel. They hoped to eliminate "size guessing" and to insure proper fit for everyone, even though the garments could not be tried on before the purchase was made. Sizes for each item were related to physical characteristics of the body. For example, the size in women's slips and night-wear was determined by combining the measurements of the bust, waist, and hip, plus the woven slip length, whereas in men's pajamas the size corresponded to the man's chest measure. The mail-order houses probably did more than manufacturers or other retailers to standardize apparel sizes and relate them to the body.

Sizing is always improved by adjusting it more realistically to the physical characteristics of the body. In 1958 the United States Department of Commerce completed a thirteen-year program to revise the standard sizes of women's clothing. A sizing standard, based on scientific body measurements of a representative sampling of women, was presented to the garment industry for voluntary acceptance. The first response to this offer came on July 1, 1958, when the National Knitted Outerwear Associated Manufacturing organization announced that women's T shirts would be manufactured and labeled in accord with the new voluntary sizing standard. The swimwear segment of the industry followed in the spring of 1959. Sweater manufacturers adopted the new standards in the fall of the same year.[32]

The purpose of the Commerce Department plan is to provide consistent sizing in all branches of women's ready-to-wear apparel. The framers of the standard hoped that various segments of the apparel industry which use different systems (dresses and coats use one system, corsets and girdles another, and blouses, lingerie, and sweaters still another) might all base their sizing on one common system developed through new knowledge of the body and its measurements.

Their standard, which most closely resembles the dress

industry system of sizing, can be applied to all women's garments with the possible exception of brassieres. It covers four classifications: Misses, Womens, Half-sizes (for shorter women), and Juniors. There are also three height groups: tall, regular, and short; and three hip types: slender, average, and full.

Thus, a 14 R Minus would be a size 14, regular height, slender hips; a 12 T Plus would be a size 12, tall, full hips; a 16 S would be a size 16, short, average hips.

The Commerce Department has reassured the garment industry that the new sizing plan is not an attempt to standardize garment dimensions, but rather an effort to provide a basis on which manufacturers could build their own sizing style. Thus, if a manufacturer wishes to fit garments more loosely, or tightly, or longer or shorter, that is his designing privilege. But underlying the "style image" will be a system of sizing based on scientific body measurements.[33]

Concern over garment sizing works to the economic advantage of the garment industry and the consumer. Consumers like to shop where clothing fits. The cost of needless returns, as well as time wasted by salesclerk and customer in trying on garments that do not fit, can be eliminated, as can expensive alterations. And one of the chief causes of consumer sales resistance—annoyance with fit—may be overcome.

Ready-to-wear has, in effect, forced the individual to adjust her body to the garment, whereas custom-made clothing allows the garment to be adjusted to her. Millions of women feel there is something wrong with their figures if they do not fit any apparel size found on the market. Of course, the need for women to "fit" a standard size helps keep the foundation-garment makers, diet specialists, and slenderizing salons in business. For if the American woman, almost totally dependent on ready-to-wear to supply her clothing needs, cannot shape her body to a standard garment size, she is at a disadvantage in a mass-produced garment system where sizes come ready-made.

FINDING A MASS MARKET. What is a "mass" market? There is no entity in society called the "mass consumer." In truth, the market is composed of differentiated groups: individuals, families, corporations and institutions, and the government. For example, a car used by the head of the household at work and by the rest of the family at play is a family car—it meets a family need. But a Model A rebuilt Ford "worn with pride" by a teen-age boy meets an individual need. On the other hand, companies buy cars for their salesmen to meet business competition, and the government needs a vast number of cars for military and civilian use. The automobile manufacturers must answer the varying needs of all these consumers.

There are conflicting demands from different consumer groups. An individual shopping for piece goods may want a fabric that is aesthetically pleasing and of good handling quality and reliable construction. But such a fabric may be hard to find because most manufacturers key their supply to the demands of their biggest customer, the manufacturer of low- to medium-priced clothing.

As a consumer of piece goods, the manufacturer of low-priced clothing, who is interested in increasing sales and lowering costs, may be willing to sacrifice aesthetics and lasting quality. Indeed, the fact that a popular color in a cheaper piece of goods is harsh in tone or that the material is printed off grain may indirectly benefit a fashion producer, for while fashion can sell a garment, a trying color or poor print may make the owner tire quickly of her dress and be willing to discard it for a new one the next year. The biggest profit to the manufacturer of low-priced garments is in fast turnover, not in slow, steady trade.

While these facts imply that the market caters only to the largest consumer groups, in truth it does not. Some companies have deliberately aimed at a small market made up of customers whose tastes or needs differ significantly from those of the general public. By designing for a comparatively small segment of the population, these firms have consciously foregone mild appeal to a large group of potential customers in favor of strong appeal to a limited number. Yet companies which seek this limited market sometimes find their products have strong mass appeal.

Lane Bryant began her rise to fame in 1904 when she first originated a maternity gown, a kind of tea gown with an accordion-pleated skirt attached to the bodice by an elastic band. Expectant mothers came to her shop in such numbers that in 1909 she decided to try quantity production. (At that time no newspaper would risk shocking its readers by advertising maternity wear, and not until 1911 did the New York *Herald* accept her first advertisement.) As her fame spread, she turned her attention to another neglected group, "larger-sized" women. Later she focused on tall women and chubby girls. Now, success in these other areas has made maternity clothes a fraction of the total sales of the Lane Bryant corporation.

A study of the population mix is helpful in spotting group demands. There is currently a large number of aged people in the United States population primarily concerned with health, and therefore, an important market for drugs. But the young adult group—under 24 years of age—shows enormous growth potential. And young adults are interested in fashion.

It was no accident that Maurice Saltzman of Bobbie Brooks, Inc., decided to focus on young women aged 15 to 24. He was interested in sales and research that had shown young adults are fashion conscious and willing to spend freely. Saltzman's strategy was simple: Pick a target group; study their clothing tastes (we constantly pursue knowledge on why and where girls select their clothes); design specifically for them; aim your fashion shows at them, with cokes and popular music; and sell to them in special junior departments.

The young adult group is certainly not the only group that shows potential for growth in fashion demand. Wives of men in management, moving from city to city and state to state, form a core of discerning shoppers. For a number of years business journals, ambitious husbands, and other propaganda agencies have been telling wives that success and a well-dressed wife go together. As a result, when five hundred distinguished young men, all presidents of companies before the age of 40, met in Miami Beach in 1960, they were accompanied by four hundred carefully groomed and gowned wives. The *New York Times* described the wives: "They dress to do credit to their husbands but never to steal his show. However, they are not above using the popular status symbols. Almost every wife has an impressive diamond ring and a mink coat or stole . . . worn cautiously, never in the heat of a Miami sun."[34]

A wife who travels with her husband on speaking tours, to conventions, and district meetings needs the same type of wardrobe she would take on a fast trip to Europe. She may use a special travel wardrobe or she may rely on mobile retailing. Picking up her favorite fashion magazine, she reads the ads to see who carries what in such-and-such a place. Then when she is in that city she is prepared for shopping. Such a woman is a member of a large group of travel-oriented consumers.

It is apparent that there are many mass markets. When any sizable group of people share the same taste and consume a noticeable quantity of any particular item, there is a mass market waiting for, and usually exploited by, some alert manufacturer.

Competition. The art of copying imports has become "big business" in the United States as well as in other countries. However, the exchange of ideas—or copying—sometimes under a license arrangement, *moves in two directions.* While Americans copy European creative goods, Europeans take out licenses on American inventions that improve popular-priced goods. These include methods for shrinkage control and resin wash-and-wear treatment.

The American textile producers, faced with increasing competition from abroad in the efficient use of resources and creative imagination, have generally chosen to retreat from the volatile fashion element in goods and concentrate on the "utility" aspect. They have stressed "easy-to-care" fabrics at low prices, principally in cotton and the man-made fibers. To gain fashion acceptance for these low status qualities, they have continually worked to give their fabrics some of the more traditionally desired elements of higher status present in silk, linen, and wool. Once the utility fabrics were accepted, however, as reflecting the "modern way" of life, they exerted a long-term effect on fashion trends. The casual and practical qualities they promoted in dress have been generally accepted as socially desirable in all strata of society.

ABILITY TO MEET CONSUMER DEMAND. Flexibility in adjusting to changing consumer demand is a requisite of any industry involved with the fashion element. Through the years there has been a change in the type of customer the ready-to-wear industry serves. However, the overall policy of the industry has been an effort to continue serving the old customer while adjusting to the demands of new groups that appear.

The first demand for ready-made clothing came from the least fastidious members of the society. Men's ready-mades originated in slopshops, so named because the clothes were made for sailors who would stow them away in slop chests during whaling and seafaring expeditions. Historians believe that shopkeepers made up special supplies for sailors who were not in port long enough to have made-to-measure clothing.

The custom of purchasing ready-made clothing was established by the markets built up by the second-hand clothing dealers. The rapid growth of the United States made domestic clothing supplies inadequate, especially for unmarried men, and the demands for second-hand clothing grew faster than the supply. The dealers not only bought unclaimed suits from tailors but also had clothes made new to be sold ready-made. Master tailors were soon buying cloth especially for this trade. By 1840 about one-half of the men's coats were ready-made and the business well established.

In addition, southern plantation owners used ready-mades to clothe their Negro laborers since it seemed more profitable to employ men in cotton-growing and cultivating than in making their own clothes. The first separate shirt factory (1832) was said to have developed as a sideline to the manufacturing of cheaper grades of outer clothing. Often planters who ordered clothing for their field hands also included an order of shirts for themselves.

As the railroads opened up the West and the South, rural stores began to carry ready-mades (some imported) in addition to yard goods. These were all relatively poor in quality and were intended to be sold at low prices.

Probably the biggest boost to clothing production came from the government orders for soldiers' uniforms during the Civil War. Because hand sewing could not fill the large army orders, factories had to be built and equipped with sewing machines. After the war, the need of returning soldiers for nonmilitary clothing and the delayed needs of the civilian population, deprived by wartime shortages, further increased demand for ready-mades. However, "store clothes" still carried the connotation of cheap and nasty goods in the minds of the well-to-do, an attitude encouraged by custom tailors who were prejudiced against machine sewing.

It was not until the economic panic of 1873 that the quality of ready-mades improved. With their money gone, many wealthy citizens were forced to buy clothing ready-made. Most at least bought ready-made pants for tailor-made coats. This group of consumers, used to having garments custom-made by tailors and dressmakers, brought a demand for better quality to the ready-to-wear market. Each depression in the next twenty-five years increased the demand for quality ready-mades.

A depression, by decreasing the purchasing power of most of the population, causes the less efficient establishments to fail, while those that survive prosper. By 1910 the large custom houses for both men and women's clothing had changed. They offered three types of garments: made-to-order; garments made up in advance but with only one of each style, called ready-to-wear; and many garments of one style known as ready-mades.

During the eighteenth and nineteenth centuries most American women took their own material to tailors, dressmakers, and mantua makers to be custom made. Commercialization of garments progressed when dressmakers and tailors began selling yard goods and experimented in making up styles in advance of orders. Soon it was possible to find suits, cloaks, and muslin underwear ready-made—suit production reaching a peak in the years 1905 to 1915.

This great demand in the early 1900's for tailored suits and shirtwaist blouses, two strictly American fashions, is related to the fact that more women were working outside the home. In 1880, 16 per cent of the women were gainfully employed in occupations outside the home. By 1910 this number had increased to 25.5 per cent, with 20.7 per cent in non-agricultural pursuit.[35] The development of the telephone and typewriter provided new jobs for persons with limited technical skill or muscular strength—it created a demand for women in office work. At work, women needed clothing that would not hamper their movements yet would have a proper business-like appearance. The tailored suit or skirt and blouse not only filled this need but seemed to express the changing political and legal status of women; they wanted to copy men's wear in cut and general style.

As the garment manufacturing industry became well established, it produced more items that had formerly been homemade. Commercially made dresses, a twentieth-century innovation, soon pushed suits into the fashion background.

In the period following World War I the American wholesale dress market became the chief customer of the Paris couturier, taking the place of many of the fashion-minded women in the international set whose fortunes had been wiped out by the war. But Americans came more as copyists than as buyers: they came to adapt Paris models to fit the needs of American mass production.

The prosperity of the middle and late 1920's, prior to the stock market crash in '29, permitted people to have more generous wardrobes, while the auto took them to more places in which they needed more clothes. To own only a house-dress and Sunday dress was obsolete; instead, a woman needed clothes for business, travel, and sports. More clothes and more simply designed clothes suited the rapid pace of the era.

This affluent picture changed with the depression of the 1930's. Budgets were curtailed. When there were no jobs to get dressed up for, informality was the rule and sportswear became a separate industry.

Thus, it is apparent that habits of consumption arise out of variations in living conditions. But no extreme changes take place; each new practice is a modification of one that preceded it. For example, better heating and the increased speed and comfort of travel have decreased our need for protective clothing. As a result, men's suits, although styled fundamentally the same as before, have become lighter in weight; men's over-coats are shorter; cotton blouses can be worn by women all year regardless of the temperature changes; and undergarments can be transparent trifles.

There is also an interrelationship among consumption habits. The use of light-weight silk stockings, begun in the early years of the century, was dependent not only on the development of the techniques of knitting and silk reeling, but also on the style changes in skirt lengths and shoes, and on the lessened need for protective clothing. Moreover, when dresses became more tightly fitted, bulky muslin underclothes gave way to closer-fitting knitted cotton or more pliable silks, rayons, and nylons.

And, basic to all these changes is the state of the economy. The income of the consumer is a significant factor in determining demand. As real incomes rise, there is a tendency for stores to begin "trading-up"—giving consumers higher quality goods and finer styles at higher prices. We see this in the increased number of stores selling line-for-line copies of original Paris models.

Trading-up is not an unmixed blessing. The hazards of this policy are discussed by Paul H. Nystrom in his book *Economics of Fashion:* "Trading-up" is "economically sound if the object is to sell the best garment the customers can afford," but, "bad if it forces customers to buy higher-priced garments than their economic position will justify."

In general, when higher-grade clothing can be produced at lowered costs it permits persons of low incomes to buy better clothing. It results in an improvement of clothing for the lower rather than the higher income groups. The benefit of mass production has come mainly to the middle- and low-income groups; wealthy people today value clothing no higher, if as high, as the early aristocracy. Although the market has risen to include many who would have depended on custom-made or couture garments in an earlier era, its biggest effect has been to expand to a greater variety of groups in the prospering middle class.

6
DISTRIBUTION

In the interrelated networks of specialized operations that produce and distribute fashion goods, the apparel manufacturer builds sales for the textile industry and for the retailer but is, in turn, dependent on the retailer for the purchase and distribution of the goods he manufactures. All three operations—textile manufacturing, apparel production, and retail distribution—are, however, ultimately dependent on consumer demand. Thus, the entire fashion industry benefits from a cooperative marketing policy focused on consumer satisfaction, with the retailer providing the most direct link to customer needs in face-to-face distribution of goods through sales.

Until recently many merchandisers viewed the mass production of consumer goods as "product-oriented" rather than "consumer-oriented." Emphasis was on the technical skill of producing efficiently a particular product and then using the power of "persuasive salesmanship" to get rid of as much of it as possible (for the seller's benefit) without regard to what the customer would do with the product he had purchased. Today, marketing policy tends to be consumer-oriented. The focus is on the buyer, satisfying the needs of customers by means of the product and the whole cluster of activities associated with creation, distribution, and consumption of goods. This consumer-oriented policy benefits the seller by first satisfying the buyer.

When marketing is viewed as a customer-satisfying rather than a goods-producing process, the retailer must be knowledgeable in two areas: (1) specific marketing facts; and (2) consumer behavior patterns. Marketing executives ask: How are products perceived by the consumer? How are they used? Is the consumer more value conscious, brand conscious, or price conscious? Fashionwise, is it time to "cover up" or time to "uncover"? Retailers cooperate with their suppliers, the manufacturing companies, to study economic, commodity, and fashion trends, attempting to spot declining trends they can avoid and to identify natural-growing trends to get with and lead if possible. As conditions change, the overall policy of the industry has been to continue serving old customers while adjusting to the demands of new groups that appear.

The constellation of goods and services, marketing know-how, and physical atmosphere offered by a retail outlet constitutes store policy, what the consumer calls "retail store image." What image should a modern store present? Do the customers want "the little shop" with an intimate one-step shopping atmosphere on a selected taste level? Or do they prefer a wide variety of substitute items with emphasis on price? Which of the countless variations in retail policies best satisfies the customers a store hopes to attract?

A close relationship exists between the establishment of a particular retail policy and consumer attitudes. A study of successful retail outlets of fashion goods at different periods in history shows that men with imagination created store images that satisfied the customers of those special times. If these stores continue in operation over a long period, it is because their managers have been able to adjust the store policy to meet new consumer demands and the mounting pressure from current types of retailing; those retail establishments that are unable to adjust must close. Therefore, there can be no letup in the observation and study of consumer behavior patterns by a long-term successful distributor of fashion goods.

Consumer Behavior Patterns

One of the chief retailing trends in the 1960's has been the efforts of the retailer to shorten his reaction time in response to customer needs. Once a retail outlet is established, data on classified merchandise can be processed by electronic computers to keep the retail buyers up-to-the-minute on sales trends, but this is information from the *past*. The retailer would like to be able to fill demands even before customers articulate them; he wants to predict the *future*.

He can predict his customers' needs only if he thoroughly understands them. He must ask himself these questions: What kind of customer lives here? Where will she shop? When will she shop? How much will she pay? What services will she need or desire?

Some of these questions can be answered by considering the population growth and purchasing power in the trading area, the type of employment and wages in the community, and the relationship between the merchandise in a particular store and the total retail trade of the area. Other answers for the future come from college students, computers, chemists, physicists, painters, musicians, and social scientists.

Sociological studies of consumer purchasing habits have shown that the store a consumer chooses is largely determined by her concept of social and economic success. Similarly, a retailer selects a store image that fits his concept of a successful retailer. A study of the consumer by Gregory P. Stone, and research into retail establishments by Louis Kriesberg illustrate these phenomena.

In his study of city shoppers and their urban identification, Stone characterized four consumer types: the economic; the personalizing; the ethical; and the apathetic.[1]

According to Stone, the economic consumer prefers large department and chain stores. She is sensitive to price, quality, and variety in merchandise. She is likely to be young, often a newcomer to the area, who has a high level of aspiration but lacks a correspondingly high income.

The personalizing consumer shops with local merchants —"where they know my name." This type of consumer may not have access to other channels of social participation, perhaps because of low social status or a large number of children, or because she spent her early life in another community. She finds that a semipersonal relationship with a store helps to compensate for her larger social losses.

The ethical consumer shops where she "ought" to—with the local independent merchant. She has a relatively high social status and long residence in the community. She dislikes the "social deterioration" of the city center that so often accompanies rapid business growth and feels it her duty to try to counteract it. In addition, shopping in an old, established store bolsters her status image since deference is paid to her position in the community. The older stores help to maintain the social distance between the high-status customer and the low-status clerk. The greater the success a long-time resident has enjoyed, the more likely she is to be this type of consumer.

The apathetic consumer shops because she "has" to. She wants to "get it over with" by a minimum of effort. Convenience outweighs all other factors in her mind. Whichever shop is the closest is the one she chooses. She feels there is little choice between local merchants and chains. Such a consumer is likely to be an older woman who has moved downward in the social scale or whose efforts to move upward have been thwarted. The less social or economic success a long-time resident has enjoyed, the more she is likely to fall into this category.

The retailer, as well as the consumer, is influenced by personal concepts of social and economic success and such concepts help determine the type of store a retailer operates. For example, a study of retail furriers by Louis Kriesberg revealed that custom furriers and business furriers had different concepts of security and success.[2]

Kriesberg found that the custom furrier thought of a "secure" furrier as one who was independent and self-sufficient because of his personal possessions—knowledge of the skills of the fur trade, and money. The custom furrier was self-oriented. But the business furrier was consumer-oriented, basing his security on the attitudes of his customers. He emphasized good workmanship, adequate advertising, and honest dealings with customers.

Today, consumer-oriented retailers dominate the retail field and merchandising policies are judged in the light of consumer reaction. The following examples illustrate the types of difficulties encountered by a retailer lacking detailed knowledge of his potential customers in the trading area.

In one area an ultrasophisticated and lavish branch store was set up to cater to a group of suburban residents who drove fancy European sports cars, belonged to country clubs, and wanted to be first with fashion—no matter what. Yet the concern did poorly. Potential customers apparently felt the store was too sophisticated; it quite literally frightened them away.

Until the store management created a less formidable image they could not attract the local residents.[3]

In another area, a branch store was established to serve a population that favored Irish jigs, lace curtains, pizza, and polkas. The store management assumed that a self-service store with low prices and low quality goods would best meet customer needs. Yet, although the majority of the families in the area were in the low-income brackets, the store managers found that merchandise of higher quality than that provided was demanded. They also discovered that in order to sell this merchandise better-than-average salespeople were needed. In addition, they learned that most of the shoppers came at night and sales events should be planned with this in mind. Because these style demands and buying habits had not been foreseen, acceptance of the store in the community came slowly and only after changes in merchandising policy had been made.[4]

The question of consumer attitudes and values affects many areas of fashion retailing. As the above examples show, members of various social strata have different buying habits and retailers must be aware of such differences. Sociological studies provide further evidence of the relationship between social status and buying habits. For example, a study of the buying tastes of a group of people in Austria revealed that those with low incomes preferred fabrics with a rubbery touch, and demanded sweet chocolate and strong-smelling flowers, while members of the upper class were partial to irregular weaves, and liked dry-tasting foods and less pungent fragrances. Paul Lazarsfeld interpreted these findings as indicating that ". . . the lower-class person is starved out for pleasant sense experiences; . . . the upper-class individual exhibits his sensual wealth by non-consumption of strong stimuli."[5]

However, the retailer must also realize that consumer stereotypes need to be continually reexamined in the light of changing economic conditions. All strata of society are profiting from increased prosperity. Thus yesterday's "poor little working girl" is no longer considered poor. In fact, where fashion is concerned, the young working girl with a steady paycheck and no babies or home to save for is one of the most vital elements of the industry. She wants the last word in fashion and is not bothered by such questions as "How long can I wear this if I pay that much for it?" She likes color, the "new look," and a variety of new clothes to attract boy friends. She is one of the greatest assets of the ready-to-wear business.

The example of the working girl, dressing to attract boy friends, illustrates a way in which fashion functions for the individual, a subject discussed in a previous chapter. Here we are concerned with how a person's view of the functions of fashion influences her buying habits. That is, how does she perceive the goods? A retailer would have a thorough knowledge of his customers if answers to questions on this subject were available.

Some explanations are offered by Barber and Lobel as a result of their investigation of the correlation between fashion advertising for women and Lloyd Warner's social classes.[6] They conclude that the functions of clothing predominating in the middle-income groups are those symbolic of two aspects of personal role: the aesthetic and the utilitarian.

The Barber and Lobel study characterizes three types of women shoppers. Women in Type I know the appropriate group status symbols and are aware of current styles which they include in their wardrobe. They are less dependent than other shoppers on store names, labels, and brands, although they are familiar with them. They are more concerned with matters such as quality of fabric, workmanship, and uniqueness of pattern. These women are regarded by the community as sellers of style or fashion.

The Type II shoppers are found among the recent arrivals in a group or among permanent members of a group who are not completely aware of the appropriate group status symbols. Price may also be a factor limiting their shopping. They depend on the store name, brand, price, and salesclerk, as well as the recommendations of their friends in selecting their purchases.

The women labeled as Type III shoppers have little interest in fashion. Many may be elderly. Their purchases are usually rather automatic and habitual; one garment replaces another of the same style. Garments are selected because they are appropriate for many use situations or are made of materials that "wear like iron." These women are concerned with the real or apparent fitness of the garment for practical purposes.

The "world customer,"[7] highlighted by Ernest Dichter as

the customer of the future, corresponds to Type I of the Barber and Lobel study. This customer breaks national boundaries, both in mind and in fact, as communications and travel expand her world. Increasingly familiar with regional products and national styles, she is concerned with uniqueness and individuality. Enlarged experiences make her better able to judge quality; consequently, she is less dependent on the opinions of others. Travel extends her market choice; she can buy her wools in England, her silks and cottons in Thailand, and have her materials tailored to her taste in Hong Kong.

The retailer must consider marketing practices from the consumer's viewpoint. Merchandising policies such as pricing of goods, selection of commodity suppliers, choice of furnishings in a store, type of advertising, and sales techniques are determined for each particular trade area. The total effect of these policies becomes recognized by the consumer, although perhaps subconsciously, as a *store image* or personality.

Merchandising Policy

Every retail firm wants to attract customers and create a favorable impression that will sell the institution as a whole. Occasionally the right formula is found. For example, Neiman-Marcus emphasizes fashions and fashion events. Macy's stresses its wide assortment of goods. Sears, Roebuck and Company in Chicago works to build an image of a friendly and comfortable family store patronized by hard-working, practical, and home-minded customers. Marshall Fields tries to maintain an elegant and sophisticated aura to attract an upper-status clientele.

Underlying the character or personality of each store is its merchandising policy. The retailer must decide between policies such as these: (1) few services and low prices; (2) service and quality goods with a correspondingly higher markup to absorb the added cost; (3) a highly promotional setup relying on bargain appeal and heavy advertising; (4) fashion leadership with initial price markups large enough to allow for markdown losses; (5) broad assortments in depth with perhaps a markup to compensate for slow turnover.

PRICE. A pricing policy will depend partly on the type of goods offered. Fashion goods do not always have a definite recognized market value, for price is based more on cost considerations and estimates of volume at different markup levels than on a set of standard prices. For example, the material and workmanship in a dress may cost the factory $10. The retailer purchases it for $12. If the retailer is a department store with big-volume business, the dress may be sold for $15.

However, a small specialty shop owner with low-volume business and higher operating costs may have to sell the dress for at least $18 to make a profit.

For many merchandisers the best markup will be at the point where the product of the dollar markup times the volume of sales is the greatest. If the large department store prices the dress at $15 it may sell 30 dresses, whereas if it prices the item at $18 it may sell only 22. ($18 \times 22 = $396 \quad $15 \times 30 = 450.) The best price, therefore, is $15 since it gives the largest product when multiplied by the number of sales. At the same time the prices must be attractive enough to assure repeat business. In short, the retailer plans in terms of volume, goodwill, and total costs.

A pricing policy is also dependent on consumer behavior patterns involved with what Ernest Dichter has called "product meaning," "purchasing morality," and "quality consciousness." For example, Dichter explains it is not enough to tell a French shopper that a garment is fashionable. She also wants to know its "trade-in" value; that is, how long the fabric will last and how many years she can wear it. To the American shopper these values may be of little interest because of her higher income and the lower prices of fashion products. Thus, products not only have different meanings to different nationalities, but the purchasing morality of the shoppers is also different: The American replaces models quite rapidly and is more conscious of change, while the European is more conscious of preservation. As to quality consciousness, Dichter feels that Americans tend to rely on the promise of a manufacturer (brand name) for quality guarantee, while a European still requires definite proof of quality.[8]

INTERIOR FURBISHINGS. Once a basic pricing policy is established a store image is further defined by the interior furbishings, classification of merchandise, character of the personnel, and the format and content of advertising. There is a current feeling among retailers that "classification merchandising" makes more sense to the consumer than price lines. Classification merchandising is a system of classifying items of merchandise into natural categories on the basis of their end use, for example, "coats" or "after five" dresses. Subclassifications are made for groups of items considered by the customer as essentially interchangeable; the broad category of "coats" might be subclassified as "fur-trimmed dress coats" or "casual untrimmed coats." In this way a customer who does not find a specific item she has in mind may find an equally desirable substitute.

Other retailers see the store of the future devoting a very large area—perhaps an entire floor—to the needs and tastes of one type of customer, such as a young adult woman, rather than to product lines. The decor would be keyed to the tastes of the group. For the young adult, for example, there would be a place to stack school books and access to free telephones.

Both systems are indicative of one-stop shopping. One specific type of clothes, shoes, and accessories—casual wear, for example—is put in one department to be purchased with one stop. Retailers believe customers dislike separate locations for each classification and systems barriers which require a separate transaction from different merchandising areas. The retailer is beginning to think in terms of assigning classifications to buyers for procurement purposes which relate to a unified market. On the other hand, for selling purposes, combinations of classifications which make up a meaningful selling department no longer need be confined to one buyer. Under these conditions, the projection and presentation of goods in a selling department can be geared to the way a customer expects to find goods. It is possible that in the future, groupings of merchandise within a department may be handled by as many as five buyers sharing one location jointly.

MAINTAINING AN IMAGE. Traditional department stores, in contrast to discount firms which attract by low prices, have stressed wider selection, fashion acumen, and dependability. Today, however, it is becoming more and more difficult for stores to maintain a distinctive image. The great stores of the past were built by creative merchants who personally supervised every aspect of the business and made their store reflect its owner's personality, but large stores today are frequently owned by corporations and the emphasis is mainly on sound, profitable management. The trend toward hiring professional managers of departments, divisions, and stores adds little to the personality of individual stores.

Furthermore, fashion competition has caused specific kinds of retailers to lose their identification with specific kinds of merchandise. Where once high fashion Paris originals could be found only in an exclusive specialty shop such as Bergdorf Goodman, line-for-line copies are now available at Macy's, and Paris-inspired designs are featured in the pages of the Sears, Roebuck catalog. Shoe stores that once carried only shoes, now carry dresses and accessories. The battle for the middle-class dollar, invading fashion as well as most other areas of retailing, helps destroy traditional lines of distinction.

In an attempt to develop a new kind of image, some large department stores have created their own "small shops" stocked with carefully selected items of one taste level but of varying price lines.

Such an experiment was attempted by Carson, Pirie, Scott and Company in Urbana, Illinois, a college community that had traditionally gone to Chicago for its quality purchases. Under Carson's supervision and management, one specially constructed section of the Lincoln Square shopping center was devoted completely to a "small shop" stocked with selected quality items for leisure time aesthetic tastes. The shop was appropriately named "Carriage Lane" and the decor hinted nostalgically at the past—a high style version of the old country store. In artistic disarray, high-priced antique Shaker cupboards and old chopping blocks were casually mixed with modern paperweights, boxes from India, Bonnie Cashin dresses, gourmet foods, handwoven pillows, and brass candlesticks. The many status items catered to the discriminating woman of taste with money to spend.

To further complicate the problems of the department store, manufacturers have come to feel it part of their function to help retailers move goods off their shelves. Nationally known brand manufacturers, such as Lady Manhattan, a division of the Manhattan shirt company, have become adjuncts of retail stores. Their salesmen take stock on basic shirts in main branches, reordering at their discretion. They service stores overnight from warehouses situated in strategic cities for quick stock fill-ins, much as the bread companies restock the bread on the grocery shelf.

Other apparel companies like The Villager, Inc., offer a whole array of vendor aids to the retail store. Their purpose is to get the Villager merchandise away from other items so it will not get lost in the shuffle. Starting with a mannequin, a simple dressmaker's form, the Villager symbol has been expanded into a wagon, a wagon-wheel rack, a double-tiered rack, and the like. The Villager has more than 400 separate shops in department stores carrying its merchandise and sends a monthly schedule of all national ads run by the company to its retail accounts.[9]

Such factors as these—increased competition in style goods and decreased product differentiation among retailers—have been forcing changes in long-established retailing policies. So, too, shifts in population and purchasing power in an urban center, especially deterioration of a business area, encourage the retailer to change his store image or move to a new location. Similarly, providing customer parking space can be a major problem to some retailers who may be unable to buy adjoining lots, tear down old buildings, and build multi-car parking garages in their immediate neighborhood.

STORE PERSONNEL: BUYERS AND SELLERS. In practice, the retailer's main link with his customer is through his employees. And one of the most important of those employees from the viewpoint of retail policy is the buyer. In the formal networks of fashion communication the buyer is an intermediary link between the consumer and the producer. When her "open to buy" figure (the number of dollars she is allowed to spend that month in her department) comes through, she looks at each line in her price category. Her "yes" or "no" as she selects styles from the jumbled racks of dresses in the showrooms on Seventh Avenue or from the salesman's sample line will determine the customers' range of choices. The designs the buyer rejects never reach the consumer market.

Today computers are often used to project demand in more staple styled goods. A computer in a retail store, if fed descriptive information such as size and color from past sales records, data on the present stock on hand, statistics on the rate of sales, and notes on the demands of consumers, is able to plot the trends in consumer buying—which type of goods the merchant should buy and promote. But where fashion goods are involved, a machine is less likely to replace the experienced buyer. The buyer is trained to recognize a design that will appeal to her customers. She wants, first, a dress that will fit or can be easily altered; second, a cut that does something for the figure problems of the wearer; and third, a dress that resembles big sellers of the past but has some spark of newness which denotes today's fashion. No machine can predict the acceptance of the "new element" before it is placed on the market.

A buyer strives to increase her sales volume—more sales this year than last—or at least to maintain a volume comparable to other departments in the store. She keeps her merchandise looking "new." She thumbs through the racks of garments, reading the tags that tell their age, and removes some to be marked down. From the consumer point of view, racks of outdated garments fill space that should be allotted to new merchandise and narrow the choice of current fashions. The efficient buyer, mentally noting that a garment did not sell, does not try to educate her customers to a certain style; she lets her customers educate her.

Because many seemingly independent stores are in reality member stores of large organizations with central buying offices, the importance of the buyer in each separate store seems to be declining. In some cases, as previously mentioned, salesmen restock a department without consulting a buyer. In other cases, fur, hat, and shoe departments are leased and operated by an outside company. Yet the store buyer's job has not disappeared, it has simply changed its form or location; it has become incorporated into a managerial position, a salesman's job, or into a New York central buying office where stacks of electronic data aid in the selection of current trends.

Even as the buyer's role has been modified, the role of the salesperson has undergone significant change. Traditionally, direct communication with the customer in the retail store was made by the salesperson. Today this contact may be completely missing as the result of a trend toward letting customers sell themselves. In many stores the customer selects the garments that appeal to her and, if permitted, ushers herself into a fitting room where she tries them on. Where a salesperson does exist she may be a young clerk untrained in the arts of salesmanship. Expectedly, the clerk soon abandons the customer to her own devices. If the customer is skilled enough, she sells herself, and the clerk appears only to take care of the mechanics of packaging and charging for the purchase.

A helpful clerk who takes time to note the fit and non-figure-flattering cut of a trial garment and then selects other more appropriate styles for the consumer to consider is rarely found except in a high-quality service store. Where once the salesperson was an integral part of a fashion apparel department, she is now considered either expendable or symbolic of a type of service that can be offered in many forms.

Thus, in deciding on a sales policy the retailer is faced with a variety of choices. He may offer no salespeople at all; a "token" sales force that replaces stock, wraps the package, and takes the payment; or one of two types of salesclerks who truly use theories of selling—the helpful salesclerk or the aggressive salesperson. The helpful salesclerk, who knows her stock and tries to help the consumer recognize that the goods for sale are those she really wants, studies people to find out what they want and then gives it to them. Consumer preference is her guide. At the other extreme, the aggressive seller concentrates on emotions and ways of arousing them. She believes that consumer demand can be molded by the appropriate emotional response. Again, consumers are studied, but this time to discover their responses to certain appeals rather than what really are their preferences.

Aware that some consumers feel a salesclerk improves service while others resist any attempt by sellers to have them buy something they do not want, the retailer decides on a policy. And the sales force, sometimes little more than a token service, becomes part of the store image.

CONSUMER CREDIT. A retail policy must also consider credit service to the customers. The three most common types of credit used in retail stores are: (1) the 30-day open book charge account; (2) revolving credit or budget accounts;

and (3) installment buying for which a separate contract is drawn up. A customer with an approved credit rating may choose which type of credit she prefers. Margaret Reid has referred to these types of credit as *merchandise credit* which she defined as "the postponement of payment for specified goods."[10]

The 30-day charge account allows a customer to postpone payment for the merchandise she buys for 30 days. She may charge as many purchases as she likes, but if the entire bill is not paid by the end of the 30-day period many stores now levy a $1\frac{1}{2}$ per cent carrying fee on the unpaid balance.

To facilitate the bookkeeping involved with credit, Filene's of Boston pioneered the use of a Charga-plate service, a device originated by the Farrington Manufacturing Company of Needham Heights, Massachusetts, in the late 1920's. This service, which provides a simple and efficient recording of credit purchases, today is in common use throughout the country. The approved customer is provided with a small metal plate containing her name, address, and account number, and her signature on the reverse side for identification. The store has a small imprinting machine in every department. When the purchase is made, the Charga-plate is inserted and the printed impression made on the sales check which has already been itemized.

The revolving credit or budget charge account plan has been in use since 1955. Customers, such as students, who have never had a credit rating may be given this type of charge account by the store, but in most cases the customer is free to choose the plan she prefers. In the revolving credit plan the customer decides how much she can afford to pay each month on her bill—she budgets her money. An automatic limit is placed on the total amount she may charge each month at that store. For example, if she can pay $5 a month, she may charge a total of $60; if she can pay $20, she may charge a total of $240. Usually a $1\frac{1}{2}$ per cent carrying charge is levied on the unpaid balance carried over from month to month. This plan differs from a straight 30-day charge account mainly in setting a minimum amount the person must pay each month and establishing a maximum amount she can charge.

Upon closer examination the revolving credit charge

account plan is truly an installment payment of charged accounts. Without drawing up a separate contract for each purchase, the store levies a carrying charge on the unpaid balance of the total bill, sometimes amounting to 20 to 25 per cent at true annual interest rates. Any type of credit on which a carrying charge is levied can be thought of as a form of cash loan with an interest charge added for the use of the money. The retail store is, in effect, the stand-in for a small loan company.

The tremendous promotion of credit with added carrying charges by retail stores has made credit more than a service to the consumer. It has become an aggressive sales tool in the fierce competition between retailers. Slogans such as "nothing down and 'so many years' to pay" or simply "charge it" have swept from car sales to the rug industry to the apparel markets. Retailers find that charge account customers tend to buy more, buy higher-priced goods, and do less shopping around.

Credit is not a new institution. Claimed by its supporters to benefit the low-income family by allowing them to enjoy products and services while paying for them, credit was, in earlier times, used to benefit the great gentlemen and ladies of the royal courts of England. Allen French recorded that "King James had neglected to pay for embroidering his daughter's wedding gown and Charles (King Charles I) paid for it (nearly £1000) when her second son was just coming of age. James did not pay for embalming his queen in 1619, a debt which his son paid fourteen years later, and Charles waited three years before paying for cloth for his father's funeral."[11]

From this glimpse of the unpaid debts of the English royal court we see that credit and problems in meeting private expenses are not unique to one time or place. In 1737 Benjamin Franklin gave "those that would be rich" in America this advice: "Consider then, when you are tempted to buy any unnecessary household stuff, or any superfluous thing, whether you will be willing to pay *interest,* and *interest upon interest* for it as long as you live; . . . He that sells upon credit, expects to lose *5 percent* by bad debts, therefore he charges on all he sells upon credit, an advance that shall make up that deficiency."[12]

Credit service is offered by the seller at some risk to himself. There is the risk of a bad debt loss, as Franklin said.

Furthermore, the seller must consider the expense of reclaiming and collecting goods, the cost of insurance to cover damage, and the bookkeeping involved in providing a finance plan.

Supporters of credit claim that it is necessary for the mass distribution of a high standard of living. Installment buying is often used by young families with low incomes to acquire in a relatively short period the large stock of consumer goods that contribute to the high standard of living in America. Because they see a long working period ahead, such a couple is willing to go into debt in the present with the belief that future income will take care of the payments. Similarly, a fashion-conscious working girl may buy her clothes on a revolving credit plan, confident of a steady income in the months ahead. Thus, credit permits temporary expansion by drawing on future expectations. Many economists believe that people buy in relation to their long-term expected income level rather than the short-term reality.

The great demand for credit indicates that consumers want it and find it useful. In theory it enlarges freedom of choice by permitting people to enjoy things they could not have otherwise. In the long run, by increasing the sales volume, it may lower costs and prices to the advantage of everyone.

Opponents of credit say that installment policies with low monthly rates and no down payment lure the families least able to pay and cause them to live beyond their means. Because people have a tendency to underestimate what they owe, they may spend on consumption goods money that should be put into capital goods. Moreover, the high cost of credit forces people with the least income to pay the most for goods, decreasing the quantity of goods a given income will buy.

Criticism of the credit system, particularly installment buying, arises periodically. The most frequent charges against it concern misrepresentation, willingness to exploit the consumer, and high interest rates.

Installment credit, which has been expanding rapidly since the 1920's, involves a three-way relationship between the consumer as buyer, the retailer, and the financing agent. Although securing immediate possession and use of the goods, the buyer does not secure title until the final payment is made.

Sometimes the contract the consumer signs is not owned

by the sales agent, the retailer, or the firm that makes the product, but is turned over to a sales finance company which buys it and so acquires the right to collect. Installment credit costs are primarily designed to insure safety of the lenders' funds (the finance company), not to serve the consumers. On the whole, lenders have found consumer finance extremely profitable. Competition for finance paper takes the form of kickbacks from the financing agency to the seller (the retailer, in this case) and longer terms for consumer payment, increasing the potential market of the seller whose goods induce the debt. However, many stores whose financial structures permit it handle their own finance paper to insure as large a financial return as possible.

Few installment sellers will quote a financing charge on a true annual interest rate. And without this information it is impossible to make price comparisons between various installment lenders. In view of the variations in finance charges—discounts, add-on rates, level or graduated charges per month, and delinquency penalties—most people have almost no idea of the actual financing rate they are paying. Usually, a monthly interest rate multiplied by twelve gives the true annual interest rate. For example, $1\frac{1}{2}$ per cent per month on the actual declining balance would be 18 per cent in a true annual interest rate. Deliberate misrepresentation as to size of future payments, charges for credit, or buyers' rights in case of default further hinder an accurate appraisal.

Critics disagree on how much control of credit should be undertaken by the government or how much should be left to the astuteness of the individual consumer. In New York, legislation requires a contract to be easily readable, the cash price to be stated, and charges to be itemized as to credit service charge and insurance premium. At least one expert, Professor Margaret Reid, feels that the finance charge should be separated from the cost of the goods and other services. "First," she explains, "so the buyer may be aware of what credit costs are; and second, that people paying cash are not paying for credit on the same basis as those who use it."[13]

In practice, the main stabilizing influence on credit is the growth in competition which tends to hold interest rates down.

COMPETITION. Competition among retailers is necessary for the proper functioning of the free-enterprise system.

American enterprise relies on competition to prevent prices greatly in excess of costs, to reduce waste, and to spread the benefits of efficiency to society as a whole. In recent years there have been two significant trends in retailing that increase competition. One centers around retailers, the other around manufacturers.

The retailers have been developing larger and stronger combines to gain an increased share of the market. This includes the development of retailing chains, million dollar corporations, and voluntary store organizations that offer geographical convenience and/or stress price advantages, and the expansion of urban branch stores into suburban areas. At the same time, manufacturers have been carrying their struggle for a greater share of the market directly to the consumer. Some manufacturers have been able to displace the retailer as the principal selector and guarantor of merchandise. In certain instances the retailer has become nothing but a distributor of presold merchandise due to the increasing prominence of national brands.

The new trends added to the traditional forms of retailing competition help to increase the competitive structure of our society. Smaller specialty shops feel they suffer in many ways from competing with large chains. They cite price discrimination (discounts to the large buyers), merchandise restrictions, refusal of apparel suppliers to sell their line to the small store, and price fixing. They suffer much the same disadvantages that the small manufacturer does in competing with the large.

However, there are some advantages that accrue to the small store. They can give personal attention to details and carry out their own ideas without interference from partners, stockholders, or bankers; they have a strong personalized direction. While the large store may suffer from lack of flexibility, the small retailer can adjust quickly to new conditions. Traditionally it was to the small specialty shops that American women looked for fashion leadership and quality service.

Forms of competition include both within-store competition between the interrelated products and services in a store, and competition between stores. Between-store competition takes several forms: competition between identical products in two different stores which stimulates price comparison; competition between similar-use products that are style differentiated in different stores; and competition between unrelated products which have equally strong consumer appeal in different stores, for example, between a new automobile and a new fur coat. Furthermore, there is competition between consumer services and consumption goods. For instance, one woman may prefer to style her own hair and increase her clothing budget, while another may choose the weekly services of a hair stylist and spend less on clothes.

However, other factors tend to reduce competition among retailers. Those that influence the fashion industry include (1) the decrease in product differentiation; (2) identical sales techniques and methods; (3) local agreements between stores on services and matters such as hours to open and hours to close; (4) informal agreements on such things as the cost of alterations or delivery; (5) a follow-the-leader policy in which one store introduces a new price line and the others follow; and (6) uninformed customers. (An alert customer who compares prices, recognizes quality, and knows the service she wants is probably the greatest stimulant to desirable competition.)

Reduced price and service competition is usually not in the consumer's best interest. It can result in the consumer paying higher prices than when competition is keen. The history of retailing in the United States shows that under changing conditions new retail policies arise to meet consumer needs, while a future-oriented retailer may actually stimulate demand by appealing to a need of which the customer is not yet aware.

The Rise of Various Forms of Retailing

The history of retailing in America reveals that specific retail images evolved from the economic and social conditions of particular eras in the country's development; but once developed, some images have continued on in altered form through succeeding generations of consumers.

Retailing began with the one-stop informal general store—

"the little shop"—that met most of the needs of a particular customer group. Later, the small general store evolved into the large department store with formally labeled categories of goods. Each succeeding form of retailing led to either larger operations or more specialized offerings of goods and services that increasingly satisfied the economic and social needs of newly recognized consumer groups.

Although new forms of retailing appeared, old forms that continued to attract customers were seldom discarded, but were modified by far-sighted managers to meet changing conditions. A current example is the return to the informal intimate atmosphere of the "little shop" image, not by local independent merchants without access to wide selections of goods, but by large impersonal retailing enterprises with urban stores, branch suburban outlets, and a variety of resource suppliers. These retailers feel this shop suits the casual nature of today's customers much as they suited the needs of the American colonists 300 years ago.

EARLY RETAIL OUTLETS: "THE LITTLE SHOP." The first retail shops in America were found in the east coast colonial settlements. By 1650 Boston was an important trading center. An early journalist, Maverick, reported in 1660 that Boston was a town "full of good shopps well furnished with all kinds of merchandize," and even in these early days customers complained bitterly of "shop keepers and merchants who set excessive prizes [prices] on their goods."[14]

During the colonial period most transactions were by barter. The word "cash" seldom appeared in the *Journal of Boston Shopkeepers*. The shops stocked such diverse items as looking glasses, candlesticks, gloves, tin lanterns, rat traps, and bottles. But gradually shopkeepers began to specialize until two distinct types evolved, the retail grocer and the store owner who carried a general line of dry goods and seamen's clothing. These retail shops catered to sailors, laborers, and the "poorer" sort of people who could not afford to buy in bulk.

People of wealth bought their goods directly from merchants. It was the merchants who supplied the retailers with their goods. They sent carts along the improved roads from Boston with loads of men's wearing apparel, such as coats, breeches, shoes, buckles, shirts, neckcloths and gloves, along with spices and seasonings to stock the shelves of the country stores.

These merchants amassed great fortunes and most small shopkeepers hoped that through shrewd management they, too, would attain *merchant status*. The great merchant (the personalized version of today's large corporation) was a ship-owner, perhaps also a shipbuilder. His vessels lay at his own wharf, beside his warehouses from which he sold goods whole-sale or retail. Often he was also engaged in some form of manufacturing such as millinery or distilling of liquor. The merchant prince of colonial towns, like the English gentle-man, desired a large domain and sank his surplus wealth into land and slaves. In the South nearly every rich Charlestonian became a planter as well as a businessman.

Some shopkeepers did succeed in their efforts to become merchants. They became part of a group which, through correspondence and constant travel, developed intimate con-nections with members of their class in other American towns, the West Indies, London, and Bristol. Representatives of one family might reside in each place. And because of their com-mon interests, members of the merchant class became a distinct social group. Under their leadership the spirit of commerce spread throughout towns and cities, infecting even women and children.

As commerce increased, retail shops grew in number and diversity. By 1773 Rebecca Amory had a small shop in Boston that specialized in the sale of such items as mourning crepes, velvets, threads, and tapes. The New York cosmetic industry was inaugurated in 1736 with the announcement by Mrs. Edwards of "An admirable Beautifying Wash for Hands, Face and Neck, it makes the Skin soft, smooth and plump, it like-wise takes away Redness, Freckles, Sun-Burning, or Pimples . . . All Sold very cheap."[15] But the most prevalent of the specialty shops were those devoted to millinery.

This growth and diversity in retail shops and products eventually led to the establishment of a combination of small shops or departments under one roof—the modern department store.

THE DEPARTMENT STORE. Sociological and technical changes in

both the Old World and the New encouraged the creation of the department store. Improved economic conditions of the masses in the mid-nineteenth century, cheap mass transportation, and the entrance of women into the labor market, enabling them to vie with the wealthy for fashionable attire, caused an almost simultaneous movement in Paris, London, and New York toward large department stores. The first of these stores was the Bon Marche which was established by Aristide Bouciant in Paris in 1852. William Whitely, Charles Harrod, and James Shoolbred were pioneers in London, while Alexander T. Stewart in New York, John Wanamaker in Philadelphia, and Marshall Field in Chicago were the leaders in America.

It is generally conceded that American department stores were foremost in innovation. Managers of European stores frequently crossed the Atlantic to pick up new ideas from their American counterparts. Today overseas buyers in the world markets link the department store systems so that there is a certain uniformity in department stores in all countries.

Most of the founders of large department stores in the United States can be placed in one of three categories: (1) emigrants who left Great Britain because of poverty; (2) Jewish emigrés who fled from oppression in Germany and Eastern Europe; and (3) descendents of seventeenth-century Quaker families. Yet whatever their background, the founders of almost all the large retail establishments had one thing in common—each began as his own buyer, clerk, window washer, and janitor.

Certainly this was the case with Irish-born Alexander Turney Stewart, who founded the A. T. Stewart store in New York. He started out in 1823 with a small wholesale-retail business in Irish linens and laces. His business prospered and he moved to bigger stores and better locations. Finally, he built two stores of his own. The first was the Marble Dry Goods Palace which was constructed at Broadway and Chambers in 1848. Then, fourteen years later, he built Stewart's Cast Iron Palace farther up Broadway in a more fashionable shopping area.

By this time he was "King of the dry-goods merchants" and his palatial retail establishments were the models for future department stores. His Cast Iron Palace was revolutionary in every way. Cast iron had just been introduced as a building material and Stewart's store illustrated what could be done with it. The outside walls were made of molded iron panels painted to simulate stone or marble. The floors were supported by iron columns, allowing creative use of open space. The central feature was a grand stairway in the rotunda which was covered with a large glass dome. The ladies' parlor on the second floor apparently created a sensation. Here women could see themselves in full-length mirrors, the first, it was said, in America.

It was Stewart's policy never to cheat a customer "even if you can." He told his staff it was their job to make each customer happy and satisfied so that he or she would return. Stewart employed well-mannered young men expert in the art of pleasing ladies, for by this time ladies were becoming more important on the consumer market.

Indeed, the feminist movement caused something of a national revolution during the 1850's. An offshoot of the demands for political freedom and female independence was a vast buying spree. Women demanded the privilege of doing their own choosing and buying in stores, without husbands or fathers deciding what must go on their backs and into their homes. They sought the right to share in the family purse and to wear more comfortable clothes.

Dry-goods stores soon became more than a place in which to buy. Women found such stores a haven and a social gathering place. They could enter unescorted and be received with deference, be catered to, and be waited upon. Women could linger—chattering, checking quality, and comparing notes. For many, shopping became a social event with prescribed forms of dress and behavior. Stores such as Stewart's, where beautiful goods were tastefully displayed in luxurious surroundings, encouraged this kind of attitude toward shopping.

Potter Palmer, a young Quaker, was so impressed by Stewart's Marble Palace that he decided to establish a similar store in bustling Chicago. He already had rented space for a dry-goods store. The question was "Would Chicago women want what New York women seemed to want: silks and fineries in the latest Paris make, gloves and fancy bonnets, point lace and rustling brocade?"[16] Palmer decided to find out, and in 1858 opened Potter's Marble Palace on Lake Street.

He established a *one-price policy*, in contrast to bargaining, and offered a *money-back guarantee* on all his goods. He appealed to his customer's pocket books inviting them to compare his prices with those of competitors. Palmer did not stock all lines of goods, but instead emphasized quality goods. He wanted his store to be known for quality goods at low prices.[17]

Palmer's store was very successful, but in 1865 his physician advised him to retire. The store was sold to Marshall Field and Levi Z. Leiter and became known as Field and Leiter. The new owners continued Palmer's retail policies. Even after the Civil War when prices were plunging, Field and Leiter held to Potter's policy of sending goods out on approval. They told their customers: "If, when you get your goods home, you do not find them entirely satisfactory, please return them and your money will be refunded."

Although the wholesale branch of the business handled by Field and Leiter was more profitable than the retail, the owners realized that there was enormous prestige to be gained from maintaining the retail division. (In later years, it was to be the retail that supported the wholesale division.) Whenever business in the retail store was temporarily set back by an economic panic or a disastrous fire, the owners staged a grand reopening. In fact, the big openings, which attracted huge crowds, became something of a civic ritual.

In 1881 Field bought out his partner and the store became Marshall Field & Company. Field became the city's ranking merchant prince. He operated his store in the belief that quality is remembered long after price is forgotten. And he told his employees that they would never lose a customer as long as they remembered that "the customer is always right."

Yet, despite his emphasis on quality Marshall Field was aware of the need for expanding the store's clientele. Thus, in 1885 he established a bargain basement. Later, in 1941, the store management responded to the demand for a top quality fashion department and created the "28 Shop."

With the increase in the number of department stores, the role of the wholesale merchant or jobber became more and more important. As the go-between of the manufacturer and retailer, the wholesale merchant set an example of departmental selling in metropolitan areas many a retailer could not match. Retailers from the country could do all their buying at one wholesale warehouse with the same ease any woman does today in a department store. The jobber, a term often used synonymously with wholesaler, assembles goods from many factories, buys and transports in large lots to keep costs down, and provides storage from which a retailer can quickly replenish his stock. He may advise the retailer on the wholesale market and help him in his ordering or, because he is in between, advise the manufacturer of changes in consumer preference and retailing conditions.

Some large department stores, however, decided to handle their own wholesale business and deal directly with manufacturers, or open their own buying offices and send buyers to all foreign markets. This move can hurt the wholesale business and lead traders to open their own retail outlets, sometimes completely abandoning their warehouses. For this reason, retail stores establish their own wholesale houses and wholesale houses sell retail. (In general, the term wholesale includes all those whose unit purchase and sale is large, while the term retail refers to selling to the consumer.)

Other large department stores not only integrated their retail-wholesale functions but expanded through the establishment of branches, becoming chain stores.

Today's department store is more than a dry-goods store. According to John Ferry, author of *A History of the Department Store,* a retail store reaches the status of a department store in the fullest sense only when it provides for most of society's material requirements. Thus, in addition to clothing, the department store is expected to supply furniture, hardware, books, jewelry, foodstuffs, and many other wares as well as such services as restaurant, beauty salon, post office, and rest room.

The modern department store serves *all* the people, the wealthy and the masses. To avoid spoiling the appearance of the main shopping levels, lower-priced goods are put below the main floor, creating the "bargain basement," and the most expensive goods, with their more exclusive appeal, are tucked away in the quiet leisurely atmosphere of an upper floor.

Changes in merchandising came with the department store. The fixed-price system replaced cheap bargaining. The return of unsatisfactory merchandise for exchange or cash refund gradually became a firmly established principle. Any buying and selling for cash enabled merchants to sell at lower prices than under extended credit or barter.

CHAIN STORES. In recent years chain stores have grown in both size and number. The movement began in the 1920's in the grocery and drug business and moved into the apparel market. There are two types of chain stores: (1) those with a centralized buying office such as Penney's or Sears; and (2) those without a completely centralized buying office. The second type is composed of autonomous stores which have voluntarily merged some of their buying steps in order to spread overhead costs and eliminate risks.

The low prices offered by chain stores are partly due to marketing efficiency, the normal advantages gained by large-scale buying and warehousing. Thus, goods can be purchased directly from the manufacturer, shipped to a warehouse and then reshipped in appropriate quantities to individual stores.

Yet the low prices found in chain stores may also be, at least partly, the result of threats and coercion—forced concessions. Pressure may be applied when the large-scale buyer meets the large-scale seller.

Chain stores have the power to go into manufacturing for themselves if the manufacturers they contact do not keep their prices at a reasonable level above cost, and they have sufficient prestige to get customers to accept their private brands in competition with national brand reputations. Some of the money that is saved by getting prices closer to the cost of production is then passed on to the consumer.

When the large-scale buyer meets the small-scale seller the coercion may be more unfair. If a seller permits his entire output to be taken by one buyer and fails to keep in contact with other buyers he can be ruined; he has little choice when his one patron asks for price concessions.

The large chain stores, with the natural advantages gained by their size and their power to elicit concessions, arouse mixed emotions—imitation, derision, admiration, and fear—among the public and their competitors. When the chain stores have been attacked as unfair competition, the Federal Trade Commission has usually ruled in their favor. The FTC has consistently stated that under a competitive system, the type of distribution which gives the greatest sum of total advantages to the consuming public will increasingly prevail.

A review of the policies of one big department store chain, Federated Department Stores, illustrates the role played by this type of chain organization.

The complex of major department stores known as Federated Department Stores started in 1929 merely as a holding company designed to spread risks among its four founding stores. After World War II, the company either had to grow or dissolve since it was making more money than could profitably be plowed back into the existing stores. In June, 1945, the choice was made to expand. A central management office was established and a policy encouraging growth was adopted. The major effort was directed at *building greater customer acceptance*. Believing that the way to increase profits was not to cut down on overhead but to build up volume, the management conducted surveys to see what the women in each trading area thought of the local Federated store. More stores were added to the chain, and by 1963, the complex contained 12 major stores, which with their branches made a total of over 60 stores.[18]

Each Federated store acts autonomously, the local management being responsible for the merchandising policy in its particular area. The focus of the chain's central headquarters is on financial matters involving the entire chain—matters such as real estate, insurance, economic research, and on predictions for long-range success based on the dominance and profitability of each store. The company attributes its profitable record to the policy of pushing responsibility down to the lowest level, the department managers within the stores. One man is essentially in charge of buying and selling all the merchandise in a single department. He is treated like an independent entrepreneur responsible for profit and loss almost as if his department were his own store.

Profits are also the result of the company's cooperative buying organization, the chain's joint ownership with a group of large independent department stores of a common resident buying office, the Associated Merchandising Corporation (started in 1918). While buying only from 10 to 15 per cent of its stores' total purchases, the representatives in the buying office in addition serve as scouts and advisers. They have the power to bring a manufacturer's line to the attention of the member stores, to discover an unknown. And they act as purchasing agents of Aimcee Wholesale Corporation, an AMC subsidiary. If they think an item will be a big seller, they may bring the pattern of the dress to the wholesale division which then turns it out at a lower cost. The purpose of Aimcee Wholesale Corporation is to bring the tremendous buying power of AMC stores to bear in dealing with resources.

Another example of a modern chain store organization is that operated by Macy's. The original store was established in New York in the 1850's. Then, in 1923 Macy's became a chain store by acquiring La Salle and Koch in Toledo. By 1956 the Macy chain extended as far west as California and included 56 department stores.

Although the Macy's store in New York is probably the best known department store in the world, the store has been faced with many problems. The organization's response to these problems over the years, such as the decision to become a chain store, provides a lesson in alert department store management that must keep a retail policy currently competitive or let the retail establishment pass from the scene.

The founder of Macy's, Rowland H. Macy, came from a seafaring Quaker family, a family of whalers, merchants, and traders. Soon after Macy started his retail store he made a major policy decision: He would undersell his competitors. The Macy slogan became "We challenge any competition—confident that we cannot be undersold." Goods were bought for cash and sold for cash at a small profit. The savings were passed on to the customer. Originally, the Macy's discount was 10 per cent, but it was later stabilized at 6 per cent less than the price offered by its competition. (Today, the policy simply attempts to undersell any competition.)

In order to provide quality goods at low prices, Macy's established its own brands. By maintaining direct relationships with manufacturers to whom they provided a steady market for a large volume of goods, Macy's was able to demand special concessions in quality and price. In 1927 the Macy Bureau of Standards was established to test Macy's own merchandise, and, sometimes, that of their rivals to compare quality and price.

To continue this low-price policy in today's market, particularly with the competition from discount houses and soft-goods supermarkets, has become a major problem for Macy's.

Underselling competition has kept profits low. And although preferring cash transactions, Macy's has had to provide a credit service. The store is caught between a no-service low-price operation on one hand and the quality service type store on the other. Macy's has tried to do both—give service and maintain low prices.

The Macy policy of aggressive advertising has also been maintained. From the start Rowland Macy used a trademark. First, it was a crowing cock, and, later, a red star. The red star on Macy's wrapping cartons, and on the sides of the smart horse-drawn delivery wagons became a well-known symbol which is still in use today.

Macy's has also made good use of newspaper advertisements. Rowland Macy appealed to the masses by advising his customers to take the public omnibusses and horse cars. "Ladies," the ads said, "if walking is too bad, just take the cars!"[19]

In order to avoid gaining a reputation for handling cheap goods, Macy's has in recent years placed increased emphasis on fashion designs and import collections. Actually, Macy's has always handled imported goods. It established the first foreign buying office in Ireland for Irish linens and lace back in 1885 and in 1893 opened an office in Paris for the purchase of chinaware, laces, and gloves. Now Macy's has extensive buying services in many foreign countries, but much of the emphasis is on fashion. The store's semiannual promotion of line-for-line Paris copies of couture fashions is currently competitive with those from Orbachs and Alexanders, two major promoters of import copies.

MAIL-ORDER HOUSES. One of the most far-reaching developments in American retail trade was the introduction of the mail-order house. For example, Richard W. Sears, a railroad station agent in a Minnesota town, apparently got the idea in 1886 when he arranged to sell by mail a consignment of watches misdirected to a local dealer. He saw the possibilities of mass distribution by mail based on volume production and reduced prices. Sears soon persuaded A. C. Roebuck to join in the venture and Sears, Roebuck and Company began operating in Minneapolis as a mail-order house.

The mail-order houses tried to answer the needs of Americans for consumer goods in economically isolated rural areas and small towns. A general catalog sent to each family pictured and listed for sale most of the items a family might use —farm implements, household furnishings, clothing, and children's toys. Customer's orders were then filled from a company-owned warehouse which was centrally located in some large city. This form of retailing enabled people to buy goods not available in local markets or to buy better quality goods at lower prices.

In addition to introducing a mail-order retail system, Sears, Roebuck and Company also pioneered in the field of retail management. The birth of professional management in retailing actually began in 1906 when Sears, Roebuck offered retail securities for public sale. At that time the company was worth approximately $50 million, and $10 million in 7 per cent preferred stock and $30 million in common stock was offered to the public. The company is now worth several billion dollars.[20]

In 1908 Sears sold his interest in the business to Julius Rosenwald. Under Rosenwald the company continued to offer merchandise for the masses, and in addition gained character by stressing expansion, efficiency, and community-mindedness through philanthropic undertakings. During this period the company started to build a network of permanent suppliers.

By the time General Robert E. Wood took over as president in 1928, Sears, Roebuck was expanding into over-the-counter retailing. Wood sensed the impact of the auto on retailing fully a quarter of a century before the coming of suburban shopping centers and realized that stores should be located close to people, near important highways, and in areas with ample parking space. Construction of Sears retail outlets began during the 1920's. So successful were the new stores that they were opening at the rate of one every two days during the twelve-month span of 1928 to 1929.

General Wood also initiated Sears' move into foreign countries. The company established stores in Latin America in 1942, and in 1953 bought Simpsons, an established mail-order house in Canada, and expanded its facilities under the name Simpsons, Sears, Ltd.

After the retirement of General Wood in 1954 his successors continued the company's contact with foreign countries.

Sears' fashion board scouts the Paris couture and import markets to bring the elegance of high fashion to their customers. Sears chose Spain (1964) as an entering wedge into one or more of the Common Market countries*—Belgium, Italy, France, Luxembourg, Netherlands, and West Germany.

Surprisingly, the general catalog, a merchandising tool of horse-and-buggy vintage, has made a sweeping comeback in the jet age. The *Wall Street Journal* described how a Chicago housewife did her Christmas shopping chores in minutes with a Montgomery Ward Catalog in her lap and a phone in her hand: ". . . the young mother of five sat in her living room and casually ordered twenty-three Christmas items." Convinced of the great future importance of catalog selling, Montgomery Ward & Company doubled the size of its catalog sales and promotion staff in 1963. Sears experienced a similar growth in sales as catalog orders outstripped across-the-counter sales in their retail stores, and the J. C. Penney Company, another retail chain, recently started a new catalog division.

Spiegel, Inc., which formerly operated a number of retail stores, closed them to concentrate on catalog selling. Modie Spiegel, chairman of the corporation, believed that for many customers the convenience of catalog buying would outweigh any disadvantages, and some customers apparently agree. They are tired of getting parking tickets, fighting their way through crowded stores, thumbing through masses of goods, and receiving inadequate service. It is easier to stay home and order by phone from a catalog. Besides, choice in catalog offerings has multiplied. In the clothing area there are high fashion designs, casual country styles, imported articles, and a tremendous number of everyday items at reasonable prices.

However, a consumer ordering fashion goods from a catalog is at a disadvantage in not being able to see the actual texture, color, or fit of a garment and may gain a false impression

* One of the most important developments which has occurred in this century to improve living standards and promote peace in Europe has been the organization and development of the European Common Market. Also known as the European Economic Community (EEC), it includes Belgium, France, Italy, Luxembourg, Netherlands, and West Germany. The EEC which became a reality in 1958 grew out of the European Coal and Steel Community (ECSC), organized in 1953 to eliminate all trade barriers on coal and steel among the six countries. A series of tariff reductions is designed to break down all trade barriers among these countries by 1970. By January, 1966, tariffs among these countries had been reduced 80 per cent.[21]

of the style from the picture. Still, she can evaluate the item in a leisurely atmosphere and, perhaps just as important, compare prices.

Competing retailers feel that the generally lower prices offered in catalogs are an important factor in accounting for the catalog boom. The increased emphasis on discount selling has made the public more price conscious than ever, with the net result that there is increased public awareness of bargains, wherever offered. Store executives generally agree that prices in their catalogs are from 5 to 10 per cent lower than identical merchandise in their retail stores.

Mail-order firms are taking advantage of a trend in their favor by increasing the personal services offered for catalog shoppers. For example, Montgomery Ward employs catalog promotion girls to give customers personal attention. Each girl has a list of catalog customers she calls personally to inform about weekly sales specials, take Christmas lists, or remind them of special occasions, such as Mother's Day. The girls keep a personal card file on each customer. If a customer is interested in a sizable item like a floor-covering, a salesman calls at her home with samples.

Mail-order firms also use modern transportation and communication to decrease the amount of time involved in at-home shopping compared to that spent visiting a store. The *Wall Street Journal* reports that more than 80 per cent of all catalog orders come in speedily by telephone, while 50 years ago some 95 per cent moved slowly by mail. And catalog men are already planning for the day when "picture phones," telephones with screens showing the speaker, are in common use. Through these they plan to preview fashions and demonstrate the operation of appliances to housewives at home.[22]

From the consumer's viewpoint these added services, if requested, are desirable. A busy housewife or an elderly woman unable to leave her home may welcome the convenience of shopping by telephone. But there is also the danger that telephone selling may become another form of aggressive salesmanship, invading the privacy of the home and recalling the unwanted door-to-door salesmen of the 30's and 40's. The relief from "pressure-to-buy" has been one reason some women prefer shopping by catalog over the retail store. Where shopping at the store was once an exciting adventure and a social event, it has become for many people a tiring and burdensome task.

SUBURBAN SHOPPING CENTERS. The retailer's desire to meet the demands of the suburban customer led to the growth of the suburban shopping center. Surveys have shown that despite the advantages offered by large downtown shopping areas, many young family consumers, especially, prefer the convenience of shopping centers close to their homes. The whole family can go shopping at night, casually attired, taking advantage of the baby-sitting services some centers provide.

In a comparison made between three suburban shopping centers and the downtown areas of Houston, Texas; Seattle, Washington; and Columbus, Ohio, findings showed that the selection of goods was larger, prices were lower, and shoppers were able to complete several errands at one time in the downtown areas. On the other hand, downtown shoppers were hampered by traffic congestion, parking difficulties, and general overcrowding. The suburban shopping centers were limited in the number of businesses represented, and the stores often had higher prices and a poorer selection of goods than those downtown. But these disadvantages were offset by the centers' convenient locations close to residential areas.[23]

Shopping center growth has been a post-World War II phenomenon, the result of the transportation revolution. Improved highways and the increased private ownership of cars have dispersed factories, stores, and people. Until recently, industry and commerce were forced to locate close to rivers and railroads, the chief means of transporting people and goods, and close to available labor. But now, most people have their own means of transportation, and trucking has changed the freight business. Today retailers and manufacturers can consider locations away from the center of the city.

In addition, branching out into new suburban areas can seem doubly desirable to the manager of a once prosperous department store in an urban center stranded in a decaying neighborhood. It may be sound economics to revitalize the store's image by starting a branch store in the suburbs where building lots are less expensive, parking space is available, and the more affluent suburban shopper is near. Besides, suburban expansion through branch stores has become fashionable—retailing imitation converts to emulation, as each downtown department store strives to have a bigger and better-located branch store than its competitor.

SOFT-GOODS SUPERMARKETS AND DISCOUNT HOUSES. Two forms of retailing that showed tremendous growth in the 1950's and 1960's were soft-goods supermarkets and discount houses. Both compete in the popular price volume bracket of virtually all types of apparel. Price cuts have been the real stimulus for these merchandising channels. The soft-goods supermarkets began to appear in the eastern states in the early 50's. By 1959, there were 110 in the New England area, with 59 located in cities elsewhere.[24]

Soft-goods supermarkets operate much like food supermarkets, and carry a wide assortment of merchandise. Their appeal is based on *low prices*. Many departments are leased, especially the shoe, millinery, and cosmetic departments, which account for from 10 to 50 per cent of the sales. The soft-goods supermarkets have an impersonal atmosphere. Generally, the merchandise is not sold under established brand names. Thus, customers must use their own judgment in selecting the qualities they feel are important—color, style, fit, or general appeal —and they tend to accept the low prices as proof of a bargain.

The acceptance of little-known brands in the soft-goods supermarket is a challenge to the manufacturers of brand-name goods and to small shop owners who feel their profits are built on customer loyalty. Many manufacturers sell merchandise under special private labels to the soft-goods supermarkets to avoid antagonizing their other retail outlets which cannot afford to sell branded goods at such low prices. Eventually new brands may emerge for supermarket selling.

The challenge of the "bargain image," where the customer hopes to find top quality at cut prices, to "brand image" and "store image" is nowhere more pronounced than in the discount houses, the successors to the "I can get it for you wholesale" dealers. The year 1964 might be called "The Year of the Discounter," so great was the expansion in the growth of discount chains. As a general result, profit margins from all retail sales were relatively lower in spite of an increased number of sales. The threat of the discount house is greater to retailing profit than to overall sales volume.

Owners of discount houses in the early 1960's had a formula for success—low overhead, quick turnover, large volume, and smart buying. Low overhead was made possible by offering a minimum of service to customers, the plain and simple display of goods, the smallest possible staff, and a low-rent location away from the main shopping areas. The store might be an "open-to-the-public" warehouse or an especially constructed building located near a suitable parking space. But today, many discount chains are raising markups to pay the costs of adding such conventional department store features as charge accounts, package deliveries, and fancy merchandise displays, and of hiring more salesclerks. They find people want an attractive environment, fashion, and broad assortments.

Big discount dealers buy when goods are priced low, sometimes in carload lots to obtain a $7\frac{1}{2}$ to 10 per cent reduction, sometimes in deals with wholesalers whose local demand has failed. A good discount buyer develops top-notch suppliers who reinvest part of their profits in labor-saving equipment, plant rearrangement, or expansion. Discount dealers want manufacturers who provide better products and/or lower costs. This enables discount houses to reduce their selling prices and attract more customers. While some discount houses sell only first quality merchandise, with a money-back guarantee (or at least enough of such goods to build a "discounting image"), others mix lower quality goods in with brand-name merchandise, develop their own brands on which prices cannot be compared, or combine outdated merchandise with new models. The customer must rely on her own knowledge of quality in goods to get what she wants in a discount house; to be classed as a genuine bargain the offering price in the discount house must be a reduction from the price on the same goods being charged by its principal competitor. The continuing growth of large discount chains indicates that discounting is a profitable business in which not all monetary gains are made by the customer.

Mergers. A new trend in company mergers and acquisitions across the traditional boundary lines of production and distribution foretells the future development in the apparel industries. For example, the giant corporation, Genesco, is a combined manufacturing, wholesaling, and retailing complex that specializes in everything to wear. Genesco enterprises include the production of undergarments for men and women, outerwear apparel such as rainwear and women's sportswear, and footwear; chain stores; standard retailing stores; and a transnational group concerned with foreign operations.

Genesco owns and operates more than a hundred manufacturing plants and more than 1,500 stores, including Bonwit Teller and Henri Bendel. Thus it is both a supplier and a retailer. While its manufactured goods are handled by other leading retailers, it is also one of the chief retail outlets for the goods it supplies. Moreover, one division of the corporation is involved with fabrics and finishes, leathers, polishes and containers. Genesco has made a success through diversification, proving that the gap between various industries created by traditional boundaries is more apparent than real. All the enterprises have much in common, requiring the same type of technical skill and know-how.

In the case of Genesco, the corporation maintains a central staff of "functional executives" to consult with the "operating executives." An "operating executive" is the general manager of one particular company, such as the president of a shoe-manufacturing concern. A "functional executive" is an expert consultant on some phase of business common to all companies, for example, capital procurement and public financing, sales promotion, or employee relations. He is retained by the corporation to add his specialized knowledge to improve overall planning between the companies and keep them in line with the corporation policy.

It has become profitable for small companies to merge with large corporations such as Genesco because of stock and tax benefits given to the owners or stockholders. In more and more mergers, the owners of the company acquired are being paid, entirely or in part, with convertible preferred stock of the corporation. These stocks pay a fixed dividend that takes priority over any payments to common stock owners, and they can be traded in for common stock at a fixed ratio, say one share of common for $50 face value of the preferred. The company seller who swaps his common stock for the corporation preferred stock does not pay taxes on any profits involved since the transaction is regarded as a nontaxable exchange of assets. Thus, a seller is less likely to hold back because of big taxes on a cash sale.

Bigness can provide certain benefits, and in big and growing markets everybody wants to get bigger. The trend toward larger companies continues in the apparel field. The "bigness" may take the form of store chains, such as J. C. Penney with over 1,699 stores; voluntary groups of stores like Federated or Allied Stores, which retain a central buying office and continuously exchange information on operations; or company mergers and acquisitions by giant multioperation corporations. Instead of viewing production and distribution as separate industries, some retailers and their suppliers are viewed as *one* industry. Major stores and major resources pool their know-how and collaborate on one common objective—the design, production, and profitable merchandising of goods to bring consumer satisfaction. In the future, the computers of important retailers will "talk" directly with the computers of important resources and result in truly scientific sales and inventory management, moving inventories from place to place with faster and more accurate timing.

Challenges in Modern Retailing

The traditional forms of retailing are being challenged.

The small specialty shops and the long-established department stores are faced with increasing competition from the new suburban shopping centers, soft-goods supermarkets and discount houses, as well as by expanding department store chains, mail-order houses, and stockholding corporations. Once again charges of unfair competition are being heard.

The cry of "unfair competition" in protest against a competitor who competes in reality as well as in name has historic roots. At the turn of the century, the mail-order firms led by Montgomery Ward and Sears, Roebuck seemed unfair to the small country retailer. They could purchase in huge quantities, and they did not have to employ salespeople or get involved in the operation of a retail store. "Trade at home" clubs were organized and club sessions were devoted to burning catalogs.

At the same time the "unfair competition" of the department store was growing. In fact, by 1895 retailers were condemning this new form of retailing that "suppressed" competition by creating a monopoly that would, they felt, cause consumers to pay higher prices.

In the 1920's the unfair competition was the chain store. It was monopolistic, used such unfair practices as loss leaders (a practice now adopted by discount houses),* and drained money from the community because of its absentee ownership. The outcry against the chains brought in the Robinson-Patman Act (1936) which charged the Federal Trade Commission with the power and responsibility for seeing that all buyers receive equal treatment—variations in price were to be based solely on cost difference. Agitation against unfair price competition has generally involved an attempt by the small retailer to check the growth of large-scale retailing. Now, the targets include both the discount houses and the tremendous pools of buying power represented by established department store chains as well as the giant corporations who may privately or through regular stock market channels buy the controlling shares in a store or company without the knowledge of some of the company's owners.

One reaction to the challenge of the discount house was reported in *Women's Wear Daily* in 1958. When a ready-to-wear shop near Baltimore tried to sell designer fashions at discount prices, specialty store owners cancelled their orders from the manufacturers involved. Most manufacturers were quoted as saying that they would not have sold to the new store had they realized it was a discount house. Other manufacturers claimed that the discount store had purchased the merchandise from jobbers and not directly from the manufacturer. Spokesmen for the hard-hit specialty stores said they would buy only from manufacturers who promised not to sell the same merchandise to discount stores. All the specialty store owners agreed that they would not attempt to meet the prices offered at the discount houses—prices reduced by 20 to 30 per cent.[25]

Other retailers have complained of similar incidents. On behalf of the small retailers, the Fair Trade Council charged

---

* A loss leader is a commodity priced to attract customers into a store or establish an "image" with the hope that once they are in the store the customer will buy other items not specially priced.

2 / FASHION: AN ECONOMIC GOOD

that discounters hurt small businesses and that price cutting tends to destroy a manufacturer's distribution system. In answer to these charges, the Federal Trade Commission and Justice Department defended discount selling. "Mere selling at reduced prices" does not violate any law administered by this agency, the FTC chairman decided. And the Justice Department declared that in passing on to customers savings resulting from lower costs, discount houses were acting "in the best tradition of our economy." The Justice Department felt the major thrust of competitive drive was against department stores much bigger and wealthier than their discount rivals. Thus, discount houses, by prodding long-established department stores to cut their profit margins, had, in fact, benefited the public.[26]

This decision of the Federal Trade Commission in favor of the discount house highlights the retailers' problems in open competition. He must prove his worth or fail. Some large department stores have met the price challenge of the discounter head-on by saying they will meet the price of any competitor. But occasionally, when a garment appears in a discount house at a price lower than that charged by a department store, the department store may buy the entire supply offered by the discount house, thus removing the goods from price competition.

Retailing success with fashion merchandise, as in other areas, goes to the distributor with the most marketing facts and current knowledge of consumer behavior patterns. Besides skill in management, information on available products and prices, and the nature of his closest competitor, a successful retailer needs imagination—ideas with which to satisfy consumer needs.

Peter Drucker, management consultant, pointed out: "A business is first *an idea*. And only individuals have ideas. No business ever grew and prospered unless there was a man—at most a few men—who dared to think for themselves and to go counter to 'what everybody knows.'" He cited as examples Richard Sears and Julius Rosenwald who some sixty years ago had the then radical idea that "the economic isolation of the American farmer was not so much an opportunity to get *from him* money for inferior goods, as it was an opportunity to do for him the rational, responsible, selective buying of superior merchandise he could not do himself."[27]

Today, as computers and automation take over menial tasks and hasten the decline in the work week, consumers are becoming better educated, increasingly mobile, and more aware of greater possibilities for individual development. As incomes increase to higher and possibly inflationary levels, what new ideas will be developed to shape the retail image of the future?

Some retailers predict that by the year 2000 there will be two basic types of retailers with *no middle ground*:
1. The elegant retail operation with more service, more luxury, and more specialization than ever.
2. The completely automated establishment (open 24 hours a day) where a consumer can drive up, deposit money, and drive off with his goods in the rear of the car.[28]

While these predictions may be plausible, the survey made here of retailing trends reveals almost the opposite possibility—a tendency toward "sameness" in retail outlets, as the result of competitive pressure and a pronounced *coming together on a middle ground*. An example is the change that has come about in many of the once exclusive specialty shops. Large specialty shops such as Neiman-Marcus, Saks Fifth Avenue, and Bergdorf Goodman originally depended on an exclusive clientele and an exclusive atmosphere. They had no bargain basements. Their policy was to provide quality merchandise, luxurious surroundings, fashion exclusivity, salespeople with taste, and fast service on special orders and deliveries. They led by showing a "look" in fashion and maintaining the highest standards.

Today, financial success in the fashion industry comes to retailers who can provide elegance with a modest price tag. Profits are found in the middle-class market. Thus the dilemma: Can specialty shops maintain their exclusive image while entering the fashion battle for the middle-class dollar?

Tracing the development of one large specialty shop provides some insight into the solution of this problem. Edwin Goodman of Bergdorf Goodman was the first American couturier to bring ready-to-wear into his custom salons. A man of impeccable taste, his knowledge of custom tailoring and dressmaking made him demand perfection in both his custom salon and, later, in ready-to-wear. From his opening in 1906 until the present, his shops have supplied custom garments for prominent stage celebrities and society women.

But after World War I, a new type of customer appeared: "The American woman with the taste to appreciate the best in clothing and the money to afford it but with neither the time nor the inclination to fritter away her mornings in fitting rooms." It was for these women that Edwin Goodman started a ready-to-wear department in the early 1920's. He insisted that elegant ready-to-wear garments could be made at a time when ready-to-wear of the quality he desired was in its infancy.[29] From then on the store carried the ready-to-wear of top American designers, while continuing its custom salon.

The social and economic changes wrought by World War II have meant that no successful retailer can afford to overlook the status-conscious middle-class woman who demands attractive, moderately priced merchandise. Specialty shops began trading down. For example, Bergdorf's added the Miss Bergdorf line and country casuals, dropping the prices of the major lines in these divisions to build low-price, high-volume departments.

At the same time, low-priced stores began trading up, with the result that stores around the country have been closing the gap between the extremes of high- and low-price lines. This leveling trend indicates that eventually there may be little difference between stores. Erasing the differences between stores heightens the retailing competition for the average consumer dollar and widens the choice for many people, although it narrows the choice for a select few who want more distinctive goods.

Under the free-enterprise system in America it remains for realistic men with ideas to shape the future course of retailing to meet the changing needs, tastes, and desires of the American people. As social and economic factors affect one segment of the population differently than another, a new type of service will be developed to satisfy the demands of this specific consumer group. Because of the close relationship between retail policy and consumer attitudes, the varied forms of retailing help to spread the benefits of efficiency to society as a whole.

7

PROMOTION AND ADOPTION

Fashion promotion, used in all phases of the industry, serves two major functions. It is used by the producers of the apparel industry to bring an awareness of new ideas to workers within the industry. Producers of fashion want to build a "like-mindedness" in all related branches, so that fashion goods presented in one season will have some characteristics in common: hats go with coats, shoes, and bags, in color, texture, and line.

At the same time promotion is used to stimulate "style consciousness" outside the industry—in the consumer. A design may be created, but if it is not identified or recognized as having distinctive characteristics it will never become a style.* Nor can a style become a "prevailing style," or fashion, without group acceptance. Thus, fashion promotion aids in establishing styles by developing group awareness of the factors that differentiate this season's designs from last season's styles. It points out the characteristics all designs at a particular time have in common.

These two forms of fashion promotion can be called (1) *interindustry* communication, and (2) *industry-consumer* communication.

Interindustry communication works far in advance of industry-consumer communication. For example, consider the promotion of seasonal colors: The colorist for the yarn company is ready to discuss fall or spring colors 18 months before the average consumer will see them in the finished garment.

---

* Webster's definition of style: A distinctive or characteristic mode of presentation, construction, or execution in any art, employment, or product.

Promotion builds a like-mindedness in all related branches of the industry.

The company sends seasonal printed color projection cards and dyed yarn swatches to its customers (knitters, weavers, and manufacturers) who, in turn, create and sell all types of apparel. Yarn companies do not carry dyed yarn stocks, but dye colors to meet customer requirements. However, they do promote certain colors as "fashion-authenticated" and suggest to their customers the timing advantage of using the dyes for which the formula is already made rather than waiting to have the formulas for special colors worked out.

In the meantime the colorists of the yarn company discuss seasonal colors with colorists from related industries and with fabric editors of high fashion magazines. Jewelry, shoes, hosiery, and all related apparel must be color coordinated. By consulting each other and fashion advisers, they become jointly aware of fashion trends. Finally, the designers take a stand and the color, fabric, and silhouette are decided for the new season. Then the real dramatization begins—the promotion from industry to the consumer.

When a new style is presented to the consumer a concerted effort is made by commercially interested backers (designers, manufacturers, retailers) to influence and change public opinion. Each wants the new style to be accepted and become a fashion, in much the same way that a politician running for public office wants to receive the majority vote. For style acceptance must come before saturation, and saturation precedes the fashion change that means turnover and volume to the industry. In this sense fashion promotion is more than a communication to identify style characteristics, it is a mass propaganda campaign to persuade.

Effective propaganda, as defined by Wilbur Schramm in his book *The Process and Effects of Mass Communication*, must (1) gain the attention of the intended audience; (2) secure their confidence; (3) understand and respect the desires of the audience so that plausible alternatives are presented; and (4) suggest a course of action that is possible in their environment. Furthermore, propaganda appeals must be carefully timed to begin at the optimum moment and must be repeated, but not beyond some point of diminishing effectiveness.[1]

This general approach to propaganda technique has been adopted by fashion promoters: A new design is introduced in some dramatized way to secure the attention of the audience. Suggestions are made as to how the garment can satisfy an individual's social and psychological needs, aesthetic needs, or desire for physical comfort. The design is differentiated from all others and made to seem unique—a style. People are told where, when, and at what price they can obtain the style.

The entire promotion may be carried on through the mass media by fashion showings, reporting, and advertising in the newspapers, magazines, television, and radio. These are media designed to spread information over a large territory and to emphasize present-mindedness: immediate needs and gains. The effectiveness of the campaign is often judged by the total sales that result.

An evaluation of the role of mass media promotions in the acceptance of new ideas involves the field of communications research. One pertinent study suggests that people go through a series of distinguishable mental stages—awareness, interest, evaluation, trial, and adoption—in the acceptance of new ideas. The time required varies with the people and with the practice or idea. Mass media communications are found to be important in the early stages of the acceptance process, the awareness and interest stages, while person-to-person communication between neighbors and friends is the deciding factor at the later stages of trial and adoption.[2] These findings suggest that the effectiveness of fashion promotion can only be judged by the number of people who are aware of new styles and whose interest is aroused, not by the number who buy the garments.

How Is Fashion Publicized?

While fashion within the industry has been decided out of season—winter fashion in summer, spring in fall—the publicity campaign aimed at the general public gathers momentum, to explode at the beginning of a major fashion season. (Spring and fall are the two major seasons in fashion apparel.)

In the fashion industry publicity may come from, or emphasize, the designer, the manufacturer, or the retailer. Which focus is dominant depends on such factors as the place of the garment in the fashion cycle of group acceptance, the price line, and the system of design under which the idea was conceived. For example, under the French haute couture system the designer is highly publicized, but under the American ready-to-wear system the designer may remain completely anonymous. However, when ready-to-wear garments approach the same high fashion qualities and price level as couture garments, the designer's name may come into prominence.

The seasonal presentations of new styles, colors, or fabrics are dependent on a formalized network of influence among designers, manufacturers, retailers, and consumers.

Designers who think and work far ahead and are uniquely sensitive to fashion and design present what they feel is right for the coming season—a fashion idea to be interpreted. Their selections are prompted by taste, experience, training, instinct, assessment of what has been selling, and the cultural climate in which they work.

Manufacturers react to the fashion products the designers have created. They interpret these fashions according to their own estimate of style trends for the coming season and their customers' probable reactions. Thus, the manufacturers add their taste, experience, and know-how to the communication network and send on new fashion suggestions of their own.

Retailers choose what they wish to promote from the wealth of fashion products offered by the manufacturers. The retailers are the ones who decide what choice the consumer will actually have. If retailers do not offer a fashion product, the consumer can never react to it, no matter how wonderful and right it was in the eyes of the designer or the manufacturer.

Consumers react to the retail offerings. They can "kill" an item by not liking and not buying it; or they can make it a whopping success by purchasing it by the millions.

The methods of promotion most appropriate to fashion goods are fashion showings, reporting, labeling, advertising, and the exposure of goods in the store. While these methods are used in some form in all levels of the industry, each one originated with or is traditionally linked with the designer, the manufacturer, or the retailer.

DESIGNERS. Dress designs are one of the last repositories for fantasy. People are curious about the designer, especially about the creators of high fashion designs that are intended to suggest the new course of fashion. High fashion needs to be displayed. Even though high fashion is worn by very few, women like to read and dream about it; its mere presence in the world stimulates imagination and adds a vicarious touch of adventure to everyone's life.

The relative secrecy surrounding the work of a couture designer sometimes arouses whispering campaigns, rumors, or even malicious gossip. While such gossip may be worth more than all the paid publicity in the world, it is usually the quality of the designs for which designers hope to achieve favorable publicity. The number of outstanding designs they create determines the amount of press notice they will get, their placement in the fashion magazines, and the coverage given to their collections. The first exposure of the designer's original model to the opinion of fashion specialists has exceptional importance. The opening of a collection causes as much undercurrent of excitement as any important society event.

The presentation of new designs that catch the eye of the intended audience is the first step in the launching of a fashion campaign. A comparison between the new designs and the old ones they replace may be the stimulus that is needed to initiate a new fashion trend. Thus, designers attempt to show elegant gowns on living models in tantalizing settings, a custom which began in the royal courts over three centuries ago.

Fashion Showings. In the aristocratic society of seventeenth- and eighteenth-century Europe, the fashion leaders were members of royalty. Their showcases were the royal courts. The best artisans were called upon to adorn the sumptuously elegant costumes that were paraded in the splendid setting of the French court.

As patrons of the theater, royal families donated their cast-off clothes to their favorite actors, making the theater a vehicle for popularizing the fashions set by the royal court. This policy continued in France until after the Revolution, when actresses and prima donnas began creating their own costumes for the stage. Unhappily, a period of deterioration followed, and it was not until the years 1875 to 1918 that the theater threw off its shoddy trappings and again became the center for fashion inspiration.

During these years the stage was for high society what the haute couture collections are today. The French theater was the mirror for society. Drawing-room comedy dominated the repertoire, and contemporary dress came to the foreground. The latest fashions were launched by the actress and her couturier who would sit for hours pouring over sketches, discussing, discarding, and creating. Stage costumes were the couturier's best advertisement. When he sent his creations to the races, only a trained eye could tell the fashion of one great house from another. But in the theater, there could be no mistake: The couturier's name was printed on the program.[3]

So great was the interest in costumes made in the famous studios that the first-night opening of a new play included a representative from every big dressmaking house. Competing designers could not afford to miss viewing a fashion theme that might become the rage. Besides, they were sure to find ideas there for other designs.

Fashions derived from stage costumes and hair styles often acquired the name of the actress who wore them: The "Langtry bang" swept over America, and women began wearing a jersey blouse and a kilted skirt, a style devised in England to show off the beautiful figure of actress Lily Langtry, who was fondly called the "Jersey Lily."

In the 30's when movies became the poor man's theater, fashions were seldom launched in the same way they had been on the stage. A major problem was the time lag, for at least six months elapsed between the creation of the dresses and their public showing, and by then it was questionable whether the styles would still be up-to-date.

Even so, two glamorous movie stars, Greta Garbo and Marlene Dietrich, caused young women to grow long, loose manes of hair and adopt cool, sophisticated manners. And the modern-art fashions of Adrian, combined with the personal style of Joan Crawford and Rosalind Russell, brought a sense of chic to small towns throughout the country. Although the movies generally failed to start specific fashion trends, they did a great deal to popularize the idea of fashion.

Following World War I, Paris began to create more

models for export. The fashion spectacle left the stage and retired into the private salons of the great couturiers. Thereafter, the twice-yearly showings of the haute couture have continued to provide the fashion drama of the season.

Each French couture designer and his assistants create around 200 new designs for a fashion opening. Invitations are printed and chairs are rented in preparation for the launching of some 2,000 new designs in six hectic days. In a hushed showroom the audience waits. The show begins. A style number is flashed and a perfectly costumed mannequin walks the length of the salon, turning and whirling ceaselessly to keep the designs from being copied. She sweeps off and pauses backstage, with mounting tension, to listen for the special murmur from a first-run audience that spells "approval." This is fashion showing at its temperamental best, with all the mystery and beauty of an artistic creation on a lovely woman.

The first American fashion show, called a "Fashion Fete," was held in November, 1914. Sponsored by *Vogue,* it was a display of designs by the New York houses presented on living models. A committee of "best-dressed women" was asked to pass on the gowns to be shown. Admission was charged and the proceeds were donated to French charity. A break with Paris was not intended. On the contrary, the show was an attempt to uphold the tradition of smart dress which was endangered by the war conditions abroad.

Today when we read that some of New York's wealthiest and prettiest women are having a champagne breakfast at some smart shop, or watching and modeling at a charity fashion show, we realize that the fashion show is carrying on in its early tradition. However, today's fashion show has spread to all levels of society—it may be used to attract customers into the local department store or to entertain prospective freshmen visiting a college campus on "Hospitality Day."

Reporting. Ideas in fashion design, like ideas in space travel or any field of creative endeavor, are news. They offer an escape from the customary way of living and their startling element attracts attention, especially in a culture such as ours that tends to believe "everything new is admirable." Accordingly, the creative couture designer and his high fashion models are widely reported in the mass media. So, too, are unusual ideas in fashion emanating from other sources.

The mass media confer status. Common experience, as well as research, shows a rise in the social standing of persons or things which command favorable attention in print or on the air. Each fashion journal, whether it caters to the fashion professionals, the high fashion world, women in general, or the young set, enjoys the trust of a large portion of the audience it serves. The items it reports are accepted as "superior" pieces and the magazine is considered an important source of information to its readers.

In the opinion of Luis Estevez, a high fashion American designer on Seventh Avenue, "*Harper's Bazaar* and *Vogue* are the two most important magazines, along with *Life*. The *Herald Tribune* [now defunct] and *Women's Wear Daily* mean the most among newspapers. All other publications are secondary."[4] Christian Dior also favored the same journals in 1956, but added the French "Bible of Fashion," *L'Officiel de la Couture*.[5] These are the mass media read by the fashion professionals—people in the industry.

Comparing the two American high fashion magazines with each other, Richard Avedon, a fashion photographer, saw *Harper's Bazaar* as the more subliminal but more contemporary, and *Vogue* as more immediate and constant. According to Avedon, fashion magazines are a creative force influencing the reader and the designer, whereas newspapers simply report and push a good thing when they see it.[6]

The first issue of *Vogue* appeared December 17, 1892, in competition with *Harper's Bazaar*, which was established in 1867. By 1913 *Vogue* began to develop as a fashion magazine and practical shopping guide, rather than simply a gazette of social activities. It wanted to show the rest of the United States what the women of New York were buying and what the New York stores, dressmakers, and milliners were offering. *Vogue's* job, as the editor conceived it, was to direct and develop the taste and manners of its readers. At the same time *Vogue* wanted to build its own class of advertising. There was a feeling that anything high priced "is better advertised in a periodical with readers of a special type: people of breeding, sophistication, and means."[7]

One of the most controversial issues in mass media reporting is the conflict between the advertising department and editorial comment. Because the mass media are mainly supported by dollars from advertisers rather than dollars from subscribers it is difficult for journals to report fashion news impartially. A trend toward major American designers owning their production firms makes it even harder for the media to remain objective. Designers become both the beneficiaries of fashion reporting which can bring fame and notoriety to their firms, and the suppliers of the advertising dollars that keep the magazines in business. This reciprocal dependency does not encourage unbiased fashion reporting.

Designer Estevez, commenting on this, said, "Magazines give my clothes editorials on their merit once in a while, but mostly because of my advertising dollar. I admire them, I love them, I hate them. . . ."[8]

When Edna Woolman Chase became editor of *Vogue* on February 1, 1914, she took a stand in the battle between editorial integrity and the advertising department. She told her advertisers, "You may get into *Vogue* through the advertising pages, but to come in the editorial door you must give us material we can be proud of." She found it difficult, however, to learn how to turn down the gowns of shops as news items and still solicit their advertising dollar.[9]

In the daily columns of our newspapers this struggle between editorial content and advertising works to the advantage of foreign designers. When there is so much fashion advertising the reporter feels free to mention only the French, Italian, or Spanish designers, since they do not advertise in American papers. If she describes an American design, sold in one store, she will be showered by protests from every other store that advertises, because they feel they also should be mentioned.

The problem of whether or not to print a story that may adversely affect an advertiser's pocketbook was solved by *Women's Wear Daily,* a daily morning newspaper for manufacturers, wholesalers, and retailers of women's and children's wear. The founder, E. W. Fairchild, Sr., was convinced that the progress and prosperity of his six trade newspapers depended on printing news alone—no editorials, no slanted stories. He believed that the readers of Fairchild Publications were better able to make decisions in their own individual cases than was any Fairchild writer and he felt his readers would be able to do this if Fairchild papers gave them *all the news*.[10]

Since it began July 10, 1910, *Women's Wear Daily* has kept its readers informed on the changing phases of fashion. Today it is a byword among the industries it serves. It employs about 25 people to cover fashion news alone and about 18 full-time fashion artists to produce authentic drawings of the markets' fashion highlights.

The pictorial reporter, the fashion photographer, can be even more important than the writer in presenting fashion news since "seeing" can be more effective than "reading" in an artistic medium such as dress. Therefore, a brief examination of the role of the fashion photographer is in order.

Edward Steichen, who started as a painter and then developed an interest in photography, was one of the top photographers for *Vogue* between 1923 and 1938. "Let photographers be workmen," he said, "and try to make good photographs and eliminate all concern as to whether their photographs are art or not." He wanted to define the words people were using: For Steichen "smart" stood for something trim and modish but artificial and devoid of any natural or human quality, while "chic" was a sort of super smartness, but in spite of this, curiously more human.[11]

Richard Avedon, who has more recently been taking unusual fashion pictures, comments on his own work, "It is what I think I see . . . like taking a walk. . . ." As a photographer he sees the excitement in fashion as change and contrast. And he adds, "Who knows what a fine photograph is? In 50 years it might be a fashion photograph that provides the clue to this time and this life."[12]

These two opinions, coming from successful fashion photographers of different eras, illustrate the wide divergence of views on the use of photography. Should photography be a faithful representation of the subject it is presenting, or, should photography be a medium through which the photographic artist, like the painter, expresses his introspective view of the world? Modern photographers, influenced by contemporary painters, and striving to make photography a "fine art," have swung toward the introspective view. Their interest lies in the expressive possibilities of photography. Consequently, a fashion photograph may first catch the reader's eye by its unusual composition and psychological impact, and only secondly by the dress it is supposed to be presenting.

The emphasis of expressive or artistic factors rather than the fashion itself has, however, caused conflict between photographers and designers. The designers feel their dresses are distorted and given a false image, while the photographers feel the designers fail to give them credit for attracting attention to their garments through an artistic presentation.

The fashion press can create problems for the designer and periodically some Paris couture houses ban the press from their showings. Designers are displeased with the selections of exaggerated and distorted designs by reporters looking for news gimmicks. The same feeling is present on Seventh Avenue in New York. As Ferdinand Sarmi, an Italian-born American designer expressed it, "I hate gimmicks. The press looks for something different whether it is bad or beautiful. The designer who just wants to be different is prostituting himself. That's not fashion."[13]

Larry Aldrich, a Seventh Avenue producer who works closely with his designer, adds this comment, "The function of the press is to report on Fashion . . . but they *Dictate Fashion* instead of reporting. I understand, however, the publication's basic function is to be interesting . . . but sometimes the grotesque is chosen—and that's a Fashion Waste."[14] There is a general feeling among the major designers that the magazine and newspaper reporters need more taste and knowledge of fashion to insure complete reporting of fashion news.

Labeling. A label, some catchy slogan built around people and events, focuses attention in any campaign. It has been suggested that before something can really become a fashion, it must be capable of being labeled. Certainly, in retrospect, it is clear that there is a name or phrase attached to most significant changes in fashion. "The New Look" of Dior that appeared after World War II brought in dresses using fantastic amounts of yardage in comparison with the rationed fabrics of the war years. Dress styles changed abruptly from severe, broad shouldered, and short, to long, graceful, and feminine. An earlier label or symbol, "The Flapper," with her languid, concave, boyish form and bobbed hair, recalls the era of the 20's.

A label is, at first, only a shorthand method of describing a new style that has been introduced by a designer or a fashion leader. One or two words serve as the symbol for a characteristic combination of lines, color, and expression. If this style becomes a mass fashion, the label will become known to many people, spread quickly over a wide territory, and become identified with that particular time. Later, to recall the one word is to recall the entire spirit of the times in which it was used. A label that wakens a uniform favorable response may be necessary for the general adoption of a style.

There is normally some ambiguity in the meaning of any symbol: The word "Mexico" to some people implies romance; to others it suggests only a backward country. A sociological study on the effect of symbols on crowd behavior has pointed out that a symbol that arouses uniform feelings toward the object is a necessary condition for uniform group action. This study analyzed the "zoot suit riots" in Los Angeles in 1943 in which sailors attacked the zoot suiters. "Zoot suits" were parodies of the normal fashions, worn by some teen-age minority groups not in the army during World War II. The coats were extremely long and the pants very baggy at the waist and tight at the ankle. A distinguishing feature was a tremendous loop of watch chain dangling almost to the ground. Because the zoot suit gained more unfavorable than favorable connotations, it did not become a general fashion.* According to the study, the mere expression "zoot suit" had been stripped of its favorable connotations until it evoked only unfavorable feelings. Once this was done, the crowd felt free to attack anyone wearing this "outside-the-normative-order" symbol.[15]

An opposite example, where a symbol received only favorable associations, is provided by the Gibson Girl of the 1890's: Her winning smile, her friendly wave, and her tempestuous petticoat bewitched thousands. In 1895 Miss Irene Langhorne, tall, aristocratic, and lovely, married a Mr. Charles Dana Gibson, an artist living in Richmond, Virginia. With his wife as the model, Gibson launched his famous "Girl" in the pages of *Life*, a popular weekly magazine devoted to satire

---

* This costume seems to parallel that worn by Les *"Incroyables"* of the late 1790's. These radical young Frenchmen wore square-cut coats, the tails of which were incredibly elongated, and they favored medallions, lorgnettes, chains, and earrings with cameos.

and humor (not to be mistaken for the present-day magazine of the same name).

While the Gibson Girl was always the essence of charm, it was not until Miss Irene Langhorne (Mrs. Gibson) was invited by Mr. Ward Waid McAllister, the dean of New York society, sometimes described as "the most omnipotent snob in America," to lead the grand march at a society ball that the Gibson Girl became the darling of America. Her hair styles, her sailor hats, even her shirtwaists and belts were lavishly cop-

Zootsuiter

2 / FASHION: AN ECONOMIC GOOD

Gibson Girl

COPYRIGHT 1909 BY P. F. COLLIER & SON

ied. With the approval of the right person, in the right place, and at the right time, she had gained the full confidence of the public as a fashion symbol.

Today the fashion reporter's need for synthesis imposes an artificial unity upon each season's fashions. The "apparent" prevailing trend is the choice of journalists and clients. Wide news distribution and the taste for slogans further accentuate the simplification.

It was the policy of Christian Dior, the designer most responsible for reviving the French couture after World War II, to cooperate fully with the press by providing a "Label" for his new designs. The christening of his new line took place in the three days between the dress rehearsals and the openings. He explained, "I draw up the press release, describing the season's trend in as precise and unliterary language as possible."[16] In the spring of 1955 Dior picked the letter A as the symbol describing his dominant silhouette. It succeeded the letter H of the preceding season.

Many examples of fashion labeling seem to support the belief that it is not possible to launch an idea as fashion unless it can be labeled. Certainly a name, easy to remember, is a desired feature of any new product fighting for attention in mass media reporting.

Limited Advertising. In France, where the individual couturier brings fame to French fashions, the designer frequently allows his name to be used in advertisements for the textile, accessory, and perfume industries, which depend on French fashion prestige to sell their products. *L'Officiel,* the high fashion magazine of the couture contains many pages of textile company advertisements featuring the designer's name and the garments that were made from their fabrics.

In America, designers' names are used very little. Unless a company is designer owned, the consumer gives little thought to the name of the designer. If the American shopper is "name" conscious at all, it is the company name rather than the designer's name that she knows. Designer identification comes mainly through the promotion methods just discussed—showings, reporting, labeling—rather than through the advertising media. In mass production, where utility, adaptability, and timing are emphasized more than creativity, and where

　　　　　　　　　　2 / FASHION: AN ECONOMIC GOOD

manufacturers frequently change designers or employ none at all, they have felt it important to emphasize the company name, not the designer's name.

MANUFACTURER. Fashion goods are generally transported directly from the manufacturer to the retailer who distributes them to the public through sales. Exceptions are the chain store operations or voluntary federations of retail stores which use a centralized buying office. In these cases the buying office becomes a substitute for the local retail-store buyers. The retailer is the direct customer for the manufacturer, although the goods are ultimately intended for a specific group of consumers, the people who wear the clothes.

Sometimes the producer feels the retail buyer is not an accurate judge of what consumers want, and would like to force the retailer to take some of each garment the company offers. On the contrary, he may feel that the retailer, as a closer link to the ultimate consumer, knows best what will sell. In either case, he tries to build his own market by fashion promotion. Some interindustry promotion goes between the producer and the retailer, but most promotion is aimed toward the ultimate consumer. The producer wants to persuade the consumer that his garment is unique, different in some respects from all other garments on the market, and in this way reduce competitive pricing.

Showings. The opening showing of each season's line, presented on live models by a dress manufacturer, is intended to introduce the new designs to the retail buyers, the salesmen, and the press. Any manufacturing firm may make such an introduction if it chooses. When a firm does not have its own showrooms, it can rent space and hire professional models to display the dresses.

Other fashion shows that are specifically producer sponsored are called designer promotions. The designer who works for the manufacturing firm is sent to the retail store and is featured by the store, along with representative garments from the company's line. This arouses consumer awareness of the company and its type of styling.

Reporting. While manufacturers, like designers and retailers, read the interindustry professional journals and papers, especially *Women's Wear Daily,* their communication to consumers is channeled through the popular mass media.

Fashions for the middle class were first transmitted by means of fashionably dressed dolls or "babes" sent to the United States from Europe. Later, fashion by magazines replaced dolls as sources of the latest style.

The first popular women's magazines contained fashion notes and illustrations as well as articles to "elevate the mind." *Godey's Lady's Book* influenced almost every middle-class household in the United States. The fashion plates, for which the magazine is now treasured, were colored at home by 150 women employees. When the correct colors ran out, others were substituted. Thus, one subscriber might have a pink dress and her neighbor the same dress in yellow. The editor finally announced to the puzzled magazine readers: "We color our plates to different patterns so that two persons in a place may compare their fashions and spot those colors most suited to their complexions."[17]

Two people made this magazine possible: Louis Antoine Godey and Sarah Josepha Hale, who ran it together from 1836 to 1877. Curiously, he lavished particular care on fashion, while she was more concerned with social reform.

The shift toward a broader appeal to the middle-class reader began with *Good Housekeeping* in 1884. Whereas the titles of the earlier magazines made it clear that they were literally directed to "ladies," by the turn of the century the magazines were for everyone, as indicated by use of the term "woman," as in *Modern Woman.* The *Ladies' Home Companion* changed to the *Woman's Home Companion* in 1895.

In more recent years, the audience of magazine readers has become fractionated, so that each fashion group has its own magazines: *Seventeen,* for the romantic girl in her teens; *Mademoiselle,* for the more sophisticated college student; *Glamour,* for the young career girl. The importance of magazines is indicated by a study by Katz and Lazarsfeld in which they found that, outside of person-to-person contact, magazines were the medium most influential in creating awareness of new fashions.[18] With the great variety of magazines available, each consumer can choose the one best suited to her needs. New magazines aimed at new blocks of readers come and go.

National Advertising. From the time a fashion is created, the sequence of promotion for new styles is mainly (1) show them; (2) label them; and (3) report them in the mass media. Once styles are introduced to the consuming public, advertising becomes important.

Advertising can be direct or indirect. Direct advertising is a product that is bought and sold and is easily recognizable. Whether or not it is read or listened to depends on the good-will of the audience. Some people tune out the commercials on television, or skip the ads in a magazine; others read the ads and ignore the editorial content.

Indirect advertising is not always recognized or recognizable. The dresses worn by television personalities, the faces and figures of fashion models, the awards to outstanding dress designers, and the store displays at Christmas are not generally considered, by the consumer, as advertisements to be coldly tuned in or out. Instead, they seem to be a natural part of some other event, and are judged and discussed in a more personal way.

Direct Advertising. A breakdown of expenditures for selected types of advertising from 1960 to 1963 shows that newspaper national advertising of wearing apparel increased from $10,818,-000 to $13,867,000 in this 3-year period, while expenditures for all newspaper national advertising declined. Comparing expenditures during the same period in other media we find that apparel, footwear, and accessories advertisements in magazines increased slightly (from $56,684,000 to $57,208,000); whereas similar advertising on television networks decreased. However, television spot advertising, or locally originating commercials, increased markedly.*

Thus, while expenditures for apparel advertising totaled more in magazines than in all other media combined, there was a noticeable shift toward increased national advertising in newspapers and in locally originating spot commercials on television.

Timeliness and local coverage in a selected market avail-

---

* Clothing, furnishings, and accessories expenditures on television spot advertising increased from $10,107,000 to $16,267,000 (1963). All data are adopted from U.S. Bureau of the Census, *Statistical Abstract of the United States: 1964* (85th ed.), Washington, D.C., 1964.

able to the consumer are attributes of apparel ads that seem to have a direct influence on consumer buying. Day-to-day price and product changes in a shopping center or a specific store (the store name is superimposed on the brand advertising) can be announced in a daily newspaper and in locally originating commercials on television.

Moreover, in the fashion field, where person-to-person contact is most influential in the adoption of new ideas, and the mass media quickly report fashion changes "as news," the consumer's need for a fashion may be aroused before the ads appear. By then her immediate concern is where to find the fashions she is "willing to buy" at a price she is "able to pay."

The consumer allows herself to be swayed by advertising in areas where it really does not matter. She may switch from one stocking brand to another, or try this or that make-up, precisely because it makes little difference which she uses. This explains why so many dollars go into national brand advertising. If the consumer can be made brand conscious and brand loyal, even in an unimportant area, it can mean financial success for a company.

The brand name in fashion can stand for the designer, the manufacturer, or the store. National brand advertising, however, originates with producers. Fashion brands always have news to report simply by showing the latest styles.

The purpose of using brands is to build a market. It is a device, sign, or symbol which is used to identify products so the advertiser can reap the benefits of any demand created. Through a brand name the manufacturer hopes to build prestige for his product, to differentiate it from others in the consumer's mind, and lessen price competition by creating loyal customers who are reluctant to accept other brands. Brand names aid consumers to repeat a purchase found satisfactory or to avoid one that is unsatisfactory.

Where apparel companies specialize in one area of design, fashion goods labels become identified with a design style, size, and occasion-type of garment, offering so much quality at a stated price. As long as the company is consistent, the brand is a guide for the consumer. But in itself, a brand tells nothing, and must be constantly reassessed by an alert consumer.

The use of brand names is a form of persuasive advertising, a type of propaganda. It is prejudiced and one sided.

It deliberately attempts to influence, persuade, and convince people to act in a way that is favorable to the propagandist.

A foundation garment company used the same layout and the same slogan for advertising in five different magazines, but in *Harper's Bazaar* and *Vogue,* a high fashion model posed in a hostess gown; in *Mademoiselle* and *Good Housekeeping* the model wore a basic street dress, spiced with high-style accessories; whereas in *Farm Journal* the whole setting changed —a "homey" model, wearing an attractive print dress, smiled at the rural reader. The ad was changed to reflect the attitudes and values of each reader group, but it never lost sight of the product symbol.

A casual survey of current terms used in fashion advertisements reveals two types: those that describe some inherent feature, such as "half-size," or "cotton knits"; and those that enhance the psychological image of the garment. This is done by suggesting added values and benefits which are not in the product but are of subjective value to the purchaser. Examples are such phrases as "endearing accents" and "great choice." This type of advertising which serves "to freight the product image with taste meanings, symbolic attributes and emotive associations" is seen by Pierre Martineau as necessary in America where goods technically are so much alike and where most people have gone beyond a subsistence economy. Consumers now want more from their products than utility.[19]

However, in this connection, a 1932 Gallup study on the attention value of ads showed that "sex" and "quality" were the appeals noticed most by men and women even at a time when "economy" and "efficiency" were the appeals in common use.[20] And still earlier, Virginia Frazee, advising on "Advertising For Women" in *Printers Ink,* May 3, 1893, had this to say about women consumers: "Women don't want too much reasoning in an advertisement; they skip it. . . ." Indeed, she felt that "a bright, catchy way of putting things always wins her, 'provided' the woman *believes* the statement made."[21]

Truth in advertising was the primary concern of merchandisers when big advertising began. In the 1870's there was a switch from patent medicine to general merchandise advertisements. Patent medicine ads had been known for their untruths, their distortion and ambiguity. To be successful, advertisers had to wipe this concept from the consumer's mind and get a fresh start.

John Wanamaker of Wanamaker's store, New York, had six advertising rules by 1889 that were unheard of before the Civil War. He believed in frank truth-telling; understatement rather than overstatement; simple, easy English; human-interest copy; reason-why writing; and mass distribution.[22] He was so frank that he often advertised the defects of an item along with its good points.

On the other hand, bargains and price appeals have been consistently used to attract the consumer. Even today a large proportion of retail advertisement consists of comparative price ads, which can be a form of false and misleading advertising. The Federal Trade Commission has set up rulings that outline the ways in which comparative pricing can be honorable and proper. But these are rulings, not laws. Consumers still need to take time to check the accuracy of prices quoted in this type of advertising.

As a result of the control it exercises over television, radio, and periodicals, advertising has been criticized for lacking social responsibility, for misrepresentation, and for stimulating irrational choice by intensifying emotion and degrading the intellect. Since it constantly exalts the materialistic virtues of consumption, advertising may become merely a propaganda device for materialism.

On the other hand, much advertising is simply disregarded by the American consumer. Bombarded with messages and too many symbols and models to follow, the American learns to tune them out, and when this is impossible, to retreat with tongue-in-cheek.

In defense of their techniques, manufacturers argue that advertising is a marketable product, developed to satisfy human needs, and that it should be thought of as reflecting rather than directing the values of the society it serves. Although the immediate aim of advertising is to make a product known, in a broader sense it helps to overcome inertia and stimulate people to action, they say. It is constantly changing its appeals. There is some question whether advertising generates a new want or whether the appeal is to a latent want, hitherto unnoticed, because it was ignored. It was the economist Frank Knight who stressed that the development of wants is really much more important than their satisfaction, that there is no poverty so deplorable as poverty of interest.

Indirect Advertising. What importance women place on television as a guide to their ultimate fashion selection is unknown. Indirect suggestion is more powerful than direct. The demonstrators of the most-advertised products—appliances, freezers, autos, and cameras—by their choice of clothes can convey to the viewer an idea of what is currently fashionable on a mass scale.

So, too, the vehicles for the ads, the programs themselves, would seem to indirectly influence observers with the clothes worn by actresses in dramas with contemporary settings, in situation comedies, soap operas, panel or variety shows, or in musical comedies. The clothes in these shows are normally chosen for characterization purposes to give visual cues as to age, status, and income groups. At the same time they may reinforce current fashion trends.

The woman viewer may be influenced in two ways: (1) seeing what is worn by members of the group (or groups) with which she identifies herself; (2) seeing what is worn by other groups outside her own. Thus, a matron who is interested in "young-marrieds" clothes notes the features characterizing youthful styles in comparison with those characterizing clothes for her age group.

The fashion influence created by television programs is, for the most part, unconscious. The viewer is not necessarily seeking fashion information, as she would from a magazine, but rather is looking for entertainment or other information. However, the fashion is there to be unconsciously accepted and digested and to reemerge as part of the viewer's attitudes and reactions toward other groups.

The fashion model who displays the clothes shown in the apparel ads has a similar effect on the reader. When you ask a college girl how she would like to look, she probably replies, "slim and smart with not a hair out of place," or "natural and touseled" (depending on the fashion). She is modeling herself after the girls in the ads of every magazine she picks up.

The fashion model is trained to be trim and modish, to catch the eye of the viewer and enhance the dress she is wearing, but not to intrude upon it. She must subordinate herself to the garment. This explains the somewhat inhuman quality of strained perfection, even in a "planned casualness," that caused a small boy at a style show to say, "Is she out of the store window, Mommy?"

Conversely, the woman of chic values the person above the clothes. She gives thought and time to selecting from the current group of fashions those which do the most *for her*. She is fashionable, but in her own distinct way. The average American girl sees pictures of many fashion models but knows few women of fashion taste; she learns how to be smart, but not how to be chic.

RETAILERS. Once the personal desires of the audience are understood, the final step in a successful promotion is to suggest possible ways to meet these needs. The retailer, as the closest link to the consumer in the total network of production and distribution of fashion goods, is concerned with timeliness and local coverage. He stocks the garments the designer has conceived and the manufacturer has produced, and makes them available to the consumers in a selected market. Here the consumer may make a choice and exchange dollars for goods.

Local Fashion Shows. Fashion shows occur on every level of the industry, but the retailer uses them as a device to attract customers into the local store. The shows may be held in the store or presented as social entertainment to groups outside the store. They can assume an exclusive air—by invitation only—or be open to the public. This will depend on the price line and the group for which the garments are intended; the higher the price line and social status of the group, the more necessary it is to give the garments rare or limited quality.

Reporting. The retailer feels the need for a report on what consumers want, as well as on what manufacturers offer, in order to choose his stock wisely. This need gave rise to another type of professional fashion reporter, the fashion consultant.

Mrs. Tobe Coller, until she died in 1962, was generally considered to be the leading fashion consultant in the business. Her syndicated column "Tobe says" had an estimated circulation of four million in 1953. She slanted fashion reporting to the needs of industry and made it a career. She advised more than 1,000 stores on fashion trends—compiling, printing, and marking weekly 50-page reports telling her clients how and where to buy the clothes customers would be demanding. When she foresaw the immense popularity of such items as dirndl skirts, sweater blouses, and slim pants, and advised her clients accordingly, she helped make these clothes the "Fords" of the fashion industry. She was, in a sense, a communications relay station between consumer demand and producer supply.

Store Labels. Like the manufacturers, the retailers use a trademark to build business and promote the store image. Their special mark is printed on shopping bags, boxes, wrapping paper, and delivery trucks. It is used in store ads, and it is sewed as a label into garments that are especially contracted for and that represent the quality of the store. Store labels are also attached to garments already possessing a manufacturer's label. This is especially true of coats or suit jackets that may be draped over a chair back when the owner is seated, thus displaying a label on the inside of the neck. The higher the quality of the garment, the more likely the store is to sew its own label in a prominent place at the neck of the garment, while the designer or company label is hidden in a side seam. Which label is more prominently displayed may depend on the prestige or favorable customer image attached to that particular symbol.

Local Advertising. The marked increase in television spot advertising and locally originated commercials was noted in the discussion of direct national advertising. Day-to-day price and style changes in a shopping center or a specific store readily available to the customer have a marked influence on consumer buying. These timely changes can be announced most easily in the newspaper and in locally originated commercials on radio and television. Often the ads combine the manufacturer's and the retailer's appeal, with the store name inserted into an already prepared brand ad. The same technique is used in magazine advertisements to promote both a manufacturer's label and a retail store name.

The retail store is at its best with indirect advertising,

illustrated by the arrangement of stock in the store, the outside window displays, and inside department displays. A good merchandiser constantly rearranges his goods in attractive ways to bring the customer back to "look again." Each time the customer walks through the store it can appear as if new stock had arrived as items unnoticed before are suddenly seen in a changed atmosphere. The display of stock is extremely effective in encouraging the fantasy and imaginative element so necessary to the promotion of fashion goods.

The climax of indirect advertising is the Christmas fashion display in the big department store. This is the season that an executive of Marshall Field and Company of Chicago called "the department store's finest hour." During November and December the nation's department stores expend for advertising and display about 18 to 22 per cent of their total annual budgets, according to the National Retail Merchants Association. In return, the Association concludes, the stores take in about 26 per cent of their annual revenues.[23]

"A woman rarely would spend over $50 for herself for a handbag," said Charles W. Folds, merchandise manager of Field's accessories division, "but she would buy one as a gift." At Christmas time Mr. Folds has on hand alligator bags ranging in price up to over $400.[24]

By adding his fashion promotion to the vast quantity flowing between industry and the consumer, the retailer completes the publicizing of new fashion designs. How effective the combined promotion—from designer, producer, retailer—is can be determined only by examining the effects of the communication and relay process as it is passed from person to person in the informal networks of fashion adoption.

At Whom Is The Publicity Aimed?

Persons so involved with fashion that they seem to be part of the fashion process come from a variety of groups in our society. A few are *innovators,* the first to present a new fashion symbol; some are *leaders,* the first to react to the message; and many are *followers,* those who receive the message last. En masse these people are called carriers of fashion.

CARRIERS OF FASHION. The upper class, as we have seen, is often concerned with fashion, especially in a society like that of the United States where wealth is a commonly accepted criterion (and expression) of success. In a healthy nation that has maintained a fairly open upper class, as have Britain and the United States, there is a natural movement upward into the elite by people of ability. Anyone may rise to the upper class, but not everyone can do so. And while many are born into this elite, not all are able to keep their places. Such an aristocracy or elite provides a renewing fashion leadership.

Included in this fashion elite are women of natural good taste who possess an authoritative stamp of their own. They know the difference between art and artifice; they pay attention to details. They often represent the "best" of everything. Wealth allows them to indulge their personal taste; to be charming, gracious, direct, and unaffected; and to have a well-bred look, even if it requires an entire wardrobe by a master designer. They become community fashion leaders and, if well known, may be considered national fashion symbols.

During the administration of John F. Kennedy, the women in the presidential clan did much to set the tone and style of the capital's taste and culture. What's more, their influence spread across the country, so dominating the fashion industry that millions of women wore pill-box hats, A-line coats, and low-heeled shoes because they were worn by the President's wife.

It is particularly "upwardly mobile" people who follow the course charted by those on a higher level. In this country most of the material advantages acquired by the rich soon fall into the hands of the not-so-rich. Cars, refrigerators, travel, sailboats, mink coats—once the prerogative of the well-to-do—now belong to hosts of people. Thus, a middle class, rising in power and wealth, becomes increasingly fashion conscious. They are able to duplicate the fashions worn by the elite even if they cannot buy their personal sense of style.

Curiously enough, the nonmobile "occupational indifferents" may also join the fashion game. An industrial society that regiments and compartmentalizes many jobs can cause a "displacement of values" from the work itself to the by-products of the work. Off-the-job activities, such as fashion emulation in hard and soft goods, are used to compensate for the worker's lack of pride in his job.

So, too, fashion often makes up in a social way what is denied some individuals in a personal way. The uprooted individual striving for a new identity seeks compensation in fashion status. Negroes, moving from the Deep South to northern cities, from legal subjection to legal equality, from feudalism to industrialism, experience a crisis of identity. And furthermore, they are frustrated because they cannot, in America, be human beings first and only secondly Negroes.

Unable to share fully in the world of the larger American society, the Negro sometimes builds a wall of "make believe." A struggle for status with material goods inside the Negro community may be an attempt to compensate for the status denied it outside by the whites. As a result, Negroes are emerging as fashion leaders among young male groups and frequently are ahead of their white peers in wearing the newest cut and color.

Closely related to the uprooted individual as a carrier of fashion is the marginal man: the person with a foot in each of two worlds, that of the majority and that of the minority. With entree into different realms, the marginal man shares the values of several groups but is ambivalent toward all. Because he views social customs as having no guarantee of either rationality or legitimacy, he often provides the insight and motivation that inspire change. For example, jazz orchestra leaders, radio and television personalities, cosmopolites—people who see things from a position partly inside and partly outside the group—are able to mix ideas in unpredictable ways and became fashion innovators. They invent new fashion symbols.

Earlier marginal individuals are represented by the fashionable demimonde of Paris from the 1860's to World War I. These "fallen women," tarts of the highest caliber, were influential fashion leaders. For although unrestrained in fashion they were obliged never to offend with vulgarity the men of taste who financed them.

Competition among the couturier made it possible for the demimonde to achieve a high fashion rating. All the Parisian dressmakers tried to outdo each other in invention and daring to assure the triumph of their latest creation when worn by a grand cocotte. Often at the opening of a race meeting, dressmakers' assistants would still be pinning gowns to be displayed that day. One famous cocotte said, "Society ladies go to this or that couturier to be dressed like cocottes: I go to Worth's to be dressed like a lady."[25]

These peculiarly uprooted individuals, marginal people living in two worlds, were pioneers of fashion. An interpretation of their fashion consciousness was suggested by Simmel when he said that in their bizarre and picturesque dress lurked an aesthethic expression of the desire for destruction. Striking out against the permanent institutions of the society which condemned them to a pariah-like existence, they found an outlet through striving for ever new forms of appearance.[26]

And yet they may have been dependent individuals, whose self-consciousness required a certain amount of attention and singularity and who gained support from the enveloping cloak of fashion. This is one reason young people are often fashion conscious. They identify so intimately with a fashion that it becomes a personal fashion. Unable to individualize their existence purely by their own unaided efforts, they may use startling outer fashions to conceal a modest inner reserve.

While women are the main carriers of fashion, today's male is increasingly style conscious. However, since the Industrial Revolution when men retreated into the business world and donned more sober attire, it has been generally accepted that women, as mothers and guardians of the home, would be the transmitters of culture. Concerned with interpersonal relationships and the development of children who can function successfully, both emotionally and socially, women consider the institution of fashion with all of its cultural meanings an important part of their mode of living.

Informal Networks of Fashion Communication. Verbal response and other reactions to fashion symbols promoted by the mass media are transmitted through informal person-to-person communication channels between people on near or adjoining social and economic levels. These channels are used by consumers in making market decisions. The communication is a direct give-and-take, usually face-to-face. The communication unit may be composed of family members, fellow students, friends and neighbors, or coworkers. Sociologists refer to these units as small groups or, when sentiment is involved, primary groups.

Katz and Lazarsfeld in their book *Personal Influence* were concerned with specific incidents of informal person-to-person communication influencing everyday situations of marketing, fashion, public affairs, and movie-going. Their study verified that verbal personal influence was the most effective type of communication in fashion situations. It was the reaction of friends and acquaintances or salespeople, on seeing a woman's hairdo or dress, that counted. In most cases, women influence other women like themselves.

That market decisions in general depend on personal influence was highlighted in William H. Whyte, Jr.'s "The Web of Word of Mouth." Noticing the peculiar arrangement of air conditioners jutting from the windows of Philadelphia row houses, Whyte discovered a pattern based on "social traffic." The air conditioners clustered around a catalytic opinion leader.

According to Whyte, discussion as to what to buy passes by informal word of mouth as neighbors sit chatting and their children play. If a person has not already sold himself or been sold by friends, he is not likely to go to the store. Whyte concluded that through this vast series of ready-made informal networks of communication the real market decisions would be made.[27]

Opinion leaders exist in all groups and on every social and economic level. They are found among the unknown and inconspicuous members of a group as well as among formal leaders. And many opinion leaders differ little from the majority in their personal and social characteristics. Their leadership position is maintained because their advice appears to be sound. They have shown their ability to use good judgment in the area of life in which they exert a rather steady influence. For example, Katz and Lazarsfeld found that the household marketing leaders were wives between 25 and 44 years of age with large families, whereas the fashion leaders were unmarried women under 35.

The leader represents the "typical" group member. In fashion, if the norm of the group is to conform, he is the most conformist; if the norm is to deviate, he is the most deviant.

There is general agreement that opinion leaders, who are

2 / FASHION: AN ECONOMIC GOOD

minor specialists and highly interested in their field of influence, form a vital middle link in what communications people refer to as the "two-step flow" in which a communication passes from the mass media to opinion leaders, and from opinion leaders to the less active parts of the population.[28] It is believed that in small informal groups the mass communication is discussed and evaluated, opinions are reinforced, and action, if any, is taken.

Opinion leaders are not to be confused with innovators. A summary of the studies of rural sociologists in "How Farm People Accept New Ideas"[29] classified people according to the time sequence in which they adopt new practices. *Innovators are the first to adopt the new.* These are independent thinkers with a wide range of contacts. Just as the parts of the world that are most fertile in ideas are those on the borderline between two civilizations, so the marginal man, with one foot in the normal world and one foot in a deviant minority, often becomes an innovator; the tension produced by interacting in opposite worlds can furnish the needed spark that introduces change. But an innovator is seldom an opinion leader.

The time sequence in the adoption of new practices is: innovator; community leader; opinion leader; the majority.

Applying this terminology and time sequence to fashion communication, it follows that once a fashion is presented by the innovator it is essentially a new idea ready to be rejected or accepted. The early adopters or community fashion leaders (perhaps a Jacqueline Kennedy or a Duchess of Windsor) react first to the new fashion. They then add their own interpretation to the fashion symbol and send the message on. The next to react are the local opinion leaders who discuss it and bring in the informal groups of later adopters, the majority. It is in this last step, where small informal groups communicate on the same level, that the fashion decisions of consumers are made.

Today, the well-off middle-class customer—the coed, the secretary, the suburban wife—is in a position to assume fashion leadership. Fast newspaper and television coverage brings the new style story in days instead of the months previously necessary. Fashion photos taken in 1964 in every section of the country showed young women wearing the same styles no matter where they happened to live.

THE FASHION BANDWAGON. *Volume* and *distribution* are the keys to fashion trends today. To the consumer, the style most promoted and most accepted is the general fashion trend. Trends result from use, exposure, and acceptance. As a result, the big distributors like Sears, Wards, and Penney's are fast becoming fashion leaders because they promote the newest things in the greatest quantity. As these companies begin to operate in Latin America, Spain, the Common Market countries, and the Far East, the American fashion bandwagon starts to tour the globe.

When a representative from Sears, Roebuck and Company, the undisputed champion for years in general merchandise retailing, attended the 1956 fashion showing in Paris, the act revealed that the American consumer was demanding better quality and more fashion styling.

This "upgrading" of taste to include more fashion, better quality, and more unusual items can be attributed to (1) a rising real income which allows more money for clothing, (2) increased education, insofar as it increases earning power and awakens new demands, (3) propaganda from the tastemakers, and (4) the American belief in self-improvement and progress.

To meet this demand, there are now better quality goods available at no greater cost. Since the mid-1950's competition has been heightened by Japanese imports that meet specified standards of quality, and yet, undersell American clothing. Italian sportswear has given us at a reasonable price the beauty of hand knitting, hand weaving, and hand embroidery—something impossible to attain under our own system. In addition, new types of retail outlets, such as discount houses where the expense and profit margins are at much lower levels than in the traditional retail store, may feature better values at lower prices. All together, these sources have increased the volume of fashion goods on the market.

The bigger the volume involved, the more retailers look to fashion to help move merchandise. They put more emphasis on the newest item because they deliberately want to date merchandise.

The Tempo of Fashion Change. The tempo of fashion change is dependent on such factors as the age of the population, the social climate of opinion, and income levels. Change in fashion, however, is most influenced by *saturation*. When the majority of people in the market promote the same fashions, the saturation point is quickly reached and the public is soon ready for new styles and colors. As Dior has said, "The most successful fashion wears itself out the quickest because it is only imitated more."[30]

Simmel explained that the more an article is subject to rapid changes of fashion, the greater the demand for *cheap* products of its kind. This is not only because the larger and therefore poorer classes have enough purchasing power to regulate industry by their demand, but also because the higher classes cannot afford to adopt the rapid change forced upon them by the imitation of lower classes.[31]

To some extent this phenomenon has occurred in the United States, so that some women of high social position patronize the same levels of ready-to-wear used by financially secure secretaries, teachers, and middle-class wives. However, in the more expensive fashion merchandise, the emphasis increasingly is on high quality, inconspicuous but intricate cut, and individual fit—impossible goals to achieve without the expense of skilled labor and time.

There seem to be two fashion currents running parallel to each other: one elevated on a high price line, and one on a lower level. Each level receives the same fashion news at the same time, but interprets it in a different way. The quickly noted style changes and the more striking colors flood the popular-priced merchandise. The more subtle designs, made from quality fabrics in an unchanging group of neutral hues (with an occasional odd color for spice) and accompanied by an expert fitter, belong to the highest fashion realm.

The short life of the radical "sack" chemise in 1957 to 1958 highlights the dilemma of fast fashion merchandising. This new loose look burst upon the fashion scene in the Paris showing of August, 1957. While expensive clientele hesitated, the coeds and secretaries took over and became avant-garde. The chemise exploded upward in young and inexpensive clothes. It was easily made and easily copied. By May, 1958, it was at its height, reaching a turning point in group acceptance. By June it was out of style.

While the high fashion designers were modifying and slightly fitting their designs, and before their more conservative and often older clientele had time to adjust, the style was killed by the market saturation of the cheap versions in stiff cotton. Women wore them too long, they were poorly fitted, and men did not like them. The style was dropped by the influential designers, partly because snobbery in the high-priced lines prevented copying the low, and partly because the market saturation came for one group before the rest had time to get used to the idea.

Later, the semifitted chemise returned to enjoy a normal fashion run of several years. In a normal fashion cycle a style is perfected and adjusted to suit both high fashion and the mass market, and given time to become established. It is accepted through evolution, not revolution.

The principal goal of the retailer in the mid-1960's is to react more quickly to his customer's demands. He turns to motivational research to help him decide what the consumer *really* wants to buy, for the retailer cannot depend entirely on what the consumer says he wants. It is up to the retailer to study how his customers live and what they think, so that he can react faster to their new requirements.

With the advent of electronic computers, top management relies less on hunches, instincts, or a mere willingness to take a risk, and more on the up-to-date data processed by computers.

Television has speeded the fashion cycle by adding visual saturation. Furthermore, the new rapidity of transportation and the tremendous cargo traffic on airlines has meant that no area is now outside the market. The speed of the jet age allows a vastly expanded world market, for soon no nation will be more than a few hours away from another.

However, *Women's Wear Daily* warns that this rapid communication and transportation may not always favor the American fashion industry. On October 21, 1964, the newspaper noted that sportswear, once considered "strictly American," now has an international tang. From Paris to London to New York the snappy young look has been switched on. Designers, manufacturers, and buyers are combing the European scene. The feverish pace of adapting and copying, old news to Seventh Avenue, has now hit the moderate price and junior sportswear markets. And *Women's Wear Daily* concludes: *"The international exchange of fashion is healthy*

. . . but why is young American sportswear losing its identity?"

A competitive market will speed change; and contrary to those who reminisce about "the good old days" (when the country store had a real monopoly) competition is growing. Direct competition from abroad and new types of business organizations at home, such as self-service soft-goods supermarkets, discount houses, mail-order catalogs containing "quality" items of unusual distinction, continually challenge old-line firms.

Moreover, new substitutes for old favorites come out of the research laboratories to vie for the consumer's attention— stretch denim slacks versus blue jeans; a stream of synthetic fibers challenge cotton and wool. New articles appear to compete for the consumer dollar: a small foreign car in place of a mink coat; a tape recorder instead of a radio. Durable goods compete with nondurables.

Although outsiders feel America has a fast tempo of life, there were periods in the historical courts of Europe which underwent more rapid changes than we have ever experienced. One of America's main fashion contributions has been in increasing the size of the fashion movement—introducing *widespread fashion change* at a comparatively rapid rate.

As incomes grow, the consumer at every income level is able to own more things. But, unless the new is more attractive, there is no reason to discard the old. Thus, while the device of fashion may tempt the producer to present a new fashion of poor quality which can make an old style, however good, seem obsolete, he knows he must deal with an increasingly better-informed consumer who wants both quality and fashion.

Challenges Facing Fashion Promotion

Fashion promotion plays many roles. In one sense it is a form of mass communication, a propaganda campaign, useful in effecting change over a wide territory. It makes fashion-conscious people aware of new design ideas and provides general information that leads to style identification. It plays an important part in creating the awareness and interest that precede the adoption of fashion change.

At the same time fashion promotion coordinates the related areas within the fashion industry so they "change together," and builds a like-mindedness among consumers, allowing mass demand to support mass production with its resulting efficiencies of scale.

From the market viewpoint, promotion is a tool used to differentiate one product from another, one store from another —to build separate markets through brand loyalty and lessen price competition.

But, from the consumer viewpoint, there is still another and broader sense in which fashion promotion is visualized. In this role, promotion is seen not as a campaign, or a tool, but rather as a necessary channel of communication linking the producer and the consumer so the consumer gets what he wants. Messages must go in *both* directions if successful communication is to result. Ideally, the consumer would like to say to the producer: This is what I want. The producer would reply: Here is the product you demanded, is it satisfactory? The consumer would answer back. . . . As in any communication, the difficulty is in "sharing" or "making common" an idea, experience, or piece of information between the sender and the receiver.

A communication is successful when it arouses the intended response. For semantic specialists, the question becomes: Is the picture in the head of the receiver the same as the picture in the head of the sender? The answer is determined by studying "feedback"—the words, gestures, and reactions of others.

Perhaps a critical analysis of the networks used in the fashion communication systems between levels of the industry and between industry and the consumer can suggest the difficulties each presents and point up the weak links in the communication systems.

VERTICAL FORMAL NETWORKS. These are the communication networks that link designers, producers, retailers, and consumers and act as a funnel narrowing consumer choice. Vertical networks of fashion communication are between people on levels not in actual contact and are rather formal in character. The communication flows through a set pattern of relay stations between sender and receiver that are linked by an intermediary system of buyers and sellers. Communication tends to become impersonal and much of the meaning is inferred. The sender and ultimate receiver seldom meet.

For example: The customer in the store buys from the saleswoman who can offer only what the retail buyer of her department or a central buying office has selected. The retail buyer, in turn, may be responsible to the merchandise manager who is trying to promote the general policy of the store. If the customer decided to send a message to the creative designer it would have to go through a vast chain of buyers and sellers before it finally reached its intended destination. It is doubtful that the message would even survive such a journey. That is why sales, indirect messages, are interpreted by producers and distributors as communication feedback: A sale is said to mean that the consumer understands and approves of the product presented. But this is only an assumed meaning, seldom verified by direct communication.

Listed below are some of the factors contributing to the difficulties in transmitting an "intended meaning" along the formal communication networks of the marketing system.

1. Long lines of communication with many links of senders and receivers tend to develop inaccuracies. Each additional link presents the possibility of compounded distortion.
2. Indirect or inferred communications (such as sales) permit false interpretations and lack the swift correcting feedback found in face-to-face communication.
3. The time lapse between the sending of the message (a consumer response to a fashion symbol) over long, indirect lines to the producer and his reply in the way of a product permits an altered climate of opinion on the part of the consumer. New cultural influences may have caused him to change his mind.
4. And finally, human behavior is hard to predict. In all communication there are problems of bias (one person affects another in unpredictable ways), ambiguity (few people have the same meaning for the same words), and forgetfulness.

This presents a partial picture of the difficulties encountered in fashion communication. A total picture must include those weaknesses inherent in a mass media promotion system.

MASS NETWORKS OF FASHION PROPAGANDA. In general, critics of the mass media used in the promotion of fashion and other consumer goods list these weak spots:

1. By its very nature it "gives out" more than it "gets back" in feedback. This one-way communication tends to build an audience unaccustomed to responding. Thus, the media cannot check on whether the message was received in the manner intended.
2. Too many signals coming in tend to confuse consumers who do not have the time or knowledge to discriminate between them.
3. The swiftness of mass communication can cause a time lag in one sense: The consumer demand is built long before the product is produced. (Production takes longer than communication.)
4. On the other hand, inadequate mass communication can help foster the traditional cultural lag, where the non-material culture is unable to keep pace with the material culture. For example, much is known about the physical characteristics of atomic energy and electronic ovens, but little is known about what to do with them.
5. The mass media can present a biased view of the world. Thus fashion promotion propaganda might not give a true picture of reality but may fictionalize the picture, thereby establishing false or misleading communication.

The presence of these weak spots in the fashion communication systems suggests that the producers and distributors in the ready-to-wear industry face the danger of lagging behind consumer demands in fashion styling. By concentrating on feedback (sales) from the late adopters (the majority) the producers and distributors get a picture of past fashion, not of the current or incoming fashion. Removing direct communication links with the customer, such as retail salespeople and local retail-store buyers, in favor of self-service stores and centralized buying offices, further eliminates the chance of correcting faulty generalizations about consumer wants by face-to-face communication. In addition, the nature of promotion through the mass media, as well as the tremendous volume of goods produced, tends to impose an artificial similarity upon all fashion styling, denying the personalized element so necessary to self-identify in dress. This results in an increased spread of fashion, but also in a uniform type of dress that seems to contradict one of the major functions of our economic system: increased consumer choice to permit greater satisfaction of individual needs.

8

A UNIFORM PACKAGE

The fashion industry, like other large modern industries, is characterized by growth and increasing mechanization. As technical innovation proves profitable in an industry which in the past was dominated by "factories" with two or three sewing machines, more machinery is installed and the trend toward bigness accelerates. At the same time, the personalized nature of the product—fashions to suit individual tastes which change in unpredictable and independent ways—calls for small-scale production. For example, consider the difficulties that may be encountered when one large firm tries to fill the shifting needs of youth groups for designs that today are flat-chested at the top and hippy below, and tomorrow are slim tubes, while also satisfying the continuing needs of thousands of women for strictly tailored suits. To satisfy this dual need for quantity production and diversified styling, the fashion market continues to operate through thousands of small producers who share the market with relatively few larger concerns. The collective output of all firms gives the quantity desired, while the individual nature of each firm produces variety in style. Every year, it is true, many small companies close down and others merge with or sell out to stronger companies, but as yet there is no "General Motors" of the fashion field, and the industry remains fiercely competitive.

This paradoxical situation (the incompatibility between large-scale production which is subject to the economic demands of efficiency and the nature of fashion which is responsive to the social dynamics of taste) results in economic compromises. A new fashion is not necessarily a "better product" in the economic sense that more output can be supplied with

227

less input of labor and other resources. For example, it took new and costly machinery to produce pointed-toed shoes in the shoe industry when all machinery then in use had been designed for shoe lasts with rounded toes. However, this did not prevent pointed-toed shoes from becoming a popular style. While new fashion products, such as machine-molded plastic dresses, may be accompanied by production utility, they are not determined by it. In fact, economist Dwight Robinson flatly states that all changes in design which are not purely the result of engineering advance can be summed up as fashion.[1] Some analysts believe changes are made because of social or aesthetic needs and not because they are "better" in the sense of economic efficiency. This differentiates those changes which constitute "fashion" from those which constitute "progress." It reemphasizes the difficulty that arises in applying the economic efficiency of large-scale production to a product which is by nature not economically oriented.

Consequently, unlike the fashion designer who is concerned with social and aesthetic change, the mass producer of fashion goods must be concerned with economic change. He makes the costs of producing goods conform to a selling price consumers are willing to pay. This involves keeping the price at such a level that the supply of labor is consistent with the demand for particular goods.

By increasing mechanization, organizing piece-work construction, and systematizing periods of fashion change, producers have lowered the price of fashion goods and made more fashions available to more people. But the adaptation of the imaginative and spontaneous element of fashion to the mechanized and efficient system of mass production has resulted in a more homogenized fashion. Each proposed fashion idea is modified: Some features are dropped, and often, only the minimum fashion characteristics are retained to mark this idea as today's style. Thus, because many styles may possess the same fashion characteristics—if only a uniform skirt length —they seem alike. This modification partially explains why imaginative fashion designers with a highly developed sense of cultural change may be unable to recognize their original dress ideas in the mass-produced garments they see hanging in retail stores. It is possible in smaller companies, however, where timing and the right style for specific group preferences take precedence over the considerations of large-scale efficiency, for more personalized styles to be produced.

Consumer Demand

Consumer demand in fashion goods is reflected in the sales performance of retail outlets such as department stores, discount stores, women's ready-to-wear specialty shops, and mail-order houses. There, distributors act as communication links between producers and consumers, coordinating supply with demand.

As might be expected, demand for garments is strengthened in periods of economic recovery. But, while aggregate expenditures for clothing rise as a result of increases in population and clothing prices, the per cent of disposable income spent on clothing tends to decline as disposable personal income increases. Clothing expenditures fell from 13 per cent of total income in 1929 to 8 per cent in 1961, measured in constant dollars. A special analysis by the Department of Commerce showed that the long-run decline was due to factors other than real income alone, including increased competition of other attractive goods and services such as houses and travel; the changing composition of the population toward a larger group of aged; the greater utility of modern fibers; a post-World War II demand for casual modes of dress which increased the sales of blouses and sportswear; and price changes in clothing in relation to other goods. (The price index for apparel rose only 1 per cent in 1961 and 3 per cent in the previous ten years (1951–1961), while the Consumer Price Index for all items rose 1.4 per cent in the same year and 15 per cent in the previous 10 years.)[2]

The composition of the population is an important factor in determining aggregate demand. In the future, as the proportion of young, fashion-conscious adults in the population rises there will be an increased per capita expenditure for clothing. On the other hand, an increase in those age groups that spend the least on clothing—people over 65 years of age and those under 15 years of age—can partially offset or reverse the trend.

As demand for fashion grows, the industry grows. In

return, increased availability of fashion goods stimulates increased demand by outmoding yesterday's garment and by arousing latent consumer wants. Through a circular movement, the fashion industry becomes self-generating, especially in a society such as ours where an abundance of goods allows more emphasis on consumption and promotion.

Newspaper and magazine advertising, radio, and television tend to build nationwide shared tastes that permit a mass demand. Fashion communication is so quick that all people can have just about the same thing at the same time. With women dressing so much alike, the traveler going from one city to another has to ask, "What city am I in?" Author Upton Sinclair as early as 1926 described this fashion phenomenon in his novel *Oil*: "This was the U.S. and the things on sale were the things known as 'nationally advertised products.' The ranchman drove to town in a nationally advertised auto, pressing the accelerator with a nationally advertised shoe; in front of the drug-store he found a display of nationally advertised magazines, containing all the nationally advertised advertisements of the nationally advertised articles he would take back to the ranch."[3]

The tendency of modern promotion methods to reenforce majority tastes makes it difficult to introduce new products or new ideas that do not already have group support. But where sufficient demand exists, most fashion items can be made available to large numbers of people.

Mink is an illustration of an "Everybody Can Have It" venture. Where once a mink coat or stole stood out as the item of apparel which set the owner apart from all others, this is no longer true. Although still a treasured item, mink today is comparable to a string of pearls; every woman who boasts any claim to smartness owns some form of mink, little or big, or she has switched to some "more individual" (because less commonly used) fur.

The fantastic growth of the mink industry is vividly illustrated by the increase in production of domestic skins from nearly 2 million in 1950 to 5 million in 1958, more than doubling in 8 years.[4]

Sharply increased production, along with the development of many new colors in mink, created problems for independent dealers and brokers. They lacked *time* to mark mink catalogs adequately and *money* and *manpower* to operate in both national and international markets. As a result there was a movement toward joint-venture operations, consolidation between two or three firms. The resulting efficiency made mink "the great leveler."

Conformity or Choice?

Demand for fashion will continue as long as social conditions mean there is a need for fashion. A study of fashion as a social need and an economic good poses questions about the quality of American life. Is there too much conformity? Are we packaged people?

When Christian Dior visited America in the 1950's he commented: "Their clothes, hair, nails and shoes are all impeccable. This is true of all classes of society from the millionaire down to the elevator operator . . . but I must at the same time admit that in the end there was something uniform about it."[5] This mild criticism has little of the vitriolic quality unleashed by an American designer against her fellow Americans. Elizabeth Hawes flicked her mental whip, decrying the way women seek solutions to their dressing problems through prescribed patterns, ". . . start looking at current fashion through your own eyes rather than at second hand, through the eyes of some fashion reporter, style commentator, or what-the-well-dressed-man-will-wear adviser."[6]

How does the fashion consumer make her choice? Does she select goods as an autonomous rational person, weighing all possible alternative choices and choosing that which will give her the most satisfaction for the least time, labor, and money spent? Or, is she a puppet pulled this way and that by advertising and emotional appeals, impulsively selecting goods in an uninformed way? It appears that a fashion choice will be partly rational and partly irrational. Since fashion desires are dependent on emulative social habits, they cannot always be formulated in a rational manner. The fulfillment of fashion needs must rely, to some degree, on social sensitivity and emotional response rather than mental calculation. In this sense, fashion selection will be irrational. But, as the functions of fashion are more clearly understood and tastes are broadened, the fashion consumer becomes increasingly sophisticated and knowledgeable—her choice is more rational. She may become so generally well informed that she needs only to be told each season what is new, just as she might catch up on any current events she has missed.

Consumers do not operate in herd fashion. Actually a "demand" may represent hundreds of millions of individual decisions. However, since man as a social being tends to select fashions for self-identification in a defined social position, consumer choices can be analyzed and classed by characteristics that represent some group within the society. The most obvious groupings are by sex and age, as we have seen. These broad categories can, then, be further subdivided into various smaller groups with recognizable social differences.

The degree to which one individual's decision will conform to a group depends on several factors: (1) the degree of sentiment or loyalty he feels toward a group; (2) the group attitude toward nonconformists; (3) his feeling of need to belong to a group (a nonconformist may feel he will not lose anything by not belonging); (4) the degree of confidence in his own opinion; (5) his position in the group (a newcomer may be more conformable than a person who holds a well-established position).

The high fashion designer utters the word "conformity" with vexation; the mass fashion producer caresses the word with affection, for he is dependent on a mass market where everyone is more or less like everyone else. High fashion— imaginative individual design—must be *first* and must be *different* to maintain status and glamour for the few women of recognized taste and authority who comprise the high fashion market. But paradoxically, a high fashion house gains status only if its designs are widely copied at a popular price; therefore, the couturier must also offer a look with "something uniform about it" to tempt the mass market which wants its fashions "familiar, but new looking." Here is reenacted in the market the ideological struggle between two cultural myths,* equality and freedom.

---

* A "myth" comes from the life of the people and has transcending, overall character. It is not literally true; it is composed of created characters. The purpose becomes to direct the ends of man and define these ends.

Man's status is assured by certain rights—Life, Liberty, and the Pursuit of Happiness. The attempt to define and implement these rights reveals a conflict between the principle of liberty or freedom and the principle of equality. If everyone is free to become whatever he is capable of becoming, that is, to pursue his own individual advantage, the result is great inequality among individuals. In this sense equality and freedom are irreconcilable. In another sense, they have a commonness. Freedom has an infinite quality; there is no end to what man might achieve in various ways; therefore, no goal to know when he has reached it. Equality also suggests, as Tocqueville said, the "indefinite perfectibility of men"; all can be free to reach an indeterminant level of human perfectibility.

Committed to both freedom and equality, American society attempts to maintain a balance between the two. Freedom is equated with control by a diffuse cultural structure rather than by a definite social organization. There is a difference between "wearing the same dress" or "eating the same foods" as the result of the impersonal process of competition than if we did so by government regulation or police order. A prevalence of equalitarian symbols and behavior patterns helps alleviate inequalities of condition; fashion available at any price has played a strong role in achieving a democracy of clothes in a democratic country.

Styles not only fail to distinguish rural and urban Americans as clearly as they once did,[7] they also cease to differentiate classes and other social segments as sharply as they do in other parts of the world. Therefore, it is not the dress per se, but rather the rate of acceptance of new fashion styles that is the significant factor in determining social role. The difference in appearance between the woman who spends thousands of dollars each year on clothes and the one who spends only a small fraction of that figure is by no means as conspicuous as the difference between the woman who is in fashion and the one who is out of fashion, or as the difference between the woman who has good taste and the woman who lacks it.

In the consumer's world of mass production, social critic E. Vanden Haag believes that "a mass-produced article, while reflecting nearly everybody's taste to some extent, is unlikely to embody anybody's taste fully. This is one source of the sense of violation which is rationalized vaguely in theories about deliberate debasement of taste."[8] The industrial system penalizes individual taste. Either your life is styled in conformity with mass tastes or undergoes a series of deprivations: material, if you cling to your taste and forego some purchases to pay for it; psychological, if you do not. Under these types of market conditions individual tastes tend to develop flexibility, the same ability to compromise that is needed in a democratic society with a fluid class structure.

Moving up in a mobile class society, with more dollars to spend, causes constant readjustments of individuals to the requirements of the next income level. As people move from one position to another in a society which has a certain fluidity and vagueness in social relations, they transfer some social habits from the old position to the new. This causes a constant changing of the social climate and, as a result, all strata seem to live and dress similarly.

This has disturbed many Americans who fear increasing similarity is a threat to individuality. While for some, conformity may be disturbing, to others it is benevolent. For example, a woman in a high-style wool coat may be a filing clerk or she may be a wealthy socialite. Thus, what appears to be uniformity among all classes may also be considered in another sense as wider choice for those from certain particular classes.

It is clear that shopping in a modern industrial system brings a uniform standard to some people and a variety of choice to others. Two shoppers of different backgrounds, approaching the same dress market, provide an illustration. One has wide contacts outside her local area: she knows the fine skill of the Chinese tailor; the fluid cut of the French couturier; the gay imagery of the Austrian peasant. To her, the American market seems full of classic styles and standard fit, extremely limited in choice.

The second shopper approaches the same market. She lives mainly within her neighborhood with few outside contacts. The market seems to bring the world to her—oriental gowns from Hong Kong, ready-to-wear from Paris, jewelry from Mexico. In addition, she sees the comfortable American classics that she likes. To her, the market is full of choice, a place of infinite diversity.

No two people see the market alike. Fashion selection is an involved matter of individual social tastes, changing in unpredictable ways, operating within the more stable framework of a mass economy. Increased freedom of choice in consumption for greater numbers of people may involve curtailing freedom of self-expression for others. It is impossible to have all freedoms for all people at one time; in any society there is a choice between conflicting freedoms. The problem is: How much freedom for each can be exercised without restricting the freedom of others? It appears that a variety of standards and values are necessary if the market is to supply the goods needed for satisfying consumption, especially in a society where fashion goods have become a significant symbol in the human socialization process.

FASHION: *A REFLECTION OF AMERICAN LIFE*

9

SYMBOLISM OF FASHION

Symbolic meanings inherent in the form of fashion, or fashion as a commodity, transform items of apparel into symbols of personal attributes and goals, social patterns and strivings. Each item is assessed and, then, selected. When the symbol "fits," it reinforces the way a person thinks about himself, becoming a message that is transmitted and received, both to his inner consciousness and to the outer world. Fashions symbolize sex, age, social position, and any given complex of acts, gestures, movements, and intentions.

At the turn of the century, the symbolic meaning of imported fashions was pronounced. Very rich American socialites built great mansions and furnished them with foreign goods, giving themselves a feeling of identification with the aristocracy of Europe. Similarly, today, the up-and-coming South Asians and Africans demand foreign goods, particularly the English bicycle, the Swiss watch, and the American fountain pen. Such items give these emerging peoples a feeling of belonging to the modern world where transportation is mechanized, time is significant because man and machines run on time, and people can read and write. It matters little that many who buy pens cannot write or those who wear watches do not tell time; the symbolic value is the important thing.[1]

Symbols

Man is a symbol-using animal. Language, gestures, and dress are examples of primary symbols with which he operates. A symbol is anything, the value or meaning of which

239

is bestowed upon it by those who use it.[2] For instance, the color "white" symbolizes death to the Chinese, who traditionally use white for funerals, while to Americans the color "black" has the same interpretation.

The meaning of symbols is always variable, and those who receive a message may interpret the symbols differently from the way the sender anticipates. Because meaning is not intrinsic in the physical form of an object but becomes identified with the object through use, the meaning of a symbol can be changed as new values are bestowed or discovered in the object. That symbols do not mean the same thing to all people at all times was illustrated during the 1960's when young intellectuals adopted long stringy hair, sloppy dress, and uncouth language to signify rebellion against the established order and to assert their right to a place in the world. To observers, these fashions seemed to symbolize sloppy thinking, moral decay, and national deterioration.

Appearance can be as important as conversation in maintaining relationships between people. Dress is a nonverbal sign which helps to set the conditions for social interaction.* We have seen how fashion functions for the group: to develop solidarity and speed communication by making the same symbols common to all members of the group. It is also used to spot outsiders—those who do not belong.

The newcomer who wishes to join a group searches for cues that symbolize its members. College freshmen scan the attire of upper classmen: Do they go barefooted? Barelegged? Do they wear sandals, loafers, short boots, knee boots, or hip boots? Ankle socks, knee socks, long stockings, tights? It takes observation and know-how to catch all the nuances of fashion symbols. However, the outward symbols of a group are more easily seen and obtained than the behavior patterns of the group, explaining the frequent discussion of consumption items among people in a mobile class society. As they adjust

---

* The degree to which clothing, *without* the fashion element, was used as a guide in social situations was analyzed by Mary Lou Rosencranz, a home economist specializing in sociology. She reported that women related clothing most often to (1) age, (2) occupation, (3) sex, (4) being well dressed, (5) occasion. Other themes included criticism, clothing of another culture, and economic status. (This study reveals nothing about the social use of "fashion" or "quality" in clothing, only about clothing where neither component was present.)[3]

their taste to changing styles, they are learning the current symbols for social interaction.

Sociologists use the term "symbol"; fashion writers use the term "style." Frequently the terms are interchangeable. When we speak of individual styles, group styles, and national styles, or of significant symbols that are used to identify individuals, groups, or nations, we are saying the same thing in two different ways. Every style is symbolic in reference.

Style

Clothes become associated with various objects and tend to be considered characteristic of the object to which they are linked. There is a "winter" coat as contrasted to a "fall" or "spring" coat; since it is characteristic of the season, it is referred to as a winter or spring style. When a customer asks for a "casual" suit, rather than a "dressy" one, she has in mind an occasion with which she associates certain types of suits. If she wants a "feminine" style or a "tailored" style, she is referring to an effect created by construction techniques. A "smartly" dressed woman gives a different impression than a "Bohemian" type. Each style has a distinguishing name which brings to mind a stereotyped picture associated with a particular set of circumstances.

To become characteristic of something implies both recognition and acceptance. If a dress design is accepted by only one person but reflects the wearer's personality and becomes recognized by others as symbolic of this person, it becomes an individual style.

INDIVIDUAL STYLE. The consumer, trying to symbolize a unique self in today's world of mass-produced clothing finds that she achieves style through *putting elements together*. A "whole picture" of the individual is formed by combining separate items of clothing in a way that relates the parts to each other and to the physical person, personality, and the life of the wearer. Each person who adopts a fashion interprets the meaning in her own way and sends the message on in altered form. Fashion has a way of so identifying with the wearer that it appears to be an integral part of the personality. It is a symbol to which others react in much the same way they react to words and gestures.

In the past, some people have portrayed themselves so successfully that their image has lasted through time. Queen Mary of England favored a particular hat design which has come to identify and symbolize her. Madame Pompadour's name was attached to a type of hair styling widely accepted and worn by women in later versions long after she was dead. In more recent times, Jacqueline Kennedy was associated with a youthful, simple way of dressing that was widely copied.

How much influence do particular individuals exercise in molding the basic dress styles of a society? The answer to this question appears to be: very little. Judgments of what is desirable vary both from society to society and through time. There is general agreement that it is the cultural factors in a society, not specific individuals, that affect style changes. The "felt" need for a change is present before the material form is adopted. However, some particular person, with whom the masses can identify, may seem to truly symbolize the spirit of the times and becomes, for a while, a desired ideal—a model for others to follow.

The wearer of clothes sees style in one way, the originator in another. A dress designer tends, like most creative artists, to develop his own style. Each year top designers conceive new ideas for dresses and when one of these satisfies him, he may execute many designs with common basic features. In this way he develops a style, chosen by himself, as representative of his work to present to consumers. This style becomes identified with its creator, much as any unique style of art becomes associated with its artist. In 1952 Dior presented to the public his new "A" silhouette, so named because the sloping shoulders and very full skirt formed a silhouette similar to the letter "A." Characteristic styles such as these are created where no "wearer" selection has been made but rather where there has been a self-selection of basic design features by the designer. This is why we say designers sell their own translation of the spirit of the times: an individual style. But manufacturers and retailers sell a collective representation of consumers' wants: a public style.

PUBLIC STYLE. Fashion is *public taste*, the result of many individual tastes simultaneously but separately selecting the same thing. Designers sell their interpretation of the style of the era: an individual style. Manufacturers and department stores sell fashion: a public style. It follows that fashion depends on public opinion and becomes a form of the dominance of the group over the individual.

Fixing the attention of the community at a given place and time, fashion seems to embody what is called the spirit of the age. It reflects the culture as no other symbol does. Each style seems completely appropriate to its epoch.

Fiction writers know that it is possible to grasp the essence of an era by describing the clothing of the times. Consider Al Joad in the *Grapes of Wrath:* "His stiff jeans, with the bottoms turned up 8 inches to show his heeled boots, his 3 inch belt with copper figures on it, the red arm bands on his blue shirt and the rakish angle of his Stetson hat. . . ."[4] This is a description of a cocky youth in rural Oklahoma of the 1930's. Now, see Natty Bumppo (Leatherstocking), in *The Pioneers:* ". . . he wore a cap made of fox skin . . . coat of dressed deerskin with the hair on, belted close to his lank body by a girdle of colored worsted. On his feet—deerskin moccasins, ornamented with porcupine quills; [his] limbs guarded with long leggings of the same."[5] While both characters represent the Western Frontier, neither character could change places with the other for each symbolizes a distinctly different phase in American development.

Fashion is time crystallized. It is because fashion mirrors so well the *immediate present* it can best recreate the past. Who knows better the place of fashion in history than Cecil Beaton, the designer of the romantic Edwardian fashions of *My Fair Lady.* He, along with Marcel Proust and Henry James, knows "how much the fleeting expression of fashion or fancy can reflect something beyond its limited time, something haunting that whispers of the nostalgia of human impermanence. . . ."[6]

With the words of Henry James we can step back into 1878 and watch Daisy Miller, a pretty American girl in Europe: "She was dressed in white muslin, with a hundred frills and flounces, and knots of pale colored ribbon. She was bareheaded; but she balanced in her hand a large parasol with a deep border of embroidery; and she was strikingly, admirably pretty."[7] This description is obviously the "desired" American fashion of that time—a national style of the era.

NATIONAL STYLE. Fashion is international in its scope, but national in its emphasis and concentration. Although the haute couture in Paris is the main fashion idea laboratory of the world, each nation accepts or adapts only those ideas which fit its own values and beliefs. Each retains a national style, symbolic of the nation's life.

America's greatest fashion export, in a sense, is the American woman from age 16 to 50. She is known the world over for her pertness, her spirit, her looks, the contours of her figure, the smartness of her clothes, and the vitality of her person. In colorful casual clothes she is a symbol of American life—its national style.

Style as it is used here does not mean a particular cut, color, or line, and not a precise shape, but rather a look or spirit. The dress style of a nation is part of that unspoken language which reflects the nation's inner core of beliefs; it is a collective representation of social identity—a national symbol. A national style is not static. The social phenomenon of fashion permits ever-changing forms to suit the changing values of the people.

In 1965 visitors to Russia noticed that Russian families wore a lot of fur in the winter. They saw a great deal of style variety among the fur coats and hats worn by women and children, an apparent paradox in a land where there is much sameness in consumer commodities. Each Russian man, woman, and child seemed to have a beautiful fur hat, and no two looked alike. While Russian-made suits, dresses, and shoes were criticized by the Russians themselves, Russian-made coats and hats were pridefully worn and quite admired by Westerners.

Where a national style is well developed and has some desired symbolic reference in other countries, it may be adopted as an international fashion. The political prominence of Russia and the superior status element attached to fur in the Western world combined to bring a strong Soviet influence into Western fashions in the late 1950's and early 1960's. The year 1957 seemed to mark the awakening of a pronounced fashion interest in Russia. By 1958 *L'Officiel,* the French high fashion magazine of the haute couture, showed two types of hats with a definite Soviet flavor. By 1959 *Vogue* and *L'Officiel* contained fashions with bold and obvious Russian characteristics, and by 1962 the Russian influence had swept through the mass fashion areas in hats, boots, and fur-trimmed coats. On the other hand, the Russians began adopting bright colors for their coat fashions.[8] Color in coats, something the U.S.S.R. had just discovered, has been characteristic of American fashions for decades.

Through the international character of fashion, any national style can affect the current image of fashion—not only in dress, but in such dimensions as "the personal characteristics" considered to be currently desirable in people. American society, for example, brought new qualities for women into fashion by translating into sportswear and short skirts the freedom and equality that characterize this nation.

Styles that emerge from a complex society have a wide range of meanings and associations for various members of the society. An analysis of a national style must focus on many aspects of everyday life. There is little doubt that an American style exists; it is talked about, advertised, catered to, and copied—but not always understood. Part III will examine the ways in which popular styles in dress reflect life in America. Various fashion traits will be traced to their origins in our culture—as they are conditioned through time and space and as they emerge an integral part of the American style of dress. Although each trait is treated separately for purposes of exposition, all are present in varying degrees at any time. Changing circumstances simply serve to emphasize one element more than another in various eras.

10

A STREAK OF CONSERVATISM

Stability in a society is clearly as important as change.

One of the functions of fashion for the nation is to maintain the social order while permitting progress and evolution. It is significant, therefore, that a streak of conservatism runs through the American character. These people whose women "walk with head held high on high sliver heels—a head taller than most, a hand smaller around";[1] whose cities rise with self-confidence into a thousand upward-pointing obelisks; who hurtle and roar in shining cars on endless million dollar superhighways—through these people runs a streak of conservatism.

The first Parisian couturier to come to America was Paul Poiret, who gave a series of lectures in the early 1900's. Suavely apologizing for any small smarts he might cause the ladies of his audience, he took them to task in this way: "It is as a creator that I wish to speak to you today, and I come to complain to you of the difficulty one has in interesting you in what is new. I have never met women more faithful than the Americans. That is not a fault, it is on the contrary a virtue, and rare enough, but when it concerns Fashion, this fidelity becomes routine, and routine is detestable. Fashion insists on change, and all creators complain of having to drag after their feet the fetters represented by the vast American mass."[2]

Paul Poiret had caught a glimpse of the conservative streak in the core of the American people. He knew that it was there beneath the trim and fashionable dress of the confident American woman. Yes, she likes change; yes, she believes change is progress; but, she is only happy to participate in change if in the process she rediscovers some of her old traditional patterns.

A probe among popular tastes for this traditional pattern in dress reveals the persistence of dress styles that are "simple" and "not too"—not too extreme; not too tight; not too dressy; not too young; not too anything. Adjusting to these demands, so easy to state but so hard to meet, the designer arrives at the desired pattern. Simplicity is that which remains when all the "not too's" of popular taste are satisfied.

In the philosophical sense, conservatism means a love of authority and tradition. Fear, habit, and education, insofar as they build respect for tradition and authority, tend to fortify and increase the hold of conservative attitudes, rationalizing them and giving them ideological content. But what kind of fear leads to conservatism? The answer is: fear of public opinion. What habit? The habit of conditioned response. What education? Mass education. Seen in this way conservatism can be considered nonthinking and reactionary. It, too, could be expressed as "not too," an unconsciously negative approach.

There is also an intelligent and positive approach to conservatism. To be conservative means to lay hold of, and make part of one's life, things worth conserving, and this includes things in the current milieu no less than things which are dated. In this sense conservatism immediately implies discrimination, and a basis of judgment. Standards are necessary to decide what to keep and what to throw away. These standards come from a conscious value-pattern, allowing a person to *discriminate between various aspects of the same thing, program, or custom.* For one purpose, or in comparison with one alternative, a thing should be conserved; for another purpose or in comparison with another alternative, the same thing should be discarded. When the points in favor of the new do not outweigh those in favor of the old, the latter is chosen.[3]

As a country, America is conditioned toward both types of philosophical conservatism. Various historical events seem to have strengthened or restored a general conservative attitude. The United States began as an English colony with a strong religious element and a basic industry of agriculture. The colonists wished to conserve their European culture. The Revolution of 1776 was basically a revolution to conserve fundamental beliefs. Later, when the middle class swept into power with Andrew Jackson, similarities between the "age of the common man" in America and "respectable" Victorian England became apparent. The grip of conservatism was loosened in the 1890's only to be abruptly restored by the Great Depression (1929–1933). Recovery in the 30's again brought a release, until overshadowed by World War II and the communist menace.

Conservatism shows in everyday dress. American women accept and even demand basic styles. Commonly called "classics," these standardized styles appear every year regardless of the fashion trend. Such a classic may once have been revolutionary, or it may at least have seemed so. Today it produces unity and tradition; it endures.

Many of today's classics are twentieth-century fashions, launched in the 30's and 40's and now uniform by popular choice. Some had their nucleus in the tailored simplicity of British styling; others yielded to Paris influence. A partial list of such styles would include (1) the Chanel type of box jacket suit; (2) the tailored suit; (3) the coat dress; (4) the shirtwaist dress; (5) the dirndl; and (6) the sheath. Occasionally classics make news—they become high fashion. Fashion writers proclaimed 1962 as the year "classics made a big comeback." Always present in popular fashion, these styles, like the cockney working girl, are lifted from their environment, groomed and embellished to take their place for a whimsical length of time in the more leisurely world of "my fair lady."

When French high fashion is *modified to suit the American taste,* intricate or unusual cut is reduced to simpler lines. Group acceptance of basic styles goes deep into our conservative past, and few American women want that which is too "different." The shirtwaist dress was developed in a dressmaker era; the cry for simplicity was raised by the English Puritan before coming to the New World. Both this particular style and the general character of clothing remain popular today.

The dress of a nation is the outer expression of the inner life of that nation; conservative dress reflects conservative traits. The historical background of American philosophical conservatism expresses the continuity of the past and present and helps explain the prevalence of current attitudes about dress.

Modern America was formed in the seventeenth century with the arrival of a large number of colonists, mainly from England. The official policy of the English government toward colonization waxed pro and con. As feeders of commerce and a source of revenue through customs' duties, the colonies strengthened the nation; as a drain on the population through emigration, they weakened it.

While the Parliamentarians and men of affairs discussed the colonial policy, the *simpler folks* went to the New World. Ideas often thought to be Puritan were the general outlook of the more sober elements of the English middle class of that period. Most New England colonists were drawn from the same reservoir of sober, God-fearing people in the home country.

Religious prejudice was strong in seventeenth-century man. He feared Rome because he remembered the Inquisition; it was not dim history, but something which might come again. Religious discussion was of serious interest even to the illiterate, and tolerance was regarded as criminal weakness. There were bitter struggles between the Anglicans, who conformed to the official Protestant church in England, and the dissenters or nonconformists.

It was the dissenters and nonconformists who came to New England, forming in 1692 the Province of Massachusetts from two colonies: the Plymouth Colony and the Colony of Massachusetts Bay. The Pilgrims and the Puritans, although differently conditioned, each tried to conserve some valued aspects of English life. The Pilgrim Fathers, who began the settlement of New England in 1620, came from the northern counties of England. These were countrymen "used to a plain country life and the innocent trade of husbandry."[4] They had sought refuge first in Holland. But several years later, fearing renewed persecution from home and not wanting their children to become Dutch but to use English and follow English customs, they looked to the New World. They were granted a patent from the Virginia Company and left for America to form the Plymouth Colony.

Nine years later another colony, a Puritan refuge, was planted on the shores of Massachusetts Bay. The Puritans in addition to religious interests had political plans. They wished to found a colony where they would be free according to ancient charters and statutes of England.

Around 700 persons sailed with the Winthrop fleet of eleven ships. These "emigrants were not a huddle of poor." They paid their passage (£5 per adult), provided tools and household utensils for use across the water, and took enough food for at least a year. "Of nearly 250 possible heads of families only 1 in 10 was of a social rank above that of yeoman."[5]

Their ministers, however, were graduates of English universities, equal in ability and culture to those who remained in the National Church, and Governor Winthrop was an Esquire. These people had singular energy and enterprise. In the Puritan colony were found the elements of vigorous growth and permanent influence that change colonies into nations. From the first it was an embryo state, containing the germ of independence.

Perhaps the essence of the Pilgrims and the Puritans is embodied in those two symbolic figures—the Statue of Liberty and Uncle Sam; one, a kind and gracious woman in a simple, flowing robe; the other, a gaunt and homey, but sometimes demanding man in a top hat. The Pilgrims gave us the lessons of patience and gentleness. They gave us the beauty and poetry of New England. To them we owe a larger tolerance, gentle manners, and purer laws. But the Puritan influence was greater in some respects: energy, enterprise, and political wisdom—a genius for creating new types of government. They shaped much of the best in our intellectual and religious life.

Today the ideas carried to America by conscious choice continue on as the unconscious conservative tradition. Middle-class America retains a strong moral orientation, with opposing views seen as good and evil rather than as conflicting interests. Television drama labels the good and the bad; audiences are disturbed if they must make the identification. College students feel secure when statements are called right or wrong, uneasy if no distinction is made. In this black and white morality only the artist seems free to see the many shades of grey. For the average critic, a line is "clean," a design is "good," a thought is "right." Words such as "good" and "right" carry a religious connotation, and religion is not debatable. Religion has often been separated from the intellect, placed in the realm of emotions where it is viewed with a certain distrust and contempt, and considered inferior to intellect.

Fashion is Morally Suspect

The term puritanism as currently used in the United States expresses a social attitude. The religious base that underlies the word is largely ignored. However, in seventeenth-century America, theology and dress had to be reconciled. The Puritan's strong religious morality fostered "a morality of taste," the dislike of ceremony and ritual in the church that introduced "simplicity" in dress.

PURITAN MORALITY. Richard Baxter, a seventeenth-century Puritan minister, "found the essence of Puritanism in two things: a serious effort to live a godly life and a desire to achieve further reformation within the church."[6] A twentieth-century historian sees the Puritan, in general terms, as a "man so dedicated to his religious or moral principles that to their practice he will subordinate everything else"; in the widest sense "Christ was a Puritan, and Paul, and Augustine, and Saint Francis." In addition to this general attitude, the Puritans had specific beliefs. They were Calvinists who believed in "predestination"—foreordained damnation for most of the human race. Motivated by dread of God and the desire to escape a gloomy fate, puritanism "rises above dogma to a moral drive, a resolve—a desperate one—to do right though even that might not save one from hell. An unformulated personal guide with no comforting ritual, no precept except the command to serve God, it produced in America the 'New England conscience.' "[7]

The church was uppermost in man's thought, and central to his experience. The minister had an authoritarian relationship with his flock: He was respected, educated, entrusted as a man of God with the exercise of moral discipline; he often shared political control with the magistrate in an age that admitted no separation of church and state. As representatives of a vested institution, the clergy could largely be counted upon to wield the spiritual sword on the side of conservatism and stability.[8]

Fashion was morally suspect since it fostered "intolerable pride in clothes and hair" and it interfered with the "natural way" (the accepted way). Samuel Sewall discusses wigs in his diary (Tuesday, June 10, 1701): "Having last night heard that Isiah Willard had cut off his hair (a very full head of hair) and put on a Wigg, I went to him this morning. Told his mother what I came about, and she call'd him. I enquired of him what Extremity had forced him to put off his own hair, and put on a Wigg? He answered, none at all. But said that his Hair wast stright, and that it parted behinde. Seem'd to argue that men might as well shave their hair off their head, as off their face. . . . God seems to have ordain'd our Hair as a Test, to see whether we can bring our minds to be content at his finding: . . ."[9]

The social relationship between the sexes was another area of moral concern. In Salem parish, Roger Williams instructed the women to always wear veils in public. "But John Cotton preached to them the next Sunday, and he proved to the dames and goodwives that veils were a sign and symbol of undue subjection to their husbands, and Salem women soon proved their rights by coming barefaced to meeting."[10] In general it was assumed that women played a subordinant role and should be kept in a separate sphere (the kitchen and the home). "The ideal middleclass female must be perfect in household accomplishments, she must have every charm, but she must be docile and self effacing. Her garments should be comely, strong and healthful, without 'toyish garnishes, or glosse of light colours,' avoiding the vanity of 'fantastic fashions.' "[11] Such was the advice from London in the 1600's.

The American woman from the first was more emancipated than her European counterpart. She had a higher value—she was a scarce product and rendered greater economic service. (In addition, property rights—the right of inheritance —in many colonies were greater than in England, and women were freer to move about without a male escort or a chaperone of their own sex.) But for all, rich and poor, the same duties remained—to be a good wife and mother. "We give nothing with our daughters, their education, health, and the customary out-set, are all that the fathers of numerous families can afford:

as the wife's fortune consists principally in her future economy, modesty, and skillful management; so the husband's is founded on his abilities to labour, on his health, and the knowledge of some trade or business."[12] The economic stability of marriage depended on the individual performance of each partner.

MODESTY. Social traits were another important matter: The modest woman was highly prized. Single men in the early days, often desperate for wives, tried to entice women from England with tales of good fortune in America. Rather than demanding a dowry, it was common for men to buy a deserving wife for the price of 100 pounds. Yet they "wou'd not receive any, but such as cou'd carry sufficient Certificate of their Modesty and good Behavior."[13]

Modesty is an ambiguous term, often poorly defined, vaguely used, heatedly discussed. This ambiguity fosters reckless accusations of right or wrong, good or bad behavior. Each person interprets modesty according to his own code and participates in the moral culture, for modesty has a moral connotation. Since modesty is not innate in man but is highly conventional, relative to a culture, it has no meaning except within a culture and within a specified time, place, and situation. Women from India are surprised that women in America wear so many hats; it seems immodest because hat wearing is a man's privilege in India. In America, it is immodest to wear cosmetics "in the wrong way"; to pursue a man "openly"; to laugh "loudly"; to wear a neckline "too low for your age."

Modesty, which arose out of an established relationship between the sexes, is essentially correlated with desire. Whereas the aim of modesty is to combat desire, in so doing it often has the opposite effect of stimulating desire. Is it less sexually inviting to hide a woman's legs behind a curtain of fabric that flutters and moves in suggestive lines, or to reveal them as stark sculptures in bone and muscle? The issue has never been decided. This ambivalence is a goad to fashion. And fashion and modesty soon tangle.

James Laver[14] sees fashion as essentially a game between prudery and style. Psychologists call it "the shifting of the erogenous zones." Believing that man can absorb only one part of the female body at once, the fashion designer plays up one part: by exposing it, exaggerating its size, or by drawing clothes tightly around it. When interest in this part of the body begins to wane from too much familiarity, or as the psychologists say "it exhausts its erotic capital," boredom sets in. Fashion shifts to another part. This explains the constant shift from, perhaps, small waists and rounded hips to long slender legs, to the cleavage in the bosom, to. . . . Once a fashion takes hold, it is worn with ease, but the shift to the next zone at first seems shocking and indecent. (A period when women cover themselves up completely is called a "period of prudery." It never lasts very long. The point beyond which you "dare not go" is the prudish part of the fashion—your skirt may show your legs, but, it must *not reveal your kneecap.)*

Americans have been trained by their Puritan heritage to keep their bodies out of their minds. Clothes serve to separate individuals from their own bodies as well as from the bodies of others. "Closeness to the bodily self is still felt inevitably as a threat to those whose standards of control and responsibility and decency have been built on its denial." The solution for this difficulty lies "in developing greater ease with our clothes on; taking them off only increases our anxiety."[15]

The bikini bathing suit was slow to achieve popularity in America. Men returning from Europe after World War II delighted in telling of the "shocking" style. By 1954 every woman on the beach at Nice, France, had one. But not until 1965 did bikinis become popular at public beaches in America. The same slow response greeted plunging necklines. As the commentators say, "The American women cannot adopt these with the same finesse as the European. The woman will fidget, and a man does not know whether to look or not." This unease can be traced to the Puritan morality and to the diversity of moral codes in American families of mixed backgrounds. There is no set reaction to the same cue. A neckline or a bikini may be met with an embarrassed averted eye, a comradely grin, an unwelcome advance, or an admiring stare. The cautious American retreats into safe conservatism.

WOMEN IN PUBLIC LIFE. Women active in public life often tend to promote the conservative ideas of their time. The first woman to edit a magazine for women was Sarah Josepha

Hale, a widow. Later she consolidated her *Ladies Magazine* with *Godey's Lady's Book* and continued as coeditor with Louis Antoine Godey until her 89th birthday. Unlike Godey, who advanced fashion with his colored fashion plates, she thought fashion undemocratic, and condemned slavish imitation of foreign modes. "Those modish ladies who appear to think themselves born only to be amused,—such a class is scarcely recognized in our republic land," she wrote. She opposed extensive decoration which served only to cultivate and gratify vanity. Ideally, she felt, "when all our ladies are possessed of 'inward greatness, unaffected wisdom and sanctity of manners' they will not find a continual flutter of fashion adds anything to the respect and affection their virtue and simple graces will inspire."[16]

The General Federation of Women's Clubs has more than once berated fashion. During the days of the demimonde in Paris when fashionable gowns were paraded by the grand cocottes (Gigi)—those "fallen women" of romantic mystery—American club leaders wrung their hands in public concern over the "demoralizing effect on our young girls." These girls would go to Paris, see the beautiful gowns, and copy them. (No Frenchman would allow his wife to wear them. Our girls "should apply the test of common sense.") "We hope the madly accelerated speed at which fashion moves today is rushing toward destruction of its empire."[17]

During the years of World War I, leaders of the Federation worked for standardization of dress. They were against the tyranny of style. Are we not "captains of our souls," with "courage to be free?" they asked. They wanted simple, becoming, modest designs in women's clothes. They favored the Biennial suit (named after their biennial convention), a style becoming to anyone when modified or adapted. They urged their fellow club members to be like men; ". . . let us standardize our street clothes . . . it is not a uniform . . . it is a principle . . . the street suit is a moral issue."[18]

Strict moral surveillance by public authorities was a seventeenth-century attitude. Because of the dominant role of the Puritan colonists in American political and economic life it is known as Puritan morality. It continues its smouldering course, erupting now and then to engulf the people settled at its base. The most massive outbursts left their mark, first, in the "New England conscience" before 1700, and second, in the "respectability" of Early Victorian England (1830–1865).

VICTORIAN RESPECTABILITY. "Victoria, roused in the early morning of June 1837 to be told that she had become Queen, appeared in a loose white nightgown, a shawl, and a nightcap which had all but fallen from her head."[19] She was 18 years old and lived to rule for 63 years. The continued soberness of her dress helped to prevent in England the extravagances present in France during the days of Empress Eugénie.

Early Victorian England had a two-fold faith in *goodness* and *progress*. Almost every event was controlled by the pressures of the Evangelical discipline, steadily rising incomes, and increasing security.

Coming into power was the new manufacturing class. Wealthy, but puritanical, its members continued simple living and did not compete by ostentation. They were proud of representing the new empire of the middle classes. They wished to shine by their own gentility, personal abilities, and fortune and not by rich and elegantly tailored attire. Under their influence men's clothes became dark and sober, and this attire was imitated by the "white collar" or clerical workers.

In the United States, as in England, it was the "Age of the Common Man," beginning with Andrew Jackson and ending with Abraham Lincoln, who preserved the union and settled the political future of the country. Over 3½ million English emigrated to the United States, driven by poverty, desire for adventure, or hope of a better life in a new world in need of skilled workmen. Many of the traits of Victoria's England are still conserved in the great middle class of twentieth-century America.

The concept of the proper relations to be maintained between the sexes caused a social barrier: Man was locked in his office—his wife in the home. While man placed emphasis on work and getting ahead, woman took her place as wife and mother, demure and self-effacing. A lady was "gentile," her dress was quiet and not obviously expensive. She "should not be conspicuous and never be talked about."

Modesty in the form of prudery reached ridiculous heights. If a young woman was making a shirt and a gentleman entered, it was considered a symptom of absolute depravity to name the article. "It's a frock, an apron, a pillow case. . . . " she would pretend. Words for articles of clothing took on moral overtones. Mrs. Trollope, an Englishwoman visiting America in 1827, reports, "A young German gentleman of perfectly good manners once came to me greatly chagrined at having offended one of the principal families in the neighborhood by having pronounced the word *corset* before the ladies of it."[20]

The prudery of the Victorian period was both cause and consequence of the failure of men and women to associate more naturally in everyday life, a difficulty not yet overcome. With slight changes, this description by Mrs. Trollope would fit many social events in conservative America today. "The women herd together at one part of the room, men at the other. The gentlemen spit, talk of elections and the price of produce, and spit again. The ladies look at each other's dresses till they know every pin by heart; talk of Parson Somebody's last sermon on the day of judgment, or Dr. T. Otherbody's pills for dyspepsia, till the 'tea' is announced, when they all console themselves. . . ."[21]

Mrs. Trollope thought the separation of the sexes objectionable in America, but habits in England were similar. At a society dinner it was customary for the ladies to linger at the table after dessert for a quarter hour while sweet wines were served. Then the gentlemen rose, opened the door for the ladies, and after they were gone drew close together around the table. They discussed subjects of local and everyday interest while drinking deeply. Each was free to join the ladies in the salon if he chose. (Queen Victoria struck a blow at this custom by requiring her gentlemen to join her in the drawing room shortly after the ladies left the dining room.) No doubt the artificial restraints of the era had a depressing effect and man could not help feeling more at ease when alone with other men; it was not, however, a favorable circumstance for the development of women. The whole attitude of the age in America made women whose brave and determined traits would have been honored in the early Colonial days martyrs to *public opinion* (i.e., abolitionists).

PUBLIC TASTE. Everyone concerned himself with everyone else; no one despised guidance. Specialists in taste arose.

A desire to direct taste suited the mental atmosphere of the time; it was compatible with the social consciousness of "respectability." Home decorations were graded as *distinctive, mediocre,* or *shoddy.*[22]

The idea of "public taste" has burgeoned in present-day America. Clothing selection is taught in our schools and dress designs are rated as *distinctive, classic, ordinary,* and *poor.* Magazines and newspapers, movies and television, museums and world fairs, industrial designers and big corporations all concern themselves with taste. Standards are developed which, if followed, will insure "correct" (approved by public opinion) taste.

The idea that "rules" will insure taste is appropriate to American confidence in law. Americans alone among the peoples of the Western world made their constitution the supreme law of the land and invested the judiciary with an almost religious power. No other people is so confident of the power of law to preserve peace in the international sphere. Lawyers have taken over politics (there were 12,600 lawyers in the metropolitan district of the capital, Washington, D.C., in 1964—a ratio of one to every sixty persons),[23] and to a large extent have permeated business. Legal ideas are a *force for conservatism.* In a way, they are a secular form of the puritan morality in America.

Today we live in a middle-class era with middle-class restrictions—moral, mental, and physical. The middle class lives for the future. (In contrast, the subculture of poverty, Oscar Lewis suggests, has a "present time" orientation with relatively little ability to defer gratification and plan for the future.)[24] The Puritans, mainly middle-class folk, first imposed restrictions on behavior in the world of the living to gain the more important and richer life in the world after death. Later, the emphasis shifted toward gain in this world, but the philosophy of inhibiting now in order to gain future benefits did not change. We still advise: Do not marry now, go to college first and you will have a richer life, mentally and materially. Or we say: Give up candy and desserts so you will have a better figure when you are older; give up the satisfaction and self-confidence which comes from accepting high fashion and buy a staple design so you will not be out-of-date in several years. This latter restrictive rationale against high fashion in favor

of more basic design is founded in the Puritan dislike for ceremony and ritual in the church.

"I Drest Plainly"

Rich dress in the Renaissance style was worn by most
Europeans of wealth and position in colonial times. The
clothing of simple people—the yeomen, small farmers, and
workingmen—was substantial and plentiful. Fashions did not
change from year to year. Garments were stored as "wealth"
and inherited as part of an estate. Grandmother, mother, and
daughter might charm three successive generations of men
with the same dress, and never be out-of-date.

PURITAN SIMPLICITY. If fashion affected style little, religious
attitude affected it greatly. Phillip Stubbes, a Puritan, published in 1586 a book called *An Anatomie of Abuses* on
the excesses of the England of his day, including excesses in
dress: "And therefore when I speak of excess of Apparel my
meaning is of the inferiour sorte only who for the most parte
do faire surpasse either noble, honorable or worshipful, ruf-
fling in Silks, Velvets, Satens, Damaske, Taffeties, Gold, Silver
and what not; . . . There is such a confuse mingle mangle of
apparel . . . so that it is verie hard to know who is noble,
who is worshipful, who is a gentleman, who is not; . . ."[25]
Stubbes disliked men of low class and little means spending so
lavishly on dress unsuited to their station.

The Puritan protest was against sumptuosity in dress, the
principle of emulation. Sumptuosity, as defined by Quentin
Bell, is "dress which has, whether fashionable or not, provoked
the respect and admiration of mankind." It is the dress of the
"privileged class *or* those who lead an ornamental as distinct
from an industrial existence."[26] The Puritan protest took the
form of plain clothes and darker colors, a political badge
adopted before and during the English civil war.

Only two political revolutions have had catastrophic influence on dress: the Puritan Revolution in England in 1642,
and the French Revolution in 1789. When a middle class re-
volts against a resurgent aristocracy, one would expect a revolt
against the principle of emulation. Puritan dress was never

quite without sumptuosity; it was always the dress of the white-collar worker.

The sumptuary laws of Massachusetts were patterned after existing laws in England, imposed mainly for class differentiation and to reduce ostentation. In 1634 the court "forbade the purchase of woollen, silk, or linen garments, with silver, gold, silk, or thread lace on them. No slashed clothes, except those with *one* slash in each sleeve and another slash in the back." Such items as gold or silver girdles, beaver hats, and hatbands were forbidden.[27] A letter from Susan Moseley of Virginia to Governor Yardley in 1650 throws some light on these rich hatbands prohibited as vain and extravagant by the Massachusetts magistrates. She tells of "the exchange of a hatband and jewel for 4 young cows, one older cow and 4 oxens, on account of her 'great want of cattle.'" Writing at Elizabeth River, Virginia, she explained "for ye hatband y't alone coste 500 gilders as my husband knows very well. . . ." (The purchasing value of 500 gilders equaled nearly $1,000 in 1903.)[28]

The Massachusetts General Court in 1651 again expressed its "utter detestation that men and women of meane condition, education, and calling should take uppon them the garbe of gentlemen by wearing of gold or silver lace, or buttons or poynts at their knees, or walke in great boots, or women of the same ranke to wear silke or tiffany hoods or scarfs." Two women brought before the court in Newbury in 1653 for wearing silk hoods and scarfs were discharged on proof that their husbands were worth £200 each. By 1682 the tables had turned and the courts were arraigning selectmen for not prosecuting offenders.[29] This type of law did not suit a flourishing and progressing America.

The Puritan attitude toward sumptuosity reflects a difference in basic belief between the Anglicans and the dissenters. The Anglican loved the ritual and ceremonies of the established English church; the Puritan liked them less. Specifically, he "did not like the use of the ring in marriage and the sign of the cross in baptism, bowing at the name of Jesus, and wearing of the surplice."[30] He found them tending too much toward Rome. The Anglicans insisted on the outward and visible signs; the Puritans on the inward and spiritual graces.

The Puritan ministers also favored a simple and unpretentious sermon. One such minister, Baxter, tells us that he carefully resisted the temptation to aim at a polished literary style; "life was too brief and too serious to waste its moments playing with words." He set down his thoughts as quickly and as forcefully as he could, and wasted no time straining after elegance or effect. The urgent sense of the value of time, so characteristic of the Puritan, supported the belief in simplicity. "Attire must be simple, lest time be wasted in the unprofitable necessity of dressing."[31]

Simple clothes to save time, energy, and money is acceptable to a nation in progress. In this form an attitude born of the religious zeal and bitter conflict of the seventeenth century has continued into modern America. Its supporters state that "to save" produces wealth; and wealth encourages progress. They firmly resist the counterview of economic analysts that the way to progress is not to save but to spend.

BENJAMIN FRANKLIN'S THRIFT. A staunch advocate of thrift and plain dress was Benjamin Franklin, who helped give the Puritan morality a more secular utilitarian footing. He wrote: "In order to secure my credit and character as a tradesman, I took care not only to be in *reality* industrious and frugal, but to avoid all appearance to the contrary. *I drest plainly.*"[32] So does the businessman today: His uniform, a neat sack unit of dull grey, or black, or brown, embodies the concept of serious responsibility to family, business, and country, as does the black broadcloth suit of the minister to God, or the black academic gown of the college graduate to learning. He shows no more frivolity than his public will accept, for his business depends on public approval. Thus, while the reason for simplicity changes, the tradition itself remains.

The "good Dr. Franklin," as the French fondly called him, added still another dimension to Puritan morality with his practical sense as a humanitarian. In *The Way to Wealth,* he renews the attack on overspending for fashion by those who cannot afford it (a trait responsible for the first sumptuary laws in Massachusetts): "Many a one for the sake of finery on the back, have gone with a hungry belly, and half starved their Families; *silks and satins, scarletans, velvets,* as Poor Richard says, *put out the kitchen fire.* These are not the necessaries of life; they can scarcely be called the *conveniences,* and yet only because they look pretty, how many *want* to *have* them. The *artificial* wants of mankind thus become more numerous than the natural; and as Poor Dick says, for *one* poor person, there are *an hundred indigent*."[33]

It may seem strange that a nation with an economy which can afford the most powerful military establishment in the world, while maintaining the highest living standards for the greatest number of people in history, has constantly returned to a tradition of simplicity and economy in clothes. It is not surprising, however, in view of the stress placed on the qualities of simplicity, economy, and serviceability by the arbiters of American taste, the fashion tastemakers.

Among the first of ten fashion secrets revealed by the Duchess of Windsor is simplicity: "I like simplicity in my clothes. I feel they should be so unobtrusive as to seem unimportant. This is a feeling developed from my practical turn of mind and from an earlier one-time lack of money when I had to select clothes with the idea of getting a lot of wear out of everything I bought. I never wear fluffy or extravagantly decorated clothes. For one thing they don't suit me, but perhaps more important, they are so immediately noticeable that their performance has a limited run."[34]

A newspaper headline proclaims: TIMELESS TASTE SURVIVES FASHION'S CHANGES. An interview in the *New York Times* in 1960 with Mrs. Robert G. Hughes, who was, before her marriage in the late 1930's, a mannequin for designer Elizabeth Hawes, states that one of her treasures is a lamé dinner gown which she wore continuously for 21 years. "Its lines will always be in style," she believes.[35]

As consumers, we are constantly reminded that with a limited budget we should beware of too sudden explosion of a fashion; choose comparatively conservative styling, we are told; choose classics. "Normal" in American fashion business has come to mean unimaginative conservatism. Fashion writers may feel that "conservative" as used by the best-dressed women does not imply dressing unimaginatively. But in the mind of the average woman it becomes just that; she wants no part of violent style changes, as the million dollar ready-to-wear industry well knows. Capitalizing on this streak of conservatism running deep in the American people are the Davidow brothers, Archie and Mel. Their suits in soft, subtle

Scotch tweeds are a trademark of refined taste and serviceability to the women who own them.

AMERICAN REVOLUTION. The American Revolution, unlike the Puritan Revolution and the French Revolution, had no effect on dress. It was a conservative revolution. There was no class conflict and no desire to change fundamental beliefs. The leaders were of good social backgrounds and thoroughly upper middle class. Many of the same men held office before and after the dividing line of the Revolution, so service before was no political obstacle to service after. The continuity brought a degree of social and political stability to the new nation rarely associated with the word "revolution." It was the first time a colonial people had successfully rebelled against the mother country without making a serious interruption in the smooth flow of development. They conserved the past, rather than repudiated it. This was no "heedless overthrow of an oppressor; it was a slowly germinating determination . . . to counter and thwart a change in their hitherto established and accepted ways of governing."[36]* Tocqueville wrote in 1840, "Social conditions and the Constitution of America are democratic but they have not had a democratic Revolution. They arrived on the soil they occupy in nearly the condition in which we see them at the present day."[37]

American independence has a peculiar character; in the process of moving away there is "at the same time a nostalgic longing to be one with the pattern of ideas from which it is derived." America is "always anxious to be independent and always concerned that it cannot escape dependence."[38]

However, attitudes and ideas became more fluid in America. The territorial sweep and abounding resources, with the resulting sense of indefinite expansion, had infused a new spirit: the right to progress; the right to a future if not a past. American conservatism is not interested in the past so much as in the future; it weighs the old against the new and selects that which best fits a particular purpose. If points in favor of

---

* After the French and Indian wars the Americans had expected to return to the freedom and lax uninterested British administration of the prewar years, especially freedom from any obligation to support imperial defenses. Instead, England, saddled with a big war debt, taxed the colonies to help bear the burden. The colonists protested; they suddenly realized they were no longer wards of Britain but a separate people capable of forging their own destiny.

the new do not outweigh those for the old, the old is retained. This process may slow down change, but it is not adverse to change. This is a conservatism aligned with progress.

Compatible Fashion Eras

In forming her own mold, America turned for fashion to France. Versailles, the citadel of fashion, was the admiration of Europe throughout the eighteenth century. The court dress of the French aristocracy was essentially urban, sophisticated, and artificial. It was the costume of the salon, a dress of idleness and pleasure; at its most characteristic it was elaborately embroidered and decorated. In fashion, wherever a more sumptuous style is encountered it tends to be imitated. The whole civilized world imitated the French. As French fashion changed, so changed Western dress.

What was the nature of style at this time? The cut in dress changed little during the decades, but the change of adornment became increasingly rapid. In France it was the "milliners" who were allowed free play of artistic inspiration; they trimmed the dresses delivered by the dressmaker, designed headgear such as caps, fichus, mantillas, lace ruches. They were the artists who gave the dress "the tone, the flash of wit and its fascinating grace." Rose Bertin, a milliner—the first King of Fashion—was introduced to Marie Antoinette, then sixteen and bored. Apparently her life became more interesting when "the milliner stuck pastel colored flowers and feathers in her wealth of blonde hair." Two years later, when Marie Antoinette became queen, her headgear rose to 36 inches.* Her constant love of finery and need for change can first be ascribed to the influence of Rose Bertin.[39]

FRENCH SIMPLICITY. The French Revolution reversed the trend of elaborate decoration prevalent in eighteenth-century styles. Modern dress can be dated from this year (1789) when the common man rose in his common clothes, loyal to his own class. The English Puritan had made the first move,

---

* The coiffure exceeded the dress trimmings in importance, and the profession of hairdresser ranked equally with that of the milliner. In 1770 there were 3,744 different hair styles.

the French *révolutionnaire* now made the second—both in the same direction: toward simplicity in dress. The Puritan had worn essentially the same dress as everyone else; he merely reduced decoration and modified those details considered exaggerated or grotesque. The French *révolutionnaire* in his zeal went much farther: He changed both the decoration and the cut of the dress.

Classical style, in the sense of Greek classicism, was proclaimed the triumph of reason, and simple attire became the symbol of bourgeois virtue. Transparent dresses, exposed bosoms, long flowing garments with high waists, and empire-line chemises in filmy white gauze were adopted. The dress "had to express freedom, and the natural shape of the body was to be neither corsetted nor disguised."[40] The stiff bodice with built-in corset, the tight lacings; the full skirts; the many elaborately embroidered underskirts—all were discarded. Close-fitting garments became the vogue.

The English fashion historian, James Laver, in analyzing this period states that Rousseau, a reactionary, found favor in the most blasé circles of French aristocracy. His belief that "civilization was essentially corrupt and that true virtue could only be found in the rural life" caused a sentimental, if theoretical, admiration for peasants. We find Marie Antoinette enamored of make-believe milkmaids and rural life. In England it was not the courtier but the country gentleman who was the dominant type. The French, too, admired the liberty, simplicity, and comparative lack of privilege he displayed. So, when they wished to discard the livery of the *salon* they tended to adopt the costume of the English country gentlemen. It was both a "Back to Nature" and a "Greek Revival" period.[41]

GREEK CLASSICISM. Both peasant simplicity and Greek classicism are compatible with the American Puritan tradition.

The Greek idea of beauty is still dominant in American education. Present books on the art of dress refer to the "Greek proportion" or "the harmony of related curves." The term "classic," commonly used to mean a fashion which has continued popular over a long period of time, is taken from the classic period of Greek art, famous for its simplicity and enduring beauty.

The Greeks were not adventurous in art. In the earliest

Doric temples the style was already formed, the relationship of elements was established. The Greeks did not change the style; their adventurousness was of an intellectual kind. For 200 years they continued refining these relationships in every detail until the imaginative sensitiveness of the artist could go no further. In this conservative attitude of the Greek lies the key to an understanding of his art.[42]

The perfection of balance between forms was a part of the Greeks' intellectual search for the true meaning of life; they made the disquieting discovery of self-consciousness. While the Egyptians had been content with vicarious entertainment (banquets with singers, dancers, and drink—a period characterized by the beautiful and crafty Cleopatra), the Greeks sought to explore the individual mind. Clothing oneself became an art, and individuality was achieved by a personalized way of wearing a garment, not by color, cut, and line. Greek women could make their dress appropriate for any occasion by changing the draping of the single length of fabric which formed the costume. They achieved a simple fluid line with soft fabrics moving freely over the body.

The American girl is often taught in public schools the Greek ideal of simplicity in dress. From a sketchy presentation, she may retain only the concept of a garment shaped to the natural body form with no distracting cut or line. She interprets this, in her life, as a standard dress—a "classic." Unaware that the Greeks with their simplicity gave freedom to individuals to "personalize by the way they wear it" their single length of fabric, she wears her dress "as is"—as it comes from the store. Thus the resistance to design noted by Poiret in his denunciation of the "fetters of the American mass" is unconsciously preserved by public education to improve taste.

CHANEL FUNCTIONALISM. Gabrielle Chanel has enjoyed a long-term success in America. To own a genuine Chanel suit was as much of a status symbol in 1963 as it was 30 years before. Her clothes have the appeal of simple functional lines, and they suit traditional Puritan morality with their deemphasis of sex. "I stay in the game," she once muttered, "to fight the vulgarity in fashion built around the great protrusions like Gina Lollobrigida and Brigitte Bardot."[43] (However, she occasionally "breaks down" and "fits" her suits to such movie personalities.)

Chanel suits are "modern design" in clothes. Although she became a success in the 1920's, modern design in furniture and housing became prominent in America only after the depression of the 30's. The appeal is the same: The structure is honest and sincere, compatible with the puritanism of virtue and modesty, clean living, and disdain for vulgar display.

This helps to explain the fashion popularity of Jacqueline Kennedy who epitomized the elegant uncluttered silhouette. *Real elegance is simplicity—nothing fussy, nothing loud, nothing busy.* Popular taste wants to identify with this image. Unable to comprehend the intricacies of true elegance (it is not in our tradition), consumers choose instead the simplicity of a classic design, reinforcing the conservative streak in the American style of dress.

Pragmatic Support

We have seen how Puritan morality and desire for simplicity directly affected dress in America. Clearly, however, economic and political factors, as well as religious beliefs, have supported a general conservative attitude. Before 1860 it was the rural culture with its isolation and home manufacturing that supported conservatism. In the twentieth century, conservatism was fostered by the Great Depression and World War II with its aftermath of communist competition in an atomic age. Under these conditions a basically religious belief in conservative dress tends to receive pragmatic support. Since the practical trait in the American style of dress is a section in itself, discussion here will be limited to the implications these events have for conservatism.

Rural Culture

America before 1860 was essentially a rural culture. "Homemade" could be applied to nearly every article in the house. The farmer and his sons raised wool and flax. The wife and daughters spun them into thread and yarn, knit them

A "classic" Chanel suit

into stockings and mittens, or wove cloth and made this into clothing. These home occupations were called "the homespun industries." We praise the durability of man-made fibers and tend to underestimate this quality in homespun materials. Alice Morse Earle reports in 1890, "I have flannel sheets a hundred years old. . . ."

The farm family looked after its own wants, forced to do so by its isolated location and general lack of wealth. Work was hard but there was satisfaction in the way of life, as illustrated by the writings of St. John de Crevecoeur, an American farmer before the Revolution. "The instant I enter on my own land, the bright idea of property, of exclusive right, of independence exalt my mind." His contentment is evident: "When I contemplate my wife, by my fire-side, while she either spins, knits, darns, or suckles our child. . . ."[44] Many fourth- and fifth-generation Americans today have some direct link with a rural past. In any event, a phrase in America that still meets with almost instant approval is that affirmation of self-dependence, "I did it myself."

We still use the terms made-at-home or homemade. A 1963 report by the National Cotton Council, based on a survey of 722 housewives in seven cities in different geographical regions, showed more than half of the housewives (54 per cent) sewed at home and 31 per cent made one or more items of clothing during 1962.[45] This activity provides the market for what has been one of America's oldest and most staid businesses, the pattern manufacturer. Most pattern sales to home sewers are simple unimaginative styles in easy-to-make form. Although now, with a more fashion-conscious customer, many companies offer a group of "designer" patterns in addition to their regular line, and one or two have achieved success with this type alone. Still, the average home sewer, an amateur who is less skilled than a professional seamstress, will inevitably prefer a simple pattern. There is a direct relationship between the skill of the performer and the difficulty of the task to be performed. The lack of dressmaking skill among amateurs or professionals (lack of wealth in trained human resources) encourages a return to simplicity in dress, simplicity in the sense of uncomplicated or basic design.

DEPRESSION. In a similar way the stock market crash on October 29, 1929, and its resultant lack of wealth in capital resources, encouraged a return to a more basic way of life, a look back to the past rather than forward to the future. Gone was the spirit of adventure of the flapper days and spicy nights of the 20's. People withdrew into their communities, into their homes. Driven by uncertainty and a longing for security they clung to the familiar. No other depression brought so many Americans so close to starvation, lasted so long, or came so near to overturning the basic institutions of American life.

Leisure was enforced rather than voluntary. People listlessly talked and chatted with their neighbors. Work, when it returned, was greeted with the same element of exhilaration and adventure generally associated with play activity. The whole culture became dedicated to the necessity for and the value of hard work. A purposeful seriousness entered all activities: Education must be "good for something"; leisure should be spent in a "profitable way"; the community is committed to "maintain prosperity" and to "attract new industries."[46] The nation recommitted itself to America. Buy American! French fashion exports sank to a grave low; American firms were cooperating with each other and buying one model between them.

The depression is recorded in *Middletown in Transition* by Robert and Helen Lynd, a study of the broad changes in a familiar community after 10 years of boom and depression. During this period the car emerged as a "must." The number of filling stations doubled, and car sales (retail dollar volume) fell by only 4 per cent compared to a 38 to 85 per cent drop in retail total volume sales between 1929 and 1933. Men's clothing was apparently more responsive to business decline than women's. Men's stores decreased in number from 15 to 11, while total sales dropped 67 per cent. Women's ready-to-wear specialty shops on the other hand increased from 9 to 10, and combined sales dropped only 47 per cent.[47]

The new emphasis was on "intelligent consumer buying habits." Not only was careful selection more necessary because of lack of wealth, but because the market was more complicated. Weighted silk and synthetic fibers that closely resembled natural silk confused the consumers. "Service and durability" and "thrift" were in the air. Americans were harking back to the common-sense notions of Benjamin Franklin, and on back to the Puritan desire to preserve time, energy, and money.

James Laver felt that skirt lengths in the early 30's, descending from the knee to just below the calf, corresponded to the new sense of social responsibility. The flapper image was gone. Fashion favored the older woman—the old maid type—but without the usual accompanying dowdiness. Although it is not possible to prove definitely that the depression was responsible for changes in the nature of fashion, it is known that the period ushered in a serious generation of Americans, intellectually timid, seeking security in a safe job, convinced the government should be a Guarantor State, and likely to cling to conservative traits.

AGE OF ANXIETY. The 40's ushered in another Age of Anxiety: World War II, the Communist Menace, and the Atomic Age. The war and its accompanying scientific discoveries had both a stimulating and a depressing effect on society. Surely tremendous things happened: new power shifts—the minority group emphasis on rights for small nations, Negroes, and women; space travel, dramatizing for those living in the twentieth century the daring search for the unknown of the fifteenth century. But the depressing effects—the bewilderment, the hunger for purpose in life, the cautious approach that comes from sitting on a bomb that may explode and blow the universe to bits—gave impetus to the development of a conservative attitude.

Throughout the emotional stress and insecurity of World War II, women's fashions remained serenely and monotonously unchanged. Fabrics were skimpy, skirts were short, shoulders were bulky. With the capture of Paris by the Germans in 1940, the French export trade was officially dead. It came to life only in the fall of 1945 when the Paris couture again set its jaunty and expensive cap to regain world leadership in fashion.

Although New York designers "prepared to carry on" in the fashion field, they failed to produce anything significantly new. They suffered from the loss of inspiration from Paris and chafed under the restrictions of the War Production Board. Order L-85 limited the amount of yardage in women's dresses, mainly by fixing skirt lengths and forbidding designs that used excessive amounts of material. The restrictions resembled the normal working rules of any mass-production house trying to cut costs and make a profit at a fixed selling price. The result was the inhibition of the creative atmosphere of high fashion couture.

The war years gave women one chance to be "free from fashion." If women were conservative by nature—unhappy with waste and change—they did not "lose caste" in the eyes of the fashion status seekers, for fashion itself did not change. Each season brought only a slight modification of the same style. Each garment could be worn out physically, if desired, but fashion would not discard it psychologically. The conservatives were "in." Americans returned to the Greek ideal; individuality was achieved not by cut, color, or line, but by the personalized way each wore the national dress.

When the change in fashion finally came, with Dior's dramatic "new look"—long skirts, miniature waists, and romantic full skirts—a turmoil arose. Would women repudiate this expensive change? (Complete wardrobes would have to be discarded.) There was an intense inward struggle between the conservative attitude nurtured through the trying war years and the desire for release, for change. Again fashion won, but with a conservative streak. American women dropped hems and remodeled suits, gradually easing into the new look until 1948 when it was completely accepted.

After the war, economic prosperity continued. But America, having solved one important problem and wanting to relax, was still harried by a dangerous world situation. There remained a combination of fear and self-satisfaction that inhibits men's minds. As Eric F. Goldman put it, "Our faces are straight, our thoughts are doggedly constructive, . . . Where are the clowns? Where are the guffaws in this country, the purifying wit and humor, the catharsis of caricature . . . ?"[48]

The Middle Class Carries On

The pattern of conservatism germinating in the New England area characterizes the small towns of the Midwest and some of the homogeneous suburbs that surround our large cities. Here live the middle classes who carry forward the conservative traditions and ideals of America.

In the first half of the eighteenth century the town was the main social unit in New England and neighborliness was very strong. But there was a key restriction: Kindliness and thoughtfulness for others became rigidly limited to townspeople. All newcomers were viewed with suspicion. Towns like Boston, Providence, and New Haven adopted a custom of "warning out" the strangers who arrived, a duty assigned to the sheriff or some other civil servant. If these strangers should prove incapable or unsuccessful or vicious, they could not become a charge of the town but could be forcibly, if necessary, returned from whence they came. This "nativism" was born of the great influx of immigrants coming to a prospering America. The hardy Scotch-Irish and the sober industrious Germans moved on to the frontier and to the midwestern colonies, partly because of the greater opportunities for their skills and partly because of the exclusive attitudes of the New England towns. This view of a town as a closed social unit with members of the "in group" repelling those who are "outside" continues today in many American small towns and metropolitan suburbs.

There are patterns of both voluntary and involuntary segregation in America today. When people settle with other people like themselves as a result of free choice, it is voluntary segregation. They may be held together by the same institutions—a Protestant church, a Catholic church, a Jewish synagogue—or they may have the same taste in landscaping or ways to spend their leisure time. In any case, they live in an area because they want to and tend to develop a coherent group held together by some common emotional response or congenial pattern of group behavior.

When people are forced to live in certain areas because of discrimination and prejudice, the segregation is involuntary. This has occurred during periods of heavy immigration and with Negroes. Huge metropolitan areas have whole sections composed of Italian, Irish, Jewish, and other ethnic groups. Many immigrants, forced at first by discriminatory practices to live in specific areas of a city, later remain in these same areas by free choice.

Groups so cohesive they tend to see "their group as the world" become conservative, resistant to ideas foreign to the group traditions. This is true whether their isolation is voluntary or involuntary. This conservatism has significance for research in consumer buying habits. Gregory Stone, in a study under the auspices of the Agricultural Experiment Station at Michigan State University, clearly established that irrespective of rural or urban residence, cosmopolites (people oriented more in their life style to society-at-large than to their neighbors) purchase significantly more items in particular wardrobe categories and pay more per item than do those whose life styles are contained by their local communities of residence.[49]

Fashion traditionally has come from outside. In America it came first from London and later from Paris. Georg Simmel felt " . . . the exotic origin of fashions seems strongly to favor the exclusiveness of the group which adopts them."[50] It seems likely that groups which more quickly adopt new fashions have an orientation to society-at-large rather than to a limited neighborhood. As cosmopolites or "world customers" continue to increase in America, the traditional conservative pattern may decline, or adapt into a new form. But conservatism is a strong tradition, one characteristic of the American style of dress not likely to soon disappear completely.

11

ACCENT ON YOUTH

Accent on youth, once considered uniquely American, is spreading throughout the western and oriental worlds of fashion, while maintaining its central position in the culture of the United States. The typical American woman, according to the advertisements, is young, beautiful, slim, well dressed, bright, and joyful. All women of middle age (35–60) are exiled from the ads, with the occasional exception of "Mom," who is a quaint, serene, gray-headed type (a Whistler's mother) sitting in a rocker with a shawl around her shoulders. The result of this emphasis on youth and slimness is that the retailer now sells ten times as many size 16's as size 40's, something not true 20 years ago. If any woman allows her figure to go beyond a size 16 she is banished to unexciting styles and conventional colors.

Today, successful apparel producers put an accent on youth either by introducing new "junior" and "casual" lines or by restyling their regular lines. An executive of the dress firm, Nelly Don, recently said: "Every woman, no matter what her age, likes to have a youthful look in her dresses without being ingénue."[1] This company began in 1916 with two workers and now has a sales volume of over $11 million.

Other manufacturers feel they must make an arrangement for designs with a very young European designer, such as Angela Cash of London who says, "I don't think clothes have an age barrier. I think if you have a young figure and the right look you can wear anything."[2] Even couture designers in France have been captured by the youth mystique. Couturier Pierre Cardin remarked on television that when a mother is 35 years old and her daughter is 15, the difference of 20 years can seem like 10—the daughter may appear to be 20; her mother, 30.

Age in America inspires little respect. In a society such as ours, where growing old gracefully is seldom cultivated, age becomes less worthy of respect, and elders have little authority. Sociologist Robin Williams, Jr., suggests that lack of a family group in which authority can be exercised, and forced early retirement deprive the older person of both his occupation and his kinship grouping. Moreover, he points out, where change in the society is slow, the elders are the great storehouse of knowledge and lore; but in rapidly changing societies, like modern America, young people in or just out of school are equipped with the most current knowledge and are the innovators and heroes. Derogatory terms like "old fogey" become common for those over 25 to 30.[3]

American adults try to alter their image in an attempt to prove they are not old. To do so, they dress in the manner of younger persons and adopt the modes of individuals considerably their juniors. Cosmetics and dress are created to erase, so far as possible, the pattern of living on a woman's face. Some parents act and look so youthful it is difficult to differentiate between teen-agers and their parents. When asked what they think about this, many young people reply that young parents are fine, but some feel there are limits which should be observed. One sixteen-year-old boy commented: "I think parents should try to act young and be young, but they can overdo it. They always tell us to act our age—and I suppose this applies to them too."[4]

The adult in a youth-oriented society is faced with the vexing issue of how to combine the allure of youth and the wisdom of age. Author Margaret Culkin Banning summed up the dilemma: "The half-grown emotional capacities of youth set the standards and most of us accept them—to be 'popular,' to be 'attractive to men,' to be a 'knockout,' or even a 'cute number.' These are the gauges by which woman's power to excite and maintain feeling are tested."[5]

The United States is in many ways a mature nation. It was the first to fully comprehend mass production, distribution, and consumption, although Britain led the way into the crude industrialization of the nineteenth century. While Britain is older in the continuity of political institutions, the American

The American woman's problem: how to combine the impulsiveness of youth with the discipline of age.

constitution, drafted in 1789, is the oldest such document still in use. America resists political change in a manner which is reminiscent of the set ways of middle age, showing signs of suspicion toward new legislative programs. Yet, paradoxically, while voters fill the seats in Congress with elderly senators, Americans also elect a 43-year-old president and select 30-year-old astronauts to pioneer landings on planets in outer space. The vigorous, youthful element in the nation counterbalances the mature elements of continuity and stability and pushes the nation ahead.

Despite some mature characteristics, America is considered both by itself and others a young nation. This attitude persists because much of the mass migration to this country took place within the past century and the frontier spirit still persists. Many towns and institutions have yet to celebrate their hundredth anniversary, while the first known colonial settlement is scarcely 400 years old. The early American settlers were mature, fully enlightened Europeans as familiar with the political views stirring Europe as the associates they left behind. But the sense of boundless opportunity encountered here gave a flexibility to these ideas that was impossible to acquire under the more rigid conditions in Europe. This flexibility laid the foundation for "the youthful myth" that tends to permeate many areas of American life.

The atmosphere of vigorous competition in business and industry has made the need for innovation the one permanent belief which many business executives profess. They expect and anticipate change as each company feels it must grow or perish. Businessmen are not afraid to speculate; they have an aggressive attitude typical of youth. The successful American executive, by sheer force, maintains vigor and vitality into his fifties, reflecting the youthful image his company seeks to convey.

At home, the tired businessman must attempt to keep up with his own sophisticated children who challenge his tastes, habits, and aspirations. Americans identify with their children, rather than with their parents. Since "youth" is considered to be "the best years of our lives," parents not only act young themselves but they also feel guilty if they mar their children's early years with unpleasant concerns like depressions and wars.

In the newly labeled "youthmania" or "youthquake" era, adults are already dancing the dances, hearing the music, and wearing the styles of their children. The trappings of youth—the jet aircraft, sportscar, electronic gadgets—surround every member of the society. While youth contributes refreshing assets of flexibility, ambition, and concern to problems of world tension, population, social orders, and morality, it also brings liabilities—lack of taste at times, lack of judgment at others.

In general, the fashion world of the 1960's ushered in weird, highly promotable gimmicks to relieve adult boredom and tempt the country's millions of teen-age youths to part with the billions of dollars they spend each year on apparel. The long-haired rock and roll singers from England, the "Beatles," introduced Edwardian elegance gone awry in fashions called "Mod" clothes. The style originated in London and took its name from dandy-like Mods, a group of finicky-dressing youngsters whose taste ran to snug-fitting fancy floral print cotton shirts, brightly colored tight trousers with low belt lines, high-heeled boots and brilliant jewelry.

At the same time, the market was flooded with the popular-priced adaptions of the space-age fashions of French designer Courrèges. Midcalf white boots for women, plastic skirts and jackets, angular seaming, and crash helmets were everywhere. Odds and ends of anything that was "crazy," "kooky," or "rock and rolly" flooded the market in a revolt against dullness. Dresses going to 8 inches above the knee (mini skirts) suddenly divided women into those under 20 years of age (certainly not over 25), and the rest of the world.

Do young fashion leaders follow Paris? "No," says Cathy McGown, fashion leader among the British teen-age Mods in 1964. "They copy us. We have to change fashions quickly before everyone has the same as us."[6]

Sociologists agree that the high evaluation of youth as a time of life is related to the rapid rate of social change. Change is assimilated more rapidly by youths than by their elders, and while older people attempt to imitate youth, at times the gap between the two widens until parents and their adolescent children literally represent subcultures.

In one obvious way America is truly a young nation: Youth is taking over numerically. In 1960 when John F. Kennedy was elected president, the average American was around 33 years old. By 1968 the mid-age will have dropped to 25 or lower, the biggest age drop ever recorded in American history in an eight-year period. The bumper crop of babies right after World War II is making young adults the most rapidly expanding age group. By 1970 ours will be literally the youngest nation in the Free World.[7]

The sheer numbers of young people have resulted in a preoccupation with education perhaps unparalleled in history. One out of every three Americans is likely to be in school, since older as well as young people are devoting a greater percentage of their lives to receiving an education. Increased education means the "psychological age" of the population becomes even younger, for students are "young" in outlook on life and politics; they still consider themselves outside the labor force with a consequent lack of responsible roles.

Pro-Youth Eras

History repeats. In the 1920's as in the 1960's, youth was the model, and age the imitator. Everything in fashion was pro-youth. Upton Sinclair, in his novel *Oil* in 1926, wrote about a rich young man, Charlie, who "had nobody to take care of him but a rather silly mother, who was still trying to be young and giddy, dressing like a debutante, and having surgical operations performed on her face to keep it from 'sagging.' "[8] When youth takes over, adults with less facile mechanisms for adjustment find it hard to keep up with fashion's fast gyrations.

Young women of the 60's have adopted many of the fashions of the 20's. Both preferred a version of the "shimmy," above-the-knee straight line shifts with low-banded waistlines. Both tried to aquire the boyish look. Sociologists Robert and Helen Lynd recorded in their study, *Middletown,* a "lawsuit in 1925 over the right of a schoolgirl to wear knickers instead of a skirt to school."[9] Girls, forty years later, were adopting a variety of pant suit styles, including the bell-bottomed trousers of the Roaring Twenties.

The dominant fashion news for girls, in 1965, was short geometric haircuts, ribbed "poor boy" sweaters, matching socks, and knee-baring skirts. In the 20's, short-haired French designer Chanel had been the first to make her clientele feel it was smart not to look rich. She stripped them to a *tricot* and skirt or a plain dress, then draped them with great gobs of costume jewelry. Her success as a fashion designer was due to her insistence that mature women should look young, and expensively poor.

These comments by Mark Sullivan in *Our Times (The United States 1900–1925)* could apply to either era: "It was an age of unkemptness and scantiness of college students' attire. This was the pose in all colleges. The vogue in clothes became a kind of competition in uncouthness."[10]

Chanel is credited with helping to promote the "bobbed hair" vogue of the 20's. The story is told in this way: As she was lighting the gas water heater in her bathroom at the Ritz, some stored-up gas exploded, spraying her long black hair with sticky soot. In a hurry to go to the Paris Opera, she cut her hair short in order to shampoo it more quickly. Already a celebrity of the day, the fame of her new hair style sent many admirers rushing to their barbers.[11]

Two celebrities that America loved introduced the short-hair craze in this country. Irene Castle, a member of the dance team of Vernon and Irene, was the embodiment of "modern" in 1911 when the tango and fox-trot were the rage. She combined a tantalizing balance of extreme femininity and boyish simplicity with a strong suggestion of allure. When she cut her hair in July, 1914, it was labeled the Castle bob.

But it remained for Anita Loos, of "Gentlemen Prefer Blondes" fame, to introduce in 1924 the extremely short cut with bangs which reappeared in 1965. Miss Loos typified "cuteness" in her crisp Peter Pan collars and her carefully combed short brilliantined bangs. When interviewed in 1963 about cutting her hair in the 20's, she commented: "I looked in the mirror and thought the only good thing I had was the shape of my head—so I went all the way and had it cut really short . . . I then went to Europe, and to a showing at Lanvin—and Mme. Lanvin asked me if I would wait after the show so her mannequins could see my hair style . . . they copied it . . . and it spread back to America!"[12] Thus, the idea of short hair for mature women was innovated by ladies of celebrated taste, picked up by fashion leaders, and popularized in a fashion which lasted for generations.

Bobbed hair, short skirts, silk-stockinged legs, suntan, and fragile one-piece bathing suits that revealed considerably more than 50 per cent of a girl's natural charms epitomized the heady years of the 20's, identifying the era with youth. A typical girl of this period is described in the fiction of Upton Sinclair. She is "Bertie," a young lady of 18, a brilliant flashing creature . . . "Her trim little legs were sheathed in the flossiest and most diaphanous silk, and her fancy pointed shoes were without a scratch. If Bertie got a dress of purple or carmine or orange or green, why then mysteriously there were stockings and shoes, and a hat and gloves and even a hand bag of the same to match; Dad said she would soon be having sport-cars to match."[13]

It was not until after 1914 that women made conscious and systematic attempts to look youthful. Prior to World War I, the ideal woman was "mature and dignified." Short hair was linked in the public mind with Bohemianism and radicalism, and makeup (unless skillfully concealed) was associated with actresses and fast women. Skirts were within 6 inches of the ground, and the point of greatest width in the female figure was at the hips or below. There was no suntan vogue; instead, systematic measures were taken to protect the complexion and hair against the damaging effects of wind, sun, and saltwater bathing.

These attitudes changed following the anxious period of World War I. An emphasis on youth, unequaled in the history of the world, developed partly because of a realization of the horrible destruction of war, partly because of the new emphasis of psychology and psychoanalysis upon training individuals in the "formative years," and partly because the industrial age placed a premium on the dexterity demanded in handling new machines. But primarily, it was the result of a desire to give children opportunity, accompanied by the means to do it. Moreover, young people could achieve economic and, to a large extent, moral and intellectual independence with comparative ease. It was possible to work one's way through college, borrow money, or obtain scholarships. Many, who would have been behind the plow a century before, remained in high school, college, or postgraduate school until close to thirty years of age.

Tired of national and world problems, people let trifles, fads, and sports win their attention. Girls, rebelling against demure attire dictated by puritanical convention, began a sort of gradual national striptease. Skirts started to ascend in 1923 and by 1927 were all the way to the knee and even above. Gone were stockings of black, brown, and white, displaced by flesh-colored tones. Gone or going was long hair (the most fashionable short version was the shingle). The ladies hairdressing business, stimulated by the acceptance of permanent waves, was booming. Fashion artists no longer made women look gentle, maidenly, demure, and rosebud-like, but sleek, sophisticated, worldly. (Not Mary Pickford, but Theda Bara the vamp was the prototype.)

GLAMOUR. The stage was set for an emphasis on "seduction," the base for the glamour pattern that infiltrated America and continues to hold a leading place in a culture geared to youth. The "youth culture" in America, as seen by sociologists Clyde Kluckholn and Henry Murray, stresses three attitudes: (1) the more or less irresponsible attitude of "having a good time" as opposed to the adult responsibility role; (2) a strong emphasis on social activities involving the opposite sex; and (3) the prominence of the "athletic hero" for the male (in sharp contrast to adult standards of a prosaic business executive), and the "glamour girl" role of the female (in contrast to her adult domestic role).[14]

The glamour pattern broke down the rigid classification of women into "respectable" married women and those that were "no better than they should be." Symbols such as smoking, cosmetics, and dress emancipation were taken over directly from the practices of types previously considered beyond the pale. The free expression of sexual attraction and impulses was allowed, but in a way that tended to segregate the sexual element from the total personality and so emphasized and segregated the sex role. For some women, sex became the weapon with which they could compete in a society where they felt inadequate to compete directly with the opposite sex on the same plane in an occupational role.

Mae West, the "sex queen" of the 30's, probably did more

than any other stage personality to complete the breakdown of the puritanical barriers against obvious physical display for sex purposes in America. She represented organized bawdiness, purified by a magic touch of humor. "Naughty, but nice" was the Mae West slogan. Dressed in tulle, furs, jewels, feathered hats—and everything plastered right to the body—she always portrayed a woman who was wealthy and wicked, but honest and loved.

Succeeded by such stars as Jayne Mansfield, Marilyn Monroe, and Brigitte Bardot, Mae West had been preceded in her emphasis on sex by the sophisticated "Gigis" of the French demimonde and by some of the leading stage personalities of the "naughty nineties," for whom silk stockings with fine lace insertions up to $500 a pair were not considered too expensive.

In fact, Americans have long had a muffled attachment to romantic love. A sentimental novel, *The Coquette*, by Mrs. Hannah Foster,[15] enjoyed an outstanding vogue for over 70 years, beginning in 1797, even though it was read surreptitiously. The book portrays a dashing young girl, Eliza Wharton—"I am young, gay, volatile"—confined by a society of moralists. It typifies the plight of youth asserting its right for exploration and adventure free from adult restrictions. However, while the heroine attains pleasure by a socially unapproved course, society also achieves justice in the end—the seduced one never enjoys a happy marriage but dies alone and unknown in a far place.

Americans are a paradoxical people: They idealize beauty, have a soft spot for youth and romance, but they still demand morality. High school and college girls frequently face a perplexing problem. The girl (and her mother) feel that she should be popular with boys if she is to be a success as a girl, yet she wants to remain acceptable by society's standards. Her entire future identity seems dependent on the projected role of wife-mother. Living in a society that frowns on single-blessedness and faced with the fact that women are beginning to outnumber men in many areas of the country, the adolescent girl is convinced that what really counts is to carry on social and emotional relations that will make her popular and ultimately attract the right boys. She puts on the mask that seems most likely to appeal.

This frustrating problem of a girl's popularity is portrayed by Scott Fitzgerald in his fiction of the 20's: "No matter how beautiful or brilliant a girl may be, the reputation of not being frequently cut in on makes her position at a dance unfortunate. Perhaps boys prefer her company to that of the butterflies with whom they dance a dozen times an evening, but youth in this jazz-nourished generation is temperamentally restless, and the idea of fox-trotting more than one full fox-trot with the same girl is distasteful, not to say odious."[16]

A youthful preoccupation with glamour continues into the adult life of many insecure American women. The American man feels he should marry a woman younger than himself, and since divorce is relatively easy to procure, prominent men of fifty, or more, may leave their wives and families to marry younger—not older—women. This practice compels wives, as well as single girls, to keep ever young, lovely, and resilient. They operate under a sporting code: If you can't keep your husband, don't complain if someone else gets him. Millions of women want to have the same sex appeal as the professional models, showgirls, and sophisticates of fashion who hold the public limelight. It is their key to a secure future.

There are no longer any secrets in the glamour trades. The fashion market booms with new beauty aids for everyone —false eyelashes, fake brows and hair pieces, foam-bolstered bosoms, and padded panties and girdles that give the wearer a well-rounded look from the back. Whereas the young man in the 20's may have known what he was getting when he picked a ripe, suntanned, and scantily clad wife from the beaches of southern California, today even the scantiest bathing suit may conceal some molded plastic foam. The figure of the modern girl can be bolstered fore and aft.

CHEESECAKE PUBLICITY AND BEAUTY CONTESTS. Movie stars and people in the entertainment world wear form-hugging dresses to gain attention. Figure display is part of their publicity, and if they wore a French couture model in good taste, no one would notice them. Promotion through cheesecake photography and beauty contests has done much to promote the cult of youthful beauty in America.

Webster defines "cheesecake photography" as photography

or photographs featuring the natural curves of shapely female legs, thighs, or trunks, usually scantily clothed—called also leg art. It has been said that this type of photograph was launched around 1912 by a *New York Journal* photographer who took a photograph of an actress seated on the rail of an incoming steamship. He discovered on developing it that it included more of her than either he or she expected.

Spectators also gasped, according to the reporters, at the revealing bathing suits worn at Atlantic City's first bathing-beauty contest in September, 1921. The winner wore an old-style suit with only her knees daringly bared, but others were less conventional. However, the new tight bathing suits brought joy to the hearts of rotogravure editors and proprietors of beach resorts. With the aid of photographers, the female form became the handmaiden of commerce.

Beauty has become big business. Many of the nation's celebrated beauty contests are frankly commercial. If they are not directly run by entrepreneurs for profit from pulchritude, they rely indirectly on commercial sponsorship for their existence. The most celebrated beauty contest was started in 1921 when the first "Miss America" was chosen from eight finalists at the beach in Atlantic City. It was not until 1958 that the pageant could boast a finalist from every state, but by 1965, there were 3,500 local preliminaries to choose 50 finalists. The budget was $500,000, compared with only $16,000 in 1942.[17]

The success of the Miss America contest inspired others run principally for profit, although the Atlantic City event is not. One of the largest of the private ventures is the "Miss Universe" contest, born of a commercial wrangle between Miss America 1951 and a Miss America pageant sponsor. The sponsor, Catalina, Inc., had stipulated that the final winner was to make her appearance around the country wearing the company's swimsuits. But Yolande Betbeze balked at the idea, arguing that she was an opera singer and not a bathing-suit model. Catalina withdrew its sponsorship of Miss America and promoted the Miss Universe contest in Long Beach, California.

The big business in beauty contests comes in the form of payments from cities eager to host the final contests, sale of television rights, and sale of the franchises for running preliminary events in resorts, amusement parks, and department stores. The evidence is in the fact that in 1959 the Kayser-Roth Company (which bought Catalina in 1954) demanded $100,000 from Long Beach to continue holding two pageants there: Miss U.S.A. (a preliminary contest to Miss Universe) and Miss Universe. The city refused and the two events were moved to Miami Beach.[18]

Corporations add further impetus to the beauty boom. "We are aware of the importance of teen-agers as consumers and we want them to think well of our hair products and to buy them," says Edward J. Breck, president of John H. Breck, Inc. Breck paid $25,000 as one national sponsor of the America's Junior Miss contest.[19]

While the sponsors sell their home permanents, automobiles, fabrics, and soft drinks, the beauty contestants also profit. The winner of the Miss America competition, for example, probably collects up to $100,000 in fees from personal appearances and scholarship money during her reign. Even losers can make money; state finalists who do not win the Miss America crown can count on averaging about $20,000 for the year on the strength of their state titles alone. Because the stakes are high, some 70,000 girls entered the Miss America preliminaries in 1965 and the number has been increasing by about 500 annually for some time.[20]

The appeal for sophisticated manners is reaching down to younger and younger children. At what age should a girl get her first permanent? When should she be allowed to wear nylons or red nail polish? These questions are debated in America as early as the third grade. A teen-age advertisement asks: Do you look ready for romance? Want to look like a dream walking?

As if to augment the problem, a new doll with a woman's body and a model's wardrobe skyrocketed to fame in 1959 and soon became a familiar name among 5- to 12-year-olds. The Barbie doll debut sparked a doll revolution. Baby dolls had dominated sales from time immemorial, and manufacturers who had tried to sell a doll with a movie star curved figure were unsuccessful. Then Barbie appeared—a sophisticated teen-age doll with a shapely figure and a variety of tiny, fashionable garments to be handmade or bought ready-made so that children could dress her in various ensembles. Little girls could play at being the teen-agers they would someday become. Barbie became by far the best selling doll in the 60's. In answer to critics who said that the Barbie doll placed undue emphasis on sex, Barbie's manufacturer countered that the doll helps little girls make the adjustment to teen years by allowing them to live the teen-age role. Playing with the doll teaches them something about clothes, and helps them learn poise.

The Youth Market

The total youth market consists of preschool children (up to 5), grade school children (6–12), teen-agers (13–19), and collegians or young adults (20–24). Consumer behavior is a product of learning that begins in childhood and develops throughout the life cycle.

THE CHILD CONSUMER. An interest in clothing begins to develop around the age of two years, primarily through the influence of parents who confer their ideas of masculinity and femininity on young children. Discussing sex differences in children's behavior, psychologist Evelyn Pitcher reports that clothes talk is not only more popular among preschool girls than boys, but girls also pay more attention to details ("see my pretty slip with the flower on it"), color, suitability, and general appearance. Boys are not very interested in the details of dress, except to identify with make-believe roles: "I want my sweater just on my shoulders, so I can be like Superman and Mighty Mouse." Miss Pitcher believes that differences between boys and girls reflect the fact that both fathers and mothers clearly regard an interest in pretty clothes, domestic habits, and families or babies as feminine, while they regard an interest in objects or ideas as masculine.[21]

From ages five to nine the child becomes more of an independent consumer. An exploratory study of the consumer behavior of children, five, seven, and nine, was made by market economist James McNeal. He found that independent purchasing by children in the middle socioeconomic classes becomes significant near age seven. After seven, increasing age results in greater parental permissiveness toward the child's desire for more independent consumer action in more complex purchases—from candy bars to toys to school supplies to family staples.

A skeptical attitude toward advertising develops early. At age seven, 40 per cent of the girls he interviewed and only 10 per cent of the boys stated that they did not believe most commercials, while in the group of nine-year-olds the suspicious attitude was about equally divided. The peer influence was also noticeable by ages seven and nine. Children made comments that implied they wanted sweets and toys like other children had. Nine-year-olds were slightly fashion conscious in the sense that they wanted such things as tennis shoes and skirts worn by other children. Girls, particularly, turned from an earlier interest in food and toys and increased their concern with clothes. There was a sex difference in the attitude toward the consumer role: By age nine the female was emerging with more interest and more experience than the male in the shopping function. McNeal suggests that this reflects the children's growing realization that shopping is usually viewed as feminine behavior in our society. Girls continue to demonstrate greater clothing awareness than boys throughout the teen years.[22]

The trend in the kid-clothes industry is toward high fashion and high prices to satisfy those mothers who are not going to make their daughters wear plain, cheap garb as they did in their third-grade class. It is possible to spend almost as much for a child's outfit as for an adult dress. Styling is important. There is a strong trend toward more style and changes in girls' dresses because, as one mother said, "kids are more knowledgeable these days and they quickly demand new styles." Big companies diversify into girls' dresses believing this part of the business is more stable than women's dresses. The children's couture is almost a miniature copy of the women's wear industry with fetching models built along the popular avant-garde styles of the older teen-age consumers.

THE TEEN-AGE CONSUMER. Youngsters in the 13–24 age group are the most fashion conscious individuals in today's population. As this sector of the market increases, analysts forecast a sharp increase in the supply of fashion goods. In contrast, market research men tend to count individuals over

65 and under 13 as only one-half a customer when forecasting economic growth in the apparel trades.

It was not until 1950 that the term "teen-ager" came into common use. The word was promoted by advertisers aiming at a new market, and by television and motion picture producers who wanted to cultivate a responsive new audience. In doing this they created an image for anyone who wanted to criticize the nation's youth and also gave the adolescent an erroneous view of himself as a member of a special group to be treated with kid gloves; given special privileges; and provided with special magazines, books, and programs.

Through convenience the terms "teen" and "teen-ager" have been used to lump together 13-year-old grade school students with 19-year-old college men and women, even though a 19-year-old college boy probably "wouldn't be caught dead" with a squealing group of 13-year-old girls. Undoubtedly, there are no points of view more divergent than those of a 13-year-old girl and an 18-year-old young woman.

In actual merchandising practice the ages are sorted out. Thirteen-year-olds are considered to be children just emerging into adolescence, while 19-year-olds are treated like young adults. The true adolescents of 13 to 16 are grouped increasingly by themselves. The market specializes in teenage merchandise *for this age bracket*; it may be called "young juniors" or "high school girl" or some other equally descriptive phrase. Younger girls belong to the children's section; older ones to various gradations of sub-debs, debs, juniors, college girls, and the like.

Normal adolescence (13–16) is the time when boys and girls waver between the safety and security of dependence on their parents and the urge to discover life as independent human beings. At this time parents whose role has been that of teacher may find themselves learners as their sons and daughters open doors to new ideas and new outlooks on the surrounding world. Both teen-ager and parent vacillate between ordering and yielding.

Sociologists believe the "adolescent subculture" is a peculiar phenomenon spawned by an industrial society. Although for some time it was most prominent in America, it is now emerging in other industrial societies. The adolescent subculture has values and activities quite distinct from those of the adult societies; its members have their most important associations within their own group. The high school, or its equivalent, has become the functioning adolescent community. Set apart in a world of their own with activities peculiar to their fellows, teens develop their own social system. They have all the things to make the system run—money, cars, freedom in association with the opposite sex, clothes, and entertainment designed especially for them. The international spread of swing music and youthful clothing fads is the consequence of economic and social changes that put adolescents into a world of their own. Before 1910 labor statistics listed all people below 16 as children, and all those older as adults. The teen-ager was not a fashion leader in those days and dress styles were full busted and matronly.

Family Structure and the Teen-ager's Role. Industrialization, particularly between 1880 and 1900, produced many changes in the American family structure and, consequently, in the role of the teen-ager. Perhaps one of the most significant changes was the decrease of patriarchism in the family. Many a father's preeminent role as authoritarian head of the family was shaken when it became possible for his daughter and even his wife to support herself and strike out against his actual or potential tyranny. In the ten years between 1880 and 1890, the number of children working increased 75 per cent. The percentage of women over sixteen who were gainfully employed jumped from 14.8 per cent in 1880 to 20.6 per cent in 1900. Among skilled workers, 56 per cent would have been without aid from other members of their families, while of the unskilled, only 9 per cent were able to support themselves and their families.[23]

Until this time the American family had closely retained its European heritage, but now a new trend began. Instead of a closely knit unit, the family became more democratic— a group of individual members dependent less on forced authority than on ethical unity and spontaneous government by free decision. As familism weakened, society had to assume a more parental role. The school and church began to undertake more rigorous programs of socialization; juvenile courts were established; education was made compulsory; school lunches, free books, and playgrounds were introduced. In other words, social centers replaced the home.

Another important change in family life caused by industrialization was a shift from the private home of the rural and small town environment to the multifamily dwelling or apartment house in the city. Urban life had its effect on the teen-ager. When not working outside the home, he was seeking social ties, also away from home. The family home was no longer a source of entertainment in itself.

Today, industrialization and rapidity of change appear to have completely taken out of some parents' hands the skill to train their child. Their own skills obsolete, they seem out of touch with the times and unable to understand, much less instill, the standards of a society that has changed since they were young. Fathers gone to the service and mothers busy in defense industries during World War II thrust youngsters into new maturity. Since then the process has accelerated as many mothers continue to work, fathers moonlight, and families move to the suburbs where fathers have even less time at home due to the extra hours spent commuting to jobs. The suburban child is in many ways a fatherless child. The town is devoid of men, but filled with children. Public sentiment becomes largely dominated by children below sixteen.*

The increased mobility of American families, the increased travel by fathers on the job, and increased complexity of living leave less time for parental supervision. As the adult world withdraws from the problems of youth, the adolescent subculture becomes stronger. It is from this culture the teenage consumer emerges.

Teen Insecurity. The lack of family supervision has had its harmful effects. Beneath a cool exterior many teen-agers are painfully insecure, questioning, and doubting, according to Lester Rand, president of a marketing service, Youth Research Institute. Although young people are often accused of snap judgments, 72 per cent of the teen-agers Rand polled said they fret and suffer when they commit themselves in what they

---

* William H. Whyte, Jr., in a study of Park Forest, Illinois, found the concerns of parenthood were so pervasive that adjustment for childless couples was almost impossible and they often adopted children.[24]

consider to be an important matter. Thirty-six per cent were perturbed when faced with any kind of choice, even a simple question of what flavor ice cream to order. Moving to a new neighborhood upsets them, as does the prospect of getting into a new group or club. Until they become acclimated, which may take a long time, they feel very unsure of themselves. And as to clothes, 36 per cent "felt funny" when they wore something new. *They thought everyone was looking at them.*

The leading worries found by Rand differed somewhat between girls and boys (16–18 years of age). The largest percentage of girls ranked their worries in this way: (1) how to act on a date; (2) school grades; (3) popularity; (4) money and allowances; (5) clothing. Boys of the same age group ranked their worries differently: (1) money; (2) future, careers, or job; (3) dating; (4) school grades; (5) popularity. Clothing was of minor concern to the boys.[25] In sum, girls tend to worry more than boys about grades, dates, social acceptance, and clothing, and less about careers.

Psychoanalyst Bruno Bettelheim believes the respected modern formula for today's girl includes: She has " 'done well' at school, at finding jobs, at finding husbands, at running homes, and at planning activities of all sorts."[26] Because these goals may conflict, difficult choices face the adolescent girl. Doing well at school or finding a job may conflict with finding a husband, since boys, who are worried about their career status, may be afraid of girls who compete with them too closely on the same level. On the other hand, a girl good at finding a husband and running a home may feel intellectually deprived if she interrupts the development of a job career. Margaret Mead believes the principle cause of adolescents' difficulties in our complicated society is the *presence of conflicting standards* and the belief that each person should make his or her own choices, coupled with a feeling that choice is an important matter.[27]

Several youthful ways-to-look have caught on in America. To paraphrase Mae West, you may appear to be "nice" *or* "naughty"—it is the artless ballet slipper versus the seduction of the high heel. The *nice* young look is bright eyed, carefree, clean, wholesome, fresh and vigorous, long legged, and graceful. This look became recognized abroad, beginning in the 1930's, as the American look. It is sometimes called the "little boy" look, or, when coupled with demure attitudes, shorter legs, and a quiet rosebud quality, the "little girl" look. In opposition to this is the *naughty* look—the more-knowing, sophisticated, glamour girl look—the flirt, the vamp, the seducer. To heed conventional middle-class morality while attracting boys, most American girls attempt to combine the two looks: They want to *appear* naughty, yet *be* nice; they want to tempt the boys, yet keep them in line.

In 1965 "the black mesh scandal suits," presented by the swimsuit company of Cole of California, Inc., seemed to capture the two-pronged image by achieving something wild for nice girls. The modest use of net was the key to the "tastefully scandalous suits," which bared enough skin to allow the wearer to get air and sun while covering up enough so the men could admire it comfortably and the wearer could be at ease. One Cole ad put it this way: "New but not nude." The well-placed publicity for this suit made it a big seller in the summer of '65 as American women grew bolder on the beach. Interestingly, reports from local stores indicate it was not the very young who were buying the suit, but women in the middle and older age brackets.

The purchase of young styles by not-so-young customers is suspected—indeed, welcomed—by editors of youth magazines. Magazines that announce themselves as "the college girls' bible" are perfectly aware that many a "middle-aged woman" is caught by their lure. Unlike the older fashion magazines, *Vogue* and *Bazaar,* magazines such as *Mademoiselle, Charm,* and *Glamour* are products of the Depression, dedicated to showing what is actually for sale in everyone's stores. Working with big stores they have opened the gates of fashion to every woman, but their chief discovery has been the rise of the young as an influence and a market.

Reaching Juvenile Markets. The general prosperity of the 1960's (like the 20's) has tended to increase choice. This is the age of economic emancipation of the juvenile. One of the by-products of almost full employment since World War II is the teen-age part-time wage earner. Teens earn billions of dollars in part-time jobs after school or on Saturday—working in local shops, supermarkets, and filling stations; baby sitting, doing odd jobs around home, and such. In the summertime

Nice . . . naughty . . . naughty but nice

the teen-age full-time working force swells into the millions. Teen-agers pocket their earnings, add liberal allowances and gifts from generous parents, and open bank accounts of their own. The young people of the 20's, brazen, irritating, and offensive to some, were undoubtedly the spearhead which broke down conventions. Today, young people do not lead such protected lives and are able to look after themselves with a certain independence.

Four important factors have resulted in increased sales pressure on teen-agers: (1) the billions of dollars in teen-age hands; (2) the indirect buying influence the teen-ager has on family consumption patterns; (3) the increasing number of teen-age marriages; and (4) the teen-age role of innovator and fashion leader.

Shortly after the juvenile market began to receive special attention from advertisers, the magazine *Consumer Reports* (March, 1957) suggested one explanation for rising teen-age influence: "In a hard-living, fast-driving, urbanized community, where adult privileges often desired by the young include alcohol, tobacco, and late hours, the parent has to say 'No' much too frequently; hence he is looking for places to say 'Yes.' . . ." A high school principal was quoted as saying, "Parents, today, feel a need to prove to their teen-age children that they are 'Good Joes.'" Consequently, *Consumer Reports* explained, parents accede to pressure from the youngster for the responsibility of spending his own money, as well as on the choice of the new family car, the family television, where to take a vacation, what movies to see, and what clothes to choose for both adult and child.[28] As an indication of the teen's indirect buying influence, 55 per cent of the teen-age girls in a survey made by *Seventeen* said they thought they had exercised at least some influence on the family's most recent automobile purchase.[29]

The lenient attitude of parents toward teen-age spending is also credited with helping establish consumption patterns in the child which are freer than the practical standards of the parent. Shopkeepers feel that when the teen-age consumer wants something he can afford, he buys it, seldom shopping around. Price comparisons are reported to be rare on records, jewelry, table radios, clothes, and cosmetics. Neither is the teen a contributor to the returned-goods problem. If he does bring something back it is usually because his parents refused to let him keep it. He fails to demand replacement when goods are faulty and also disapproves of his parents' return of goods. Apparently, foolish expenditures fail to produce the same awareness of wasted dollars in son or daughter as they do in "Pop" who has his money tied up in rent, car payments, electric bills, and other household expenses.[30]

What seem to be wasteful buying habits in the youthful consumer are often the result of his aforementioned insecurity. Embarrassed at making a poor buy, he may try to hide the fact in not calling attention to the situation by demanding his rights. His buying habits also reflect certain family-size funds as well as the parents' permissive attitude. Rather than calling for good consumer education, however, merchandisers expect the young to persuade the parent that what he buys is right.

A third reason for the market's concentration on the teen-ager is the rapidly increasing number of teens who become brides and grooms. The trend to teen marriage seems more pronounced in the United States than anywhere else. Girls no longer have to choose between marriage and a career as a result of increased opportunities for employment among young married women with above-average education. Before World War II, universities might expel students who married, especially girls, who were considered a bad influence in dormitories. Now, marriage in college becomes increasingly more commonplace.

In an interview with *U.S. News and World Report* on early marriages (June 6, 1960), Margaret Mead suggested that "everybody is pushing, to a degree," young people into premature responsibilities and early marriages. She mentions that World War I, the Depression, World War II, and the Korean War have all discouraged the adult world, the people who are the parents of today's youth. Having lived through all these traumatic times, the parents' attitude is: We want you to have fun now; take some enjoyment in life while you can get it; the future is totally uncertain. Similarly, anxiety over atomic war and unsettled world conditions drives young people into snatching at happiness for fear it is going to disappear. Teen-agers feel that if they are not married and settled and have a career and a house before they are twenty-five they may never get these things.[31] Such security-seeking attitudes lead to early retiring into domesticity and young marriages.

A final, and fourth reason for the popularity of the young consumer, especially in the fashion market, is his role as innovator and fashion leader. The Katz and Lazarsfeld study on personal influence showed that fashion interest was highly correlated with the life cycle. The greatest concentration of fashion opinion leaders was among the group called *Girls* (single females under 35 years), and each successive life cycle position was associated with declining leadership rate.[32]

While older people are often suspicious of the new or different, young people expect and anticipate change; they are willing to try a new product or switch to a new brand. The juvenile consumer exudes optimism for the future. Feeling sure tomorrow will be better than today, he continues to expand consumption, increasing his relative amounts of pleasure and the area of his purchasing power. He finds virtues not in curbing desires, but rather in realizing himself by acquiring the necessary goods and services such as a hi-fi set, clothing, or an automobile. What adults consider a luxury, young people consider a necessity to keep pace with today's living. They can be won by enterprising merchandising techniques, but swiftly lost if advertisers become complacent. Their standards are shifting, and in whatever direction youthful enthusiasm flows, so flows production.

MARKET RESPONSE TO TEEN-AGE DEMANDS. While the boy buys sports equipment, the teen-age girl spends far more on clothes than the average for the total population. She is well groomed and spends heavily to stay that way. Her prime focus from her early years is attracting boys. In 1959 sociologists Arthur Vener and Charles Hoffer, interested in adolescent orientations to clothing, explored the relationship between clothing awareness and the social characteristics of adolescents. They found that while girls show more clothing awareness than boys, both boys and girls who are more other-directed, that is, more sensitive to the feelings and opinions of others, tend to be most aware of clothing. Conversely students, both boys and girls, with greater confidence have less clothing awareness. (This latter finding seems to concur with that of Mary Ryan (1953) who found a slight tendency for boys and girls displaying the least general security—shyness, difficulty in making friends—to have higher clothing interest than those who demonstrated high general security.)[33]

Among students who experienced a strong feeling of clothing deprivation, clothing became a subject of decreasing interest. It is as if the socially deprived individual who lacks the money to purchase clothes eases his feeling of frustration by a decreasing interest in clothes. The higher the clothing awareness, the age-grade, the social confidence, and the occupation of the father, the less likely the adolescent is to experience a feeling of clothing inadequacy.[34]

Individuals whose opinions are most important to the adolescent in assessing his own clothing behavior are his mother and his peers. However, Vener and Hoffer found that youngsters in the 12th grade, as a group, tend to refer less than do younger adolescents to *specific* other persons as clothing models. By this time, approved rules related to dress seem to have become unconscious and generalized.[35]

These findings are confirmed by other research. A marketing report on teen-age girls (14–17) by the United States Department of Agriculture suggests sixteen as the age of shopping independence. Both mothers and daughters feel that by this time a girl is "old enough to do her own shopping and pick out her own clothes." The USDA report shows that teen-age girls talk with other people (mothers and friends), consult magazines and newspapers, window-shop, and look in several stores before buying. *Only a few make more than one actual shopping trip* to select the dress or skirt they buy. Mother's influence is strongest on price and the girl's need for the item; least on color and style. The pattern runs like this: After mother has decided whether an article of clothing is needed and the price acceptable, after mutual agreement on fabric and what stores to shop in, daughter has relatively free rein to decide upon the item. The report suggests that retail promotion on price, durability, and ease of care in fibers is best directed to mothers, while style promotion should be aimed at the teen-age daughter.[36]

The rise of teen-age influence in the market has resulted in some youthful styles aimed at 13- to 19-year-olds. The birth of the Junior dress, a major change in styling, came in the early 1930's. It was strictly an American development that was eventually to influence Europe. The style was born in St. Louis where Irving L. Sorger, one-time general manager of Kline's women's specialty shop, passed Washington University on his way downtown each day. Noticing what the girls were wearing to classes, Sorger had manufacturers incorporate fads he observed into clothing styles sold at Kline's. He also persuaded a teacher in design at the School of Fine Arts to give the class a problem in dress design. The best designs were manufactured by a local firm, and became immediate successes. One particularly popular style was a young princess dress, very short waisted, with quite a bit of gingerbread trimming. This, Sorger felt, was the real beginning of junior styling. He developed junior sizing by taking the average measurements of girls on the Washington University campus.[37]

Junior dresses were at first youthful styles in youthful sizes. It remained for the firm of Bobbie Brooks, in more recent years, to promote the concept of junior as an *age* rather than a size by persuading stores to emphasize the age-group approach.

By the mid-60's the retail market jumped on the teen-age bandwagon in earnest. According to *Seventeen*, in 1965 teen-age girls composed 11 per cent of the population and purchased 20 per cent of the apparel and 23 per cent of the cosmetics sold in this country. Their ranks were increasing by 1.8 million every year, as 12-year-olds turned the corner.[38] *Seventeen* also emphasized that teens bought almost 72 million hosiery items and over 6 million pieces of costume jewelry, 4 million belts and 3.5 million wallets during back-to-school sales of the previous year.[39]

A new type of fashion model, Twiggy, a 17-year-old cockney from northwest London, made looking 17 and starved a fashion image for 1967. With 91 pounds scattered over a 5' 7" frame she seemed to be the world's narrowest girl and the personification of youth. Her mini-bosom suited the mini-skirt age. With wide open gray eyes that radiated the precious innocence of the schoolgirl, and her underdeveloped boyish figure, she made a virtue of all the terrible things of gawky, miserable adolescence—when teen-age spending power was never greater. In no other era would such a girl have become a fashion model.

No one dares overlook the booming teen-age market.

For example, fur coats are displayed in a New York street-level showroom—everything helter-shelter; nothing forbidding about it; the kind of place that says "come in and browse"— as an invitation to buy for the working girl and all the young. Fabric retailers have presented "making-it-easy preprinted 'mock-frocks,' " sold by the dress, ready to cut out and stitch up. Department stores have organized fashion councils composed of local high school sudents who attend monthly store meetings and model their own garments at the store.

Even the J. C. Penney Company, reputedly the world's biggest buyer of dresses, increased its interest in young fashions, a sharp contrast for a company which has traditionally frowned on the "jive crowd" by stressing moderation and the Golden Rule. *Women's Wear Daily*, February 10, 1965, reported the opinion of one merchandiser who had been with Penney since 1944: "About 50 per cent of the women in this country are under the age of 25. We're going after that group. They're repeat customers, they buy more than one dress at a time and represent a sizable portion of business." As a result, the Penney Company signed contracts with three European designers, all of whom have demonstrated great appeal to young people.[40]

Young designers have been quite successful at designing young clothes, perhaps because they are more familiar with the tastes of those in their own age group. Vicki Tiel, who at age 21 designed a group of swimsuits and accessories for a junior line, flatly states: "Clothes are meant to be thrown away. . . . These women who walk around with their dirty smelly three-year-old Chanels . . . they can have their stupid suits. . . . I think clothes should be simple, basic, fun, and inexpensive."[41] (Paper dresses for $1 that could literally "be thrown away" first appeared in 1966.)

Curiously, these ideas on clothes expressed by a modern young designer almost echo those of the French designer Chanel whose suits women *will not throw away*. The two designers' ideas seem to differ in only one major respect, the importance of quality. It was Chanel who, over 40 years ago, first insisted that women should look *young, simple, charming,* and *natural*—"expensively" *poor*. She, too, believes that fashions are made to throw away. But, in the French couture tradition, she also believes in the luxurious elegance of excellent fabrics, workmanship, and fit, qualities which women learn to value in her clothes and which prevent them from throwing her suits away.

The French couture, with the exception of Chanel, had not traditionally been interested in the young look. Chanel's fellow couturiers did not like her flat-chested boyish styling in the 20's; however, enthusiastic American buyers made her styles famous. Haute couture emphasis has been "elegance," and elegance demands poised women of at least thirty years of age who have the composure and bearing to complement elegant clothes. The recent French attitude that promotes "youth" is probably the result of the tremendous influence of American buyers on a group of young French designers who gained prominence in the late 1950's and 1960's.

Guy Laroche was the first couture designer to successfully emphasize the junior look, achieving his initial success in 1957. Like the American junior market which supposedly aimed at a size not an age, Laroche attracted private clientele with an outlook that was youthful even if their chronological age was not. He aims to maintain two facets to his fashion identity—youthfulness and simplicity. Stylists suggest that part of his youthful concept may have developed during two years on Seventh Avenue where he designed collections for several American manufacturers to gain ready-to-wear experience before opening his own couture house. At the same time, a compatriot, Pierre Cardin, who began in 1952, scored his first American success with "young coats" in 1958. Since then Cardin has gone on to execute successful versions of the young look in the current mode and has had a strong design influence on the rising French ready-to-wear market.

Probably the youngest and most celebrated of the French couture designers in the 1960's is Yves St. Laurent. When Christian Dior died in 1958, Yves, at 21, became the head designer of the House of Dior. Devoted to the young and feminine look, he startled the couture world with his first fashion triumph, "the trapeze" (a high-waisted shift). Later, as master of his own house, he started another Paris couture revolution by opening a snappy young boutique on the Left Bank. He planned to keep his shop open until midnight, cater to the young, and sell clothes at moderate prices ($60). He saw his *Rive Gauche look* as: trouser suits—with turtleneck pullovers; sleeveless shifts with side slits; classic raincoats. Yves believes that the young and the less young will be able to wear his clothes: "All you need is the right frame of mind—think of seduction before elegance."[42]

The greatest blow to the traditionally elegant look of the Paris couture system was struck by the controversial André Courrèges, onetime master tailor for Balenciaga, who appeared as a designer with his own house in 1964, quietly vanished by 1966, but returned to the scene once more in 1967. In his first appearance on the couture scene Courrèges introduced a revolutionary concept of styling for contemporary space-age clothes: boots, goggles, dresses three inches above the knee. More junior than adult, more sportswear than salon, the main features of his boxy, uncluttered look spread throughout the fashion world. Anyone young enough to wear the Courrèges look, wore it. The rest felt suddenly "old."

Oldsters in a Youth-Oriented Society

The mannerisms of youth are gay, timid, friendly, and mischievous, while the characteristics of age are quiet, poised, formal, and dignified. Youth is quick, graceful, airy; age is deliberate, firm, decisive. Youth goes forth to seduce life and the unknowable; age settles back and wisely contemplates. Young bodies are firm, yet pliable; mature bodies are uniquely and individually formed, resistant to change. With such divergent characteristics, how do two age groups—youngsters and oldsters—meet on the common ground of fashion? How do they blend the current styles until the apparent gap between the ages is almost (but never quite) closed?

Advantages in a ready-to-wear system seem to accrue to the young. A mass market relies for its sales on color, fashion, and standardized styling, as opposed to the intricate cut, high quality, and personalized fit of a couture system. In this way ready-to-wear is keyed to youth, for the young consumer is more interested in color and style than in quality of workmanship, fabric, or fit. The older person, on the other hand, requires the type of service only a couture system can supply. No longer at her physical best, she needs the flattery of subtle drapings and well-cut designs, not clothing that leaps out and demands attention or makes for "fashion news." Her individual body shape demands personalized fit, and the depth of her experience and the dignity of her bearing demand quality in clothes—fabrics that enhance through association the diminishing vigor of her body. In short, she needs all the things time, money, and skill can produce, if she is to portray, with her clothes, those qualities that belong to age: poise, dignity, and assurance. Selecting from a market styled for youth, the qualities of age take second place. It is seldom possible for the same dress to look as well on a woman of seventy as on a girl of seventeen.

On the other hand, a ready-to-wear market which idealizes the slim, long-legged figures of youth may have a psychological value for the older woman. Most dresses produced for the American mass market are designed to slenderize the waist and hips, emphasize the face, and make a woman appear tall and slender. Any design that "ages" its wearer is sifted out; those that give a youthful look become best sellers. The middle-aged consumer is not treated as a member of a special group, but simply as *one of the girls, with a sizing problem*. Foundation garment designers, cosmeticians, and health specialists work to make her appear on an equal level with all females. While she is not honored for her age, neither is she shunted out of the society. Instead, she is offered all the accouterments of beauty that will give her the illusion of youth in a youth-oriented culture.

American society believes age is a matter of mental attitude—that the key to effective aging is a program that requires activity of body and mind. The fashion market puts all women in slender high-heeled shoes, uplift brassieres, and stretch girdles to make them feel part of the active world and accepted by it, instead of "old" and "ready for the shelf."

"A Marketing Profile of the Senior Citizen Group" by David E. Wallen (1957) outlined three characteristics of this group: (1) Unlike children and teens, its wants parallel those of other groups, except for some special health and comfort items. (2) This group has less economic identity in common with other groups, since large concentrations are at the base of the scale and it is larger than average at the top. (3) Group members resist identification, partly, Wallen believes, because of the youth-infatuated society and partly because age is losing its meaning. Improved status, physically and economically, makes the senior citizen want to be treated like everyone else.[43]

He found that the elderly man is not as conservative as is generally thought. He likes argyle socks and gaudy shirts and sportswear, possibly because he had to dress conservatively at work and now in his retirement is less restricted. Wallen found the elderly woman less predictable, however. She dresses conservatively and appears to put comfort ahead of style. She likes a certain propriety in her dress—long sleeves because her arms age easily—and is partial to soft full lines.[44]

In many ways, old age is a period of social isolation. Because of the great significance of occupation status in American society, as Kluckholn points out, retirement not only cuts ties to the job itself, but also greatly loosens those to the community of residence. In addition, as children become independent through marriage and occupation, there is the isolation of the parental couple left without attachment to any continuous kinship group.

Normally the adult role is one of specialization; as man narrows his field of concentration, his ability to share common interests with others decreases until there may be little to bind him to others of comparable status in his community. It is not surprising, then, that market research shows the expenditures for clothing decrease as age advances, regardless of the income, social, and cultural level of older people. This finding can be related not only to the older person's decrease in social activity, but also to his purchase of more conservative clothing, and reluctance to accept fashion change.

Man seems to operate in this way: As his experience with the environment increases, he begins to classify and catalog things in relation to his needs and interests. This enables him to sift out and retain from an overwhelming mass of incoming facts and impressions only those he can use. As he grows older and less energetic, his catalog system grows harder and firmer; he rejects messages that do not fit its structure, or distorts them so they do. He becomes suspicious of the new or different, more set in his ways, and harder to sell. In the language of the market economist, his choice becomes more stable.

In 1956 I made an examination of choice stability in specific design features in dresses among 304 married women over 18 years of age. Choice stability was assumed to occur when one woman chose *the same* design features in two "well-liked" dresses in separate years. The survey showed that choice stability for women in general was greatest for three aspects of silhouette: waistlines, sleeves, and bodice fit. Since fashion change is likely to affect silhouette, this finding suggests a conflict between the stability of women's choice and fashion. The two items showing the least stability were "type of design in the fabric" and "hue, value, and intensity of color." Since these are surface aspects of dresses rather than structural features, it is not surprising that fashion change in these areas met with little resistance.

Choice stability also increased with age. This was particularly noticeable in four items of silhouette: necklines, waistlines, sleeves, and skirts. This increased choice stability among older women implies they may resist more strongly than other groups fashion influence which affects these aspects of silhouette.

The more open attitude of American women toward color change, revealed in this study, strongly suggests the influence of the mass market, which depends more on color change than on cut for garment salability. Or, it may reflect the youth-oriented nature of our culture. Uninhibited use of color is one way to level the difference between ages.

Since color is merely reflected light, it can change the particular light it reflects in the individual instance. That is, it can change the complexion of the woman who wears it— make her look paler, sallow, rosier. Variable factors—the brightness and color of eyes, the exact shade of hair, and especially the habitual expression—determine what colors each woman will wear. In the final analysis, color depends on the woman's courage and opportunity to experiment, to try this color and that and study what it does to enhance or diminish her good looks. Many of the wonderful color possibilities unleashed by twentieth-century chemistry will never find their way into the clothes market unless the customer insists on a wider, freer palette of colors to choose from.

American women have liked color for some time. Cecil Beaton reported that Mrs. Nancy Tree, a "taste leader" in the 1940's, brought a welcome love of color and feeling for comfort to the English scene. But color in fashion did not become prevalent until after World War II when people felt a compulsion to be light, bright, and cheerful for a change. Expanding markets were ready for anything, aided by perfected dyes, with better clarity, depth, and performance. Sober-coated Germans were amazed to see the bright red and green coats worn by American women.

Color, styles, silhouette. . . . While fashion influence tends to pass mainly between members of the same age group, there are clear indications that trends set by young fashion leaders are adopted by older women. The youth movement has influenced the color spectrum and markets for all ages. The long-run effect of an accent on youth has been a general leveling of age differences. Fashion paradoxically supplies the needs of maturity while catering to youth—in eyeglasses, make-up, foundation garments, hair coloring. A generation ago a woman of 60 was ready for her shawl and rocker. Today she tries the newest hairdo and goes to the newest plays. She wants to look fashionable and make the most of her figure which is not the figure of her 18-year-old granddaughter.

Aware of all age groups, the competitive American market makes a play for "oldsters" as well as youngsters. However, each group retains its unique characteristics, preventing the same styles from enhancing both groups equally well. The young still remain more facile at adopting fashion change than the old; the mischievous spark of youth matches extreme cuts and colors that catch the eye, throwing them away quickly. But the dignity of age demands subtle lines and keeps them a long time. Curved young figures seduce when discreetly exposed, older more rigid and imperfect bodies look elegant in knowing-concealment. The "smart to be 60" market wants quality merchandise and services instead of gimmicks. Alert merchandisers are aware that some adjustments for age are necessary, even in a youth-oriented culture in which the fashion industry identifies its oldsters by size instead of age.

12

THE CASUAL LOOK

A shift toward casualness has been occurring at every level in American life. In an attempt to persuade John F. Kennedy when he was President of the United States that he should wear a hat, a British men's fashion magazine asked how a hatless man could properly greet a lady. In an editorial speculating on the question, the magazine suggested that he could make a brief and courteous bow, offer a hearty hand-shake, or, it added, he could use "that peculiarly American greeting—the flat palm of the hand sliding upwards and out-wards across the greeter's face and the cheerful injunction 'Hi.'" None of these techniques would do, however, if the President greeted a lady like Queen Elizabeth II, was the editorial verdict.[1]

The American in casual dress piques the curiosity of foreign observers. They meet her in the streets, museums, and theaters of Russia—an American tourist. What are those "crude, slipper-like shoes" on her feet? (The loafers.) Why does she wear shapeless, loose sweaters and coarse wool cloth in her suits, and tie her head in a kerchief? Surely in America there is a choice of hats. And why does she wear a kerchief so wrinkled and soiled? Each Russian girl, no matter how small her wardrobe, traditionally takes pride in her freshly washed and pressed kerchief, folding it carefully as she wears it to keep it unwrinkled.

At home, the American is even more careless and relaxed. Women shoppers in pants, dangling large handbags, and ac-companied by one to five children make up the casually dressed contingent in suburban shopping centers. Children seem to be dressed in whatever the mother finds first: unmatched colors, skirts either too long or too short, a little boy's pants leg dragging the floor while the other leg is rolled up to his calf.

It is all part of the casual look. In a symbolic gauging of formality and informality—caviar or hot dogs, five-course dinners or buffet—modern man adjusts his social index. In the nineteenth century, peasants who came to America felt above the immigrant class only if they wore a hat. Soon, everyone had a hat. No one knew why; it became an unwritten law enforced by parents, churches, and schools. In the twentieth century, when almost everyone can afford a hat, few people wear them.

The "casual look" is somewhere between the working look and the dressy look and is symbolized by this century's unique contribution to fashion: the sweater and skirt. In broader terms it is the "spectator sports" look, designed for people who go to games, look like they might play, but do not.

When asked what is *American* fashion, the French editor of *Elle,* a widely read French fashion publication, said, "Sportswear . . . especially Texas sportswear. The blue jeans dress . . . that was pure Texas. American fashion is good when it's really American . . . sweaters . . . leather coats with tricot sleeves. . . ."[2]

A casual style has three characteristics that supplement one another. First, it reduces formality by decreasing the emphasis on "proper clothes." Unpretentious and friendly, informal styles seem to symbolize the feeling of a democracy. Second, it is versatile; it is nonspecialized in use. Being a marginal style, neither strictly for work or strictly for play, it is acceptable in either world and still fulfills all the requirements of health, durability, and social decorum. Consequently, it has a third characteristic: It is practical—or, rationally functioning.

It was the proper and impractical aspects of women's dress that aroused the ire of dress reformers after the Civil War. One such reformer, Elizabeth Stuart Phelps, wrote: "I lay especial stress upon the close waist and long skirt . . .; when I see women stay indoors the entire forenoon because their morning-dress trails the ground a half a yard . . .; when I read of the sinking of steamers at sea, with 'nearly all the women and children on board,' and the accompanying comments, 'Every effort was made to assist the women up the masts and out of danger till help arrived, but they could not climb, and we were forced to leave them to their fate. . . .' "[3]

Such restricted behavior for women is no longer forced by clothing styles. The casual look brought in a new way of acting as well as a new style of garment. The new attitude is illustrated by Scott Fitzgerald's description of Miss Baker, a golf champion who is one of his characters in *The Great Gatsby:* "I noticed that she wore her evening-dress, all her dresses, like sports clothes—there was a jauntiness about her movements as if she had just learned to walk upon golf courses on clean crisp mornings."[4] Similarly, boys in tuxedos and girls in evening dress, laughing together on stair steps as they "sit-it-out" during intermission at a school dance, convinced André Maurois, a noted French writer, that American kids can make even a formal dance seem informal. It is plain that young people and sporting events both break tradition, ignore conventions, and add unexpected fluidity to the social scene.

The casual look is a purely twentieth-century phenomenon. It is rooted in the gradual rise of organized sports and the revolt of youth in the 20's. But the movement received a marked boost in the economic depression of the 30's which forced the average man to stay home, save money, and entertain himself. Further impetus came as the result of emergency working conditions of World War II, when women were placed on the same level with men in factory jobs. Today, casualness finds new advocates in mushrooming suburban developments and high school and college students who make up an increasingly larger proportion of the burgeoning population. Sustaining the adoption of casual dress are four typically American attitudes: a modern tendency to romanticize the "old days" of the frontier and the western movement; a belief in equality and freedom; a youth orientation (discussed in the preceding chapter); and a pragmatic approach to life.

The Western Movement

Nearly every American changes his city of residence several times during the course of his life, and many

Americans have at some time in their lives changed occupations. This mobility and familiarity creates a climate of equality, frankness, and simplicity in human relations, combined, as Maurois saw it, with a "certain pleasant timidity, the sort found in nomads."[5] These are the qualities that keep alive the informal attitudes of youth and cause Americans to attempt to relive in spirit the adventure of an immense Western story.

"The frontier" and "pushing west" were synonymous terms in the mid-nineteenth century. Men on the frontier were rough and boisterous; they recognized no authority but their own. Respectable women were scarce and treated with an awed, almost idolatrous, respect,* but the favors of "fancy ladies" helped increase the popularity of dance halls where cowboys often gathered just for sociability and a good time.

"Out West," work was hard and people were far apart. When they did get together at barbecues, backwoods balls, log rollings, and camp meetings, they intended to enjoy themselves. There was rollicking gaiety at the dances as couples kept time to the spirited beat of the fiddler whipping out the Virginia reels, country jigs, and shakedowns. Such functions were popular, and cowboys gathered in full dress (silk handkerchief, fancy vest, chaps, and spurs) from as far as two hundred miles away. As Foster Dulles phrased it, "It is the West's exuberant spirit of fun, its refusal to allow itself to be cramped by traditional tabus, the spirit typified by the comment that while the church might be tolerated, the saloon and the dance hall were regarded as necessities, that had its influence on the attitude of the country as a whole toward work and play."[6]

Western style dress—blue jeans, shoe-string ties, cowboy belts, and fancy boots—are never completely off the American market. Occasionally they reach a peak in popularity and become a fashion craze. For example, the Western influence spread like a prairie wind among the young set in America during 1965 and 1966, apparently initiated by the high fashion boots and cowboy hats designed by French couture designer

---

* Wyoming was the first territory to adopt women's suffrage in 1865 and kept it when it won statehood a quarter of a century later. The West was willing to reward its women for the hard work of pioneering; the East was too antagonistic to the suffrage movement for early progress; and the South, far too chivalrous, determined its women should not be degraded by "rights."

Courrèges in '64. Boys achieved a lean, sexy, and hippy look with figure-hugging jeans in a variety of fabrics and color and in high-heeled, pointed-toed, highly polished boots. Girls wanted their jeans with a leather patch on the derriere or hip.

Jeans have become even more desirable as the result of a "durable press"* treatment that keeps them neat looking with little effort. To insure equitable distribution of jeans during the '65–'66 craze, a major producer, Levi Straus and Company, found it necessary to set up an allotment plan for their sales on men's jeans.

Sportswear and Leisure Living

Changes in dress since the mid-nineteenth century have been brought about almost entirely through the reflected influence of outdoor sports. The rise of sportswear followed the rise of sports, both moving from the upper classes down to every man. Sports clothes are English in origin. However, they have been made more colorful in America, and spectator sports apparel garments that simulate the appearance of utility rather than art and constitute most of the casual dress seen today are American products.

America has provided broad opportunities for play so that people may choose in accordance with their needs and interests. In the cities many people watch rather than participate in sports, but the rise of spectator sports has served to keep an interest in active sports alive. An examination of the development of modern sports in America reveals that, at first, sports were adjusted to the formalized dress and manners of the wealthy world of fashion, but decades later, when sports became recreation for the masses, dress and manners were adjusted to the sports.

---

* "Durable pressed" garments, according to their producers, do not wrinkle regardless of how they are worn, and never need ironing. The process involves a resin treatment of the fabric as well as special treatment after the garment is cut or manufactured, either in what is known as a "hot head" press or in a large oven, which, in effect, bakes the finish into the garment. It is being used especially in men's work clothes and shirts, and women's blouses. (Standards on the process for the overall industry, as on stretch fabrics and "wash and wear," can only be maintained through voluntary compliance.)

THE FASHIONABLE WORLD AND PLAY (BEFORE 1900). The sudden rise of an American interest in sports after the Civil War is difficult to explain. It is linked by some writers to a national concern over the deteriorating health and general lack of exercise among the people. Thomas Wentworth Higginson wrote in the first issue of the *Atlantic Monthly* in 1858: "Even the mechanic confines himself to one set of muscles, the blacksmith acquires strength in his right arm and the dancing teacher in his left leg. But the professional or business man, what muscles has he at all?"[7]

The primary spur to sports was their adoption by people of fashion, in a postwar atmosphere that intensified an instinct for pleasure. By 1887 most of the people at Bar Harbor were dressed in costumes suggestive of tennis or boating or mountaineering. The society world, the only persons with the necessary leisure and financial means, pioneered in the formation of sports. The leisure classes initiated baseball, croquet, and swimming. It was even hoped by the social leaders who introduced roller skating that it could be restricted to the educated and refined classes. Distinguished guests were invited to watch tastefully dressed young men and girls glide through the maze of the march as if impelled by magic powers. But soon rinks were built everywhere.

Although the world of society set the standards for play, the masses soon caught on, causing the people of fashion to shift to more expensive sports. It is not competition but expense that makes a sport "fashionable." Highly commercialized sports such as boxing and wrestling set no fashions, and in fact, they may be considered slightly vulgar. On the other hand, horse racing has set many fashions. Upper-class leisure activities are valued not as relaxation from work, but as independent symbols of status. Thus, the sport that provides the most futile expenditure holds the highest rank. To enhance the status image, sports were forced to fit a formal and fashionable atmosphere.

In this tradition, James Gordon Bennett, Jr., made sports his entree into society in 1898. He sailed yachts and fought his way to the proud post of commander of the New York Yacht Club. He took up coaching and drove his four-in-hand at the Newport parade; he introduced polo.[8] Although anyone could watch horse races, only the very wealthy could support a stable. Country clubs near the shore promoted yachting and sailing while others emphasized hunting, pony races, and polo. Golf began to take hold after 1880. Scottish in origin, golf was considered "preeminently a game of good society."

At that time spectators were amazed to see gentlemen in scarlet coats furiously digging up the turf in fenzied and wholly serious efforts to drive a little white ball into a little round hole some hundreds of yards away. They wore elaborate leg-wrappings to protect themselves from the gorse indigenous to Scottish hills but quite foreign to this country, and pulled down over their foreheads visored caps in the best Sherlock Holmes tradition.[9]

The pioneer American sport, baseball, was first played in 1842 by a group of New York business and professional men. As with other sports of the period, baseball was made to fit the formal and fashionable times. It is reported that in keeping with their high social status the members of the first team played in neat uniforms of blue trousers, white shirts, and straw hats, while the formal dance that followed was considered as important as the game.[10]

Tennis was a very genteel sport, too refined to offer any attractions for the lower orders of society. Women players suffered only the slightest handicap in having to hold up their long dragging skirts; they were not expected to actually run for the ball. It was patted gently back and forth over a high net stretched across any level space of lawn. Tennis did not involve the present smashing drives and hard overhand serve until after 1900. Instead, it was considered a feminine game which offered a chance to sport white flannels and gaily colored blazers, rather than to exercise.

Croquet brought men and women out-of-doors in an activity they could enjoy together. They were instructed to hold the mallet in a "gentlemanly and ladylike manner." The pendulum swing, between the legs, was not for ladies unless they wore bloomers, and those wearing hoop skirts were obviously at a disadvantage.

The most spectacular craze of all was bicycling, daring riders on a postage-stamp size saddle atop a 60-inch wheel. The Club of Wheelmen banded together to make cycling a sport. Sober pedestrians watched awestruck as they mounted to the bugle call "Boots and Saddle" and wheeled past in military formation.[11] Woman's role was limited but recognized. She was given the tricycle, a step toward her emancipation from an inactive indoor life. It was the clothing needs of women on horseback and on bicycles that encouraged the development of the divided riding skirt, one of the first casual fashions attributed to American influence.

Bathing was an outdoor recreation more open to all classes of people—men and women of whatever age, young people, and children—than any other sport. Old prejudices against men and women going into the surf together had completely disappeared. However, the prudent female still went into the water fully clothed. *Godey's Lady's Book* advertised a costume of Turkey Red "consisting of a yoke polonaise and full drawers to be worn with a sash around the waist, long black stockings and a straw hat."[12]

While the question today is, Am I wearing "too much"? the concern at the turn of the century was, Am I wearing "too little"? Changes in the styles of bathing suits have reflected the degree of free association between men and women acceptable to society as a whole. A by-product of outdoor sports was the breach in the separation of the sexes so prevalent in the Victorian era. This lessening of formal constraint would lead in a few decades to greater equality among all members of the society and a general relaxation in dress.

RECREATION FOR THE MASSES (1920–1930). "It was a world," wrote Upton Sinclair in the 20's, "in which some people worked all the time, and others played all the time. . . . They talked about their play, just as solemnly as if it had been work; tennis tournaments, golf tournaments, polo matches— all sorts of complicated ways of hitting a little ball about a field! . . . Bunny looked at these fully grown men and women with their elaborate outfits of 'sport clothes'. . . ."[13] Their tanned skins proved they were not city workers, but could bask in the sunlight of the Mediterranean.

Beach complexion fads are an American-originated fashion. Besides being a status symbol, the suntan look in the 20's was apparently also a form of revolt of youth against tradition. The previous ideal for feminine beauty had been one of unfreckled fairness; tanned skins were condemned by honest women. Soon the beach tan became so customary as to seem respectable, and even desirable. It is so prized today by Americans that it may be artificially produced by cosmetics or a sunlamp, if there is no direct sunlight available. A tan still symbolizes the leisure life: Florida—skiing—Palm Springs. A belief exists that the beach-browned American could have obtained his tan almost anywhere in the world, thanks to jet airplanes and the automobile.

The automobile was originally intended for the upper status groups—a plaything for the rich, a sport comparable to yachting or riding to the hounds. Special clothing was necessary at first since roads were chokingly dusty and most cars were open. Men went prepared for any emergency, laden down with leather gloves, goggles, umbrellas, raincoats, dusters. Women had to be even more careful to protect their fashionable dress. Large picture hats on imposing pompadours were secured by long veils knotted tightly under the chin, fine gowns were protected by long linen dusters, and lap robes were tucked securely around the legs.

By 1914 Henry Ford's mass-produced Model T's (at $400) were beginning to reach the public, including the working-man and the farmer. Only in the United States did a high standard of living and mass production make possible a general ownership of cars which permitted motoring on a gigantic scale. The wealthy had made the fashionable tour in 1825, the well-to-do built up the beach resorts in 1890, but every Tom, Dick, and Harry toured the country in the 20's and 30's—in his own shiny automobile. The availability of the auto stimulated the whole outdoor movement and broke down the isolation of the country. Camping was possible; lake resorts, golf courses, fishing streams, and mountain scenery were within everyone's reach. Touring and pleasure driving became the popular recreation. The car completed the transformation of Sunday (a change which had begun in the nineteenth century) from a day of rest and worship to a day of recreation. From then on the travel industry became an economic as well as a social phenomenon.

Lured by the joys of the open road—"seeing America first"—families pushed their loaded cars with stalled engines up muddy hills, patched flat tires, and headed for the horizon. They pitched tents that leaked in sudden downpours, sloshed happily in and out of national parks, rode shaggy burros up bleak mountain trails, sweated in the desert sun, and forgot the work back home in a childlike orgy of exploring nature. They were tourists and proud of it.

Americans now began to dress down, not up, for vacations. Men liked the khaki pants, colored shirts with no ties, raincoats, and hiking shoes that were made especially for travel. Knickers for women reached their height as a fashion in 1921 along with bobbed hair and the cloche. Little girls wore knickers, too, and young boys put on the masculine version of knee pants. All members of the family looked alike and, comfortably attired to suit the occasion, all helped in the chores of camping out. Clothing was now being truly adjusted to the sport rather than the sport adjusted to the clothing.

Dressing down continues to be a trait of the average American tourist. Although he now does the things that would have been only the prerogative of the wealthy in former times, such as flying by jet plane to all places on the globe, he approaches his vacation as a man-on-the-job seeking relaxation from his work, not as a member of the elite seeking independent symbols of status. He wants a change of pace—from the formality of the city, the working routine, and the opinions of others. He wants to do as much as he can with the money that he has and be temporarily free from responsibility.

Taste arbiters feel that when an American visits nice places on his vacation—restaurants, downtown areas of cities and towns, theaters, museums, art institutes, lavish motels—he should dress accordingly. The market offers suits with relaxed jackets, quiet good looks and clean lines that will travel smoothly. But the desire to "let down" when away from home persists. The average American is more likely to visit the capital of the United States or the changing of the guard outside Buckingham Palace dressed in sweat shirts and shorts than in a travel suit of formal design. He is not there to be seen but to see.

SOCIALIZED LEISURE (1930–PRESENT). Modified sports clothes were the real beginning of casual dress for the masses. By 1928 they were coming into general use and were referred to as "spectator sports styles" by fashion periodicals.

The expansion of active sports for all was accelerated during the depression of the 30's by community-planned recreation and the increased organization of out-of-school life through "youth" agencies, such as Boy Scouts, YWCA, and YMCA. The socialization of leisure facilities for both participant and spectator, under the government's Federal Emergency Recreation Act, was a significant development of these years. Free programs for adults—concerts, square dances, and amateur nights—were held in the parks and high schools. New swimming pools were built to cater to all classes of people. Cities constructed public playgrounds, athletic fields, softball diamonds, public tennis courts, and golf courses, sometimes with the help of the PWA, a federal program designed to give work to the unemployed youths. This increased public provision of local leisure time activities was intended to help counteract the acute emphasis upon competitive jobs, possessions, and spending brought on by enforced rather than retired leisure. Democracy was making good its promise that everyone should be able to play the games formerly limited to the small class that had the wealth and leisure to escape the city.

Entertainment in the depression years was informal and inexpensive, featuring less planning and more "dropping in." Instead of dressing up for dinner at the country club, you came-as-you-were and had supper on the back porch. Buffets and back-yard barbecues became popular. The outdoor living room of the 30's with its fireplace and rock garden has been superceded in popularity only by the charcoal grill, the patio, and the rose bed of the 60's. People stayed home and listened to a new toy, radio. Gardening was popular for day, while the game of bridge was an inexpensive guarantee against a dull evening.

The movies became the poor man's theater where glamour stars of the 30's gave a promise to life that was often missing in the real world. Prophetically, the enigmatic Greta Garbo, with huge black eyelashes and pale ethereal face, portrayed the essence of romantic illusion on the screen, but was a sportive casual in real life. Straight blonde hair cut like a medieval page, she strode along in low-heeled shoes, cowboy belt, and a hat hiding her face.

The years around 1925 and those around 1935 were found by the Lynds, in their study of "Middletown," to be two periods with widely different implications for leisure. The first period was full of both promise and reality. For the businessman there was golf, midwinter trips to Florida, and the vague hope of retiring into a land where every day would be like Sunday; for the working man there were the tangible realities of the radio and the automobile. The second period, with its abundance of enforced leisure, soured the taste for this once-coveted condition and men emerged from the depression more than ever committed to work.[14] It is not surprising, then, that the 1960 census showed Americans moving to Florida and California in greater numbers than to any other sections of the country. Nor is the recent emphasis on fun with a purpose, such as addition of workshops to vacation resorts, unexpected. Combining the attitudes of the 20's and the 30's, the sober middle-class American works hard to get his leisure, and once he has it, turns leisure into work.

Recreation, outdoor living, sports, vacations, and travel are all becoming more important in the American way of life. People are living better, eating better, and enjoying more leisure time. Rising incomes of the 50's caused a boom in water sports. Spending for pleasure-boats jumped, and homes with private swimming pools increased over thirty 'imes in a ten-year period. Uses of leisure have multiplied for many people. The auto, travel, and active sports, such as boating and water skiing, hunting and fishing, camping, golf, and bowling, draw people away from the home. But gardening, the barbecue pit and patio, like the private swimming pool and colored television set, center attention in the home.

Suburbia. It is suburban living, the result of the widespread availability of the automobile, that permits the leisurely, casual life. If you do not participate in any sports, you can at least look like you do. If you do not swim, *watch the swimmers,* but dress in a non-swimsuit designed for plain pool or beach sitting. What starts as a style for suburban life may sweep the city areas as well, as in the sportive look in the early 60's.

The sportive look started as a casual look for women during the day—textured stockings and low-heeled shoes shown for wear with an open type of suit and sweater. The style was meant for suburban life, the country life, or a certain casual city life when a woman did not want to appear dressed up.

Basically, it was not a new look. Women who live in the country or go shooting, especially in England, Scotland, or Spain, always have had superb sport clothes. Heavy stockings for long walks, beautifully tailored suits, woolen scarves, and leather shoes with a high shine all denote a life of money and servants or service.

When the sportive look hit Seventh Avenue, however, it ran rampant. Suddenly everyone wore shaggy furs, checked tweeds and heavy sweaters, textured hose and boots. It did not matter if the weather was good or bad, the wearer young or old, short or tall. The sporting look invaded smart city restaurants as well as the suburban drive: A new mass fashion had been adopted.

The boom in suburban living, following World War II, has caused a dramatic change in the type of clothing women

Suburbia

want. Multitudes are experiencing the feel of a new, more casual way of life. The clothing they demand is shown by the production figures of the apparel industries. Between 1947 and 1960 skirt production rose a startling 325 per cent; blouses rocketed 100 per cent; play garments, including pedal pushers, shorts, and such, boomed 400 per cent; slacks, standard wear for supermarket shopping, rose 300 per cent; and sweaters rode in on the trend with a 150 per cent increase.[15]

In general, a study of American spending habits is a picture of a luxurious, but casual, way of life, centered in the home, with a growing concern about health, outdoor recreation, and education.

College Life. The adult sees education as the key that unlocks the world for his children. Every year an increasing proportion of the population attends high school and college. An unprecedented emphasis on education, beginning in the 20's, has brought the college student into the fashion limelight where he carries on his crusade for casual dress.

Blind faith in education crowded the colleges in 1920, much as it does today. College life still retained an aura from the past when only the rich and high-born aristocracy were students. Uninhibited by anxiety about his role in society and learning a trade, the student in the 20's went to college to play as well as learn. It was a place boys and girls could gain self-identity in relative isolation, with an environment and milieu of their own. College was a tree-shaded campus, a benevolent professor, and the excitement of dating and dancing with the opposite sex.

A stereotype of college life evolved from the drawings of John Held, Jr. He portrayed boys with patent-leather hair and raccoon coats resisting the attention of collegiate flappers with scanty skirts and incredibly slim legs, high heels, and two circles of rouge just below the cheek bones. The real-life college girls wore sweaters belted at the hips, sported long strings of beads, and wore felt hats like inverted tumblers. There was an informal yet dapper air to college fashions in the 20's.

During the depression, a more sober viewpoint toward school on the part of parents and children developed. Some boys withdrew from college and went to work. Girls, on the other hand, went to school in even greater numbers to study to be teachers, a profession not in acute competition with men. There was the added inducement that a coeducational college might provide an enhanced opportunity for finding a mate.

The roots of present-day attitudes toward education lie in the viewpoint of the 30's. To justify the increased cost to the taxpayer of the delay in his children "settling down to work," education had to be not only good, but be "good for something"—a benefit to both the individual and the community. There was confusion over the purpose of education in general: Parents wanted their children to get skills and knowledge, as well as the symbolic label of an educated person; the community wanted to bring backward students up to a formula standard by social guidance; and the teacher, loyal to his own code and philosophy, felt school was a place for developing thought. The idea that education should develop individual differences seemed in sharp contrast with the emphasis on solidarity and group action of organized labor and the government relief programs. The criterion of quantitative efficiency rather than quality in education gained ascendancy: A good teacher was the one who received the largest quantity of education.[16]

Today, these sober attitudes of the 30's, reinforced by continuous world tension, scientific advancement, and automation, have culminated in increased professionalization in one area of study and increased seriousness of students. Everything now depends on "meritocracy"—the grades and records of the high school student determine which college he can enter, his undergraduate achievement determines his eligibility for graduate study, and graduate work is the key to his future job.

As the college curriculum becomes more trade-centered and less a place to play and learn as one pleases, clothing of college students has become more functional and casual. While seldom a fashion innovator (with a few exceptions, such as Radcliffe, where the girls are pace-setters), the college student is among the first to adopt casual styles once they have been introduced. Since each college group acts as a homogeneous community in adopting a similar look, the mass display of one style can have an impact outside the college campus.

For example, the dirndl skirt, one of the few important fashion contributions of the 30's, was taken to the heart of almost every college girl for campus or party wear. (Mothers also used it for lounging, country and evening wear, and the style made possible attractive mother-daughter fashions because both looked so young and fresh in their full skirts.)

Another coed favorite, the sweater, was first adapted from garments of the working class and introduced in a Paris collection of 1926 by Lanvin. But it was not until the 30's, when the British, shivering from the cold, wore a cashmere cardigan over a matching pullover, added a string of pearls, and started the "twin set" fad, that the sweater became a college classic. About the same time, American college girls were putting cardigans on backwards to get a new effect out of old sweaters during the depression.

The sweater has gone through all design stages from tight to loose, trim to bulky. In 1935 Lana Turner, spotted by a Hollywood talent scout at the age of fifteen, skyrocketed to movie fame as the "sweater girl." Tight sweaters were the fashion until World War II when the fitted look gave way to the loose and baggy "Sloppy Joe," a classic sweater worn several sizes too large (usually size 40), so that the shoulders drooped down the upper arm and the length fell well below the hips. The style was worn with a prim white collar in every college in the country.

Subsequently, this oversized look evolved into the bulky sweaters that accompanied slim pants from the mid-50's on into the 60's. Italian fluffy mohair knits also found a huge American market. Since then, sweaters have been ribbed to fit close to the body (the French girls "poor" sweater of 1965), crocheted, patterned, combined with suede for men, and redesigned in every possible way. Sweaters have become an indispensable part of the college wardrobe and have been adopted by secretaries and society matrons; indeed, by all branches of society.

The college girl's craze for men's clothing made news in the September 30, 1940, issue of *Life*. This trend reached its peak when the boys were away at war and women adopted their slacks, loose sweaters, crew shirts, moccasins, and raincoats. However, girls had already begun to adopt boys' clothing in the mid-30's: blue jeans, tailored shirts, dirty saddle shoes, and yellow slickers. The college shops advertised coats of "exclusive men's wear plaids—patterned exactly after your beau's coat." The velvet-collared Chesterfield became a college classic. Since then, sneakers, socks of all types, trench coats, and scarves have been added.

Clothing worn by both men and women tends to acquire a bisexual look and can no longer be used to identify the sex of the wearer. In general, the college trend is toward color and gaiety, informality and greater comfort, with sportswear separates as the dominating fashion. This is the way they go to college—the "conservatives," the "sorority set," the Bohemian "hang-loose crowd," the "dorm" girl, or the "commuter." Each group influences the other, but there is a general casual way of dressing—tweeds, flannels, and plaids . . . loafers and sneakers . . . sweaters and skirts . . . jumpers, a few suits . . . perhaps, wool slacks . . . Bermudas—all fashions that are purely functional. Upperclassmen who work summers in college shops of retail stores advise incoming freshmen of the current college whim as they shop for their fall wardrobes.

College students working at summer jobs in their campus clothes, and college graduates who fill positions in urban centers, carry with them some of their attachment to the casual look of their college days. They become, unwittingly, one of the major promoters of informal attire. Certainly casual dress looks best on the young, and college students are young people with status. Casual dress becomes, then, a desired symbol of youth. When worn by mature people, it breaches the gap between various age groups and between men and women, breaking down the rigidity of roles.

Role Flexibility

When roles are well defined and strictly enforced by a powerful social authority, dress becomes specialized and formal, as in political systems where royalty still exists. Queen Elizabeth II of England dresses precisely to fit each ceremony she attends in her role as queen. The government insists that she observe traditional rules of protocol—behavior and dress—

which make the occasion more formal than if there were no rules and the structuring was left to the individual performing the state ceremony. The Paris couture, with a background of royal tradition, also upholds a formal code for dress. The houses know precisely which textures, lines, and colors in dress are appropriate for every hour of the day, every season of the year, and each type of occasion.

Americans, on the other hand, follow an unstructured or informal tradition. Democratically, they believe in "offering opportunities"—a wide selection from which individual choices can be made in recreation, in consumption goods, or in self-advancement in a career. Control is exercised by a diffuse cultural structure (often public opinion) rather than by a defined social organization with power. As a result, roles are more flexible and vary between times and places; dress, too, tends to become unspecialized and informal. A well-designed dress, to an American, is appropriate for work, for dinner, and for the theater; in every instance the one style seems exactly right. Furthermore, it can be worn all day in a car or plane and still look fresh.

EQUALITY OF THE SEXES. A change in the twentieth-century attitude toward the sex role has been accompanied by changes in dress. Casual dress, the prototype of functional, informal, and nonspecialized attire, permits a great deal of role flexibility: Women may dress like men, and men may adapt any of women's fancies they desire. Children can look like children, or like miniature adults, and adults may wear childlike garments. Construction workers dress up in fashionable work clothes and businessmen dress down in working slacks. The net result is less marked external differentiation in the social structure of the society, although characteristic forms of identity for each group are still retained.

Informality in dress reflects easy companionship between the sexes as well as between children and adults. Women borrow items of men's wear, such as trench coats, shirts, and pants, while men adapt general trends from women's fashions —a greater style consciousness, softer lines, and beauty aids.

Decline in the rigid relative position of men and women has influenced and been reflected in fashion. The old pattern —the dominant aggressive male and the submissive female, or the work-oriented husband and the home-oriented wife—is no longer the only alternative. Instead, the sex role in marriage may be decided by agreement between two cooperating partners, according to the interests and abilities of each. Both may work, and both may share tasks at home, or the woman may concentrate on the social and spiritual environment of the family while the man focuses on the economic condition. Society will not condemn either choice as long as the family is physically and socially healthy and there are job opportunities for all in the labor market. So, too, the single woman and the single man, a state not completely adapted to the present social structure, have greater opportunities to choose a way of life that best suits their needs. Roles, like casual dress, have become more flexible, with new identities and new complexities.

Women Adopt Men's Clothes. Psychologist Esther Rothman, principal of a school for disturbed adolescent girls aged 12 to 18 notes: "Our worst days are when we have a snowstorm because, realistically, the girls say they have to wear slacks. . . . This is the day we know there are going to be at least 10 fights. When they dress in a way that gives them greater freedom, . . . in a somewhat masculine way, they are going to act up. But no girl particularly wants to act up when her hair is well done, when she has had a manicure, when she's made up . . . she doesn't want to bother; she doesn't want to disturb it."[17]

While these students are problem girls to the New York public school system, their reaction to dress is fairly normal. American women historically have adopted men's clothing as a sign of freedom, to denote rebellion against unfair restrictions made on the basis of sex.

In 1836, facing a world where women were highly regarded and often dominant within the family but where social control was entirely in male hands, Lucretia Mott, Quakeress, founded the American feminist movement. The movement's manifesto set the tone for all future American feminism: "Men and women were created equally, provided by the Creator with inalienable rights. . . ."

At that time, women rallied to the cry of "women's rights"—to vote, have jobs, to wear "sensible" clothes. They wore adaptions of masculine attire to emphasize their viewpoint. For example, Mrs. Elizabeth Smith Miller, daughter of Congressman Gerret Smith of New York, startled Washington around 1849 by appearing dressed in somewhat Turkish style. Above the waist her costume was conventional. Below, however, she wore a skirt which extended barely beyond the knee, underneath which were full baggy trousers of broadcloth gathered together at the ankle with an elastic band.[18]

Not content with startling one city, several months later, wearing the same garb, she strode into Seneca Falls, New York, to visit her cousin, Mrs. Stanton. The costume caught the eye of several other feminist leaders, including Mrs. Stanton, Susan B. Anthony, Lucy Stone, and also Mrs. Dexter Bloomer who ran a journal called *The Lily*. Through the columns of her paper, Mrs. Bloomer immediately launched a campaign of reform in women's dress based on the new costume, and the ensuing notoriety linked her name inseparably with it. The trousers might have accurately been called "Mrs. Bloomer's Millers,"[19] but they became known instead as "Bloomers." The movement was called Bloomerism, and its followers were Bloomerites. The fight to reform dress was never won, and women eventually stopped wearing the garment because of the ridicule it caused. Mrs. Bloomer was perhaps the last to give it up, holding on for eight years. (Fifty years later, black bloomers became an accepted style for girls' gym suits and short filmy versions in pastel colors or printed ruffled ones are occasionally worn yet.)

In 1873 the relative position of men and women was clearly defined by the styles each adopted. Men's wear was simple, compact, and durable, fitted for labor and travel, and consistent with all the requirements of health. Women's dress, on the other hand, was complicated, voluminous and burdensome; flimsy in texture, calculated to impede body movement, except in a state of repose.

Unlike today's woman in her casual attire, nineteenth-century woman was a servant (in the best European tradition) to specialized dress. She might make at least ten changes in one day. Starting with a morning dress, if she was to receive callers at home, or a housekeeping dress, if she had to do menial tasks, she might change to a walking costume, with a skirt 2 inches to 4 inches from the ground, or a tailor-made costume for church or travel. In the afternoon she might don a carriage dress which was a charming bright-colored silk confection she could display riding with the coach top down, or she might slip into an opera dress for a matinee. She had to remember that a promenade costume had a train and that dinner gowns should be changed for ball gowns at ten o'clock.

Some women, coming home from summer outings by the sea, mountains, and forests, where they walked and climbed in gymnastic suits, voted never to wear trailing skirts again, no matter what the dressmakers might say.

It was, finally, the freedom of sports clothes, perhaps more than anything else, that expressed the American woman's desire for independence. Women who went to the beach in the 20's and 30's dressed for the demands of the sport instead of following the "tabus of an outworn prudery." From then on, women would insist on their right to adopt any type of dress. Feminized versions of men's slacks—lounging pajamas for the beach—were fashionable during the 20's and 30's, but it remained for the alluring Marlene Dietrich, in 1933, to hide her legendary legs in a typical mannish slack suit. This was the true beginning of the era of slacks and shorts for all.

The feminine trend toward adopting articles of men's clothing became more than a fashion whim; it became a necessity when women were called to replace men in factory jobs during World War II. Because women were learning to rivet, to weld, and to operate lathes and milling machines, a new requirement was added to women's clothing—"safety." For example, a one-piece slack suit, with plenty of room for reaching and stooping, but with no extra fullness to catch on moving machinery, was designed by the Bureau of Home Economics.

Slacks spread from sportswear to work, and to all fields of feminine activity from air raid duties to an evening at home. The *New York Times Magazine*, March 1, 1942, reported what women thought: "Right now it is a matter of comfort—being able to move around without worrying about pulling your dress down, being warm, being crisp and efficient looking, and also being economical, because slacks cut down on stockings, dry cleaners and laundry bills."[20]

Filenes in Boston installed three "Slack Bars"; Marshall Field's, the Fair, and Goldblatt Brothers in Chicago reported trouser sales five to ten times greater than the previous year.

Executives, such as Lieutenant Commander R. R. Darron of the Alameda Naval Air Station in California, ordered women employed in the machine shops to wear pants to work.[21]

The American woman did a man's job in the factories, and she wore men's clothes. Companion clothes for husband and wife appeared: polo shirts, raincoats, and sportswear of all types were designed alike for "His" and "Hers." When socially prominent married couples were photographed in *Vogue* in 1951 wearing tennis shirts designed by the former French amateur champion, René Lacoste, the "His" and "Hers" fad was under way.[22]

The American woman now has her choice of two worlds, male and female, and refuses to admit there are social differences between the sexes. However, while demanding equal privileges with men in the business and political worlds, she still exacts a personal consideration and attention that is a carryover from the chivalrous pioneer age when women were both rare and in real need of protection. While this makes the European say the American woman is selfish, it may not be personal selfishness so much as the feeling she owes it to her sex to expect deferential treatment.

One writer suggests a four-sex division: the woman at work (more masculine); the woman at play (more feminine); the man at work; the man at play. Yet others call the masculine clothing adapted for women, and women's foibles adapted to men, "the bi-sexual look"—part male and part female. In either case, the result is a fashionwise coming together of the sexes.

Today, slacks and shorts are considered essential to women's wardrobes. Pants are for walking the dog, riding bicycles and horses in Central Park, skiing, flying airplanes, yachting, traveling, getting into bed, driving the kids to school, carrying screens, gardening, entertaining at home, and even for attending movies and the opera. More than 100 years after "Mrs. Bloomer's Millers" appeared, pants for women are no longer considered "items" but are part of the basic stock in retail stores because of their widespread acceptance, particularly by suburban dwellers and college girls. Women have appropriated men's trousers for their own use, first as symbols of revolt, next as sports clothes and work clothes, and now as leisure wear. They move freely about in greater convenience

and safety (they reason), wearing a happy feeling of equality with men.

Men Relax and Adopt Feminine Foibles. Historically, an interrelationship between men's and women's fashions has existed when there is a very high interest in fashionable dress. In France prior to the revolution in 1789 both sexes wore colorful and fancy clothing. During the English Restoration period of 1660 to 1688, men of nobility outshone the women. It is not surprising that men who have tended to lag behind women in twentieth-century fashion leadership have finally become conscious of changing styles and grooming in a very fashion-conscious era.

Masculine fashions from the past fifty years have shown two main trends: one toward more comfortable and colorful clothes; the other toward increased style consciousness on the part of men. During the war years women wore trousers and dressed like men. But later, men followed the fashion lead of women into gay beach costumes and sports clothes. While modern women have directly borrowed *items* of men's attire for their own use, modern men have tended to adopt *general trends* from women's fashions—the use of color; softer, more flexible materials and styles; increased style consciousness; and beauty aids.

Style Consciousness. When skin-tight pants, needle-pointed shoes, and pleated shirts with lace at collar and cuff are topped by the moplike hairdos popularized by the Beatles, "you can't tell the boys from the girls without a program," notes one observer of the fashion scene.[23] These are styles adopted by male teen-agers, quick to ape the often bizarre costume of the youthful musicians on television and in the London discotheques. The styles are also picked up by art students and intellectual leaders of dissent on the college campus, who quickly change from one current craze to the next. Because the young set and the marginal male are willing to make a more extreme statement in their clothes than the average businessman, their tastes influence men's style.

Increased male interest in current masculine fashion (style consciousness) began in the early 1930's. Whether or not wives and sweethearts were responsible for the trend is not known, but men began to buy ensembles: shirts, neckties, handkerchiefs, and socks to harmonize with each other and with suits.

In the ten-year period between 1945 and 1955 men were exposed to a series of sudden style changes. In 1947 there was the Bold Look, with bright colors, wide and exaggerated shoulders; by 1950 the Casual Look, with tweedy squire effects, had arrived. The year 1953 brought the Ivy League Look (the no-shoulders look) which was modified into the Slim Look, which was transmitted into the Continental Look. . . .

The true impact of style consciousness was revealed by the speed with which men accepted the "Ivy League Look" in the early 50's. This suit model, characterized by a sack coat with natural body lines, decreased shoulder padding, and thin lapels, and worn with a narrow dark tie, indicated a long-term trend away from wide padded shoulders, wide lapels, and wide ties toward a slimmer, trimmer look. The fashion reached a peak in 1954 and was still popular several years later.

"Paring down" became the fashion revolution of the 60's. *Vogue* explained that this trend started in Italy when tailors modified the Ivy idea into a more conservative look. Everything from hats to shoes was pared down. When men accepted the skimpy cuts, tight pants, tight armholes, and narrow cuffs of these fashions after being propagandized for years on comfort in clothes, they had undoubtedly climbed on the fashion bandwagon.

Fashion consciousness in men is largely related to the adoption of television, the rise of the "expense account aristocrat," and a change in the general public's attitude toward fashion for men. Television has made both sexes more fashion conscious by transmitting direct promotion from clothing and fabric producers who encourage male interest in fashion as a business stimulant. But more importantly, it transmits indirect advertising by showing the dress of popular entertainers, such as male singing stars, who provide a model for the teenage boy to follow. One of the first to adopt new styles, teenagers help set the fashion trends.

But fashion awareness will not bring adoption of new styles without sufficient income to expend and the desire to waste it. The conservative American male, unlike the female, has not traditionally discarded his suit when it is out of style, but rather when it is worn out. He has considered himself rational and economically minded; by his reasoning a fashionable person cannot be an economic man because fashion is wasteful. For fashion to flourish in the business world some new development had to break this pattern of behavior. The development was the rise of the "expense account aristocrats," men on generous company accounts which permit them to frequent upper-class places of entertainment where suitable dress is required and high fashion styles are seen. This not only makes fashion an economic necessity for business but also provides the impetus for imitation and emulation so necessary to the rise of fashion. In addition it allots an income specifically to "waste."

The final obstacle in the development of a fashion-conscious male—the public attitude toward a fashionably dressed man—has been modified in recent years. Fortunately for the fashion business, a man's fear of being classed as a homosexual, when fashionably attired, has been diminished due to findings in the social sciences. Psychiatrists have explained that a wholly masculine man or a wholly feminine woman does not exist, and sociologists note that the male is frequently the more brilliantly attired in most species.

The direction of men's fashions in the 1960's shows lack of consensus on the need for masculinity. While some styles appear "feminized," others, under the Western influence, are ruggedly topped with full-blown masculine beards. Some men's wear makers say that new styles simply reflect a continued effort to pry men out of their accustomed rut and start a change. However, novelist and critic Leslie Fiedler recently called new male styles a manifestation of "a general retreat from male aggressiveness to female allure."[24]

Male Cosmetics. The term "male cosmetics" (a sociological classification) is controversial in popular usage, while the term "men's toiletries" is readily accepted. Any suggestion that certain fashions are not "manly" will discourage male customers from using them. Yet the term "cosmetics," if defined as an external application intended to beautify, cleanse, or protect the skin, nails, hair, and eyes, would include not only the traditional colognes, shaving creams, after-shave lotions, and deodorants used by men, but also the newer and increasingly accepted skin cleansers, wrinkle creams, hair-coloring products, and lotions. It appears that male cosmetics are in general use.

Are male cosmetics truly used or are they purchased by women as gifts and merely tossed out or abandoned on the closet shelf by the men who receive them? *Vogue,* in support of the latter possibility, reports that 54 per cent of all male colognes are purchased by women.[25] However, *The Drug and Cosmetic Catalogue* which lists most of America's drugs and cosmetics, claims that many men do chose their own cosmetics, and most of them are healthy, all-American males.[26]

The growth of hair-styling shops for men, exemplified by Jerry's in New York and Sebrings in Los Angeles, is another indication of how widely male beauty aids are accepted. Emulating the beauty shops for women, this type of male shop gives special hair "stylings," designed to make the man look slimmer, taller, younger, or handsomer. A full styling treatment includes cutting and shaping the hair, combing the hair into place, spraying with a setting lotion while the hair is covered with a net. As the *Wall Street Journal* reports, "The customer finishes with a session under the dryer, perhaps puffing on a cigar while a manicurist buffs his nails."[27]

There are definite indications not only of increased use of male cosmetics but of a mushrooming market rather than a steady growth. For a nominal sum almost any man today can buy a perfumed after-shave lotion, which in the days of his grandfather would have been prohibitively priced for the common man. What is really new is the attention that makers of women's beauty aids are paying to the male market. Clairol, Inc., which manufactures hair coloring for women, is creating a product aimed specifically at men who do not want to go gray; Elizabeth Arden's line for men includes cream mask and after-bath talcum; while Evan W. Mandel, vice-president of Revlon, Inc., says: "Fragrances and hair coloring for men are accepted. The next thing will be wrinkle cream—after all a lot of men borrow their wives' now."[28]

A casual survey reveals that shaving supplies—pre-shave or after-shave lotions, shaving creams, and colognes—as well as hair creams and shampoos are in general use. Shaving lotions are believed necessary because users feel they perform the functions the ads claim: promoting the general well-being of the face, alleviating the abrasive effects of the razor, and preventing infection. As for hair preparations, men use them to project an acceptable image, to cushion their self-esteem, and to give them a feeling of "togetherness" with fellow Americans. If he is a Negro, his hair is brilliantined or clipped to the proper straightness; if a teen-ager, it is molded into the current fad; if a Madison Avenue type, it may be greaselessly brushed across the forehead. Some men employ hair coloring, massage, and beauty treatments to improve their appearance for economic reasons; the apparent increased vigor and youth is an advantage in the competitive world of business that wants to maintain a youthful image.

There is an ambivalent attitude toward male cosmetics. Some men condemn them as effeminate, others praise them as aesthetic and healthful. An examination of advertising and periodicals presents unclear conclusions about the acceptability of perfumes for men. *McCall's* claims that today we are free of "Puritan taboos from the innocent pleasure of indulging the sense of smell . . . the American nose has been liberated," and illustrates its point with an article about an ex-Marine who uses four different scents.[29] However, the advertising market continues to feel unsure that the male nose has been completely liberated, emphasizing the masculinity of their products with names such as "Jet" or "Monsieur" and indicating that the scent of the product is very male: grass or spice or tobacco. The Owens-Illinois Container Corporation, in masculine-slanted advertising, claims in trade journals that its containers are not only convenient to use but also full of masculine vigor in shape.[30]

"The Rugged Set" or *"Feminized Male?"* Theoretically, the typical American male is a "he-man" oriented toward the world of work: rugged, strong, and stable both emotionally and physically. The concept of the role of the American male leaves little room for the gentle, the sensitive, or the creative. According to Margaret Mead, the American male carries this role for two reasons. First, the emphasis on aggressiveness is a throw-back to the days of early America when the male fought the wilds of the prairies in the West and the wilds of Wall Street in the East. Second, the Great American Dream suggests that if one fights, pushes, and shoves sufficiently, he will

3 / FASHION: A REFLECTION OF AMERICAN LIFE

reach the top, even if his origins are lower class. Under either of these two premises, weakness is intolerable and inopportune, if not dangerous. These norms were once understood and shared by all males and as a result there was little friction over the male role.

The acceptance of a fixed role throughout the whole culture at a particular time is no sign that the roles of male and female are automatically derived from their sex. The child is identified as male or female and then taught the appropriate role. It is possible to find roles within the same society differing through time and place. Today, a boy is no longer instilled with a traditional role. He may not be taught the same role as his father, just as his future son may not play a role identical to his own. Many boys are taught to accept a changed attitude toward the female role: to cooperate rather than to dominate, to become more sensitive. Others, however, learn the established dominant male role. Thus, there is no longer a stable consensus, but a choice of a variety of roles ranging from traditional patriarchy, stressing male domination of the female, to extreme cooperation between children and parents, with accompanying equality of male and female.

The "Leveling Effect" of Sportswear

Ceremony appears to be in continuous retreat in most areas of American life. In high society, the Duke of Windsor noted the decline in male elegance in 1965 and remarked that "men look too sloppy these days."[31] On the professional level: the doctor makes his rounds in an open-necked sports shirt, slacks, and canvas-top foam-rubber shoes. A few years back he would not have dared appear in less than a suit coat, vest, and tie. The businessman removes his coat any time he pleases and wears Dacron short-sleeved shirts to the office. The man in the factory, no longer requiring protective clothing since the advent of automation, discards his bib overalls and twill shirts and dons colorful sports shirts and slacks.

The fashion of workers in the factory "dressing up" in sports clothes is just as revolutionary as the relaxed look in business of men "dressing down" in similar attire. The formalized restrictive dress of the middle-class male and the easy sensible garb of the workingman have met on the common ground of sportswear. The resultant leveling effect has made it difficult for the casual observer to discover who sets the fashion pace.

Some manufacturers believe high school and college students set the pace for work clothes. They point out that students used to wear army twills but now have switched over to new types of garments, and the workers, especially the younger ones, follow the trend. Then, too, increased wages allow factory workers to purchase clothes without any pressure to imitate the conventional businessman's taste.

The fashion influence on work clothes began in the early 1950's when matched sets of work pants and shirts became popular. By 1955 matched sets were replaced by slacks with contrasting shirts. A factor in the growth of style consciousness was the increased leisure time and the do-it-yourself ideas that made people want more style in the clothes they used at home. At work, the general trend toward installing lockers in the factory encouraged working men to wear sports clothes to work, displaying no special badge of occupational identity, and change to work clothes at the plant.

Curiously, the manufacturers of work garments comment that one difficulty in low-priced style items is telling one style from another. For example, in 1960 there were two popular styles of trousers, the Western and the Continental, both with front slit pockets and narrow tapered legs. To help the consumer tell the two apart, the manufacturer had to print the style on the label. Work-clothes manufacturers do not pretend to be style leaders; in their price range they merely compete by being the first to copy.

Men's-wear manufacturers scout the European scene for fashion ideas, with particular attention to Italy, innovator of the "pared down" look, and London, the traditional pacesetter for men's fashions. London has developed two widely divergent sources of men's styles: (1) the excellent custom tailors of Seville Row, whose influence filters down, and (2) the swing-singers and teen-age sets, working in offices, shops, and factories, whose influence on mass fashions filters up. British custom tailors started the "natural shoulder suit" of the 1920's, a revolt against the overpadded and freak suits of the previous era, but the commercialized singing "Beatles" switched crew-cut kids to bangs and boots in the 60's, while the "Mods," a fashion-conscious group of British boys and girls who lived at home with their parents, introduced hipster slacks, white levis, gay colorful shirts, and short skirt styles.

However, the success of a new style at critical points in the United States rather than in Great Britain or Western Europe is what determines the effect of the style on the American fashion market for men. Young men's fashions often start at Ivy colleges in the East, such as Princeton. Teen-age fashions may start simultaneously throughout the country through the impact of television. Mature men look to the prominent business executives (35–45 years of age), who, in turn, adopt fashions introduced at Palm Beach, at ski resorts, Acapulco, or wherever the leisured and socially prominent males relax.

Many new ideas for men begin in the sportswear area where more innovations are possible than in business attire, and where new styles are more readily accepted. At the beginning of a vacationing season there are many types of clothes, but by the close of the season the style is fairly well set. The men return home in socially accepted styles which are copied by friends and spread in ever widening circles.

THE "CASUAL REVOLUTION" FOR MEN. In most periods the clothes of the middle classes have been stiff, sober, and restrictive, while the fashion of the workers has been free, easy, and sensible, suited to a strenuous life. Men in the business world, while flexible in the adoption of new ideas, historically have been rigidly bound by custom in dress (as noted in Chapter 2). Their consumption of conservative or stable clothing, economist Leland Gordon suggests, may offset the versatility and uncertainty of their business occupation.[32]

Since man voluntarily adopted the formalism of the dark business suit as his badge of respectability, he has been divided in his allegiance to it. Aware that few things can equal the heat generated by the human torso hermetically sealed at the top by a collar and at the bottom by a belt, informed by critics that his uniform was unhygienic, inartistic, and depressing, the businessman was still convinced that it had many merits. The plain lines follow the feeling of modern art and always seem contemporary. A well-pressed and tailored fabric that refrains from bulging gives the illusion of a lean athletic figure underneath. There are plenty of pockets to hold things, and the dark neutral color does not show spots. The style does not pinch, unless the size is wrong; and the unpicturesque look has the merit of longevity and relative cheapness.

Because his attitude is two-sided, man has periodically rebelled against the limitations of his uniform. An early revolt against the rigidity of business dress—a long-term trend toward less, looser, lighter weight, and more colorful clothing—began in the 1920's. Men just home from World War I were tired of uniforms and determined to wear more comfortable clothes in spite of the civilian style setters who advocated more binding styles. The returned soldiers got their way and clothing has been cut fuller ever since. Army men were also responsible for bringing about the acceptance of the shirt with an attached soft collar, initiating the demise of the separate starched collar.

The 30's continued the "casual revolution" against the orthodox male dress. A British men's reform party proposed some radical changes, such as abolishing the suit coat by replacing the shirt with a blouse designed as a respectable outergarment so men would not feel obliged to wear coats in the presence of ladies, and replacing tubular pants with shorts or kilts. The group considered hats unnecessary and suggested that sandals be worn instead of shoes. Fashion designer Elizabeth Hawes waged a more realistic campaign for the liberated male: She proposed an invention called a *slack suit*—a pair of loose trousers and a shirt to match. (At first these were worn in the country and to sports events in the city, but not to work. By 1940 they were a smash hit.)

The "casual revolution" gained headway in the 40's when the California casual look emerged as a distinct fashion force across the nation. Man changed his clothes to suit the tempo of the times, or more exactly, the seasons of the year. In the summer he wore polo shirts with short sleeves, ventilated oxfords, cool porous underwear, and wash trousers and shorts made of sturdy seersucker, providing his figure was suitable.

Partly because of the controversy over the excess of men's clothing and partly because of a new invention, air conditioning, the Harvard University School of Public Health ran an experiment to learn why air conditioned public buildings were too hot for men and too cold for women. Men in their customary 5 pounds of clothing were comfortable at 72°, but women, in only 1.8 pounds of clothing, felt cold unless the temperature was increased to 80°. The scientists arrived at the obvious conclusion: Men dressed too heavily in summer; women too lightly in winter.[33] In 1941 *Life* reported that a woman could be completely clothed in only 21 ounces, while the average weight of a man's summer outfit totaled 7 pounds.[34] Regulated temperatures in office buildings made it necessary for the weight of wearing apparel to be more equally distributed between the sexes: If women would not put more on, men must take something off.

The climax in the struggle for the liberation of modern man from the orthodox male uniform, that began after World War I, was reached following World War II. The major effects of World War II were not on style but on textiles and clothing construction. Chemically derived fibers—nylon, Dacron, and Orlon—allowed lighter weight fabrics without loss of strength or protection for the body. Construction was simplified; stiffening and padding were reduced or eliminated for men's suits.

By the early 50's, the overheated male was truly liberated in the open-neck sport shirt, its tail flying in the breeze. The style seemed "immoral" to the advocates of puritanical restrictive dress who felt there must be some middle ground between discomfort and flopping shirttails. But the supporters of the style reminded people that the sensible Cuban wore a *guyaberra,* a cool white jacket type shirt made of the finest linen that looked elegant and felt comfortable on the hottest day, principally because the *neck is open* and the *shirttail is free.*

When Clark Gable took off his shirt and exposed a bare torso in *It Happened One Night,* he struck a blow for informality and, incidentally, jolted the undershirt business throughout the country. Thousands of timid males followed his lead: If a "he-man" like Clark Gable could do without an undershirt why couldn't they? Even hats were discarded. A survey of office rules in 1952 showed the gains made in "the cult of informality": three-fourths of the companies interviewed allowed men employees to remove their suit coats at any time and 13 per cent more allowed sport shirts at the office. Ten years earlier, this practice was practically unheard of.[35]

A feature writer in *Reader's Digest,* J. P. McEvoy, was

able to report that only 12 years after the *Life* report that men wore 7 pounds of clothing, he was wearing less than 3 pounds on a sizzling summer day in New York. This included his shantung silk suit that weighed 1½ pounds; his nylon-mesh foam-rubber shoes, ½ pound; his orlon socks, dacron shorts, sheer batiste shirt (short sleeves, open neck) about 14 ounces. However, he stated, "I don't push my luck. I always carry a spare necktie in my pocket and have a jacket handy to put on whenever necessary to soothe a supercilious headwaiter or reassure a fussy female."[36]

The casual revolution has reached a victorious conclusion. Increased style consciousness of men has combined with the trend toward more casual clothes to produce a studied air of relaxation, a fashionable look in sportswear. Sport coats and slacks, short socks without garters, brightly colored Bermuda shorts, Hawaiian shirts, and fast-changing teen-age fashions are giving men freedom of color, comfort, and informality. While the badges of occupational dress are still present, they are less pronounced today than in other eras. The working class, the white collar man, the business executive, the professionals, and the leisure class all wear a relaxed look.

In today's casual era, minor degrees of fashion, quality, and formality in clothes identify class and occupational differences. The Duke of Windsor retains a hint of formality in his gray checked suit and striped shirt, while incorporating subtle elements of casual dress. The middle-age business executive still clings to the conventional attire, but the college professor and the younger working man move closer to the pronounced informality of the college student. The total projected image is one of greater similarity between the classes and occupational groups.

EQUALITY OF AGE GROUPS. The bars between youth and middle age are being removed in all areas of American life. Man is closer to his dream of "agelessness" in this century than in any previous era. Emphasis on sports, advance in medical science, and new trends in child development and family relations tend to draw age groups together and counterbalance the effect of fast technological change which pulls them apart.

Fashions no longer filter down from the avant-garde to heads of families to teen-agers; they now go the other way.

Mother-daughter fashions with their extreme coming-together, agewise, are styles of youth, not those of maturity. These look-alike styles dramatized, in the beginning, new trends in child development.

For example, three covers of the *Ladies' Home Journal* in 1939 featured the "Journal Twins," a mother and daughter dressed alike. This pair appeared annually on *Journal* covers until 1952. A letter in the "Readers'" section illustrates the results of the adoption of the fashion:

> DEAR EDITOR: Following your fashion series . . . , I put the idea into practice and found that clothes can fasten comradeship between my eight-year-old daughter and me.

The editor answered:

> That's how these covers started. Years ago the editor bought her daughter a dress just like hers and was delighted with her daughter's joy.[87]

Ads for mother-daughter dresses read like this: "To feel young—to make your daughter feel gratifyingly grown up—dress as she does." Mothers liked the implication in the phrase: "these two young generations."

Concepts of child psychology had undergone a startling transformation between 1914 and 1945. Originally, the infant was believed to be endowed with strong and dangerous impulses which could grow beyond control; parents were warned not to play with their children, but to enforce strict and rigorous discipline. Children were considered to be only children pure and simple—so many little creatures to be washed, dressed, schooled, fed, and whipped, according to certain general and well-understood rules. By 1930 advances in the social sciences made it obvious that the human character was more complex than ever before suggested. Scholars focused on a new area, personality growth. A child with an unbearable disposition might properly say to her parents, "You've made me that way! No child ever has a bad disposition unless it's her family's fault. Whatever I am, you did it!" Finally, in 1942 to 1945, the baby came to be viewed more as a completely harmless individual or, in other words, a pool of latent possibilities waiting to be developed. The new psychology in child rearing said father must be a pal to his son and mother a chum to her daughter. These changing conceptions of children helped to establish general attitudes toward play: At first it was "wicked" to play with the child; then, it became "harmless"; and now, "you must."[38]

The Democratic Family and Casual Dress. The reduction of strict obedience and enforced silence of children in the presence of their elders marked a step toward the democratic family in the same way the increased companionship between men and women reduced the "battle of the sexes." The family life that evolved was based more on affectional ties and less on duty. Rather than an authoritarian family where father was the "law of the home and mother the gospel," the whole family began sharing in power and tasks. Clothing began to reflect and reinforce this pattern. Casual dress, by blurring the differences in age and sex groups, makes companionship more of a reality in family groups, and the family can indeed become "the gang."

The Choice-Makers' Dilemma

Relaxed standards from one area cross into others. Because standards become less rigid, materials like burlap and denim, not traditionally fibers of prestige, can achieve status through the skill of the designer and the finesse of the wearer. However, as role identity becomes more flexible, confusion can result.

Ginette Spanier, directrice of the couture house of Pierre Balmain, on a two-week visit to New York in 1960 observed, "At lunchtime, French women dress very simply. American women, in their dressy hats, look more like French women at cocktail time."[39] A French graduate student at the University of Chicago was frankly puzzled by the women she observed: "Why do some American women wear rhinestones and high-heeled shoes to shop in the grocery store? . . . And why do others have their hair on hair curlers?"

Part of the casual look is the privilege to dress as one pleases at most functions. An informal cocktail party that crosscuts the intellectual, social, and artistic worlds might well have guests variously attired. Some will be in traditional gowns, others in tweeds and sweaters, and still others in pants and tops. Each one subtly displays his own occupational trademark and no one will be ostracized. It is as if a silent pact had been signed between cultural groups. "I will accept your dress and say nothing, if you, in turn, will accept mine." In fact, we tend to believe that diversity does add diversion—on most occasions.

The housewife, shopping in the grocery store, faces a similar freedom, one which often presents her with a dilemma. She represents many occupations in one person; which phase of her occupational role shall she depict? Is she Veblen's conspicuous consumer for her husband's ego? Is she simply an errand girl shopping for the family larder? Or, is she a responsible member of the community, president of the Mother's Club? Depending on the circumstances of the moment she will choose one role. Other wives, meanwhile, make their separate decisions. Thus, a grocery store and a cocktail party, in America, display much the same disparity of dress.

Because the customs of one culture are seldom understood by observers from another, choice-making for the "world citizen" can be a serious matter. A State Department wife just back from the Far East explained a dilemma posed at an official dinner attended by dignitaries from America and the host country. "I was embarrassed by the way our women dressed," she said, ". . . they came in simple wool dresses. The Oriental believes that the more richly you dress, as a guest, the more honor you do your host. Silk is still *their* highest status fabric . . . you can see how those simple wool dresses seemed a direct insult, to them." "What did you wear?" she was asked. "A silk brocade made in Hong Kong, and some dynasty earrings," she replied.

The simple dress of the other American guests was not deliberate sabotage of the American image abroad. They had made their decision by reasoning in this way: These people think Americans are extremely materialistic; we will show them *we* are not. We will dress simply, in good taste—"underdone." We will wear neat wool dresses and discreet jewelry. The result was they not only failed in their intent but added insult as well, because through incomplete knowledge of protocol in a highly structured situation, they overlooked the traditions of the host country.

Freedom in choice-making requires dedicated effort on the part of the chooser. The less structured the situation by society, the more knowledge the individual must possess to structure it for himself.

Practical, Simple, Functional Clothes

When roles become more flexible and relaxed, dress grows more restrained in design. This seeming disparity is the outgrowth of "function." Flexible roles require clothing that adjusts, not more specialized in design, but so unspecialized as to contain some elements common to all roles. Suits, separates, shirtwaist dresses, these are the styles in which Americans live. They are "fashion hybrids"—the result of cross-pollinization between active sports and the business world—and they function with great flexibility to move us from boat to business, from suburb to city.

Conflicts among the casual look, an accent on youth, and the conservatism of the American people are resolved in the styling of the sportswear classics. Such garments as sweaters and skirts, with an informal and unspecialized air, are youthful to look at, yet conservative in cut. Futhermore, as simplified designs, they can be changed with color, fabric, and decorative details to satisfy the demand for fashion, yet they fit smoothly into a mass-production system.

When modern woman entered the business world, her clothing concern was aptly voiced by Claire McCardell: ". . . I have little time to make up to the dress; I want the dress to make up to me."[40] Miss McCardell, a designer of the American Look, felt that clothes should be worn in comfort and that only comfort can create sense-making styles. By promoting separates and breaking tabus, she helped introduce into business clothes some of the flexibility of sportswear.

Judged solely by a standard of utility, in a purely physical sense, clothing should be both warm and cool enough for any combination of temperature plus humidity (sometimes referred to as the "discomfort index"), yet light weight enough to travel easily by air. It should move freely with the body, avoiding any pressure or pull on yielding parts like the throat; it should clean easily and cheaply; be durable; reasonable in cost; and suited to its purpose.

Functionalism as a basis for sound design was present in America before 1850 in the Stonecutter's Creed of Horatio Greenough:

> By beauty I mean the promise of function,
> By action I mean the presence of function,
> By character I mean the record of function.[41]

Tocqueville, visiting America during the same period, said our country preferred the useful to the beautiful and would require that the beautiful be useful. (This creed ultimately found expression in the work of Frank Lloyd Wright.)

Oriented toward a pragmatic attitude of mind, Americans historically have been less concerned with the purely aesthetic and intellectual interests, or veneration of the past, than with the world of here and now. Life is viewed as a constant choosing between alternatives (ideally, by intellectual objectivity) and choices are weighed on the basis of their good consequences. As the consequence falls out, so William James observed, "things are judged . . . true or false; good or evil."

Most American contributions to fashion have been pragmatic or functional solutions to immediate American problems. For example, Western style clothes for children seem more comfortable, practical, and durable to visitors from India and Pakistan than their own traditional Eastern dress. To the American housewife, faced with no outside help and high prices, "ease of care" and "durability" are important considerations. However, the Easterners point out, where cotton is low in price and labor is cheap, as in their home countries, "ease of care" and "durability" are not problems. Their clothes are hand-laundered and easily replaced by others that are made at home by a seamstress or a professional tailor at nominal cost.

The adoption of boys' clothing for little girls, once the major obstacle of tradition had been overcome, was accelerated by the busy American mothers' practical decision that greater warmth, protection, and easy care are offered by, for example, knit shirts and corduroy slacks than by dainty batiste dresses.

The shirtwaist dress (a style never approved by Paris)

evolved from the shirtmaker blouse and separate skirt worn by women "white collar" workers—secretaries and typists who entered the business world in significant numbers after the typewriter was invented. For office work, they needed less hampering and more easily kept clothes. Consequently, the bustle declined, the skirt shortened and decreased in size, and separate tailored blouses with long sleeves and stiff cuffs came into vogue. As a trend toward women's suits developed to complement the sober attire of the businessman, the shirtwaist blouse and separate skirt gradually merged into a one-piece dress.

The cocktail dress developed for after-office play much as the shirtwaist dress evolved for office work. The low-necked street-length dress, designed by Ceil Chapman in the late 30's, became the symbol par excellence of American sophistication, answering a need for a dress somewhere in between a street dress and a dinner dress. The "cocktail party" was popularized during the depression as a method of large-scale entertaining that required less help and was less costly to give than dinners or balls. It has since become a permanent part of the social scene and serves as a social medium for impersonal groups of people who are held together, if at all, by some slight bond of business or social relationships. As a type of entertaining, the cocktail party has become increasingly important in a highly mobile society.

Mobility has also caused an emphasis in America on multipurpose, easy-to-pack clothing as people commute greater distances to work, travel more extensively by jet planes, and shift quickly from work to play. Skirts may have matching jackets for business, and blouses for after work; the auto coat and the raincoat are designed to wear with everything.

Mobility and technological advances have been largely responsible for changes in peoples' attitudes and values toward textile fibers and designs. To measure these attitudes, a study of the comfort characteristics of clothing with varying fiber content was made by Jane Werden, M. K. Fahnestock, and Ruth Galbraith of the departments of Home Economics and Mechanical Engineering at the University of Illinois. They were concerned with questions such as these: Is there a difference in the comfort of clothing based on the fiber content as the general public tends to believe? Do such comments as, "I never wear nylon in the summer, it is too hot," or "I always change to cotton slips in hot weather because they are more comfortable" have any basis in fact?

To test these statements, women in complete outfits made of nylon, cotton, acetate, and Arnel were checked at temperatures from 70° to 94°F. at both medium and low humidities. Such factors as the rectal temperature, skin temperatures, evaporative weight loss and a subjective evaluation on comfort were recorded. The research concluded that either with or without large quantities of sweat on the skin and in the clothing, no difference in thermal comfort as measured by comfort votes and skin temperature could be attributed to fiber content.[42]

Textiles of the future may include fabrics that air condition their wearers, cottons with increased heat endurance, and wrinkle-free clothes with dirt-repellent finishes that require no washing. Developments in clothing being designed for astronauts may lead to suits with mechanized arms that reach out and work at the push of a button. This type of functional approach to clothing, developed for some specific purpose but having novelty appeal when applied to another area, is wholly American in concept.

The zipper is such a development. A useful gadget for closings and high in novelty appeal, the zipper has been universally adopted wherever it has been introduced. After World War II, during which Stalin stood by and watched the United States Army put zippers on everything from Eisenhower jackets to jungle hammocks and airplane flaps, the Soviet Union dismantled and shipped to Russia the foremost German zipper factory.

While the basic idea for the closure was invented in 1893 by Whitcomb L. Judson, the name "zipper" did not appear until 1922 after the slider was put on the "zipper," popular rubber galoshes manufactured by B. F. Goodrich. In 1924 the Prince of Wales (now the Duke of Windsor) arrived in the United States with trousers boasting a zipper; again, zipper sales zoomed. Then in 1933, in mid-depression, a woman's garment manufacturer, seeking a novelty to boost sales, put zippers in a line of dresses. The idea needed a boost from Paris, however, before it took hold. Madame Schiaparelli used the idea in some gowns exported to this country, and the zipper was on the back of American women forevermore.

As the zipper example shows, utility in clothing may inadvertently introduce novelty, but it clearly ignores art for art's sake and the relationship of clothing to personality. It may in truth merit the bitter denunciation of Poiret who exclaimed, "But what is charm to an American? Everything is utility or necessity. They do not know how to invent the superfluous, which, for us, is more indispensable than the necessary."[43]

In its aesthetic rigidity, and continuing desire for novelty, casual dress can dull a sensitivity to "line," just as an undue emphasis on function opposes imaginative waste. This taste is exported to the Paris market of the haute couture through the buyers for American stores. When Chanel made her comeback in 1954 after World War II, she was panned by Paris newspapers. She had created nothing new; they said she was designing her "same old styles." But Americans rejoiced; they wanted those "same old styles."

Not beautiful, but "functioning," the American in casual dress goes everywhere. A symbol of democratic society—long legged and slender, a little rumpled, yet courageous—the American woman tackles traditions and prestige wherever they may be: on the college campuses or the streets of Moscow, at the diplomat's table or the Paris market. Reflecting the conservatism of her Puritan heritage, combined with the effects of mobility and democracy, she is a focus of the American ethic—while high fashion may not be available to everyone there is some fashion for all. A curious phenomenon intriguing to watch, she is often misunderstood but seldom mislabeled as America's major contribution to the international fashion scene.

NOTES

INTRODUCTION: *Nature of Fashion*

1. Paul H. Nystrom, *Economics of Fashion* (New York: The Ronald Press Co., 1928), pp. 4–5.

CHAPTER 1: *The Rise of Fashion*

1. Gabriel Tarde, *The Laws of Imitation* (translated from the French) (New York: Henry Holt & Co., Inc., 1903), p. 193.
2. *Ibid.,* p. 221.
3. Georg Simmel, "Fashion," *International Quarterly,* X (Oct., 1904), 140.
4. Samuel Sewall, *Samuel Sewall's Diary* (abridgment), edited by Mark Van Doren, Macy-Masius, 1927 (first published in 3 vols., Massachusetts Historical Society, 1878–1882), p. 52.
5. Carl Bridenbaugh, *Cities in the Wilderness* (New York: Alfred A. Knopf, Inc., 1955), p. 411.
6. Alice Morse Earle, *Two Centuries of Costume in America* (New York: Macmillan Co., 1903), II, 655.
7. Wilson, *Memorial History of New York I,* p. 349, quoted in Bridenbaugh, p. 98.
8. Bridenbaugh, pp. 95, 133.
9. Allen French, *Charles I and the Puritan Upheaval* (Boston: Houghton Mifflin Co., 1955), pp. 49–53.
10. Frances Trollope, *Domestic Manners of the Americans* (New York: Alfred A. Knopf, Inc., 1949), p. 88.
11. Harriet Beecher Stowe, *Old Town Folks and Sam Lawson* (Boston and New York: Houghton Mifflin Co., 1899), I, 57–58.
12. Benjamin Franklin, *The Autobiography of Benjamin Franklin* (New York: Doubleday, Page and Co., 1924), Introduction, p. v.
13. Theodore Dreiser, *The Financier* (New York: Dell Publishing Co., Inc., 1964), p. 227.
14. "Jay Gould," *Chicago Sunday Tribune,* Dec. 3, 1961.

15. Robert S. Lynd and Helen M. Lynd, *Middletown* (New York: Harcourt, Brace & Co., Inc., 1929), p. 162.
16. Upton Sinclair, *Oil* (New York: Grosset & Dunlap, Inc., 1926), p. 27.
17. John Useem, Pierre Tangent, and Ruth Hill Useem, "Stratification in a Prairie Town," *American Sociological Review*, VII (June, 1942), 331–42.
18. W. Lloyd Warner, *American Life*, Revised edition, Phoenix books (Chicago: University of Chicago Press, 1953 and 1962), pp. 146–52.
19. Carl Becker, "Progress," in Edwin R. A. Selgeman (ed.), *Encyclopedia of the Social Sciences* (New York: Macmillan Co., 1934) XII, 495–99.
20. David Riesman, Nathan Glazer, and Reuel Denney, *The Lonely Crowd* (New York: Doubleday & Co., Inc., 1955), p. 100.
21. Alexis de Tocqueville, *Democracy in America* (New York: Vintage Books, 1954 [first published, 1840]), II, 35.
22. Robert S. Lynd and Helen M. Lynd, *Middletown in Transition* (New York: Harcourt, Brace & Co., Inc., 1937), p. 7.
23. Henry Adams, *The Education of Henry Adams* (Boston and New York: Houghton Mifflin Co., 1918), p. 328.

CHAPTER 2: *The Functions of Fashion*

1. Ernest Becker, "Socialization, Command of Performance, and Mental Illness," *American Journal of Sociology*, LXVIII (March, 1962), 494–95.
2. Gregory P. Stone and William H. Form, "The Local Community Clothing Market: A Study of the Social and Social Psychological Contexts of Shopping," *Technical Bulletin No. 262*, Michigan State University, Agr. Exp. Sta., p. 8.
3. Gregory P. Stone, "Appearance and the Self," in A. M. Rose (ed.), *Human Behavior and Social Processes: An Interactionist Approach* (New York: Houghton Mifflin Co., 1962), pp. 86–118.
4. Ernst Harms, "The Psychology of Clothes," *American Journal of Sociology*, XLIV (Sept., 1938), 239–50.
5. Edmund Bergler, *Fashion and the Unconscious* (New York: Brunner, 1953), p. 136.
6. Harms.
7. Esther Warner, *Art, an Everyday Experience* (New York: Harper and Row, 1963), pp. 22–24.
8. Melvin Seeman and John W. Evans, "Apprenticeship and Attitude Change," *American Journal of Sociology*, LXVII (Jan., 1962), p. 368.
9. *Ibid.*
10. *Ibid.*
11. *Ibid.*

12. Stone and Form, p. 3.
13. W. Lloyd Warner, *American Life*, Revised edition, Phoenix books (Chicago: University of Chicago Press, 1953 and 1962), pp. 66–67.
14. Margaret Mead, *Male and Female* (New York: William Morrow and Co., 1949). (Complete discussion on sex role.)
15. Elihu Katz and Paul Lazarsfeld, *Personal Influence* (Glencoe, Illinois: Free Press), p. 178.
16. William H. Whyte, Jr., "Consumer in the New Suburbia," in L. H. Clark (ed.), *Consumer Behavior*, Vol. I, issued by Consumer Behavior, Inc. (New York: Harper and Brothers, 1954).
17. "Hold That Hemline," *Wall Street Journal*, Dec. 11, 1964, p. 1.
18. William H. Form and Gregory P. Stone, "The Social Significance of Clothing in Occupational Life," *Technical Bulletin 247*, Michigan State University, Agr. Exp. Sta., June, 1955, pp. 4–6.
19. Kenneth D. Benne, "The Uses of Fraternity," printed in *Journal of the American Academy of Arts and Sciences; Daedalus*, Spring, 1961, pp. 241–42.
20. "The English Switch-on," *Women's Wear Daily*, Sept. 29, 1964, p. 5.
21. Benne, pp. 238–40.
22. Dwight E. Robinson, "The Economics of Fashion Demand," *Quarterly Journal of Economics*, LXXV (Aug., 1961), 376–98.
23. "Norman Norell," *Women's Wear Daily*, Apr. 16, 1963, p. 5.
24. Russel Lynes, *The Tastemakers* (New York: Harper and Brothers, 1954), p. 340.
25. Harriet Martineau, *Society in America* (2nd ed.; London: Saunders and Otley, 1837), III, 93.
26. Horatio Algier, Jr., *Tattered Tom* (Philadelphia: The John C. Winston Co., 1899), p. 189.
27. Joyce Carey, "The Mass Mind," *Harper's*, March, 1952.
28. Anny Latour, *Kings of Fashion* (New York: Coward-McCann, Inc., 1958; Germany, 1956), p. 41.

CHAPTER 3: *Economics of Fashion*

1. U.S. Department of Commerce, *Survey of Current Business*, July, 1964.
2. Paul H. Nystrom, *Fashion Merchandising* (New York: The Ronald Press Co., 1932), Preface, p. iii.
3. Eric Larrabee and David Riesman, "Autos in America: Manifest and Latent Destiny," Mimeographed draft, Nov., 1955, p. 10.

1. "Dictator by Demand," *Time,* March 4, 1957, p. 33.
2. Anny Latour, *Kings of Fashion* (New York: Coward-Mc-Cann, Inc., 1958; Germany, 1956), p. 191.
3. "One-man Design Factory," *Women's Wear Daily,* Nov. 12, 1958, p. 4.
4. "Galanos Says: Manufacturer's Viewpoint Alone Not Good for Designer," *Women's Wear Daily,* Dec. 22, 1958, p. 4.
5. Jeanette A. Jarnow and Beatrice Judelle, *Inside the Fashion Business* (New York: John Wiley & Sons, Inc., 1965), p. 73.
6. Rolf Meyersohn and Elihu Katz, "Notes on a Natural History of Fads," *American Journal of Sociology,* LXII (July, 1956–May, 1957), 594–601.
7. Georg Simmel, "Fashion," *International Quarterly,* X (Oct., 1904), 153.
8. Latour, p. 6.
9. Report of the General Executive Board, ILGWA, May 12, 1965, p. 96.
10. Latour, p. 58.
11. "High Fashion Yields Paris Great Prestige But Scanty Profits," *Wall Street Journal,* July 21, 1964.
12. "Note on Paris," *Women's Wear Daily,* Dec. 9, 1964.
13. "Costs High, Profits Low at Dior," *Chicago Tribune,* March 8, 1965.
14. "Note on Paris."
15. "High Fashion Yields Paris . . .".
16. *Ibid.*
17. 12th Census of United States, Vol. IX: *Manufactures,* Part III, p. 300.
18. U.S. Department of Commerce, *Survey of Current Business,* July, 1964.
19. Printer's Ink Staff, "Survey Shows How American Women Buy," reprinted in James U. McNeal, *Dimensions of Consumer Behavior* (New York: Appleton-Century-Crofts, 1965).

CHAPTER 5: *Production*

1. "Brita Believes," *Women's Wear Daily,* Oct. 20, 1964, p. 5.
2. "British Stores Set To Buy U.S. Fashions and Textiles," *Women's Wear Daily,* Dec. 2, 1963, p. 1.
3. "Soviet Group Looks on U.S. R & U With Appreciative Eye," *Women's Wear Daily,* Dec. 2, 1963, p. 20.
4. Christian Dior, *Christian Dior and I* (New York: E. P. Dutton & Co., Inc., 1957), p. 76.
5. Thomas Jefferson, *Notes on the State of Virginia* (Philadelphia: R. T. Rawle Publisher, 1801), p. 323.
6. Benjamin Franklin, Pamphlet (1784): "Information About America," reprinted in Herbert W. Schneide (ed.), *The Auto-*

biography and Selections From His Other Writings, The American Heritage Series (New York: Liberal Arts Press, 1952).

7. Alice Morse Earle, *Home Life in Colonial Days* (New York and London: Macmillan Co., 1898), pp. 180–87.

8. *Ibid.*

9. U.S. Bureau of the Census, *Statistical Abstract of the United States, 1964* (Washington, D.C., 1964).

10. Alexander Hamilton, *Report on Manufactures,* II, 227.

11. Harriet Martineau, *Society in America* (2nd ed.; London: Saunders and Otley, 1837), III, 245.

12. "Textile Men Quietly Oust King Cotton," annual meeting of American Textile Manufacturers Institute at Hollywood Beach, Florida, reported in *Women's Wear Daily,* March 26, 1965.

13. Letter from Charles H. Rutledge, Manager, Product Information, E. I. Du Pont de Nemours & Co., Inc., Wilmington, Delaware, Textile Fiber Department, Nov. 27, 1946.

14. "The Import Story," *Women's Wear Daily,* Feb. 24, 1967, pp. 6–7.

15. Tom McDermott, "American Exporters Group Set To Tie Up Foreign Mart," *Women's Wear Daily,* Feb. 20, 1967.

16. Margaret Brew, *American Clothing Consumption 1879–1909,* unpublished thesis, Chicago, Illinois, University of Chicago, Sept., 1945.

17. "How To Attract the Ladies Without Starting a Riot," *Forbes,* Oct. 15, 1964, p. 22.

18. "Combines 3 Operations," *Women's Wear Daily,* Sept. 16, 1958.

19. *Genesco Annual Report,* Nashville, Tennessee, 1965.

20. "Research Group Mails 1st Journal to Apparel Makers," *Daily News Record,* Nov. 22, 1965.

21. Discussed more fully in articles based on a series of lectures given at the Fashion Institute of Technology by Bertrand Frank, author of *The Progressive Sewing Room,* published by Fairchild Publications, Inc., New York. Reported in *Women's Wear Daily,* March 17, 1951.

22. Florence S. Richards, *The Ready-To-Wear Industry 1900–1950* (New York: Fairchild Publications, Inc., 1951), pp. 27–28.

23. Paul Jacobs, "David Dubinsky: Why His Throne Is Wobbling," *Harper's,* Dec., 1962, p. 77.

24. Richards, pp. 12–14.

25. *Ibid.*

26. John R. Commons *et al., History of Labor in the United States* (New York: Macmillan Co., 1936), I, 15, quoted in *American Journal of Sociology,* Sept., 1963, p. 184.

27. Melvin W. Reder, *Labor in a Growing Economy* (New York: John Wiley & Sons, Inc., 1957), p. 104.
28. Jacobs, pp. 76–82.
29. *Ibid.*
30. "Sheer Brassiere: 2 Points of View, U.S. Brand Bras Bow in Russia," *Women's Wear Daily,* Feb. 25, 1965.
31. "Size Standards Revolution," *Women's Wear Daily,* Feb. 18, 1965, p. 7.
32. Commercial Standard CS 215–58, U.S. Department of Commerce, Office of Technical Services; "Body Measurements for the Sizing of Women's Apparel," U.S. Government Printing Office, Washington, D.C.
33. "The Sizing Triangle," Commodity Standards, U.S. Department of Commerce.
34. "Success and a Well-Dressed Wife Go Together for Young Executives," *New York Times,* Apr. 2, 1960.
35. Josepha A. Hill, "Women in Gainful Occupations, 1870–1920," Census Monograph IX, U.S. Government Printing Office, Washington, D.C., 1929, p. 30.

CHAPTER 6: *Distribution*

1. Gregory P. Stone, "City Shoppers—Urban Identification," *American Journal of Sociology,* LX (1954–1955).
2. Louis Kriesberg, "The Retail Furrier—Concepts of Security and Success," *American Journal of Sociology,* LVII (March, 1952), 478–85.
3. "A Tale of Two Branches—Class, Mass—Alas, Alas," *Women's Wear Daily,* Sept. 23, 1958, pp. 1 and 10.
4. *Ibid.*
5. Paul Lazarsfeld, "Reflections on Business," *American Journal of Sociology,* LXV (1959), 5.
6. Bernard Barber and Lyle S. Lobel, "Fashion in Women's Clothes and the American Social System," *Social Forces,* XXXI (Dec., 1952), 124–31.
7. Ernest Dichter, "The World Customer," *American Fabric Magazine,* No. 60 (Spring, 1963), 87–91.
8. *Ibid.*
9. "The Villager, Inc.," *Women's Wear Daily,* March 14, 1966, p. 18.
10. Margaret Reid, *Consumers and the Market* (New York: Appleton-Century-Crofts, 1942), p. 283.
11. Allen French, *Charles I and the Puritan Upheaval* (Boston: Houghton Mifflin Co., 1955), p. 40.
12. Benjamin Franklin, Pamphlet (1784): "Information About America," reprinted in Herbert W. Schneide (ed.), *The Autobiography and Selections From His Other Writings.* The

American Heritage Series (New York: Liberal Arts Press, 1952), p. 86.

13. Reid, p. 312.
14. Carl Bridenbaugh, *Cities in the Wilderness* (New York: Alfred A. Knopf, Inc., 1955), p. 41.
15. *Ibid.,* p. 340.
16. Lloyd Wendt and Herman Kogan, *Give the Lady What She Wants!* (Chicago, New York, and San Francisco: Rand McNally & Co., 1952), pp. 21–22.
17. *Ibid.,* p. 24.
18. "First Family of Retailing," *Forbes,* March 15, 1961.
19. Margaret Case Harriman, *And the Price Is Right (The R. H. Macy Store)* (Cleveland and New York: World Publishing Co., 1958).
20. Samuel Feinberg, From Where I Sit: "Sears Went Professional When It Went Public," *Women's Wear Daily,* Dec. 6, 1963.
21. R. W. Bartlett, "Some Achievements of the European Common Market," *Illinois Research,* College of Agriculture, Urbana, Illinois, Vol. VIII, No. 2 (Spring, 1966), pp. 3–4.
22. "Convenience and Price Lure More Customers To Buy From Catalogs," *Wall Street Journal,* Dec. 20, 1963, p. 1.
23. C. T. Jonassen, "The Shopping Center vs. Downtown: A Motivation Research on Shopping Habits and Attitudes in Three Cities," Review by Richard C. Wilcox, *American Journal of Sociology,* LXII (1956), 113.
24. G. B. Tallman and Bruce Blomstrom, "Soft Goods Join the Retail Revolution," *Harvard Business Review,* XXXVII (1960), 113–43.
25. "Stores Cancel Fashions Sold by Discounters," *Women's Wear Daily,* Sept. 23, 1958.
26. "FTC Justice Agency Defends Discount Selling Before Senate Group," *Wall Street Journal,* June 26, 1958.
27. Peter F. Drucker, "If I Were a Company President" (The Easy Chair) *Harper's,* April, 1964, p. 16.
28. "Panel Predicts Retailers Head for a Bright Era," *Women's Wear Daily,* March 16, 1966, p. 14.
29. Booton Herndon, *Bergdorf's on the Plaza* (New York: Alfred A. Knopf, Inc., 1956).

CHAPTER 7: *Promotion and Adoption*

1. Wilbur Schramm, *The Process and Effects of Mass Communication* (Urbana, Illinois: University of Illinois Press, 1954), pp. 482, 530.
2. "How Farm People Accept New Ideas," *North Central Regional Publication No. 1* of the Agr. Ext. Serv., Ames, Iowa, Iowa State College, Nov., 1955.

3. Anny Latour, *Kings of Fashion* (New York: Coward-Mc-Cann, Inc., 1958; Germany, 1956), p. 130.
4. "Luis Says," *Women's Wear Daily*, March 13, 1964, p. 5.
5. Christian Dior, *Christian Dior and I* (New York: E. P. Dutton & Co., Inc., 1957), pp. 42, 48.
6. "Richard Avedon," *Women's Wear Daily*, Jan. 6, 1965, p. 5.
7. Edna Woolman Chase and Ilka Chase, *Always in Vogue* (Garden City, New York: Doubleday & Co., Inc., 1954), p. 66.
8. "Luis Says."
9. Chase and Chase, p. 108.
10. Printer's Ink Staff, "The Fairchilds of 12th St.: Salvation in Printing the News," *Printer's Ink*, Jan. 23, 1959, reprint.
11. Chase and Chase, p. 174.
12. "Richard Avedon."
13. "Sarmi Says So,"*Women's Wear Daily*, Sept. 9, 1964, p. 4.
14. "The Subject Is Fashion," *Women's Wear Daily*, Sept. 14, 1964, p. 5.
15. Ralph Turner and Samuel Surace, "Zoot Suits and Mexicans: Symbols in Crowd Behavior," *American Journal of Sociology*, LXII (July 1956–May 1957), 14–20.
16. Dior, p. 127.
17. Ruth E. Finley, *The Lady of Godey's* (Philadelphia: J. B. Lippincott Co., 1938), p. 54.
18. Elihu Katz and Paul Lazarsfeld, *Personal Influence* (Glencoe, Illinois: Free Press, 1955), p. 178.
19. Pierre Martineau, "Motivation in Advertising," in C. H. Sandage and V. Fryberger (eds.), *The Role of Advertising* (Homewood, Illinois: Richard D. Irwin, Inc., 1960), p. 193.
20. George Gallup, *Factors of Reader Interest in 261 Advertisements* (New York: Liberty Publishing Co., 1932).
21. Sandage and Fryberger, p. 550.
22. Joseph H. Appel, "Growing Up With Advertising," *The Business House*, 1940, p. 96.
23. "All Set for Santa," *Wall Street Journal*, No. 23, 1964, p. 1.
24. *Ibid.*
25. Latour, p. 122.
26. Georg Simmel, "Fashion," *International Quarterly*, X (Oct., 1904), 146.
27. William H. Whyte, Jr., "The Web of Word of Mouth," *Fortune*, Nov., 1954.
28. Rolf Meyersohn and Elihu Katz, "Notes on a Natural History of Fads," *American Journal of Sociology*, LXII (July, 1956–May, 1957), 594–601.
29. "How Farm People Accept New Ideas."
30. Dior, p. 249.
31. Simmel, p. 152.

CHAPTER 8: *A Uniform Package*

1. Dwight E. Robinson, "The Economics of Fashion Demand," *Quarterly Journal of Economics*, LXXX (Aug., 1961), 376–90.
2. U.S. Department of Agriculture, Agr. Res. Serv., "Supplies and Prices of Clothing and Textiles," a talk by Virginia Britton, Nov. 16, 1962.
3. Upton Sinclair, *Oil* (New York: Gosset & Dunlap, Inc., 1926), p. 18.
4. "Mink—A Dynamic Story," *Women's Wear Daily*, Dec. 16, 1958, p. 22.
5. Christian Dior, *Christian Dior and I* (New York: E. P. Dutton & Co., Inc., 1957), pp. 75–76.
6. Elizabeth Hawes, *It's Still Spinach* (Boston: Little, Brown and Co., 1954), p. 10.
7. Gregory Stone and William Form, "Clothing Inventories and Preferences Among Rural and Urban Families," *Technical Bulletin No. 246*, Michigan State University, Agr. Exp. Sta.
8. Ernest Van Den Haag, "Of Happiness and Despair We Have No Measure," in Bernard Rosenberg and D. M. White (eds.), *Mass Culture* (Glencoe, Illinois: Free Press, 1958).

CHAPTER 9: *Symbolism of Fashion*

1. Hartley C. Grattan, "The Things the World Wants," *Harper's*, Nov., 1956.
2. Leslie A. White, "The Symbol," *Philosophy of Science*, VII (1940), 451–63.
3. Mary Lou Rosencranz, "Clothing Symbolism," *Journal of Home Economics*, LIV, No. 1 (Jan., 1962).
4. John Steinbeck, *Grapes of Wrath* (New York: Viking Press, Inc., 1939), pp. 114, 115.
5. James Fenimore Cooper, *The Pioneers* (Boston, New York: Houghton Mifflin & Co., 1898), p. 20.
6. Cecil W. H. Beaton, *The Glass of Fashion* (Garden City, New York: Doubleday & Co., Inc., 1954), pp. 1–4.
7. Henry James, *Daisy Miller* (New York: Dell Publishing Co., Inc., 1965), p. 130.
8. "The Russian Way," *Women's Wear Daily*, March 5, 1965.

CHAPTER 10: *A Streak of Conservatism*

1. Archibald McLeish, quote from public talk given at the University of Illinois, 1961.
2. Paul Poiret, *King of Fashion* (Philadelphia and London: J. B. Lippincott Co., 1931), p. 289.

3. Dr. James A. Pike, "The Art of Being Conservative," *Vogue,* Jan., 1962, pp. 112–13.

4. Ezra Hoyt Byington, D.D., *The Puritan in England and New England* (London: Sampson Low Marston and Co., Ltd., 1896), Chap. 1, pp. 84–89.

5. Allen French, *Charles I and the Puritan Upheaval* (Boston: Houghton Mifflin Co., 1955), p. 362.

6. Gerald R. Cragg, *Puritanism in the Period of the Great Persecution, 1660–1688* (Cambridge, London, Cambridge at the University Press, 1957), p. 194.

7. Allen French, pp. 236–37.

8. Carl Bridenbaugh, *Cities in the Wilderness* (New York: Alfred A. Knopf, Inc., 1955), p. 100.

9. Samuel Sewall, *Samuel Sewall's Dairy* (abridgement), edited by Mark Van Doren, Macy-Masius, 1927 (first published in 3 vols., Massachusetts Historical Society, 1878–1882), pp. 161, 162.

10. Alice Morse Earle, *Home Life in Colonial Days* (New York: Macmillan Co., 1898), p. 285.

11. French, in Markham, *Countrey Contentments,* p. 58.

12. J. Hector St. John de Crevecoeur, *Letters From an American Farmer* (London, reprint 1926; original, Philadelphia, 1783), p. 176.

13. Robert Beverly, *The History of the Present State of Virginia in Four Parts, 1673–1722* (London: R. Parker, 1705), p. 287.

14. James Laver, "What Will Fashion Uncover Next?" *This Week Magazine,* Dec. 10, 1961, pp. 16–20.

15. Margaret Mead, *Male and Female* (New York: William Morrow and Co., 1949), p. 79.

16. Sarah J. Hale, *Sketches of American Character* (originally appeared in the *Ladies Magazine*) (Boston: Putman, Hunt, Carter, and Hendee, 1830), pp. 103–5.

17. Mrs. John C. Hessler, "Better Dress Standards," *Journal of Home Economics,* 1912, p. 471.

18. Pear MacDonald, "Club Women Approve Sensible Styles in Dress," *Journal of Home Economics,* VII (1915), 201.

19. G. M. Young, *Early Victorian England, 1830–1865* (Oxford University Press, Humphrey Milford, 1934), I, 100.

20. Frances Trollope, *Domestic Manners of the Americans* (New York: Alfred A. Knopf, Inc., 1949, p. 136.

21. *Ibid.*

22. Young, p. 117.

23. Joseph Kraft, "The Washington Lawyers," *Harper's,* April, 1964.

24. Oscar Lewis, *The Children of Sanchez* (New York: Vintage Books, 1963), Introduction, p. 26.

25. Phillip Stubbes, *Anatomie of Abuses,* in Alice Morse Earle,

Two Centuries of Costume in America (New York: Macmillan, 1910), p. 16.

26. Quentin Bell, *On Human Finery* (New York: A. A. Wyn, Inc., 1949), p. 21.
27. Earle, p. 61.
28. *Ibid.*, p. 123.
29. *Ibid.*, p. 62.
30. Allen French, p. 238.
31. Cragg, p. 211.
32. Benjamin Franklin, *The Autobiography and Selections From His Other Writings* (New York: The Illustrated Modern Library, copyright 1944 by Random House, Inc.), p. 75.
33. *Ibid.*, p. 222.
34. "Ten Fashion Secrets of the Duchess of Windsor," *This Week Magazine*, Sept., 27, 1959.
35. Carrie Donovan, "Timeless Taste Survives Fashion's Changes," *New York Times*, Apr. 18, 1960, p. 33.
36. Carl N. Degler, *Out of Our Past* (New York: Harper and Brothers, 1959), p. 84.
37. Alexis de Tocqueville, *Democracy in America* (New York: Vintage Books, 1954) (first printed in 1840), II, 7.
38. Harold J. Laski, *The American Democracy* (New York: Viking Press, Inc., 1948), p. 400.
39. Anny Latour, *Kings of Fashion* (New York: Coward-McCann, Inc., 1958; Germany, 1956), pp. 12–18.
40. *Ibid.*, p. 29.
41. James Laver, *Taste and Fashion* (London: George G. Harrap and Co., Ltd., 1937), p. 24.
42. Helen Gardner, *Art Through the Ages* (New York: Harcourt, Brace & Co., Inc., 1926, 1931), p. 130.
43. Anne Chamberlin, "The Fabulous Coco Chanel," *Life*, Oct., 1963, p. 165.
44. De Crevecoeur, p. 25.
45. David C. Hull, "Housewives' Opinions of and Experiences With Easy-Care, Wash-Wear Clothing," *Journal of Home Economics*, LV, No. 10 (Dec., 1963), 773–76.
46. Robert S. Lynd and Helen M. Lynd, *Middletown in Transition* (New York: Harcourt, Brace & Co., Inc., 1937), pp. 242–45.
47. *Ibid.*, pp. 10, 11
48. Eric F. Goldman, "Good-By to the 'Fifties—and Good Riddance," *Harper's*, Jan., 1960, p. 29.
49. L. H. Clark (ed.), *Consumer Behavior*, Vol. XI, issued by Consumer Behavior, Inc. (New York: Harper and Brothers, 1954), Introductory Comments by Gregory Stone.
50. Georg Simmel, "Fashion," *International Quarterly*, X (Oct., 1904), 130–55.

1. Letter from Beulah Spillsbury, Director of Public Relations for Nelly Don, Kansas City, Mo., March 11, 1964.
2. Quoted in: Feature column by Carol Bjorkman, *Women's Wear Daily,* Feb. 17, 1965, p. 16.
3. Robin Williams, Jr., *American Society* (New York: Alfred A. Knopf, Inc., 1951), p. 67.
4. Lester Rand, "To Parents: Be Young, But Not Kids," *Des Moines Tribune,* Aug. 22, 1963, p. 30.
5. Margaret Culkin Banning, "Size Sixteen," in Elizabeth Bragdon (ed.), *Women Today* (Indianapolis and New York: The Bobbs-Merrill Co., Inc., 1953).
6. "Mods and Rockers," *Women's Wear Daily,* Sept. 11, 1964.
7. Peter F. Drucker, "American Directions: A Forecast," *Harper's,* Feb., 1965, p. 42.
8. Upton Sinclair, *Oil* (New York: Grosset & Dunlap, Inc., 1926), p. 294.
9. Robert S. Lynd and Helen M. Lynd, *Middletown in Transition* (New York: Harcourt, Brace & Co., Inc., 1937), p. 167.
10. Mark Sullivan, *Our Times, The United States 1900–1925,* Vol. VI, *"The Twenties"* (New York: Charles Scribner's Sons, 1935), p. 453.
11. Anne Chamberlin, "The Fabulous Coco Chanel," *Life,* Oct., 1963, pp. 165–70.
12. Interview recorded in "Carol Says" by Carol Bjorkman, *Women's Wear Daily,* Nov. 1, 1963.
13. Sinclair, p. 127.
14. Clyde Kluckholn and Henry A. Murray, *Personality in Nature, Society and Culture* (New York: Alfred A. Knopf, Inc., 1948).
15. Hannah Foster,*The Coquette or The History of Eliza Wharton,* reproduced from the original edition of 1797 with an introduction by Herbert Ross Brown. Produced for the Facsimile Text Society of Columbia University Press, N.Y., p. 25.
16. F. Scott Fitzgerald, "Bernice Bobs Her Hair," short story in a collection: *Flappers and Philosophers* (New York: Charles Scribner's Sons, 1920).
17. "Mi$$ America et al," *Wall Street Journal,* Sept. 10, 1965, pp. 1 and 10.
18. *Ibid.*
19. *Ibid.*
20. *Ibid.*
21. Evelyn Goodenough Pitcher, "Male and Female," *The Atlantic Monthly,* CCXI (March, 1963), 87–91.
22. James U. McNeal, "An Exploratory Study of the Consumer Behavior of Children," in the book *Dimensions of Consumer*

Behavior (New York: Appleton-Century-Crofts, 1965), pp. 190–209.

23. Carl N. Degler, *Out of Our Past* (New York: Harper and Brothers, 1959), pp. 352, 354.

24. William H. Whyte, Jr., "Consumer in the New Suburbia," in L. H. Clark (ed.), *Consumer Behavior,* Vol. I, issued by Consumer Behavior, Inc. (New York: Harper and Brothers, 1954).

25. Lester Rand, "Youth Finds Plenty To Fret About," *Des Moines Tribune,* Jan. 22, 1959, p. 12.

26. Bruno Bettelheim, "Growing Up Female," *Harper's,* Oct., 1962, pp. 120–28.

27. Margaret Mead, *Coming of Age in Samoa,* a Mentor Book (New York: New America Library of World Literature, Inc., 1928), p. 154.

28. "Teenage Consumers," *Consumer Reports,* March, 1957, pp. 139–41.

29. "Do Ad Men Understand Teenagers?" *Printer's Ink,* CCLXXII (July, 1960), 21, 23, 26.

30. "Teenage Consumers."

31. Margaret Mead, "A New Look at Early Marriages," an interview reported in *U.S. News and World Report* (June 6, 1960), pp. 80–86.

32. Elihu Katz and Paul Lazarsfeld, *Personal Influence* (Glencoe, Illinois: Free Press), p. 178.

33. Arthur M. Vener and Charles R. Hoffer, "Adolescent Orientations to Clothing," *Technical Bulletin 270,* Michigan State University, Agr. Exp. Sta., March, 1959.

34. *Ibid.*

35. *Ibid.*

36. "Teenage Girls Discuss Their Wardrobes and Their Attitudes Toward Cotton and Other Fibers," *Marketing Research Report No. 155,* U.S. Department of Agriculture, Washington, D.C.

37. *St. Louis Post Dispatch,* Feb. 16, 1964.

38. "Stores Leap Atop Teen Bandwagon," *Women's Wear Daily,* March 22, 1965.

39. "Seventeen Plans Idea Boutique," *Women's Wear Daily,* May 2, 1965.

40. "Penny Pitch," *Women's Wear Daily,* Feb. 10, 1965, p. 1.

41. "Vicki," *Women's Wear Daily,* March 31, 1965.

42. "Yves St. Laurent *Rive Gauche,*" *Women's Wear Daily,* Oct. 11, 1965.

43. David E. Wallen, "A Marketing Profile of the Senior Citizen Group," in Robert L. Clewett (ed.), *Marketing's Role in Scientific Management* (Chicago: America Marketing Association, 1957); reprinted in James U. McNeal.

44. *Ibid.*

1. "Is a Hatless Kennedy Polite?" *Des Moines Tribune,* July 5, 1963.
2. James W. Brady, "Two-Gun Lazareff," *Women's Wear Daily,* Apr. 16, 1964.
3. W. G. Marshall, "America and the Americans" (pamphlet) (London, 1877).
4. F. Scott Fitzgerald, *The Great Gatsby* (New York: Charles Scribner's Sons, copyright 1925, renewed 1953), p. 51.
5. André Maurois, "What I Like About America," *This Week Magazine,* Dec. 27, 1959, p. 7.
6. Foster Rhea Dulles, *America Learns To Play: A History of Popular Recreation 1607–1940* (New York and London: D. Appleton-Century Co., Inc., 1940), pp. 179–81.
7. *Ibid.,* p. 183.
8. *Ibid.,* p. 239.
9. *Ibid.,* p. 242.
10. *Ibid.,* pp. 186–87.
11. *Ibid.,* pp. 195–96.
12. *Ibid.,* p. 202.
13. Upton Sinclair, *Oil* (New York: Grosset & Dunlap, Inc., 1926), p. 294.
14. Robert S. Lynd and Helen M. Lynd, *Middletown in Transition* (New York: Harcourt, Brace & Co., Inc., 1937), p. 246.
15. Bernard Groger, "Do Coats Need New Needle?" *Women's Wear Daily,* Apr. 14, 1963.
16. Lynd and Lynd, pp. 221–26.
17. Esther P. Rothman, "Reaching the Disturbed Adolescent Girl," *What's New in Home Economics,* Feb., 1964, p. 54.
18. Russel Crouse, *Mr. Currier and Mr. Ives* (New York: Garden City Publishing Co., Inc., 1930), pp. 61–64.
19. *Ibid.*
20. "Slacks," *New York Times Magazine,* Mar. 1, 1942, p. 16.
21. "Pants," *New York Times,* Apr. 13, 1942, p. 18.
22. "The Talberts," *Vogue,* May 1, 1951, p. 112.
23. "The Rugged Sex?" *Wall Street Journal,* Aug. 5, 1965, p. 1.
24. *Ibid.*
25. "The Truth About Men and Their Looks," *Vogue,* Nov. 1, 1963, p. 155.
26. *The Drug and Cosmetic Catalogue, 1958–59* (New York: Drug and Cosmetic Industry, 1958), p. 218.
27. "The Rugged Sex?"
28. *Ibid.*
29. "Perfume for Everybody," *McCall's,* Nov., 1955, pp. 146–47.
30. *The Drug and Cosmetic Catalogue, 1958–59.*
31. "The Wonderful Windsors," *Women's Wear Daily,* Oct. 7, 1965, pp. 4–5.

32. Leland J. Gordon, *Economics for Consumers* (New York: American Book Co., 1961), p. 129.
33. "Clothes Make the Man Hot," *Newsweek*, Oct. 20, 1941.
34. J. P. McEvoy, "Revolt of the Overdressed Male," *Reader's Digest*, Sept., 1953, pp. 141–43.
35. Frederick L. Allen, *The Big Change* (New York: Harper and Brothers, 1952), p. 232.
36. J. P. McEvoy.
37. "Our Readers Write Us," *Ladies' Home Journal*, Oct., 1941, p. 3.
38. M. Woeferstein, "The Emergence of Fun Morality," *Journal of Social Issues*, VII (1951), 15–25.
39. "Behind the Scenes of a Couture House," *Women's Wear Daily*, March 17, 1960, p. 5.
40. Claire McCardell, *What Shall I Wear?* (New York: Simon and Schuster, Inc., 1956. Introduction excerpted from *Time*, May 2, 1955).
41. Horatio Greenough (Horatio Bender), *The Travels, Observations, and Experience of a Yankee Stonecutter* (Gainsville, Florida: Scholars' Facsimilies and Reprints, 1958).
42. Jane E. Werden, M. K. Fahnestock, and Ruth L. Galbraith, "Thermal Comfort of Clothing of Varying Fiber Content," *Textile Research*, Urbana, University of Illinois, Aug. 1959, pp. 640–51.
43. Paul Poiret, *King of Fashion* (Philadelphia and London: J. B. Lippincott Co., 1931), p. 270.

INDEX

prestige, 27–28, 37–39
segregation, 274–75

Haag, E. Vanden, on mass production, 233
Hair fashions, 283–84, 337–38
Hale, Sarah Josepha, *Godey's Lady's Book*, 204, 255
Half-size, 71. *See also* Sizing
Harms, Ernst, on "psycho-social" fashions, 25, 26
Harper's Bazaar, 195, 207, 296
Haute couture, 72–92
  challenges, 89–92
  clientele, 76–78, 89
  copying, 90–91
  couture houses, 81, 89
  defined, 77
  showings, 79, 85–86
  subsidy, government, 89
  training, 80–85
Hawes, Elizabeth, 231, 263, 342
Held, John, Jr., on college fashions, 324
Hepburn, Audrey, 80
High fashion
  defined, xii, 28
  designs, 37
  and mass market, 232
High-style consumer groups, 53
"His and Hers" styles, 332
Historical aspects of fashion, 250–52, 254–55
Hochman, Julius, union head, 128
Hoffer, Charles, on adolescents, 300–301
Home Economics, Bureau of, 134, 331
Howe, Elias, Jr., 122
Huffmann (Forstmann and Huffmann), 119
Hunt, Walter, inventor, 122

Imitation in fashion, 4, 15–16, 219
Immigrants, 125
Imports, copying of, 139
India, 114
Individual style, 16–17, 241
Industrial development, American fashions, 107
Industrial revolution, 18, 42–43, 111–12
Industry, fashion. *See* Fashion
Innovation, in fashion, xii, 334. *See also* Fashion innovators

Installment buying, 160
Intellectual attitude, in fashion, 88
International Ladies Garment Workers Union, 126–29
Ireland, 68
Italy, 68, 218, 340
Ivy League look, 335

J. C. Penney Company, 170, 175, 181, 218, 303
James, Henry, 243
James, William, 349
Japan, 120, 218
Jefferson, Thomas, on clothing production, 107–8
Jerry's, men's hairstyles, 337
Jonathan Logan, Inc., 130
Journalism, fashion, 202. *See also* Fashion reporting
Junior dress, 301
Junior Miss contest, 289

Katz, Elihu, on fashion interest, 32, 66, 204, 216, 300
Kayser-Roth Company, 288
Kennedy, Jacqueline, fashions worn by, 268, 281, 311
Kluckhohn, Clyde, on youth culture, 285, 307
Knight, Frank, on advertising, 208
Kriesberg, Louis, on retailing, 147

Labeling, 198, 211
Labor
  and cotton manufacturing, 114
  and garment industry, 125–27, 228
  Unions, 126–30
Lacoste, René, tennis fashions, 332
Ladies' Home Companion, 204
Ladies' Home Journal, 345
Langhorne, Irene, Gibson Girl, 200
Langtry, Lily, 193
Lanvin, Jeanne, 70
Laroche, Guy, 304
Laurent, Yves, St. *See* St. Laurent, Yves
Laver, James, on fashion trends, 254, 266, 272
Law
  impact on American traditions, 259
  and style piracy, 91